A Confederate Girl's Diary

SARAH FOWLER MORGAN

A Confederate Girl's Diary

SARAH MORGAN DAWSON

INTRODUCTION BY
WARRINGTON DAWSON

Edited with a Foreword and Notes by
JAMES I. ROBERTSON, JR.

Civil War Centennial Series

INDIANA UNIVERSITY PRESS

Bloomington

NOTE

A few passages of this diary, referring especially to the relations between white and black during the Civil War, have appeared in French in Mr. Warrington Dawson's book, "Le Nègre aux États Unis." They are reproduced here in the original by permission of the French publisher, Monsieur E. Guilmoto.

MANUFACTURED IN THE UNITED STATES OF AMERICA
LIBRARY OF CONGRESS CATALOG CARD NUMBER:
60-8310

To

Those Who Endured and Forgave

CONTENTS

ILLUSTRATIONS

FOREWORD

ONE has only to move down library shelves and thumb through Civil War soldiers' narratives to encounter the streamlets of horror and hardship that merge to form the pool of a war so destructive its toll remains unequalled in American history. Yet the baleful and barbarous impressions often left by contemporary military accounts have been leavened by the diaries and reminiscences of women on both sides — much as its inhumanity at the time was softened by their activities. Their observations and experiences give to the war touches of human interest and warmth that contrast sharply (and generally agreeably) with the gory accounts of how it was where the bullets flew "thicker'n a hornet's nest."

The Confederacy was blessed with a number of talented feminine diarists whose several published journals present a vivid panorama of Southern life behind the battle lines. Supplementing the military campaigns of the East are such works as Mary Boykin Chesnut, *A Diary from Dixie* (New York, 1905, and three later editions), Sally Brock Putnam, *Richmond during the War* (New York, 1867), Constance Cary Harrison, *Recollections Grave and Gay* (New York, 1912), Eliza Frances Andrews, *The War-Time Journal of a Georgia Girl* (New York, 1908), and many others of lesser merit. For later generations of Americans who have been curious to know what happened in the lower Mississippi Valley between 1861 and 1865, there were a handful of women who faithfully recorded their daily experiences and feelings Their published memoirs are often as revealing as their observations were keen, and much of what we know about the war in that remote area is due in part to their diaries. This is particularly true of Louisiana, where the journals of three perceptive and literate women give us a clear insight into the civilian life of both country and city. The recently published reminiscences of Kate Stone, *Brokenburn*, edited by John Q. Anderson (Baton Rouge, 1955), present a brutally candid picture of plantation life and war. *The Journal of Julia LeGrand*, edited by Kate M. Rowland and Mrs. M. L. Croxall (Richmond, 1911), recounts the trials and tribulations of a Victorian socialite caught in the turmoil of occupied New Orleans.

The third of these Louisiana diaries is the best. Indeed, it is generally considered one of the three most interesting diaries written by Confederate women.[1]* First published in 1913, Sarah Morgan Dawson's *A Confederate Girl's Diary* has enjoyed a wide and merited popularity since the day it was released. Reviewers in 1913 and 1914 characterized this journal as "a deeply touching, dramatic and tragic story," "fraught with an unexpected wisdom and comprehension of the larger movements of the

* For notes see page xxv.

war," and "one of the most remarkable diaries penned by an American." [2] The test of time has proved its value, for more recent appraisals are equally laudatory. Douglas S. Freeman praised its fairness and superb style. [3] E. Merton Coulter termed it "one of the best war diaries related to the Confederacy." [4] No adverse criticism has been found denying its appeal.

Sarah Ida Fowler Morgan was brought up in circumstances equal to the most favorable then available in America. Her father, Thomas Gibbes Morgan, was a transplanted Pennsylvanian who served as Collector for the Port of New Orleans and then, in 1850, returned to Baton Rouge to resume his post as magistrate for the judicial district encompassing the state capital. Her mother, Sarah Fowler, was also of wealthy lineage, though Judge Morgan took her from an orphanage to make her his second wife. The Sarah Morgan of this diary was born in New Orleans February 28, 1842. The seventh child of a seventh child (her mother), she was considered by many to possess the supernatural powers associated with people of that birth. [5] Like her five brothers and three sisters, Sarah was tutored largely by her parents. The ten months of formal schooling she is alleged to have received must have been superficial at the most. That she became proficient in French, history, and the classics is demonstrated by many entries in her diary.

The Morgans were always noted for their strong

family bonds. Then, almost overnight, the family unity fell asunder. In May, 1861, Harry Morgan, the second of the five sons, was killed in a duel as unnecessary as most such barbaric episodes. Six months later Judge Morgan died, to the last abhorring the secession now upon his state. The storm of civil war further divided the family. The eldest son, Philip Hickey Morgan, while taking the Federal oath of allegiance, refused to bear arms against the South and became a New Orleans magistrate. A brother-in-law of Sarah's, Richard C. Drum, stayed with the Federal forces in the Far West. The remaining three Morgan brothers — Gibbes, George and Jimmy — all enlisted in Confederate service. Only one returned alive at the end. Left at the two-storied Morgan mansion on Church Street (now Fourth Street in downtown Baton Rouge) were Sarah, her excitable mother, two sisters (one of whom, Eliza, was burdened with five children), and Eliza's husband, Count Charles de la Noue, who was ill-fitted for coping with the abnormal conditions of war.

Not until the spring of 1862 did the war come forcibly to Baton Rouge. Federal troops, having occupied New Orleans, moved unmolested up the Mississippi and took over Sarah's city on the bluffs on May 9. Just prior to the seizure of the town, Sarah commenced her diary. She was barely twenty, strikingly tall (at least five feet, seven inches), with clear blue eyes and golden hair tinged faintly with red. Her snow-white complexion was matched by an hour-glass figure that was the pride of both Sarah and her brother Jimmy, the famous "Rebel Reefer" of Confederate Navy exploits.[6] As attested by diary notations Sarah had a soprano voice beautiful enough to win the admiration of both Confederate and Federal soldiers who occupied the town. They often congregated before the Morgan home when she sang. She frequently accompanied herself on the guitar. And it is evident from the number of suitors who crossed her threshold, no matter where she lived, that she had a radiant personality — though the diary clearly reflects strong and peculiar feelings about each caller.

For three months after the fall of Baton Rouge the Morgan girls scoffed at the Federal yoke upon their town and were confident that the Stars and Stripes waving atop the Arsenal was but a temporary sight. Early in August, 1862, the Confederates made their first and only concentrated effort to recapture the city. The family sought temporary shelter with friends in the country, and, after the inconsequential Battle of Baton Rouge (August 5), made only two visits back to their sacked house, which Sarah termed the "most shockingly treated home in the whole area." For seven months the refugees enjoyed a happy exile at "Linwood," the plantation home of Albert G. Carter twenty miles from town in East Feliciana Parish.[7] When Federal operations began against Port Hudson — only three miles from

Linwood — in the spring of 1863, the Morgans were forced to seek safety elsewhere. In the meantime, Sarah had suffered a serious injury. (See page 281.) While visiting one of the Port Hudson army camps, she fell from a moving carriage and struck her spine on the steel rim of the buggy wheel. She was confined to her bed for six months and was a semi-invalid the remainder of her life. More particularly at that time, she had to be borne wherever and whenever the family moved — and that was often in the next few months.

Yet the hospitality of many friends sustained the displaced Morgans. For short periods they lived in Clinton, Madisonville, and in several intermediate rural homes. They traveled by rail along the eastern shore of Lake Pontchartrain, and thence by boat to New Orleans, where, against the wishes of Sarah and the stubborn resistance of her mother, they took the loyalty oath in order to gain refuge in the home of Judge Philip Morgan. In New Orleans Sarah lived out the last bitter months of the Confederacy. Here she saw the ragged remnants of the defenders of Vicksburg and Port Hudson confined in the Customs House; here she learned of the deaths of her brothers Gibbes and George; and here she was daily surrounded by a pro-Union sentiment she unfalteringly disdained.

War's end found the family scattered and shattered. The Baton Rouge home place was a shambles. Within a year Sarah's three sisters had all married and moved to other sections of the United States. Sarah and her mother remained in New Orleans entirely dependent upon Philip Morgan. It was a situation Sarah found far from agreeable, but for a year there was no alternative. The homecoming of her brother Jimmy in 1866 from service in Egypt brought a welcome change. The two women accompanied him on a pleasure-trip to New York, then journeyed with him to Wade Hampton's Congaree River plantation, which Jimmy had purchased upon his return to the States. For the next six years Sarah enjoyed life as much as Reconstruction in South Carolina allowed. Even when the mortgaged plantation had to be sold and the Morgans were forced to move to Charleston, they retained a degree of happiness. But when Jimmy married in 1873, custom and prudence dictated that mother and daughter seek lodging elsewhere.

The two women moved into the Gadsden home on Meeting Street. Their accommodations in this private and spacious residence were secured largely through the efforts of Francis Warrington Dawson, the young and fiery [illegible] of the Charleston *News and Courier*. A handsome widower, Dawson had been born in London in 1840, christened Austin John Reeks, and had written several successful plays by the time he was nineteen. He gave up a promising career to run the blockade and offer his services to the Confederacy. Because of his father's apprehension that the name of Reeks would be disgraced if he were hanged as a spy, the son assumed the pseudonym he carried to his grave. His Civil War career was both versatile and brilliant. It included service on blockade runners and in Lee's army.[8] His postwar career as one of the leading spokesmen of the New South was even more distinguished.[9]

Dawson quickly recognized in Sarah's writings definite marks of journalistic skill. Despite the custom that women should remain out of newspaper work, Dawson accepted and published many of her literary efforts. Her contributions included articles, book reviews, and even editorials — all written under the pseudonyms of "Mr. Fowler" or "Feu Follet." From this journalistic association came affection, which Sarah initially was reluctant to return, since Dawson's first wife, Virginia, died of tuberculosis only a few months after Sarah first met him. The mourning period at last over, however, the couple were married January 27, 1874, at the Gadsden home. Their married life was comparatively short but was filled with mutual devotion.[10] In the next decade Sarah made several voyages to France, a land she loved intensely. (It should be remembered that she had been nurtured in a French atmosphere.) During the same period she provided her husband with the children he greatly wanted, although childbirth was always a particularly painful ordeal to her because of the injury to her spine. A daughter, Ethel, was born in 1874; four years later came a son, Warrington.[11] The death of her mother in 1876 was not unexpected to Sarah and apparently left few lasting scars of sadness. Her greatest grief came on March 12, 1889. On that date Dawson was killed by a Charleston physician under circumstances that for the most part still remain a mystery.[12] For the next ten years Sarah continued to live in a shroud of loneliness that seemed to press down harder each year on her Bull Street home. In her grief she turned down at least two wedding proposals, though she willingly consented to her daughter's marriage in 1898.

The following year Sarah sold her interest in the *News and Courier* and with her son moved permanently to Paris. Her last years were spent in desired contentment. At her home in the Faubourg Saint Germain she wrote ardently. One of her works, *Les Aventures de Jeannot Lapin* (1903), a French version of the Brer Rabbit stories, was so well received it was in time adopted as a textbook for all French schools and gave the graying lady an additional financial security.[13] Sarah died in Paris May 5, 1909, at the age of sixty-seven. Death was attributed to pneumonia, contracted as a result of a visit she felt compelled to make during a rainy, chilly day.

(Francis) Warrington Dawson, the first editor of his mother's diary, was in the Kenya country of Africa at the time of her death. Born in Charleston September 27, 1878, he was largely responsible for Sarah's move to France. Mr. Dawson had a varied and active career. He was Theodore Roosevelt's private secretary during the ex-President's famous big game hunt, 1909-1910. During World War I Mr. Dawson performed several special missions crammed with dangers that crippled and invalided him for life. For many years he was Special Attaché at the American Embassy in Paris. He also acted as chief researcher in France for documents relative to the restoration of Colonial Williamsburg. Yet his fame rests more on his reputation as an author. Among his works are seven novels, including *The Scar* (1906), *The Gift of Paul Clermont* (1921), and *The Guardian Demons* (1926). Besides editing his mother's diary, Mr. Dawson also annotated the wartime memoirs of William Graves Sharp, American Ambassador to France, 1914-1919. Awarded the Commandeur de la Légion by the French government, he now resides in Versailles as one of only two persons ever named an honorary citizen of that city. He has never married.

Sarah Morgan was a remarkable young woman, possessing many traits not found in most Civil War diarists. Her sympathies were as divided as her family. This is not to imply that she did not have strong feelings about Federal troops; quite the contrary was true. Like most Louisiana women, she possessed and displayed a violent detestation of General Benjamin "Beast" Butler. Moreover, soon after her arrival in New Orleans as a refugee she wrote of her Federal overseers: "O that from the Atlantic to the Rio Grande their vile foot steps should have been allowed to press our soil! Give up to them? Rather than submit, I would that, all gathered together, we should light our own funeral pyre, and old men, brave soldiers, fair women and tender children should all perish hand in hand in the bright flames we would send up to Heaven as a memorial to our toil, sorrow and suffering. If I was a man! O if I was only a man!" [14]

Yet if Sarah despised the Federal army as a whole, she came to admire the civility of many of its individual officers, notably General Thomas Williams, the benevolent commander of Baton Rouge after its fall. At the same time, while she could greet her captors with a Confederate flag emblazoned across her bosom and a pistol concealed in the folds of her dress, she too was sharply critical of those Southerners (especially the feminine variety) whose lips uttered Confederate praises she knew their hearts did not feel. Of them she wrote on June 16, 1862: "Loud women, what contempt I have for you! How I despise your vulgarity!" In an unpublished entry for that same date, she reminded each "Patriotic woman" that "there are no 'Politics' in Heaven!" Her patriotism for the Confederacy was strong, but it ran second to a more intense feeling: a yearning for peace — a yearning that increased as the war years passed. Not a member of the planter class and seldom stubbornly loyal to the South, Sarah often thought in terms of the welfare of the nation as a whole. For that reason she refused to fall prey to the sectional hatred and blind intolerance so characteristic of many of her neighbors.

At first fascinated by the struggle, Sarah soon came to view it with horror. For example, in her first weeks as a refugee she humorously referred to herself as "Noah's Duck," waddling in a sea of war. Very quickly, however, her wanderings became stale. After a sojourn in one town she cried out in her diary: "I would stand another four months of Yankee rule, rather than live that long in Clinton. Yes! and would undergo a weekly shelling besides!"[15] By the last year of the war her entries reflect a dreariness of spirit illustrative of those caught in the webs of defeat and despair.

Sarah Morgan acquired a judicious calm from her father that often was the sole pillar of support for her family. This calmness which surmounted all crises was easily her greatest virtue. Though she could and did at times display signs of recklessness—such as expending precious time to gather up trinkets at her home while it was under bombardment —Sarah possessed a self-control, initiative, and fortitude quite remarkable in a girl who, in her growing years, had known nothing akin to the brutality of war. She had a natural concern for love and marriage, and clearly displayed it in her diary. She lamented the fact that the nicest callers at the Morgan home were married men. She never allowed herself to become flirtatious or facetious, but rather evinced a friendly and dignified behavior that gained her much more male attention than coquettishness would have achieved. As one writer said of her: "Her good sense and self-composed coolness somewhat curb, but are far from inhibiting, the romantic and heroic ideals of a young Louisianian brought up on Walter Scott." [16]

Her diary is a vivid self-portrait. It is feminine, fresh and frank. It is a panorama of Southern life, painted with local colors, framed in social history, and situated on the easel of "The Brother's War." To say more approaches redundancy, so let the diary speak for itself — let Sarah Morgan tell her story.

In editing this new edition of *A Confederate Girl's Diary*, I strove for two objectives: first, merely to supplement the introduction of Warrington Dawson, and secondly, to identify the persons and explain the events found in the diary itself. To ensure the accuracy of the text I compared it word for word with the original four journals, now in the Duke University Library.[17] As Mr. Dawson stated in his introduction, certain passages were omitted from the published version of 1913. For the most part they treat of such things as childhood reminiscences, love of family, and short treatises on irrelevant topics.

In cases where I felt particular omissions were important to the narrative, I have either quoted or summarized them in the notes at the end of the diary. I have made an earnest effort to identify all persons to whom Sarah gave more than casual mention. A few failures ensued. For these I apologize, and rationalize by saying that even Grant and Farragut had difficulty bringing the lower Mississippi Valley under complete control.

It is a pleasure to acknowledge the unselfish assistance of many persons in the preparation of this new edition. The Honorable Warrington Dawson kept the trans-Atlantic mails busy with enough data on the Morgan-Dawson families to render much further research unnecessary. For his suggestions and encouragement I am grateful. Charles E. East of the Baton Rouge *State-Times* volunteered to become my liaison in his area and aided immeasurably in the identification of local citizens mentioned in the diary. His assistance, enthusiasm, and devotion to this project cannot be overpraised. Sincere thanks go to ten of my students who helped me compare the written and printed diaries — even when I warned them that "apple-polishing" would not apply to this particular enterprise. For aid, individual and invaluable, I am indebted to Dr. James Z. Rabun of Emory University, Richard B. Harwell and Ray D. Smith of Chicago, Judge Cecil Morgan of New York, Miss Mattie Russell of Duke

University Library, and David E. Estes of Emory University Library. Lastly, to my wife, who tolerated neglect and held in check two Rebels as rambunctious as Taylor's Louisianians, I dedicate this new edition. She deserves it.

JAMES I. ROBERTSON, JR.

March 28, 1959

1. Excerpts from the diary have been published in at least eight anthologies. For example, see E. Merton Coulter, *The Confederate States of America, 1861-1865* (Baton Rouge, 1950), 511; Katherine M. Jones, *Heroines of Dixie* (Indianapolis, 1955), 121-123, 128-138, 168-171; Francis P. Simkins and James W. Patton, *The Women of the Confederacy* (Richmond, 1936), *passim*.

2. *New York Tribune*, September 27, 1913; *The Review of Reviews*, November, 1913; *Mississippi Valley Historical Review*, I (1914-1915), 150. See also *Philadelphia Enquirer*, September 27, 1913; *Chicago Tribune*, October 11, 1913; *Milwaukee Free Press*, October 20, 1913; *Confederate Veteran*, XXI (1913), 577.

3. D. S. Freeman, *The South to Posterity* (New York, 1939), 139-148.

4. E. Merton Coulter, *Travels in the Confederate States* (Norman, 1948), 68.

5. Sarah reputedly predicted the death of her neighbor, Felix Brunot (see page 47), a Confederate soldier, almost at the precise moment it occurred on the battlefield. Letter to the editor from Warrington Dawson, December 26, 1958.

6. Jimmy enjoyed proving, to their mutual pleasure, that he could enclose Sarah's waist with his thumbs and forefingers.

7. Linwood is presently owned and occupied by Malcolm Daugherty.

8. Dawson recounted his own war experiences in *Reminiscences of Confederate Service, 1861-1865* (Charleston, 1882), published in a limited edition of only one hundred copies.

9. See C. Vann Woodward, *Origins of the New South, 1877-1913* (Baton Rouge, 1951), 134, 145-147, 250. Woodward classified Daw-

son as one of the few men who tried to rebuild the South with "metropolitan and unprejudiced eyes." *Ibid.*, 146.

10. Ever in frail health because of her fall, Sarah once wrote her cousin: "I owe my life to the ceaseless care my husband takes of me. . . . We both enjoy my dependence upon him." Sarah Dawson to William G. Waller, February 20, 1876, Probate Records, East Baton Rouge Parish. In like vein Dawson wrote of his wife in 1882: "It is little enough, in the hurry of a busy life, to do for one who, year after year and so long as I have known her, has strengthened my faith by believing in me, and enlarges my hope always by her confidence and love." Dawson, *Reminiscences*, 180.

11. A third child, Philip, was born in 1880, but died two years later of heat prostration while the family was en route to a vacation in the mountains of North Carolina.

12. Sarah returned from one of several trips abroad with a Swiss governess for her children. One day this young girl complained to Dawson that Dr. Thomas B. McDow, whose home adjoined the Dawson's back yard, was making improper advances to her, despite the fact that he had a family. Dawson went to the physician's home for an explanation. McDow, the only one who lived to recount the episode, maintained Dawson was clubbing him with a cane when he shot him in self-defense. However, the doctor could never give a valid reason for trying to bury Dawson under his steps — or why the editor was found shot in the back. Yet the jury acquitted McDow on grounds of justifiable homicide. S. Frank Logan presents a detailed discussion of this affair in his study, "Francis W. Dawson, 1840-1889: South Carolina Editor" (unpublished master's thesis, Duke University, 1947). More recently, and after further research, Warrington Dawson published additional information on the subject in an article in the Charleston *News and Courier*, August 24, 1958.

13. Elizabeth Vignier, "Sarah Morgan Dawson," *The Southern Club Woman*, IV (1929), 1-2. The best biographical sketch of Sarah is in *The National Cyclopaedia of American Biography* (48 vols., New York, 1892-1952), XXIII, 300-301.

14. Unpublished entry for April 30, 1862.

15. Unpublished entry for October 26, 1862.

16. Edmund Wilson, "Three Confederate Ladies," *The New Yorker*, November 5, 1955, 179.

17. There is a fifth journal, containing Sarah's daily activities during the Reconstruction years. Never published, it is in the possession of Warrington Dawson.

INTRODUCTION

It is perhaps due to a chance conversation, held some seventeen years ago in New York, that this Diary of the Civil War was saved from destruction.

A Philadelphian had been talking with my mother of North and South, and had alluded to the engagement between the Essex and the Arkansas, on the Mississippi, as a brilliant victory for the Federal navy. My mother protested, at once; said that she and her sister Miriam, and several friends, had been witnesses, from the levee, to the fact that the Confederates had fired and abandoned their own ship when the machinery broke down, after two shots had been exchanged: the Federals, cautiously turning the point, had then captured but a smoking hulk. The Philadelphian gravely corrected her; history, it appeared, had consecrated, on the strength of an official report, the version more agreeable to Northern pride.

"But I wrote a description of the whole, just a few hours after it occurred!" my mother insisted. "Early in the war I began to keep a diary, and continued until the very end; I had to find some vent for my feelings, and I would not make an exhibition of myself by talking, as so many women did. I have written while resting to recover breath in the midst of a stampede; I have even written with shells bursting over the house in which I sat, ready to flee but waiting for my mother and sisters to finish their preparations."

"If that record still existed, it would be invaluable," said the Philadelphian. "We Northerners are sincerely anxious to know what Southern women did and thought at that time, but the difficulty is to find authentic contemporaneous evidence. All that I, for one, have seen, has been marred by improvement in the light of subsequent events."

"You may read my evidence as it was written from March 1862 until April 1865," my mother declared impulsively.

At our home in Charleston, on her return, she unstitched with trembling hands a linen-bound parcel always kept in her tall, cedar-lined wardrobe of curled walnut. On it was scratched in ink "To be burned unread after my death"; it contained, she had once told me, a record of no interest save to her who had written it and lacked the courage to re-read it; a narrative of days she had lived, of joys she had lost; of griefs accepted, of vain hopes cherished.

From the linen, as the stitches were cut, fell five blank books of different sizes. Two, of convenient dimensions, might have been intended for diaries; the other three, somewhat unwieldy, were partly used ledgers from Judge P. H. Morgan's office. They were closely written in a clear, firm hand; the ink, of poor quality, had faded in many places to a pale brown scarcely darker than the deep yellow to which time had burned the paper. The effort to read under such conditions, and the tears shed over the scenes evoked, might well have cost my mother her sight; but she toiled for many weeks, copying out the essential portions of the voluminous record for the benefit of the Northerner who really wished to know.

Her transcription finished, she sent it to Philadelphia. It was in due course returned, with cold regrets that the temptation to rearrange it had not been resisted. No Southerner at that time could possibly have had opinions so just or foresight so clear as those here attributed to a young girl. Explanation was not asked, nor justification allowed: the case, tried by one party alone, with evidence seen from one standpoint alone, had been judged without appeal.

Keenly wounded and profoundly discouraged, my mother returned the diaries to their linen envelope, and never saw them again. But my curiosity had been roused by these incidents; in the night, thoughts of the records would haunt me, bringing ever the ante-bellum scent of the cedar-lined wardrobe. I pleaded for the preservation of the volumes, and succeeded at last when, beneath the injunction that they should be burned, my mother wrote a deed of gift to me with permission to make such use of them as I might think fitting.

Reading those pages for myself, of late, as I transcribed them in my turn, I confess to having blamed the Philadelphian but lightly for his skepticism.

Here was a girl who, by her own admission, had known but ten months' schooling in her life, and had educated herself at home because of her yearning for knowledge; and yet she wrote in a style so pure, with a command of English so thorough, that rare are the pages where she had to stop for the alteration of so much as one word. The very haste of noting what had just occurred, before more should come, had disturbed the pure line of very few among these flowing sentences. There are certain uses of words to which the twentieth century purist will take exception; but if he is familiar with Victorian literature he will know that these points have been solved within the last few decades — and not all solved to the satisfaction of everyone, even now.

But underlying this remarkable feat of style, are a fairness of treatment and a balance of judgment incredible at such a period and in an author so young. On such a day, we may note an entry denouncing the Federals before their arrival at Baton Rouge; another page, and we see that the Federal officers are courteous and considerate, we hear regrets that denunciations should have been dictated by prejudice. Does Farragut bombard a town occupied by women and children, or does Butler threaten to arm negroes against them? Be sure, then, that this Southern girl will not spare adjectives to condemn them! But do Southern women exaggerate in applying to all Federals the opprobrium deserved by some? Then those women will be criticized for forgetting the reserve imposed upon ladies. This girl knew then what history has since established, and what enlightened men and women on both sides of Mason and Dixon's line have since acknowledged: that in addition to the gentlemen in the Federal ranks who always behaved as gentlemen should, there were others, both officers and privates, who had donned the Federal uniform because of the opportunity for rapine which offered, and who were as unworthy of the Stars and Stripes as they would have been of the Stars and Bars.

I can understand, therefore, that this record should meet with skepticism at the hands of theorists committed to an opinion, or of skimmers who read guessing the end of a sentence before they reach the middle. But the originals exist to-day, and have been seen by others than myself; and I pledge myself here to the assertion that I have taken no liberties, have made no alterations, but have strictly adhered to my task of transcription, merely omitting here and there passages which deal with matters too personal to merit the interest of the public.

Those who read seriously, and with unbiased mind, will need no external guarantees of authenticity, however; for the style is of that spontaneous quality which no imitation could attain, and which attempted improvement could only mar. The very construction of the whole — for it does appear as a whole — is influenced by the circumstances which made the life of that tragic period.

The author begins with an airy appeal to Madame Idleness — in order to forget. Then, the war seemed a sacred duty, an heroic endeavor, an inevitable trial, according as Southerners chose to take it; but the prevailing opinion was that the solution would come in victory for Southern arms, whether by their own unaided might or with the support of English intervention. The seat of war was far removed, and but for the absence of dear ones at the front and anxiety about them, Southern women would have been little disturbed in their routine of household duties. But presently the roar of cannon draws near, actual danger is experienced in some cases, suffering and privation must be accepted in all. Thenceforth, the women are part of the war; there may be interludes of plantation life momentarily secure from bullets and from oppression, yet the cloud is felt hanging ever lower and blacker. Gradually, the writer's gay spirit fails; an injury to her spine, for which adequate medical care cannot be found in the Confederacy, and the condition of her mother, all but starving at Clinton, drive these Southern women to the protection of a Union relative in New Orleans. The hated Eagle Oath must be taken, the beloved Confederacy must be renounced at least in words. Entries in the Diary become briefer and briefer, yet are sustained unto the bitter end, when the deaths of two brothers, and the crash of the Lost Cause, are told with the tragic reserve of a broken heart.

I have alluded to passages omitted because too personal. That the clearness of the narrative may not suffer, I hope to be pardoned for explaining briefly, here, the position of Sarah Morgan's family at the outbreak of the Civil War.

Her father, Judge Thomas Gibbes Morgan, had been Collector of the Port of New Orleans, and in 1861 was Judge of the District Court of the Parish of Baton Rouge. In complete sympathy with Southern rights, he disapproved of Secession as a movement fomented by hotheads on both sides, but he declared for it when his State so decided. He died at his home in Baton Rouge in November, 1861, before the arrival of Farragut's fleet.

Judge Thomas Gibbes Morgan's eldest son, Philip Hickey Morgan, was also a Judge, of the Second District Court of the Parish of Orleans. Judge P. H. Morgan (alluded to as "Brother" and his wife as "Sister" throughout the Diary) disapproved of Secession like his father, but did not stand by his State. He declared himself for the Union, and remained in New Orleans when the Federals took possession, but refused to bear arms against his brothers and friends. His position enabled him to render signal services to many Confederate prisoners suffering under Butler's rule. And it was a conversation of his with President Hayes, when he told the full, unprejudiced truth about the Dual Government and the popular sentiment of Louisiana, which put an end to Reconstruction there by the Washington Government's recognition of General Francis T. Nicholls, elected Governor by the people, instead of Packard, declared Governor by the Republican Returning Board of the State. Judge P. H. Morgan had proved his disinterestedness in his report to the President; for the new Democratic régime meant his own resignation from the post of Associate Justice of the Supreme Court of Louisiana which he held under the Republicans. He applied then to himself a piece of advice which he later was to give a young relative mentioned in the pages of this Diary: "Always remember that it is best to be in accord with the sentiments of the vast majority of the people in your State. They are more apt to be right, on public questions of the day, than the individual citizen."

If Judge Thomas Gibbes Morgan's eldest son stayed within the Union lines because he would not sanction Secession, his eldest daughter — Lavinia — was on the Federal side also, married to Colonel Richard Coulter Drum, then stationed in California, and destined to become, in days of peace, Adjutant-General under President Cleveland's first administration. Though spared the necessity of fighting against his wife's brothers, Colonel Drum was largely instrumental in checking the Secession movement in California which would probably have assured the success of the South.

In the early days of Secession agitation, another son of Judge T. G. Morgan, Henry, had died in a duel over a futile quarrel which busybodies had envenomed. The three remaining sons had gone off to the war. Thomas Gibbes Morgan, Jr., married to Lydia, daughter of General A. G. Carter and a cousin of Mrs. Jefferson Davis, was Captain in the Seventh Louisiana Regiment, serving under Stonewall Jackson; George Mather Morgan, unmarried, was a Captain in the First Louisiana, also with Jackson in Virginia. The youngest, James Morris Morgan, had resigned from Annapolis, where he was a cadet, and hurried back to enlist in the Confederate navy.

At the family home in Baton Rouge, only women and children remained. There was Judge Morgan's widow, Sarah Fowler Morgan; a married daughter, Eliza or "Lilly," with her five children; and two unmarried daughters, Miriam and Sarah. "Lilly's" husband, J. Charles La Noue, came and went; unable to abandon his large family without protector or resources, he had not joined the regular army, but took a part in battles near whatever place of refuge he had found for those dependent on him. We note, for instance, that he helped in the Confederate attack on Baton Rouge, together with General Carter, whose age had prevented him from taking regular service.

A word more as to the author of this Diary, and I have finished.

The war over, Sarah Morgan knitted together the threads of her torn life and faced her present, in preparation for whatever the future might hold. In South Carolina, under Reconstruction, she met a young Englishman, Captain Francis Warrington Dawson, who had left his home in London to fight for a cause where his chivalrous nature saw right threatened by might. In the Confederate navy under Commodore Pegram, in the Army of Northern Virginia under Longstreet, at the close of the war he was Chief Ordnance officer to General Fitzhugh Lee. But although the force of arms, of men, of money, of mechanical resources, of international support, had decided against the Confederacy, he refused to acknowledge permanent defeat for Southern ideals, and so cast his lot with those beside whom he had fought. His ambition was to help his adopted country in reconquering through journalism and sound politics that which seemed lost through war. What he accomplished in South Carolina is a matter of public record to-day. The part played in this work by Sarah Morgan as his wife is known to all who approached them during their fifteen years of a married life across which no shadow ever fell.

Sarah Morgan Dawson was destined to outlive not only her husband, but all save three of her eight brothers and sisters, and most of the relatives and friends mentioned in the pages which follow; was destined to endure deep affliction once more, and to renounce a second home dearer than that first whose wreck she recorded during the war. Yet never did her faith, her courage, her steadfastness fail her, never did the light of an almost childlike trust in God and in mankind fade from her clear blue eyes. The Sarah Morgan who, as a girl, could stifle her sobs as she forced herself to laugh or to sing, was the mother I knew in later years.

I love most to remember her in the broad tree-shaded avenues of Versailles where, dreaming of a distant tragic past, she found ever new strength to meet the present. Death claimed her not far from there, in Paris, at a moment when her daughter in America, her son in Africa, were powerless to reach her. But souls like unto hers leave their mark in passing through the world; and, though in a foreign land, separated from all who had been dear to her, she received from two friends such devotion as few women deserve in life, and such as few other women are capable of giving.

She had done more than live and love: — she had endured while endurance was demanded; and, released from the house of bondage, she had, without trace of bitterness in her heart, forgiven those who had caused her martyrdom.

WARRINGTON DAWSON.

VERSAILLES, FRANCE,
July, 1913.

A CONFEDERATE GIRL'S DIARY

BOOK I

BATON ROUGE, LOUISIANA,
March 9th, 1862.

HERE I am, at your service, Madame Idleness, waiting for any suggestion it may please you to put in my weary brain, as a means to pass this dull, cloudy Sunday afternoon; for the great Pike clock over the way has this instant struck only half-past three; and if a rain is added to the high wind that has been blowing ever since the month commenced, and prevents my going to Mrs. Brunot's before dark, I fear I shall fall a victim to "the blues" for the first time in my life. Indeed it is dull. Miriam went to Linewood with Lydia yesterday, and I miss them beyond all expression. Miriam is *so* funny! She says she cannot live without me, and yet she can go away, and stay for months without missing me in the slightest degree. Extremely funny! And I — well, it is absurd to fancy myself alive without Miriam. She would rather not visit with me, and yet, be it for an hour or a month, I never halfway enjoy myself without her, away from home. Miriam is my "Rock ahead" in life; I'll founder on her yet. It's a grand sight for people out of reach, who will not come in contact with the breakers, but it is quite another thing to me, perpetually dancing on those sharp points in my little cockleshell that forms so ludicrous a contrast to the grand scene around. I am sure to founder!

I hold that every family has at heart one genius, in some line, no matter what — except in our family, where each is a genius, in his own way. Hem! And Miriam has a genius for the piano. Now I never could bear to compete with any one, knowing that it is the law of my being to be inferior to others, consequently to fail, and failure is so humiliating to me. So it is, that people may force me to abandon any pursuit by competing with me; for knowing that failure is inevitable, rather than fight against destiny I give up *de bonne grâce*. Originally, I was said to have a talent for the piano, as well as Miriam. Sister and Miss Isabella said I would make a better musician than she, having more patience and perseverance. However, I took hardly six months' lessons to her ever so many years; heard how well she played, got disgusted with myself, and gave up the piano at fourteen, with spasmodic fits of playing every year or so. At sixteen, Harry gave me a guitar. Here was a new field where I would have no competitors. I knew no one who played on it; so I set to work, and taught myself to manage it, mother only teaching me how to tune it. But Miriam took a fancy to it, and I taught her all I knew; but as she gained, I lost my relish, and if she had not soon abandoned it, I would know nothing of it now. She does not know half that I do about it; they tell me I play much better than she; yet they let her play on it in company before me, and I cannot pretend to play after. Why is it? It is *not* vanity, or I would play, confident of excelling her. It is not jealousy, for I love to see her show her talents. It is not selfishness; I love her too much to be selfish to her. What is it then? "Simply lack of self-esteem" I would say if there was no phrenologist near to correct me, and point out that well-developed hump at the extreme southern and heavenward portion of my Morgan head. Self-esteem or not, Mr. Phrenologist, the result is, that Miriam is by far the best performer in Baton Rouge, and I would rank forty-third even in the delectable village of Jackson.

And yet I must have some ear for music. To "know as many songs as Sarah" is a family proverb; not very difficult songs, or very beautiful ones, to be sure, besides being very indifferently sung; but the tunes *will* run in my head, and it must take *some* ear to catch them. People say to me, "Of course you play?" to which I invariably respond, "Oh, no, but Miriam plays beautifully!" "You sing, I believe?" "Not at all — except for father" (that is what I used to say) — "and the children. But *Miriam* sings." "You are fond of dancing?" "Very; but I cannot dance as well as Miriam." "Of course, you are fond of society?" "No, indeed! Miriam is, and she goes to all the parties and returns all the visits for me." The consequence is, that if the person who questions is a stranger, he goes off satisfied that "that Miriam must be a great girl; but that little sister of hers —! Well! a *prig*, to say the least!"

So it is Miriam catches all my fish — and so it is, too, that it is not raining, and I'm off.

April 7th.

Until that dreary 1861, I had no idea of sorrow or grief. . . . How I love to think of myself at that time! Not as *myself*, but as some happy, careless child who danced through life, loving God's whole world too much to love any particular one, outside of her own family. She was more childish then — yet I like her for all her folly; I can say it now, for she is as dead as though she was lying underground.

Now do not imagine that Sarah has become an aged lady in the fifteen months that have elapsed since, for it is no such thing; her heart does ache occasionally, but that is a secret between her and this little rosewood furnished room; and when she gets over it, there is no one more fond of making wheelbarrows of the children, or of catching Charlie or mother by the foot and making them play lame chicken. . . . Now all this done by a young lady who remembers eighteen months ago with so much regret that she has lost so much of her high spirits — might argue that her spirits were before tremendous; and yet they were not. That other Sarah was ladylike, I am sure, in her wildest moments, but there is something hurried and boisterous in this one's tricks that reminds me of some one who is making a merit of being jolly under depressing circumstances. No! that is not a nice Sarah now, to *my* taste.

The commencement of '61 promised much pleasure for the rest of the year, and though Secession was talked about, I do not believe any one anticipated the war that has been desolating our country ever since, with no prospect of terminating for some time to come. True the garrison was taken, but then several pleasant officers of the Louisiana army were stationed there, and made quite an agreeable addition to our small parties, and we did not think for a moment that trouble would grow out of it — at least, we girls did not. Next Louisiana seceded, but still we did not trouble ourselves with gloomy anticipations, for many strangers visited the town, and our parties, rides, and walks grew gayer and more frequent.

One little party — shall I ever forget it? — was on the 9th of March, I think; such an odd, funny little party! Such queer things happened! What a fool Mr. McG—— made of himself! Even more so than usual. But hush! It's not fair to laugh at a lady — under peculiar circumstances. And he tried so hard to make himself agreeable, poor fellow, that I ought to like him for being so obedient to my commands. "Say something new; something funny," I said, tired of a subject on which he had been expatiating all the evening; for I had taken a long ride with him before sunset, he had escorted me to Mrs. Brunot's, and here he was still at my side, and his conversation did not interest me. To hear, with him, was to obey. "Something funny? Well —" here he commenced telling something about somebody, the fun of which seemed to consist in the somebody's having "knocked his *shins*" against something else. I only listened to the latter part; I was bored, and showed it. "Shins!" was I to laugh at such a story?

April 12th.

Day before yesterday, just about this time of evening, as I came home from the graveyard, Jimmy unexpectedly came in. Ever since the 12th of February he has been waiting on the Yankees' pleasure, in the Mississippi, at all places below Columbus, and having been under fire for thirteen days at Tiptonville, Island No. 10 having surrendered Monday night; and Commodore Hollins thinking it high time to take possession of the ironclad ram at New Orleans, and give them a small party below the forts, he carried off his little aide from the McRae Tuesday morning, and left him here Thursday evening, to our infinite delight, for we felt as though we would never again see our dear little Jimmy. He has grown so tall, and stout, that it is really astonishing, considering the short time he has been away. . . . To our great distress, he jumped up from dinner, and declared he must go to the city on the very next boat. Commodore Hollins would need him, he must be at his post, etc., and in twenty minutes he was off, the rascal, before we could believe he had been here at all. There is something in his eye that reminds me of Harry, and tells me that, like Hal, he will die young.

And these days that are going by remind me of Hal, too. I am walking in our footsteps of last year. The eighth was the day we gave him a party, on his return home. I see him so distinctly standing near the pier table, talking to Mr. Sparks, whom he had met only that morning, and who, three weeks after, had Harry's blood upon his hands. He is a murderer now, without aim or object in life, as before; with only one desire — to die — and death still flees from him, and he Dares not rid himself of life.

All those dancing there that night have undergone trial and affliction since. Father is dead, and Harry. Mr. Trezevant lies at Corinth with his skull fractured by a bullet; every young man there has been in at least one battle since, and every woman has cried over her son, brother, or sweetheart, going away to the wars, or lying sick and wounded. And yet we danced that night, and never thought of bloodshed! The week before Louisiana seceded, Jack Wheat stayed with us, and we all liked him so much, and he thought so much of us; — and last week — a week ago to-day — he was killed on the battle-field of Shiloh.

April 16th.

Among the many who visited us, in the beginning of 1861, there was Mr. Bradford. I took a dislike to him the first time I ever saw him, and, being accustomed to say just what I pleased to all the other gentlemen, tried it with him. It was at dinner, and for a long while I had the advantage, and though father would sometimes look grave, Gibbes, and all at my end of the table, would scream with laughter. At last Mr. Bradford commenced to retaliate, and my dislike changed into respect for a man who could make an excellent repartee with perfect good-breeding; and after dinner, when the others took their leave, and he asked permission to remain, — during his visit, which lasted until ten o'clock, he had gone over such a variety of subjects, conversing so well upon all, that Miriam and I were so interested that we forgot to have the gas lit!

April 17th.

And another was silly little Mr. B——r, my little golden calf. What a — don't call names! I owe him a grudge for "cold hands," and the other day, when I heard of his being wounded at Shiloh, I could not help laughing a little at Tom B——r's being hurt. What was the use of throwing a nice, big cannon ball, that might have knocked a man down, away on that poor little fellow, when a pea from a popgun would have made the same impression? Not but what he is brave, but little Mr. B——r is so soft.

Then there was that rattle-brain Mr. T——t who, commencing one subject, never ceased speaking until he had touched on all. One evening he came in talking, and never paused even for a reply until he bowed himself out, talking still, when Mr. Bradford, who had been forced to silence as well as the rest, threw himself back with a sigh of relief and exclaimed, "This man talks like a woman!" I thought it the best description of Mr. T——t's conversation I had ever heard. It was all on the surface, no pretensions to anything except to put the greatest possible number of words of no meaning in one sentence, while speaking of the most trivial thing. Night or day, Mr. T——t never passed home without crying out to me, "*Ces jolis yeux bleus!*" and if the parlor were brightly lighted so that all from the street might see us, and be invisible to us themselves, I always nodded my head to the outer darkness and laughed, no matter who was present, though it sometimes created remark. You see, I knew the joke. Coming from a party escorted by Mr. B——r, Miriam by Mr. T——t,[1] we had to wait a long time before Rose opened the door, which interval I employed in dancing up and down the gallery — followed by my cavalier — singing, —

"Mes jolis yeux bleus,
Bleus comme les cieux,
Mes jolis yeux bleus
Ont ravi son âme," etc.;

[1] Note added at the time: "O propriety! Gibbes and Lydia were with us too."

which naïve remark Mr. B——r, not speaking French, lost entirely, and Mr. T——t endorsed it with his approbation and belief in it, and ever afterwards called me "*Ces jolis yeux bleus*."

April 19th, 1862.

Another date in Hal's short history! I see myself walking home with Mr. McG—— just after sundown, meeting Miriam and Dr. Woods at the gate; only that was a Friday instead of a Saturday, as this. From the other side, Mr. Sparks comes up and joins us. We stand talking in the bright moonlight which makes Miriam look white and statue-like. I am holding roses in my hand, in return for which one little pansy has been begged from my garden, and is now figuring as a shirt-stud. I turn to speak to that man of whom I said to Dr. Woods, before I even knew his name, "Who is this man who passes here so constantly? I feel that I shall hate him to my dying day." He told me his name was Sparks, a good, harmless fellow, etc. And afterwards, when I did know him, [Dr. Woods] would ask every time we met, "Well! do you hate Sparks yet?" I could not really hate any one in my heart, so I always answered, "He is a good-natured fool, but I will hate him yet." But even now I cannot: my only feeling is intense pity for the man who has dealt us so severe a blow; who made my dear father bow his gray head, and shed such bitter tears.

The moon is rising still higher now, and people are

hurrying to the grand Meeting, where the state of the country is to be discussed, and the three young men bow and hurry off, too. Later, at eleven o'clock, Miriam and I are up at Lydia's waiting (until the boat comes) with Miss Comstock who is going away. As usual, I am teasing and romping by turns. Harry suddenly stands in the parlor door, looking very grave, and very quiet. He is holding father's stick in his hand, and says he has come to take us over home. I was laughing still, so I said, "Wait," while I prepared for some last piece of folly, but he smiled for the first time, and throwing his arm around me, said, "Come home, you rogue!" and laughing still, I followed him.

He left us in the hall, saying he must go to Charlie's a moment, but to leave the door open for him. So we went up, and I ran in his room, and lighted his gas for him, as I did every night when we went up together. In a little while I heard him come in and go to his room. I knew nothing then; but next day, going into mother's room, I saw him standing before the glass door of her armoir, looking at a black coat he had on. Involuntarily I cried out, "Oh, don't, Hal!" "Don't what? Is n't it a nice coat?" he asked. "Yes; but it is buttoned up to the throat, and I don't like to see it. It looks —" here I went out as abruptly as I came in; that black coat so tightly buttoned troubled me.

He came to our room after a while and said he was going ten miles out in the country for a few days. I begged him to stay, and reproached him for going away so soon after he had come home. But he said he must, adding, "Perhaps I am tired of you, and want to see something new. I'll be so glad to get back in a few days." Father said yes, he must go, so he went without any further explanation.

Walking out to Mr. Davidson's that evening, Lydia and I sat down on a fallen rail beyond the Catholic graveyard, and there she told me what had happened. The night before, sitting on Dr. Woods's gallery, with six or eight others who had been singing, Hal called on Mr. Henderson to sing. He complied by singing one that was not nice.[1] Old Mr. Sparks got up to leave, and Hal said, "I hope we are not disturbing you?" No, he said he was tired and would go home. As soon as he was gone, his son, who I have since *heard* was under the influence of opium, — though Hal always maintained that he was not, — said it was a shame to disturb his poor old father. Hal answered, "You heard what he said. We did *not* disturb him." "You are a liar!" the other cried. That is a name that none of our family has either merited or borne with; and quick as thought Hal sprang to his feet and struck him across the face with the walking-stick he held. The blow sent the lower part across the balcony in the street, as the spring was loosened by it, while the upper part, to which was fastened the sword — for it was father's sword-cane — remained in his hand.

[1] Note by Mrs. Dawson in 1896: "Annie Laurie!"

I doubt that he ever before knew the cane could come apart. Certainly he did not perceive it, until the other whined piteously he was taking advantage over an unarmed man; when, cursing him, he (Harry) threw it after the body of the cane, and said, "*Now* we are equal." The other's answer was to draw a knife,[1] and was about to plunge it into Harry, who disdained to flinch, when Mr. Henderson threw himself on Mr. Sparks and dragged him off.

It was a little while after that Harry came for us. The consequence of this was a challenge from Mr. Sparks in the morning, which was accepted by Harry's friends, who appointed Monday, at Greenwell, to meet. Lydia did not tell me that; she said she thought it had been settled peaceably, so I was not uneasy, and only wanted Harry to come back from Seth David's soon. The possibility of his fighting never occurred to me.

Sunday evening I was on the front steps with Miriam and Dr. Woods, talking of Harry and wishing he would come. "You want Harry!" the doctor repeated after me; "you had better learn to live without him." "What an absurdity!" I said and wondered when he would come. Still later, Miriam, father, and I were in the parlor, when there was a tap on the window, just above his head, and I saw a hand, for an instant. Father hurried out, and we heard several voices; and then steps going away. Mother came down and asked who had been there,

[1] Note by Mrs. Dawson: Bowie knife.

but we only knew that, whoever it was, father had afterward gone with them. Mother went on: "There is something going on, which is to be kept from me. Every one seems to know it, and to make a secret of it." I said nothing, for I had promised Lydia not to tell; and even I did not know all.

When father came back, Harry was with him. I saw by his nod, and "How are you, girls," how he wished us to take it, so neither moved from our chairs, while he sat down on the sofa and asked what kind of a sermon we had had. And we talked of anything except what we were thinking of, until we went upstairs.

Hal afterwards told me that he had been arrested up there, and father went with him to give bail; and that the sheriff had gone out to Greenwell after Mr. Sparks. He told me all about it next morning, saying he was glad it was all over, but sorry for Mr. Sparks; for he had a blow on his face which nothing would wash out. I said, "Hal, if you *had* fought, much as I love you, I would rather he had killed you than that you should have killed him. I love you too much to be willing to see blood on your hands." First he laughed at me, then said, "If I had killed him, I never would have seen you again."

We thought it was all over; so did he. But Baton Rouge was wild about it. Mr. Sparks was the bully of the town, having nothing else to do, and whenever he got angry or drunk, would knock down anybody he chose. That same night, before Harry met him, he had slapped one man, and had dragged another over the room by the hair; but these coolly went home, and waited for a *voluntary apology*. So the mothers, sisters, and intimate friends of those who had patiently borne the blows, and being "woolled," vaunted the example of their heroes, and asked why Dr. Morgan had not acted as *they* had done, and waited for an apology? Then there was another faction who cried only blood could wash out that blow and make a gentleman of Mr. Sparks again, — as though he ever *had* been one! So knots assembled at street corners, and discussed it, until father said to us that Monday night, "These people are so excited, and are trying so hard to make this affair worse, that I would not be surprised if they shot each other down in the street," speaking of Harry and the other.

Hal seemed to think of it no more, though, and Wednesday said he must go to the city and consult Brother as to where he should permanently establish himself. I was sorry; yet glad that he would then get away from all this trouble. I don't know that I ever saw him in higher spirits than he was that day and evening, the 24th. Lilly and Charlie were here until late, and he laughed and talked so incessantly that we called him crazy. We might have guessed by his extravagant spirits that he was trying to conceal something from us. . . .

He went away before daybreak, and I never saw him again.

April 26th, 1862.

There is no word in the English language that can express the state in which we are, and have been, these last three days. Day before yesterday, news came early in the morning of three of the enemy's boats passing the Forts, and then the excitement began. It increased rapidly on hearing of the sinking of eight of our gunboats in the engagement, the capture of the Forts, and last night, of the burning of the wharves and cotton in the city while the Yankees were taking possession. To-day, the excitement has reached the point of delirium. I believe I am one of the most self-possessed in my small circle; and yet I feel such a craving for news of Miriam, and mother, and Jimmy, who are in the city, that I suppose I am as wild as the rest. It is nonsense to tell me I am cool, with all these patriotic and enthusiastic sentiments. Nothing can be positively ascertained, save that our gunboats are sunk, and theirs are coming up to the city. Everything else has been contradicted until we really do not know whether the city has been taken or not. We only know we had best be prepared for anything. So day before yesterday, Lilly and I sewed up our jewelry, which may be of use if we have to fly. I vow I will not move one step, unless carried away. Come what will, here I remain.

We went this morning to see the cotton burning — a sight never before witnessed, and probably never again to be seen. Wagons, drays, — everything that can be driven or rolled, — were loaded with the bales and taken a few squares back to burn on the commons. Negroes were running around, cutting them open, piling them up, and setting them afire. All were as busy as though their salvation depended on disappointing the Yankees. Later, Charlie sent for us to come to the river and see him fire a flatboat loaded with the precious material for which the Yankees are risking their bodies and souls. Up and down the levee, as far as we could see, negroes were rolling it down to the brink of the river where they would set them afire and push the bales in to float burning down the tide. Each sent up its wreath of smoke and looked like a tiny steamer puffing away. Only I doubt that from the source to the mouth of the river there are as many boats afloat on the Mississippi. The flatboat was piled with as many bales as it could hold without sinking. Most of them were cut open, while negroes staved in the heads of barrels of alcohol, whiskey, etc., and dashed bucketsful over the cotton. Others built up little chimneys of pine every few feet, lined with pine knots and loose cotton, to burn more quickly. There, piled the length of the whole levee, or burning in the river, lay the work of thousands of negroes for more than a year past. It had come from every side. Men stood by who owned the cotton that was burning or waiting to burn. They either helped, or looked on cheerfully. Charlie owned but sixteen bales — a matter of some fifteen hundred dollars;

but he was the head man of the whole affair, and burned his own, as well as the property of others. A single barrel of whiskey that was thrown on the cotton, cost the man who gave it one hundred and twenty-five dollars. (It shows what a nation in earnest is capable of doing.) Only two men got on the flatboat with Charlie when it was ready. It was towed to the middle of the river, set afire in every place, and then they jumped into a little skiff fastened in front, and rowed to land. The cotton floated down the Mississippi one sheet of living flame, even in the sunlight. It would have been grand at night. But then we will have fun watching it this evening anyway; for they cannot get through to-day, though no time is to be lost. Hundreds of bales remained untouched. An incredible amount of property has been destroyed to-day; but no one begrudges it. Every grog-shop has been emptied, and gutters and pavements are floating with liquors of all kinds. So that if the Yankees are fond of strong drink, they will fare ill.

Yesterday, Mr. Hutchinson and a Dr. Moffat called to ask for me, with a message about Jimmy. I was absent, but they saw Lilly. Jimmy, they said, was safe. Though sick in bed, he had sprung up and had rushed to the wharf at the first tap of the alarm bell in New Orleans. But as nothing could be done, he would probably be with us to-day, bringing mother and Miriam. I have neither heard nor seen more. The McRae, they said, went to the bottom with the others. They did not know whether any one aboard had escaped. God be praised that Jimmy was not on her then! The new boat to which he was appointed is not yet finished. So he is saved! I am distressed about Captain Huger, and could not refrain from crying, he was so good to Jimmy. But I remembered Miss Cammack might think it rather tender and obtrusive, so I dried my eyes and began to hope he had escaped. Oh! how glad I should be to know he has suffered no harm. Mr. Hutchinson was on his way above, going to join others where the final battle is to be fought on the Mississippi. He had not even time to sit down; so I was doubly grateful to him for his kindness. I wish I could have thanked him for being so considerate of me in my distress now. In her agitation, Lilly gave him a letter I had been writing to George when I was called away; and begged him to address it and mail it at Vicksburg, or somewhere; for no mail will leave here for Norfolk for a long while to come. The odd part is, that he does not know George. But he said he would gladly take charge of it and remember the address, which Lilly told him was Richmond. Well! if the Yankees get it they will take it for an insane scrawl. I wanted to calm his anxiety about us, though I was so wildly excited that I could only say, "Don't mind us! We are safe. But fight, George! Fight for us!" The repetition was ludicrous. I meant so much, too! I only wanted him to understand he could best defend us there. Ah! Mr. Yankee! if you had but your brothers in this world, and their lives hanging by a thread, you too might write wild letters! And if you want to know what an excited girl can do, just call and let me show you the use of a small seven-shooter and a large carving-knife which vibrate between my belt and my pocket, always ready for emergencies.

April 27th.

What a day! Last night came a dispatch that New Orleans was under British protection, and could not be bombarded; consequently, the enemy's gunboats would probably be here this morning, such few as had succeeded in passing the Forts; from nine to fifteen, it was said. And the Forts, they said, had *not* surrendered. I went to church; but I grew very anxious before it was over, feeling that I was needed at home. When I returned, I found Lilly wild with excitement, picking up hastily whatever came to hand, preparing for instant flight, she knew not where. The Yankees were in sight; the town was to be burned; we were to run to the woods, etc. If the house had to be burned, I had to make up my mind to run, too. So my treasure-bag tied around my waist as a bustle, a sack with a few necessary articles hanging on my arm, some few quite unnecessary ones, too, as I had not the heart to leave the old and new prayer books father had given me, and Miriam's, too;—pistol and carving-knife ready, I stood awaiting the exodus. I heaped on the bed the treasures I wanted to burn, matches lying ready to fire the whole at the last minute. I may here say that, when all was over, I found I had omitted many things from the holocaust. This very diary was not included. It would have afforded vast amusement to the Yankees. There may yet be occasion to burn them, and the house also. People fortunately changed their minds about the *auto-da-fé* just then; and the Yankees have not yet arrived, at sundown. So, when the excitement calmed down, poor Lilly tumbled in bed in a high fever in consequence of terror and exertion.

[A page torn out]

I was right in that prophecy. For this was not the Will Pinckney I saw last. So woebegone! so subdued, careworn, and sad! No trace of his once merry self. He is good-looking, which he never was before. But I would rather never have seen him than have found him so changed. I was talking to a ghost. His was a sad story. He had held one bank of the river until forced to retreat with his men, as their cartridges were exhausted, and General Lovell omitted sending more. They had to pass through swamps, wading seven and a half miles, up to their waists in water. He gained the edge of the swamp, saw they were over the worst, and fell senseless. Two of his men brought him milk, and "woke him up," he said. His men fell from exhaustion, were lost, and died in the swamp; so that out of five hundred, but one hundred escaped. This he told quietly and sadly, looking so heartbroken that it was piteous to see such pain. He showed me his feet, with thick clumsy shoes which an old negro had pulled off to give him; for his were lost in the swamp, and he came out bare-footed. They reached the Lafourche River, I believe, seized a boat, and arrived here last night. His wife and child were aboard. Heaven knows how they got there! The men he sent on to Port Hudson, while he stopped here. I wanted to bring his wife to stay with us; but he said she could not bear to be seen, as she had run off just as she had happened to be at that moment. In half an hour he would be off to take her to his old home in a carriage. There he would rejoin his men, on the railroad, and march from Clinton to the Jackson road, and so on to Corinth. A long journey for men so disheartened! But they will conquer in the end. Beauregard's army will increase rapidly at this rate. The whole country is aroused, and every man who owns a gun, and many who do not, are on the road to Corinth. We will conquer yet.

May 5th.

Vile old Yankee boats, four in number, passed up this morning without stopping. After all our excitement, this "silent contempt" annihilated me! What in the world do they mean? The river was covered with burning cotton; perhaps they want to see where it came from.

May 9th.

Our lawful (?) owners have at last arrived. About sunset, day before yesterday, the Iroquois anchored here, and a graceful young Federal stepped ashore, carrying a Yankee flag over his shoulder, and asked the way to the Mayor's office. I like the style! If we girls of Baton Rouge had been at the landing, instead of the men, that Yankee would never have insulted us by flying his flag in our faces! *We* would have opposed his landing except under a flag of truce; but the men let him alone, and he even found a poor Dutchman willing to show him the road!

He did not accomplish much; said a formal demand would be made next day, and asked if it was safe for the men to come ashore and buy a few necessaries, when he was assured the air of Baton Rouge was very unhealthy for Yankee soldiers at night. He promised very magnanimously not to shell us out if we did not molest him; but I notice none of them dare set their feet on *terra firma*, except the officer who has now called three times on the Mayor, and who is said to tremble visibly as he walks the streets.

Last evening came the demand: the town must be surrendered immediately; the Federal flag Must be raised; they would grant us the same terms they granted New Orleans. Jolly terms those were! The answer was worthy of a Southerner. It was, "The town was defenseless; if we had cannon, there were not men enough to resist; but if forty vessels lay at the landing, — it was intimated we were in their power, and more ships coming up, — we would not surrender; if they wanted, they might come and

Baton Rouge - Sarah's Home

Take us; if they wished the Federal flag hoisted over the Arsenal, they might put it up for themselves, the town had no control over Government property." Glorious! What a pity they did not shell the town! But they are taking us at our word, and this morning they are landing at the Garrison.

"All devices, signs, and flags of the Confederacy shall be suppressed." So says Picayune Butler. *Good.* I devote all my red, white, and blue silk to the manufacture of Confederate flags. As soon as one is confiscated, I make another, until my ribbon is exhausted, when I will sport a duster emblazoned in high colors, "Hurra! for the Bonny blue flag!" Henceforth, I wear one pinned to my bosom — not a duster, but a little flag; the man who says take it off will have to pull it off for himself; the man who dares attempt it — well! a pistol in my pocket fills up the gap. I am capable, too.

This is a dreadful war, to make even the hearts of women so bitter! I hardly know myself these last few weeks. I, who have such a horror of bloodshed, consider even killing in self-defense murder, who cannot wish them the slightest evil, whose only prayer is to have them sent back in peace to their own country, — *I* talk of killing them! For what else do I wear a pistol and carving-knife? I am afraid I *will* try them on the first one who says an insolent word to me. Yes, and repent for it ever after in sackcloth and ashes. *O!* if I was only a man! Then I could don the breeches, and slay them with a will!

If some few Southern women were in the ranks, they could set the men an example they would not blush to follow. Pshaw! there are *no* women here! We are *all* men!

May 10th.

Last night about one o'clock I was wakened and told that mother and Miriam had come. Oh, how glad I was! I tumbled out of bed half asleep and hugged Miriam in a dream, but waked up when I got to mother. They came up under a flag of truce, on a boat going up for provisions, which, by the way, was brought to by half a dozen Yankee ships in succession, with a threat to send a broadside into her if she did not stop — the wretches knew it *must* be under a flag of truce; no boats leave, except by special order to procure provisions.

What tales they had to tell! They were on the wharf, and saw the ships sail up the river, saw the broadside fired into Will Pinckney's regiment, the boats we fired, our gunboats, floating down to meet them all wrapped in flames; twenty thousand bales of cotton blazing in a single pile; molasses and sugar thrown over everything. They stood there opposite to where one of the ships landed, expecting a broadside, and resolute not to be shot in the back. I wish I had been there! And Captain Huger is not dead! They had hopes of his life for the first time day before yesterday. Miriam saw the ball that had just been extracted. He will probably be lame for the rest of his life. It will be a glory to him. For even the Federal officers say that never did they see so gallant a little ship, or one that fought so desperately as the McRae. Men and officers fought like devils. Think of all those great leviathans after the poor little "Widow Mickey"! One came tearing down on her sideways, while the Brooklyn fired on her from the other side, when brave Captain Warley put the nose of the Manassas under the first, and tilted her over so that the whole broadside passed over, instead of through, the McRae, who spit back its poor little fire at both. And after all was lost, she carried the wounded and the prisoners to New Orleans, and was scuttled by her own men in port. Glorious Captain Huger! And think of his sending word to Jimmy, suffering as he was, that "his little brass cannon was game to the last." Oh! I hope he will recover. Brave, dare-devil Captain Warley is prisoner, and on the way to Fort Warren, that home of all brave, patriotic men. We'll have him out. And my poor little Jimmy! If I have not spoken of him, it is not because I have lost sight of him for a moment. The day the McRae went down, he arose from his bed, ill as he was, and determined to rejoin her, as his own boat, the Mississippi, was not ready. When he reached the St. Charles, he fell so very ill that he had to be carried back to Brother's. Only his desperate illness saved him from being among the killed or wounded on that gallant little ship. A few days after, he learned the fate of the ship, and was told that Captain Huger was dead. No wonder he should cry so bitterly! For Captain Huger was as tender and as kind to him as his own dear father. God bless him for it! The enemy's ships were sailing up; so he threw a few articles in a carpet-bag and started off for Richmond, Corinth, anywhere, to fight. Sick, weak, hardly able to stand, he went off, two weeks ago yesterday. We know not where, and we have never heard from him since. Whether he succumbed to that jaundice and the rest, and lies dead or dying on the road, God only knows. We can only wait and pray God to send dear little Jimmy home in safety.

And this is WAR! Heaven save me from like scenes and experiences again. I was wild with excitement last night when Miriam described how the soldiers, marching to the depot, waved their hats to the crowds of women and children, shouting, "God bless you, ladies! We will fight for you!" and they, waving their handkerchiefs, sobbed with one voice, "God bless you, Soldiers! Fight for us!"

We, too, have been having our fun. Early in the evening, four more gunboats sailed up here. We saw them from the corner, three squares off, crowded with men even up in the riggings. The American flag was flying from every peak. It was received in profound silence, by the hundreds gathered on the banks. I could hardly refrain from a groan. Much as I once loved that flag, I hate it now! I came back and made myself a Confederate flag about five inches long, slipped the staff in my belt, pinned the flag to my shoulder, and walked downtown, to the consternation of women and children, who expected something awful to follow. An old negro cried, "My young missus got her flag flyin', anyhow!" Nettie made one and hid it in the folds of her dress. But we were the only two who ventured. We went to the State House terrace, and took a good look at the Brooklyn which was crowded with people who took a good look at us, likewise. The picket stationed at the Garrison took alarm at half a dozen men on horseback and ran, saying that the citizens were attacking. The kind officers aboard the ship sent us word that if they were molested, the town would be shelled. Let them! Butchers! Does it take thirty thousand men and millions of dollars to murder defenseless women and children? O the great nation! Bravo!

May 11th.

I — I am disgusted with myself. No unusual thing, but I am *peculiarly* disgusted this time. Last evening, I went to Mrs. Brunot's, without an idea of going beyond, with my flag flying again. They were all going to the State House, so I went with them; to my great distress, some fifteen or twenty Federal officers were standing on the first terrace, stared at like wild beasts by the curious crowd. I had not expected to meet them, and felt a painful conviction that I was unnecessarily attracting attention, by an unladylike display of defiance, from the crowd gathered there. But what was I to do? I felt humiliated, conspicuous, everything that is painful and disagreeable; but — strike my colors in the face of the enemy? Never! Nettie and Sophie had them, too, but that was no consolation for the shame I suffered by such a display so totally distasteful to me. How I wished myself away, and chafed at my folly, and hated myself for being there, and every one for seeing me. I hope it will be a lesson to me always to remember a lady can gain nothing by such display.

I was not ashamed of the flag of my country, — I proved that by never attempting to remove it in spite of my mortification, — but I was ashamed of my position; for these are evidently gentlemen, not the Billy Wilson's crew we were threatened with. Fine, noble-looking men they were, showing refinement and gentlemanly bearing in every motion. One cannot help but admire such foes! They set us an example worthy of our imitation, and one we would be benefited by following. They come as visitors without either pretensions to superiority, or the insolence of conquerors; they walk quietly their way, offering no annoyance to the citizens, though they themselves are stared at most unmercifully, and pursued by crowds of ragged little boys, while even men gape at them with open mouths. They prove themselves gentlemen, while many of our citizens have proved themselves boors, and I admire them for their conduct. With a conviction that I had allowed myself to be influenced by bigoted, narrow-minded people, in believing them to be unworthy of respect or regard, I came home wonderfully changed in all my newly acquired sentiments, resolved never more to wound their feelings, who were so careful of ours, by such unnecessary display. And I hung my flag on the parlor mantel, there to wave, if it will, in the shades of private life; but to make a show, make me conspicuous and ill at ease, as I was yesterday, — never again!

There was a dozen officers in church this morning, and the psalms for the 11th day seemed so singularly appropriate to the feelings of the people, that I felt uncomfortable for them. They answered with us, though.

May 14th.

I am beginning to believe that we are even of more importance in Baton Rouge than we thought we were. It is laughable to hear the things a certain set of people, who know they can't visit us, say about the whole family. . . . When father was alive, they dared not talk about us aloud, beyond calling us the "Proud Morgans" and the "Aristocracy of Baton Rouge" . . . But now father is gone, the people imagine we are public property, to be criticized, vilified, and abused to their hearts' content. . . .

And now, because they find absurdities don't succeed, they try improbabilities. So yesterday the town was in a ferment because it was reported the Federal officers had called on the Miss Morgans, and all the gentlemen were anxious to hear how they had been received. One had the grace to say, "If they did, they received the best lesson there that they could get in town; those young ladies would meet them with the true Southern spirit." The rest did not know; they would like to find out.

I suppose the story originated from the fact that we were unwilling to blackguard — yes, that is the word — the Federal officers here, and would not agree with many of our friends in saying they were liars, thieves, murderers, scoundrels, the scum of the earth, etc. Such epithets are unworthy of ladies, I say, and do harm, rather than advance our cause. Let them be what they will, it shall not make me less the lady; I say it is unworthy of anything except low newspaper war, such abuse, and I will not join in.

I have a brother-in-law in the Federal army whom I love and respect as much as any one in the world, and shall not readily agree that his being a Northerner would give him an irresistible desire to pick my pockets, and take from him all power of telling the truth. No! There are few men I admire more than Major Drum, and I honor him for his independence in doing what he believes right. Let us have liberty of speech and action in our land, I say, but not gross abuse and calumny. Shall I acknowledge that the people we so recently called our brothers are unworthy of consideration, and are liars, cowards, dogs? Not I! *If* they conquer us, I acknowledge them as a superior race; I will not say that we were conquered by cowards, for where would that place us? It will take a brave people to gain us, and that the Northerners undoubtedly are. I would scorn to have an inferior foe; I fight only my equals. These women may acknowledge that *cowards* have won battles in which their brothers were engaged, but I, I will ever say *mine* fought against brave men, and won the day. Which is most honorable?

I was never a Secessionist, for I quietly adopted father's views on political subjects without meddling with them. But even father went over with his State, and when so many outrages were committed by the fanatical leaders of the North, though he regretted the Union, said, "Fight to the death for our liberty." I say so, too. I want to fight until we win the cause so many have died for. I don't believe in Secession, but I do in Liberty. I want the South to conquer, dictate its own terms, and go back to the Union, for I believe that, apart, inevitable ruin awaits both. It is a rope of sand, this Confederacy, founded on the doctrine of Secession, and will not last many years — not five. The North Cannot subdue us. We are too determined to be free. They have no right to confiscate our property to pay debts they themselves have incurred. Death as a nation, rather than Union on such terms. We will have our rights secured on so firm a basis that it can never be shaken. If by power of overwhelming numbers they conquer us, it will be a barren victory over a desolate land.

We, the natives of this loved soil, will be beggars in a foreign land; we will not submit to despotism under the garb of Liberty. The North will find herself burdened with an unparalleled debt, with nothing to show for it except deserted towns, burning homes, a standing army which will govern with no small caprice, and an impoverished land.

If that be treason, make the best of it!

May 17th.

One of these days, when peace is restored and we are quietly settled in our allotted corners of this wide world without any particularly exciting event to alarm us; and with the knowledge of what is now the future, and will then be the dead past; seeing that all has been for the best for us in the end; that all has come right in spite of us, we will wonder how we could ever have been foolish enough to await each hour in such breathless anxiety. We will ask ourselves if it was really true that nightly, as we lay down to sleep, we did not dare plan for the morning, feeling that we might be homeless and beggars before the dawn. How unreal it will then seem! We will say it was our wild imagination, perhaps. But how bitterly, horribly true it is now!

Four days ago the Yankees left us, to attack Vicksburg, leaving their flag flying in the Garrison without a man to guard it, and with the understanding that the town would be held responsible for it. It was intended for a trap; and it succeeded. For night before last, it was pulled down and torn to pieces.

Now, unless Will will have the kindness to sink a dozen of their ships up there, — I hear he has command of the lower batteries, — they will be back in a few days, and will execute their threat of shelling the town. If they do, what will become of us? All we expect in the way of earthly property is as yet mere paper, which will be so much trash if the South is ruined, as it consists of debts due father by many planters for professional services rendered, who, of course, will be ruined, too, so all money is gone. That is nothing, we will not be ashamed to earn our bread, so let it go.

But this house is at least a shelter from the weather, all sentiment apart. And our servants, too; how could they manage without us? The Yankees, on the river, and a band of guerrillas in the woods, are equally anxious to precipitate a fight. Between the two fires, what chance for us? It would take only a little while to burn the city over our heads. They say the women and children must be removed, these guerrillas. Where, please? Charlie says we must go to Greenwell. And have this house pillaged? For Butler has decreed that no unoccupied house shall be respected. If we stay through the battle, if the Federals are victorious, we will suffer. For the officers here were reported to have said, "If the people here did not treat them decently, they would know what it was when Billy Wilson's crew arrived.

They would give them a lesson!" That select crowd is now in New Orleans. Heaven help us when they reach here! It is in these small cities that the greatest outrages are perpetrated. What are we to do?

A new proclamation from Butler has just come. It seems that the ladies have an ugly way of gathering their skirts when the Federals pass, to avoid any possible contact. Some even turn up their noses. Unladylike, to say the least. But it is, maybe, owing to the odor they have, which is said to be unbearable even at this early season of the year. Butler says, whereas the so-called ladies of New Orleans insult his men and officers, he gives one and all permission to insult any or all who so treat them, then and there, with the assurance that the women will not receive the slightest protection from the Government, and that the men will all be justified. I did not have time to read it, but repeat it as it was told to me by mother, who is in utter despair at the brutality of the thing. These men our brothers? Not mine! Let us hope for the honor of their nation that Butler is not counted among the gentlemen of the land. And so, if any man should fancy he cared to kiss me, he could do so under the pretext that I had pulled my dress from under his feet! That will justify them! And if we decline their visits, they can insult us under the plea of a prior affront. Oh! Gibbes! George! Jimmy! never did we need your protection as sorely as now. And not to know even whether you are alive! When Charlie joins the army, we will be defenseless, indeed. Come to my bosom, O my discarded carving-knife, laid aside under the impression that these men were gentlemen. We will be close friends once more. And if you must have a sheath, perhaps I may find one for you in the heart of the first man who attempts to Butlerize me. I never dreamed of kissing any man save my father and brothers. And why any one should care to kiss any one else, I fail to understand. And I do not propose to learn to make exceptions.

Still no word from the boys. We hear that Norfolk has been evacuated; but no details. George was there. Gibbes is wherever Johnston is, presumably on the Rappahannock; but it is more than six weeks since we have heard from either of them, and all communication is cut off.

May 21st.

I have had such a search for shoes this week that I am disgusted with shopping. I am triumphant now, for after traversing the town in every direction and finding nothing, I finally discovered a pair of *boots* just made for a little negro to go fishing with, and only an inch and a half too long for me, besides being unbendable; but I seized them with avidity, and the little negro would have been outbid if I had not soon after discovered a pair more seemly, if not more serviceable, which I took without further difficulty. Behold my tender feet cased in crocodile skin, patent-leather tipped, low-quarter boy's shoes, No. 2! "What a fall was there, my country," from my pretty English glove-kid, to sabots made of some animal closely connected with the hippopotamus! A *dernier ressort, vraiment!* for my choice was that, or cooling my feet on the burning pavement *au naturel;* I who have such a terror of any one seeing my naked foot! And this is thanks to war and blockade! Not a decent shoe in the whole community! *N'importe!* "Better days are coming, we'll all" — have shoes — after a while — perhaps! Why did not Mark Tapley leave me a song calculated to keep the spirits up, under depressing circumstances? I need one very much, and have nothing more suggestive than the old Methodist hymn, "Better days are coming, we'll all go right," which I shout so constantly, as our prospects darken, that it begins to sound stale.

May 27th.

The cry is "Ho! for Greenwell!" Very probably this day week will see us there. I don't want to go. If we were at peace, and were to spend a few months of the warmest season out there, none would be more eager and delighted than I: but to leave our comfortable home, and all it contains, for a rough pine cottage seventeen miles away even from this scanty civilization, is sad. It must be! We are hourly expecting two regiments of Yankees to occupy the Garrison, and some fifteen hundred of our men are awaiting them a little way off, so the fight seems inevitable. And we must go, leaving what little has already been spared us to the tender mercies of Northern volunteers, who, from the specimen of plundering they gave us two weeks ago, will hardly leave us even the shelter of our roof. O my dear Home! How can I help but cry at leaving you forever? For if this fight occurs, never again shall I pass the threshold of this house, where we have been so happy and sad, the scene of joyous meetings and mournful partings, the place where we greeted each other with glad shouts after even so short a parting, the place where Harry and father kissed us good-bye and never came back again!

I know what Lavinia has suffered this long year, by what we have suffered these last six weeks. Poor Lavinia, so far away! How easier poverty, if it must come, would be if we could bear it together! I wonder if the real fate of the boys, if we ever hear, can be so dreadful as this suspense? Still no news of them. My poor little Jimmy! And think how desperate Gibbes and George will be when they read Butler's proclamation, and they not able to defend us! Gibbes was in our late victory of Fredericksburg, I know.

In other days, going to Greenwell was the signal for general noise and confusion. All the boys gathered their guns and fishing-tackle, and thousand and one amusements; father sent out provisions; we helped mother pack; Hal and I tumbled over the libraries to lay in a supply of reading material; and all was bustle until the carriage drove to the door at daylight one morning, and swept us off. It is not so gay this time. I wandered around this morning selecting books alone. We can only take what is necessary, the rest being left to the care of the Northern militia in general. I never knew before how many articles were perfectly "indispensable" to me. This or that little token or keepsake, piles of letters I hate to burn, many dresses, etc., I cannot take conveniently, lie around me, and I hardly know which to choose among them, yet half *must* be sacrificed; I can only take one trunk.

May 30th, GREENWELL.

After all our trials and tribulations, here we are at last, and no limbs lost! How many weeks ago was it since I wrote here? It seems very long after all these events; let me try to recall them.

Wednesday the 28th, — a day to be forever remembered, — as luck would have it, we rose very early, and had breakfast sooner than usual, it would seem for the express design of becoming famished before dinner. I picked up some of my letters and papers and set them where I could find them whenever we were ready to go to Greenwell, burning a pile of trash and leaving a quantity equally worthless, which were of no value even to myself except from association. I was packing up my traveling-desk with all Harry's little articles that were left to me, and other things, and I was saying to myself that my affairs were in such confusion that if obliged to run unexpectedly I would not know what to save, when I heard Lilly's voice downstairs, crying as she ran in — she had been out shopping — "Mr. Castle has killed a Federal officer on a ship, and they are going to shell —" *Bang!* went a cannon at the word, and that was all our warning.

Mother had just come in, and was lying down, but sprang to her feet and added her screams to the general confusion. Miriam, who had been searching the libraries, ran up to quiet her; Lilly gathered her children, crying hysterically all the time, and ran to the front door with them as they were; Lucy saved the baby, naked as she took her from her bath. only throwing a quilt over her. I bethought me of my "running-bag" which I had used on a former case, and in a moment my few precious articles were secured under my hoops, and with a sunbonnet on, I stood ready for anything.

The firing still continued; they must have fired half a dozen times before we could coax mother off. What awful screams! I had hoped never to hear them again, after Harry died. Charlie had gone to Greenwell before daybreak, to prepare the house, so we four women, with all those children and servants, were left to save ourselves. I did not forget my poor little Jimmy; I caught up his cage and ran down. Just at this moment mother recovered enough to insist on saving father's papers — which was impossible, as she had not an idea of where the important ones were. I heard Miriam plead, argue, insist, command her to run; Lilly shriek, and cry she should go; the children screaming within; women running by without, crying and moaning; but I could not join in. I was going I knew not where; it was impossible to take my bird, for even if I could carry him, he would starve. So I took him out of his cage, kissed his little yellow head, and tossed him up. He gave one feeble little chirp as if to ascertain where to go, and then for the first and last time I cried, laying my head against the gate-post, and with my eyes too dim to see him. Oh, how it hurt me to lose my little bird, one Jimmy had given me, too!

But the next minute we were all off, in safety. A square from home, I discovered that boy shoes were not the most comfortable things to run in, so I ran back, in spite of cannonading, entreaties, etc., to get another pair. I got home, found an old pair that were by no means respectable, which I seized without hesitation; and being perfectly at ease, thought it would be so nice to save at least Miriam's and my tooth-brushes, so slipped them in my corsets. These in, of course we must have a comb — that was added — then how could we stand the sun without starch to cool our faces? This included the powder-bag; then I must save that beautiful lace collar; and my hair was tumbling down, so in went the tucking-comb and hair-pins with the rest; until, if there had been any one to speculate, they would have wondered a long while at the singular appearance of a girl who is considered as very slight, usually. By this time, Miriam, alarmed for me, returned to find me, though urged by Dr. Castleton not to risk her life by attempting it, and we started off together.

We had hardly gone a square when we decided to return a second time, and get at least a few articles for the children and ourselves, who had nothing except what we happened to have on when the shelling commenced. She picked up any little things and threw them to me, while I filled a pillow-case jerked from the bed, and placed my powder and brushes in it with the rest. Before we could leave, mother, alarmed for us both, came to find us, with Tiche.[1] All this time they had been shelling, but there was quite a lull when she got there, and she commenced picking up father's papers, vowing all the time she would not leave. Every argument we could use was of no avail, and we were desperate as to what course to pursue, when the shelling recommenced in a few minutes. Then mother recommenced her screaming and was ready to fly anywhere; and holding her box of papers, with a faint idea of saving something, she picked up two dirty underskirts and an old cloak.

By dint of Miriam's vehement appeals, aided by a great deal of pulling, we got her down to the back door. We had given our pillow-case to Tiche, who added another bundle and all our silver to it, and had already departed.

As we stood in the door, four or five shells sailed over our heads at the same time, seeming to make a perfect corkscrew of the air, — for it sounded as

[1] Mrs. Morgan's negro maid, Catiche.

though it went in circles. Miriam cried, "Never mind the door!" mother screamed anew, and I stayed behind to lock the door, with this new music in my ears. We reached the back gate, that was on the street, when another shell passed us, and Miriam jumped behind the fence for protection. We had only gone half a square when Dr. Castleton begged us to take another street, as they were firing up that one. We took his advice, but found our new street worse than the old, for the shells seemed to whistle their strange songs with redoubled vigor. The height of my ambition was now attained. I had heard Jimmy laugh about the singular sensation produced by the rifled balls spinning around one's head; and here I heard the same peculiar sound, ran the same risk, and was equal to the rest of the boys, for was I not in the midst of flying shells, in the middle of a bombardment? I think I was rather proud of it.

We were alone on the road, — all had run away before, — so I thought it was for our especial entertainment, this little affair. I cannot remember how long it lasted; I am positive that the clock struck ten before I left home, but I had been up so long, I know not what time it began, though I am told it was between eight and nine. We passed the graveyard, we did not even stop, and about a mile and a half from home, when mother was perfectly exhausted with fatigue and unable to proceed farther, we met a gentleman in a buggy who kindly took charge of her and our bundles. We could have walked miles beyond, then, for as soon as she was safe we felt as though a load had been removed from our shoulders; and after exhorting her not to be uneasy about us, and reminding her we had a pistol and a dagger, — I had secured a "for true" one the day before, fortunately, — she drove off, and we trudged on alone, the only people in sight on foot, though occasionally carriages and buggies would pass, going towards town. One party of gentlemen put their heads out and one said, "There are Judge Morgan's daughters sitting by the road!" — but I observed he did not offer them the slightest assistance. However, others were very kind. One I never heard of had volunteered to go for us, and bring us to mother, when she was uneasy about our staying so long, when we went home to get clothes. We heard him ring and knock, but, thinking it must be next door, paid no attention, so he went back and mother came herself.

We were two miles away when we sat down by the road to rest, and have a laugh. Here were two women married, and able to take care of themselves, flying for their lives and leaving two lorn girls alone on the road, to protect each other! To be sure, neither could help us, and one was not able to walk, and the other had helpless children to save; but it was so funny when we talked about it, and thought how sorry both would be when they regained their reason! While we were yet resting, we saw a cart coming, and, giving up all idea of our walking to

Greenwell, called the people to stop. To our great delight, it proved to be a cart loaded with Mrs. Brunot's affairs, driven by two of her negroes, who kindly took us up with them, on the top of their luggage; and we drove off in state, as much pleased at riding in that novel place as though we were accustomed to ride in wheelbarrows. Miriam was in a hollow between a flour barrel and a mattress; and I at the end, astride, I am afraid, of a tremendous bundle, for my face was down the road and each foot resting very near the sides of the cart. I tried to make a better arrangement, though, after a while. These servants were good enough to lend us their umbrella, without which I am afraid we would have suffered severely, for the day was intensely warm.

Three miles from town we began to overtake the fugitives. Hundreds of women and children were walking along, some bareheaded, and in all costumes. Little girls of twelve and fourteen were wandering on alone. I called to one I knew, and asked where her mother was; she did n't know; she would walk on until she found out. It seems her mother lost a nursing baby, too, which was not found until ten that night. White and black were all mixed together, and were as confidential as though related. All called to us and asked where we were going, and many we knew laughed at us for riding on a cart; but as they had walked only five miles, I imagined they would like even these poor accommodations if they were in their reach.

The negroes deserve the greatest praise for their conduct. Hundreds were walking with babies or bundles; ask them what they had saved, it was invariably, "My mistress's clothes, or silver, or baby." Ask what they had for themselves, it was, "Bless your heart, honey, I was glad to get away with mistress's things; I did n't think 'bout mine."

It was a heart-rending scene. Women searching for their babies along the road, where they had been lost; others sitting in the dust crying and wringing their hands; for by this time we had not an idea but what Baton Rouge was either in ashes, or being plundered, and we had saved nothing. I had one dress, Miriam two, but Tiche had them, and we had lost her before we left home.

Presently we came on a guerrilla camp. Men and horses were resting on each side of the road, some sick, some moving about carrying water to the women and children, and all looking like a monster barbecue, for as far as the eye could see through the woods, was the same repetition of men and horses. They would ask for the news, and one, drunk with excitement or whiskey, informed us that it was our own fault if we had saved nothing, the people must have been —— fools not to have known trouble would come before long, and that it was the fault of the men, who were aware of it, that the women were thus forced to fly. In vain we pleaded that there was no warning, no means of foreseeing this; he cried, "*You* are ruined; so am I; and my brothers, too! And by —— there is nothing left but to die now, and I'll die!" "Good!" I said. "But die fighting for us!" He waved his hand, black with powder, and shouted, "That I will!" after us. That was the only swearing guerrilla we met; the others seemed to have too much respect for us to talk loud.

Lucy had met us before this; early in the action, Lilly had sent her back to get some baby-clothes, but a shell exploding within a few feet of her, she took alarm, and ran up another road, for three miles, when she cut across the plantations and regained the Greenwell route. It is fortunate that, without consultation, the thought of running here should have seized us all.

May 31st.

I was interrupted so frequently yesterday that I know not how I continued to write so much. First, I was sent for, to go to Mrs. Brunot, who had just heard of her son's death, and who was alone with Dena; and some hours after, I was sent for, to see Fanny, now Mrs. Trezevant, who had just come with her husband to bring us news of George. A Mrs. Montgomery, who saw him every day at Norfolk, said Jimmy was with him, and though very sick at first, was now in good health. The first news in all that long time! When the city was evacuated, George went with his regiment seven miles from Richmond, Jimmy to the city itself, as aide to Com. Hollins. This lady brought George's opal ring and diamond pin. Howell and Mr. Badger, who had just joined the guerrillas as independents, spent the day with me. We were all in such confusion that I felt ashamed: every one as dirty as possible; I had on the same dress I had escaped in, which, though then perfectly clean, was now rather — dirty. But they knew what a time we had had.

To return to my journal.

Lucy met mother some long way ahead of us, whose conscience was already reproaching her for leaving us, and in answer to her "What has become of my poor girls?" ran down the road to find us, for Lucy thinks the world can't keep on moving without us. When she met us, she walked by the cart, and it was with difficulty we persuaded her to ride a mile; she said she felt "used" to walking now. About five miles from home, we overtook mother. The gentleman had been obliged to go for his wife, so Mary gave her her seat on the cart, and walked with Lucy three miles beyond, where we heard that Lilly and the children had arrived in a cart, early in the day. All the talk by the roadside was of burning homes, houses knocked to pieces by balls, famine, murder, desolation; so I comforted myself singing, "Better days are coming" and "I hope to die shouting, the Lord will provide"; while Lucy toiled through the sun and dust, and answered with a chorus of "I'm a-runnin', a-runnin' up to glo-ry!"

It was three o'clock when we reached Mr. David's and found Lilly. How warm and tired we were! A hasty meal, which tasted like a feast after our fatigue, gave us fresh strength, and Lilly and Miriam got in an old cart with the children to drive out here, leaving me with mother and Dellie to follow next day. About sunset, Charlie came flying down the road, on his way to town. I decided to go, and after an obstinate debate with mother, in which I am afraid I showed more determination than amiability, I wrung a reluctant consent from her, and, promising not to enter if it was being fired or plundered, drove off in triumph. It was a desperate enterprise for a young girl, to enter a town full of soldiers on such an expedition at night; but I knew Charlie could take care of me, and if he was killed I could take care of myself; so I went.

It was long after nine when we got there, and my first act was to look around the deserted house. What a scene of confusion! armoirs spread open, with clothes tumbled in every direction, inside and out; ribbons, laces on floors; chairs overturned; my desk wide open covered with letters, trinkets, etc.; bureau drawers half out, the bed filled with odds and ends of everything. I no longer recognized my little room. On the bolster was a little box, at the sight of which I burst out laughing. Five minutes before the alarm, Miriam had been selecting those articles she meant to take to Greenwell, and, holding up her box, said, "If we were forced to run for our lives without a moment's warning, I'd risk my life to save this, rather than leave it!" Yet here lay the box, and she was safe at Greenwell!

It took me two hours to pack father's papers, then I packed Miriam's trunk, then some of mother's and mine, listening all the while for a cannon; for men were constantly tramping past the house, and only on condition our guerrillas did not disturb them had they promised not to recommence the shelling. Charlie went out to hear the news, and I packed alone.

It seems the only thing that saved the town was two gentlemen who rowed out to the ships, and informed the illustrious commander that there were no men there to be hurt, and he was only killing women and children. The answer was, "He was sorry he had hurt them; he thought of course the town had been evacuated before the men were fools enough to fire on them, and had only shelled the principal streets to intimidate the people." These streets were the very ones crowded with flying women and children, which they must have seen with their own eyes, for those lying parallel to the river led to the Garrison at one end and the crevasse at the other, which cut off all the lower roads, so that the streets he shelled were the only ones that the women could follow, unless they wished to be drowned. As for the firing, four guerrillas were rash enough to fire on a yawl which was about to land without a flag of truce, killing one, wounding three, one of whom afterwards died.

They were the only ones in town, there was not a cannon in our hands, even if a dozen men could be collected, and this cannonading was kept up in return for half a dozen shots from as many rifles, without even a show of resistance after! So ended the momentous shelling of Baton Rouge, during which the valiant Farragut killed one whole woman, wounded three, struck some twenty houses several times apiece, and indirectly caused the death of two little children who were drowned in their flight, one poor little baby that was born in the woods, and several cases of the same kind, besides those who will yet die from the fatigue, as Mrs. W. D. Phillips who had not left her room since January, who was carried out in her nightgown, and is now supposed to be in a dying condition. The man who took mother told us he had taken a dying woman — in the act of expiring — in his buggy, from her bed, and had left her a little way off, where she had probably breathed her last a few moments after. There were many similar cases. Hurrah for the illustrious Farragut, the Woman Killer! ! !

It was three o'clock before I left off packing, and took refuge in a tub of cold water, from the dust and heat of the morning. What a luxury the water was! and when I changed my underclothes I felt like a new being. To be sure I pulled off the skin of my heel entirely, where it had been blistered by the walk, dust, sun, etc., but that was a trifle, though still quite sore now. For three hours I dreamed of rifled shells and battles, and at half-past six I was up and at work again. Mother came soon after, and after hard work we got safely off at three, saving nothing but our clothes and silver. All else is gone. It cost me a pang to leave my guitar, and Miriam's piano, but it seems there was no help for it, so I had to submit.

It was dark night when we reached here. A bright fire was blazing in front, but the house looked so desolate that I wanted to cry. Miriam cried when I told her her piano was left behind. Supper was a new sensation, after having been without anything except a *glass* of clabber (no saucers) and a piece of bread since half-past six. I laid down on the hard floor to rest my weary bones, thankful that I was so fortunate as to be able to lie down at all. In my dozing state, I heard the wagon come, and Miriam ordering a mattress to be put in the room for me. I could make out, "Very well! you may take that one to Miss Eliza,[1] but the next one shall be brought to Miss Sarah!" Poor Miriam! She is always fighting my battles. She and the servants are always taking my part against the rest of the world. . . . She and Lucy made a bed and rolled me in it with no more questions, and left me with damp eyes at the thought of how good and tender every one is to me. Poor Lucy picked me a dish of blackberries to await my arrival, and I was just as grateful for it, though they were eaten by some one else before I came.

Early yesterday morning, Miriam, Nettie, and Sophie, who did not then know of their brother's death, went to town in a cart, determined to save

[1] Lilly.

some things, Miriam to save her piano. As soon as they were halfway, news reached us that any one was allowed to enter, but none allowed to leave the town, and all vehicles confiscated as soon as they reached there. Alarmed for their safety, mother started off to find them, and we have heard of none of them since. What will happen next? I am not uneasy. They dare not harm them. It is glorious to shell a town full of women, but to kill four lone ones is not exciting enough.

June 1st, Sunday.

From the news brought by one or two persons who managed to reach here yesterday, I am more uneasy about mother and the girls. A gentleman tells me that no one is permitted to leave without a pass, and of these, only such as are separated from their families, who may have left before. All families are prohibited to leave, and furniture and other valuables also. Here is an agreeable arrangement! I saw the "pass," just such as we give our negroes, signed by a Wisconsin colonel. Think of being obliged to ask permission from some low plowman to go in or out of our own house! Cannon are planted as far out as Colonel Davidson's, six of them at our graveyard, and one or more on all the other roads. If the guerrillas do not attempt their capture, I shall take it upon myself to suggest it to the very next one I see. Even if they cannot use them, it will frighten the Yankees, who are in a state of constant alarm about them. Their reason for keeping people in town is that they hope they will not be attacked so long as our own friends remain; thereby placing us above themselves in the scale of humanity, since they acknowledge we are not brute enough to kill women and children as they did not hesitate to do.

Farragut pleads that he could not restrain his men, they were so enraged when the order was once given to fire, and says they *would* strike a few houses, though he ordered them to fire solely at horses, and the clouds of dust in the street, where guerrillas were supposed to be. The dust was by no means thick enough to conceal that these "guerrillas" were women, carrying babies instead of guns, and the horses were drawing buggies in which many a sick woman was lying.

A young lady who applied to the Yankee general for a pass to come out here, having doubtless spoken of the number of women here who had fled, and the position of the place, was advised to remain in town and write to the ladies to return immediately, and assure them that they would be respected and protected, etc., but that it was madness to remain at Greenwell, for a terrific battle would be fought there in a few days, and they would be exposed to the greatest danger. The girl wrote the letter, but, Mr. Fox, we are not quite such fools as to return there to afford you the protection our petticoats would secure to you, thereby preventing you from receiving condign punishment for the injuries and loss of property already inflicted upon us by you. No! we remain *here;* and if you are not laid low before you pass the Comite Bridge, we can take to the woods again, and camp out, as many a poor woman is doing now, a few miles from town. Many citizens have been arrested, and after being confined a while, and closely questioned, have been released, if the information is satisfactory. A negro man is informing on all cotton burners and violent Secessionists, etc.

Sunday night.

The girls have just got back, riding in a mule team, on top of baggage, but without either mother or any of our affairs. Our condition is perfectly desperate. Miriam had an interview with General Williams, which was by no means satisfactory. He gave her a pass to leave, and bring us back, for he says there is no safety here for us; he will restrain his men in town, and protect the women, but once outside, he will answer neither for his men, nor the women and children. As soon as he gets horses enough, he passes this road, going to Camp Moore with his cavalry, and then we are in greater danger than ever. Any house shut up shall be occupied by soldiers. Five thousand are there now, five more expected. What shall we do? Mother remained, sending Miriam for me, determined to keep us there, rather than sacrifice both our lives and property by remaining here. But then — two weeks from now the yellow fever will break out; mother has the greatest horror of it, and we have never had it; dying is not much in the present state of our affairs, but the survivor will suffer even more than we do now. If we stay, how shall we live? I have seventeen hundred dollars in Confederate notes now in my "running-bag," and three or four in silver. The former will not be received there, the latter might last two days. If we save our house and furniture, it is at the price of starving. I am of opinion that we should send for mother, and with what money we have, make our way somewhere in the interior, to some city where we can communicate with the boys, and be advised by them. This is not living. Home is lost beyond all hope of recovery; if we wait, what we have already saved will go, too; so we had better leave at once, with what clothing we have, which will certainly establish us on the footing of ladies, if we chance to fall among vulgar people who never look beyond. I fear the guerrillas will attack the town to-night; if they do, God help mother!

General Williams offered Miriam an escort when he found she was without a protector, in the most fatherly way; he must be a good man. She thanked him, but said "she felt perfectly safe on *that* road." He bit his lip, understanding the allusion, and did not insist. She was to deliver a message from parties in town to the first guerrillas they met, concerning the safest roads, and presently six met them, and entered into conversation. She told them of the proffered escort, when one sprang forward crying, "Why did n't you accept, Miss? The next time, *ask* for one, and if it is at all disagreeable to you, *I* am the very man to rid you of such an inconvenience! I'll see that you are not annoyed long." I am glad it was not sent; she would have reproached herself with murder forever after. I wonder if the General would have risked it?

BATON ROUGE, June 3d.

Well! Day before yesterday, I almost vowed I would not return, and last evening I reached here. Verily, consistency, thou art a jewel! I determined to get to town to lay both sides of the question before mother; saving home and property, by remaining, thereby cutting ourselves off forever from the boys and dying of yellow fever; or flying to Mississippi, losing all save our lives. So as Mrs. Brunot was panic-stricken and determined to die in town rather than be starved at Greenwell, and was going in on the same wagon that came out the night before, I got up with her and Nettie, and left Greenwell at ten yesterday morning, bringing nothing except this old book, which I would rather not lose, as it has been an old and kind friend during these days of trouble. At first, I avoided all mention of political affairs, but now there is nothing else to be thought of; if it is not burnt for treason, I will like to look it over some day — if I live. I left Greenwell, without ever looking around it, beyond one walk to the hotel, so I may say I hardly know what it looks like. Miriam stayed, much against her will, I fear, to bring in our trunks, if I could send a wagon.

A guerrilla picket stopped us before we had gone a mile, and seemed disposed to turn us back. We said we must pass; our all was at stake. They then entreated us not to enter, saying it was not safe. I asked if they meant to burn it; "We will help try it," was the answer. I begged them to delay the experiment until we could get away. One waved his hat to me and said he would fight for me. Hope he will — at a distance. They asked if we had no protectors; "None," we said. "Don't go, then"; and they all looked so sorry for us. We said we must; starvation, and another panic awaited us out there, our brothers were fighting, our fathers dead; we had only our own judgment to rely on, and that told us home was the best place for us; if the town must burn, let us burn in our houses, rather than be murdered in the woods. They looked still more sorry, but still begged us not to remain. We would, though, and one young boy called out as we drove off, "What's the name of that young lady who refused the escort?" I told him, and they too expressed the greatest regret that she had not accepted. We met many on the road, nearly all of whom talked to us, and as they were most respectful in their manner (though they saw us in a mule team!), we gave them all the information we could, which was all news to them, though very little. Such a ride in the hot sun, perched up in the air! One of the servants remarked, "Miss Sarah ain't ashamed to ride in a wagon!" With truth I replied, "No, I was never so high before."

Two miles from home we met the first Federal pickets, and then they grew more numerous, until we came on a large camp near our graveyard, filled with soldiers and cannon. From first to last none refrained from laughing at us; not aloud, but they would grin and be inwardly convulsed with laughter as we passed. One laughed so comically that I dropped my veil hastily for fear he would see me smile. I could not help it; if any one smiled at me while I was dying, I believe I would return it. We passed crowds, for it was now five o'clock, and all seemed to be promenading. There were several officers standing at the corner, near our house, who were very much amused at our vehicle. I did not feel like smiling then. After reducing us to riding in a mule team, they were heartless enough to laugh! I forgot them presently, and gave my whole attention to getting out respectably. Now getting *in* a wagon is bad enough; but getting out —! I hardly know how I managed it. I had fully three feet to step down before reaching the wheel; once there, the driver picked me up and set me on the pavement. The net I had gathered my hair in, fell in my descent, and my hair swept down halfway between my knee and ankle in one stream. As I turned to get my little bundle, the officers had moved their position to one directly opposite to me, where they could examine me at leisure. Queens used to ride drawn by oxen hundreds of years ago, so I played this was old times, the mules were oxen, I a queen, and stalked off in a style I am satisfied would have imposed on Juno herself. When I saw them as I turned, they were perfectly quiet; but Nettie says up to that moment they had been in convulsions of laughter, with their handkerchiefs to their faces. It was not polite!

I found mother safe, but the house was in the most horrible confusion. Jimmy's empty cage stood by the door; it had the same effect on me that empty coffins produce on others. Oh, my birdie! At six, I could no longer stand my hunger. I had fasted for twelve hours, with the exception of a mouthful of hoe-cake at eleven; I that never fasted in my life! — except last Ash Wednesday when Lydia and I tried it for breakfast, and got so sick we were glad to atone for it at dinner. So I got a little piece of bread and corn beef from Mrs. Daigre's servant, for there was not a morsel here, and I did not know where or what to buy. Presently some kind friend sent me a great short-cake, a dish of strawberry preserves, and some butter, which I was grateful for, for the fact that the old negro was giving me part of her supper made me rather sparing, though she cried, "Eat it all, honey! I get plenty more!"

Mother went to Cousin Will's, and I went to Mrs. Brunot's to sleep, and so ended my first day's ride on a mule team. Bah! A lady can make anything respectable by the way she does it! What do I care if I had been driving mules? Better that than walk seventeen miles.

I met Dr. DuChêne and Dr. Castleton twice each,

this morning. They were as kind to me as they were to the girls the other day. The latter saved them a disagreeable visit, while here. He and those three were packing some things in the hall, when two officers passed, and prepared to come in, seeing three good-looking girls seemingly alone, for Miriam's dress hid Dr. Castleton as he leaned over the box. Just then she moved, the Doctor raised his head, and the officers started back with an "Ah!" of surprise. The Doctor called them as they turned away, and asked for a pass for the young ladies. They came back bowing and smiling, said they would write one in the house, but they were told very dryly that there were no writing accommodations there. They tried the fascinating, and were much mortified by the coldness they met. Dear me! "Why was n't I born old and ugly?" Suppose I should unconsciously entrap some magnificent Yankee! What an awful thing it would be! !

Sentinels are stationed at every corner; Dr. Castleton piloted me safely through one expedition; but on the next, we had to part company, and I passed through a crowd of at least fifty, alone. They were playing cards in the ditch, and swearing dreadfully, these pious Yankees; many were marching up and down, some sleeping on the pavement, others — picking odious bugs out of each other's heads! I thought of the guerrillas, yellow fever, and all, and wished they were all safe at home with their mothers and sisters, and we at peace again.

What a day I have had! Here mother and I are alone, not a servant on the lot. We will sleep here to-night, and I know she will be too nervous to let me sleep. The dirt and confusion were extraordinary in the house. I could not stand it, so I applied myself to making it better. I actually swept two whole rooms! I ruined my hands at gardening, so it made no difference. I replaced piles of books, crockery, china, that Miriam had left packed for Greenwell; I discovered I could empty a dirty hearth, dust, move heavy weights, make myself generally useful and dirty, and all this is thanks to the Yankees! Poor me! This time last year I thought I would never walk again! If I am not laid up forever after the fatigue of this last week, I shall always maintain I have a Constitution. But it all seems nothing in this confusion; everything is almost as bad as ever. Besides that, I have been flying around to get Miriam a wagon. I know she is half distracted at being there alone. Mother chose staying with all its evils. Charlie's life would pay the penalty of a cotton burner if he returned, so Lilly remains at Greenwell with him. We three will get on as best we can here. I wrote to the country to get a wagon, sent a pass from Headquarters, but I will never know if it reached her until I see her in town. I hope it will; I would be better satisfied with Miriam.

June 4th.

Miriam and Mattie drove in, in the little buggy, last evening after sunset, to find out what we were to do. Our condition is desperate. Beauregard is about attacking these Federals. They say he is coming from Corinth, and the fight will be in town. If true, we are lost again. Starvation at Greenwell, fever and bullets here, will put an end to us soon enough. There is no refuge for us, no one to consult. Brother, whose judgment we rely on as implicitly as we did on father's, we hear has gone to New York; there is no one to advise or direct us, for, if he is gone, there is no man in Louisiana whose decision I would blindly abide by. Let us stay and die. We can only die once; we can suffer a thousand deaths with suspense and uncertainty; the shortest is the best. Do you think the few words here can give an idea of our agony and despair? Nothing can express it. I feel a thousand years old to-day. I have shed the bitterest tears to-day that I have shed since father died. I can't stand it much longer; I 'll give way presently, and I know my heart will break. Shame! Where is God? A fig for your religion, if it only lasts while the sun shines! "Better days are coming" — I can't!

Troops are constantly passing and repassing. They have scoured the country for ten miles out, in search of guerrillas. We are here without servants, clothing, or the bare necessaries of life: suppose they should seize them on the way! I procured a pass for the wagon, but it now seems doubtful if I can get the latter — a very faint chance. Well! let them go; our home next; then we can die sure enough. With

God's help, I can stand anything yet in store for me. "I hope to die shouting, the Lord will provide!" Poor Lavinia! if she could only see us! I am glad she does not know our condition.

5 P.M.

What a day of agony, doubt, uncertainty, and despair! Heaven save me from another such! Every hour fresh difficulties arose, until I believe we were almost crazy, every one of us.

As Miriam was about stepping in the buggy, to go to Greenwell to bring in our trunks, mother's heart misgave her, and she decided to sacrifice her property rather than remain in this state any longer. After a desperate discussion which proved that each argument was death, she decided to go back to Greenwell and give up the keys of the house to General Williams, and let him do as he pleased, rather than have it broken open during her absence. Mattie and Mr. Tunnard were present at the discussion, which ended by the latter stepping in the buggy and driving Miriam to the Garrison. General Williams called her by name, and asked her about Major Drum. It seems all these people, native and foreign, know us, while we know none. Miriam told him our condition, how our brothers were away, father dead, and mother afraid to remain, yet unwilling to lose her property by going away; how we three were alone and unprotected here, but would remain rather than have our home confiscated. He assured her the house should not be touched, that it would be respected

MIRIAM MORGAN

in our absence as though we were in it, and he would place a sentinel at the door to guard it against his own men who might be disposed to enter. The latter she declined, but he said he would send his aide to mark the house, that it might be known. A moment after they got back, the aide, Mr. Biddle (I have his name to so many passes that I know it now), came to the door. Mr. Tunnard left him there, uncertain how we would receive a Christian, and I went out and asked him in. He looked uncertain of his reception, too, when we put an end to his doubt by treating him as we invariably treat gentlemen who appear such. He behaved remarkably well under the trying circumstances, and insisted on a sentinel; for, he said, though they would respect the property, there were many bad characters among the soldiers who might attempt to rob it, and the sentinel would protect it. After a visit of ten minutes, devoted exclusively to the affair, he arose and took his leave, leaving me under the impression that he was a gentleman wherever he came from, even if there were a few grammatical errors in the pass he wrote me yesterday; but "thou that judgest another, dost thou sin?"

Well, now we say, fly to Greenwell. Yes! and by to-night, a most exaggerated account of the whole affair will be spread over the whole country, and we will be equally suspected by our own people. Those who spread useless falsehoods about us will gladly have a foundation for a monstrous one. Did n't

Camp Moore ring with the story of our entertaining the Federal officers? Did n't they spread the report that Miriam danced with one to the tune of "Yankee Doodle" in the State House garden? What will they stop at now? O! if I was only a man, and knew what to do!

Night.

We were so distressed by the false position in which we would be placed by a Federal sentinel, that we did not know what course to pursue. As all our friends shook their heads and said it was dangerous, we knew full well what our enemies would say. If we win Baton Rouge, as I pray we will, they will say we asked protection from Yankees against our own men, are consequently traitors, and our property will be confiscated by our own Government. To decline General Williams's kind offer exposes the house to being plundered. In our dilemma, we made up our minds to stay, so we could say the sentinel was unnecessary.

Presently a file of six soldiers marched to the gate, an officer came to the steps and introduced himself as Colonel McMillan, of 21st Indiana Volunteers. He asked if this was Mrs. Morgan's; the General had ordered a guard placed around the house; he would suggest placing them in different parts of the yard. "Madam, the pickets await your orders." Miriam in a desperate fright undertook to speak for mother, and asked if he thought there was any necessity. No, but it was an additional security, he said.

"Then, if no actual necessity, we will relieve you of thc disagreeable duty, as we expect to remain in town," she said. He was very kind, and discussed the whole affair with us, saying when we made up our minds to leave, — we told him after we could not decide, — to write him word, and he would place a guard around to prevent his men and the negroes from breaking in. It was a singular situation: our brothers off fighting them, while these Federal officers leaned over our fence, and an officer standing on our steps offered to protect us. These people are certainly very kind to us. General Williams especially must be a dear old gentleman; he is so good.

How many good, and how many mean people these troubles have shown us! I am beginning to see my true friends, now; there is a large number of them, too. Everybody from whom we least expected attention has agreeably surprised us. . . .

General Williams will believe we are insane from our changing so often.

His guard positively refused.

June 5th.

Last night I determined to stay. Miriam went after our trunks at daylight. A few hours after, Lilly wrote we must go back. McClellan's army was cut to pieces and driven back to Maryland, by Jackson; the Federals were being driven into the swamp from Richmond, too. Beauregard is undoubtedly coming to attack Baton Rouge; his fire would burn the town, if the gunboats do not; the

Yankees will shell, at all events, if forced to retire. It cannot stand. We can't go to New Orleans. Butler says he will lay it in ashes if he is forced to evacuate it, from yellow fever or other causes. Both must be burned. Greenwell is not worth the powder it would cost, so we must stand the chance of murder and starvation there, rather than the certainty of being placed between two fires here. Well, I see nothing but bloodshed and beggary staring us in the face. Let it come. "I hope to die shouting, the Lord will provide."

June 6th.

We dined at Mrs. Brunot's yesterday, and sitting on the gallery later, had the full benefit of a Yankee drill. They stopped in front of the house and went through some very curious manœuvres, and then marched out to their drill-ground beyond. In returning, the whole regiment drew up directly before us, and we were dreadfully quiet for five minutes, the most uncomfortable I have experienced for some time. For it was absurd to look at the sky, and I looked in vain for one man with downcast eyes whereon I might rest mine; but from the officers down to the last private, they were all looking at us. I believe I would have cried with embarrassment if the command had not been given at that moment. They drilled splendidly, and knew it, too, so went through it as though they had not been at it for an hour before. One conceited, red-headed lieutenant smiled at us in the most fascinating way; perhaps he smiled to think how fine he was, and what an impression he was making.

We got back to our solitary house before twilight, and were sitting on the balcony, when Mr. Biddle entered. He came to ask if the guard had been placed here last night. It seems to me it would have saved him such a long walk if he had asked Colonel McMillan. He sat down, though, and got talking in the moonlight, and people passing, some citizens, some officers, looked wonderingly at this unheard-of occurrence. I won't be rude to any one in my own house, Yankee or Southern, say what they will. He talked a great deal, and was very entertaining; what tempted him, I cannot imagine. It was two hours before he thought of leaving. He was certainly very kind. He spoke of the scarcity of flour in town; said they had quantities at the Garrison, and asked permission to send us a barrel, which of course we refused. It showed a very good heart, though. He offered to take charge of any letters I would write; said he had heard General Williams speak of Harry; and when he at last left, I was still more pleased with him for this kindness to us. He says Captain Huger is dead. I am very, very much distressed. They are related, he says. He talked so reasonably of the war, that it was quite a novelty after reading the abusive newspapers of both sides. I like him, and was sorry I could not ask him to repeat his visit. We are unaccustomed to treat gentlemen that way; but it won't do in the present state to act as we please. Mob governs.

Mother kept me awake all night to listen to the mice in the garret. Every time I would doze she would ask, "What's that?" and insist that the mice were men. I had to get up and look for an imaginary host, so I am tired enough this morning.

Miriam has just got in with all the servants, our baggage is on the way, so we will be obliged to stay whether we will or no. I don't care; it is all the same, starve or burn. Oh! I forgot. Mr. Biddle did *not* write that pass! It was his clerk. He speaks *very* grammatically, so far as I can judge! !

June 8th, Sunday.

These people mean to kill us with kindness. There is such a thing as being too kind. Yesterday General Williams sent a barrel of flour to mother, accompanied by a note begging her to accept it "in consideration of the present condition of the circulating currency," and the intention was so kind, the way it was done so delicate, that there was no refusing it. I had to write her thanks, and got in a violent fit of the "trembles" at the idea of writing to a stranger. One consolation is, that I am not a very big fool, for it took only three lines to prove myself one. If I had been a thundering big one, I would have occupied two pages to show myself fully. And to think it is out of our power to prove them our appreciation of the kindness we have universally met with! Many officers were in church this morning, and as they passed us while we waited for the door to be opened, General Williams bowed profoundly, another followed his example; we returned the salute, of course. But by to-morrow, those he did not bow to will cry treason against us. Let them howl. I am tired of lies, scandal, and deceit. All the loudest gossips have been frightened into the country, but enough remain to keep them well supplied with town talk. . . . It is such a consolation to turn to the dear good people of the world after coming in contact with such cattle. Here, for instance, is Mr. Bonnecase on whom we have not the slightest claims. Every day since we have been here, he has sent a great pitcher of milk, knowing our cow is out; one day he sent rice, the next sardines, yesterday two bottles of Port and Madeira, which cannot be purchased in the whole South. What a duck of an old man! That is only one instance.

June 10th.

This morning while I was attending to my flowers . . . several soldiers stopped in front of me, and holding on the fence, commenced to talk about some brave Colonel, and a shooting affair last night. When all had gone except one who was watching me attentively, as he seemed to wish to tell me, I let him go ahead. The story was that Colonel McMillan was shot through the shoulder, breast, and liver, by three guerrillas while four miles from town last night, on a scout. He was a quarter of a mile from his own men at the time, killed one who shot him, took the other two prisoners, and fell from his horse himself, when he got within the lines. The soldier said these two guerrillas would probably be hanged, while the six we saw pass captives, Sunday, would probably be sent to Fort Jackson for life. I think the guerrilla affair mere murder, I confess; but what a dreadful fate for these young men! One who passed Sunday was Jimmy's schoolmate, a boy of sixteen; another, Willie Garig, the pet of a whole family of good, honest country people. . . .

These soldiers will get in the habit of talking to me after a while, through my own fault. Yesterday I could not resist the temptation to ask the fate of the six guerrillas, and stopped two volunteers who were going by, to ask them. They discussed the fate of the country, told me Fort Pillow and Vicksburg were evacuated, the Mississippi opened from source to mouth; I told them of Banks's and McClellan's defeat; they assured me it would all be over in a month, — which I fervently pray may be so; told me they were from Michigan (one was Mr. Bee, he said, cousin of our General); and they would probably have talked all day if I had not bowed myself away with thanks for their information.

It made me ashamed to contrast the quiet, gentlemanly, liberal way these volunteers spoke of us and our cause, with the rabid, fanatical, abusive violence of our own female Secession declaimers. Thank Heaven, I have never yet made my appearance as a Billingsgate orator on these occasions. All my violent feelings, which in moments of intense excitement were really violent, I have recorded in this book; I am happy to say only the reasonable dislike to seeing my country subjugated has been confided to the public ear, when necessary; and that even now, I confess that nothing but the reign of terror and gross prejudice by which I was surrounded at that time could justify many expressions I have here applied to them. Fact is, these people have disarmed me by their kindness. I expected to be in a crowd of ruffian soldiers, who would think nothing of cutting your throat or doing anything they felt like; and I find, among all these thousands, not one who offers the slightest annoyance or disrespect. The former is the thing as it is believed by the whole country, the latter the true state of affairs. I admire foes who show so much consideration for our feelings.

Contrast these with our volunteers from New Orleans — all gentlemen — who came to take the Garrison from Major Haskins. Several of them passing our gate where we were standing with the Brunots, one exclaimed, "What pretty girls!" It was a stage aside that we were supposed not to hear. "Yes," said another; "beautiful! but they look as though they could be fast." Fast! and we were not even speaking! not even looking at them! Sophie and I were walking presently, and met half a dozen. We had to stop to let them pass the crossing; they did not think of making way for us; No. 1 sighed — such a sigh! No. 2 followed, and so on, when they all sighed in chorus for our edification, while we dared not raise our eyes from the ground. That is the time I would have made use of a dagger. Two passed in a buggy, and trusting to our not recognizing them from the rapidity of their vehicle, kissed their hands to us until they were out of sight! All went back to New Orleans vowing Baton Rouge had the prettiest girls in the world. These were our own people, the élite of New Orleans, loyal Southerners and gentlemen. These Northerners pass us satisfied with a simple glance; some take off their hats, for all these officers know our name, though we may not know theirs; how, I can't say.

When I heard of Colonel McMillan's misfortune, mother conspired with me to send over some bandages, and something Tiche manufactured of flour under the name of "nourishment," for he is across the street at Heroman's. Miriam objected on account of what "our people" will say, and what we will suffer for it if the guerrillas reach town, but we persuaded her we were right. . . . You can imagine our condition at present, many years hence, Sarah, when you reflect that it is the brave, noble-hearted, generous Miriam who is afraid to do that deed on account of "public opinion," which indeed is "down" on us. At Greenwell they are frantic about our returning to town, and call us traitors, Yankees, and vow vengeance. . . . A lady said to me, "The guerrillas have a black list containing the names of those remaining in town. All the men are to be hanged, their houses burned, and all the women are to be tarred and feathered." I said, "Madam, if I believed them capable of such a vile *threat*, even, much less the execution, I would see them cut down without a feeling of compassion" (which is not true), "and swear I was a Yankee rather than claim being a native of the same country with such brutes." She has a long tongue; when I next hear of it, it will be that *I* told the story, and called them brutes and hoped they would be shot, etc. And so goes the world. No one will think of saying that I did not believe them guilty of the thought, even. Our three brothers may be sick or wounded at this minute; what I do for this man, God will send some one to do for them, and with that belief I do it. . . .

June 11th.

Last evening mother and Miriam went to the Arsenal to see if they would be allowed to do anything for the prisoners. General Williams received them, and fascinated Miriam by his manner, as usual. Poor Miriam is always being fascinated, according to her own account. He sent for little Nathan Castle and Willie Garig, and left them alone in the room with them, showing his confidence and delicacy by walking away. The poor young men were very grateful to be remembered; one had his eyes too full of tears to speak. Mr. Garig told Miriam that when the story of her refusing the escort was told in camp, the woods rang with shouts of "Three cheers for Miss Morgan!" They said they were treated very well, and had no want, except clean clothes, and to let their mothers know they were well and content.

I have been hard at work mending three or four suits of the boys' clothing for those poor young men. Some needed thread and needle very much, but it was the best we could do. So I packed them all up — not forgetting a row of pins — and sent Tiche off with the bundle, perched real Congo fashion on her many-colored head-handkerchief, which was tied in the most superb Creole style in honor of the occasion.

June 16th, Monday.

My poor old diary comes to a very abrupt end, to my great distress. The hardest thing in the world is to break off journalizing when you are once accustomed to it, and mine has proved such a resource to me in these dark days of trouble that I feel as though I were saying good-bye to an old and tried friend. Thanks to my liberal supply of pens, ink, and paper, how many inexpressibly dreary days I have filled up to my own satisfaction, if not to that of others! How many disagreeable affairs it has caused me to pass over without another thought, how many times it has proved a relief to me where my tongue was forced to remain quiet! Without the blessed materials, I would have fallen victim to despair and "the Blues" long since; but they have kept my eyes fixed on "Better days a-coming" while slightly alluding to present woes; kept me from making a fool of myself many a day; acted as lightning rod to my mental thunder, and have made me happy generally. For all of which I cry, "Vivent pen, ink, and paper!" and add with regret, "Adieu, my mental Conductor. I fear this unchained lightning will strike somewhere, in your absence!"

BOOK II

"I hope to die shouting, the Lord will provide!"

Monday, June 16th, 1862.

THERE is no use in trying to break off journalizing, particularly in "these trying times." It has become a necessity to me. I believe I should go off in a rapid decline if Butler took it in his head to prohibit that among other things. . . . I reserve to myself the privilege of writing my opinions, since I trouble no one with the expression of them. . . . I insist, that if the valor and chivalry of our men cannot save our country, I would rather have it conquered by a brave race than owe its liberty to the Billingsgate oratory and demonstrations of some of these "ladies." If the women have the upper hand then, as they have now, I would not like to live in a country governed by such tongues. Do I consider the female who could spit in a gentleman's face, merely because he wore United States buttons, as a fit associate for me? Lieutenant Biddle assured me he did not pass a street in New Orleans without being most grossly insulted by *ladies*. It was a friend of his into whose face a lady *spit* as he walked quietly by without looking at her. (Wonder if she did it to attract his attention?) He had the sense to apply to her husband and give him two minutes to apologize or die, and of course he chose the former.[1] Such things are enough to disgust any one. "Loud" women, what a contempt I have for you! How I despise your vulgarity!

Some of these Ultra-Secessionists, evidently very recently from "down East," who think themselves obliged to "kick up their heels over the Bonny Blue Flag," as Brother describes female patriotism, shriek out, "What! see those vile Northerners pass patiently! No true Southerner could see it without rage. I could kill them! I hate them with all my soul, the murderers, liars, thieves, rascals! You are no Southerner if you do not hate them as much as I!" *Ah ça!* a true-blue Yankee tell me that I, born and bred here, am no Southerner! I always think, "It is well for you, my friend, to save your credit, else you might be suspected by some people, though your violence is enough for me." I always say, "*You* may do as you please; my brothers are fighting for me, and doing their duty, so that excess of patriotism is unnecessary for me, as my position is too well known to make any demonstrations requisite."

This war has brought out wicked, malignant feelings that I did not believe could dwell in woman's heart. I see some of the holiest eyes, so holy one would think the very spirit of charity lived in them, and all Christian meekness, go off in a mad tirade of abuse and say, with the holy eyes wondrously

[1] This passage was later annotated by Mrs. Dawson as follows: "*Friend* (Farragut). *Lady* (I know her, alas!). *Husband* (She had none!)."

changed, "I hope God will send down plague, yellow fever, famine, on these vile Yankees, and that not one will escape death." O, what unutterable horror that remark causes me as often as I hear it! I think of the many mothers, wives, and sisters who wait as anxiously, pray as fervently in their faraway homes for their dear ones, as we do here; I fancy them waiting day after day for the footsteps that will never come, growing more sad, lonely, and heart-broken as the days wear on; I think of how awful it would be if one would say, "Your brothers are dead"; how it would crush all life and happiness out of me; and I say, "God forgive these poor women! They know not what they say!" O women! into what loathsome violence you have abased your holy mission! God will punish us for our hard-heartedness. Not a square off, in the new theatre, lie more than a hundred sick soldiers. What woman has stretched out her hand to save them, to give them a cup of cold water? Where is the charity which should ignore nations and creeds, and administer help to the Indian and Heathen indifferently? Gone! All gone in Union versus Secession! *That* is what the American War has brought us. If I was independent, if I could work my own will without causing others to suffer for my deeds, I would not be poring over this stupid page; I would not be idly reading or sewing. I would put aside woman's trash, take up woman's duty, and I would stand by some forsaken man and bid him Godspeed as he closes his dying eyes. *That* is woman's mission! and not Preaching and Politics. I say I would, yet here I sit! O for liberty! the liberty that *dares* do what conscience dictates, and scorns all smaller rules! If I could help these dying men! Yet it is as impossible as though I was a chained bear. I can't put out my hand. I am threatened with Coventry because I sent a custard to a sick man who is in the army, and with the anathema of society because I said if I could possibly do anything for Mr. Biddle — at a distance — (he is sick) I would like to very much. Charlie thinks we have acted shockingly in helping Colonel McMillan, and that we will suffer for it when the Federals leave. I would like to see any *man* who *dared* harm my father's daughter! But as he seems to think our conduct reflects on him, there is no alternative. Die, poor men, without a woman's hand to close your eyes! We women are too *patriotic* to help you! I look eagerly on, cry in my soul, "I wish —"; you die; God judges me. Behold the woman who dares not risk private ties for God's glory and her professed religion! Coward, helpless woman that I am! If I was free —!

June 17th.

Yesterday, and day before, boats were constantly arriving and troops embarking from here, destined for Vicksburg. There will be another fight, and of course it will fall. I wish Will was out of it; I don't want him to die. I got the kindest, sweetest letter from Will when Miriam came from Greenwell. It was given to her by a guerrilla on the road who asked if she was not Miss Sarah Morgan.

June 18th.

How long, O how long, is it since I have lain down in peace, thinking, "This night I will rest in safety"? Certainly not since the fall of Fort Jackson. If left to myself, I would not anticipate evil, but would quietly await the issue of all these dreadful events; but when I hear men, who certainly should know better than I, express their belief that in twenty-four hours the town will be laid in ashes, I begin to grow uneasy, and think it must be so, since they say it. These last few days, since the news arrived of the intervention of the English and French, I have alternately risen and fallen from the depth of despair to the height of delight and expectation, as the probability of another exodus diminishes, and peace appears more probable. If these men would not prophesy the burning of the city, I would be perfectly satisfied. . . .

Well! I packed up a few articles to satisfy my conscience, since these men insist that another run is inevitable, though against my own conviction. I am afraid I was partly influenced by my dream last night of being shelled out unexpectedly and flying without saving an article. It was the same dream I had a night or two before we fled so ingloriously from Baton Rouge, when I dreamed of meeting Will Pinckney suddenly, who greeted me in the most extraordinarily affectionate manner, and told me that Vicksburg had fallen. He said he had been chiefly to blame, and the Southerners were so incensed at his losing, the Northerners at his defending, that both were determined to hang him; he was running for his life. He took me to a hill from which I could see the Garrison, and the American flag flying over it. I looked, and saw we were standing in blood up to our knees, while here and there ghastly white bones shone above the red surface. Just then, below me I saw crowds of people running. "What is it?" I asked. "It means that in another instant they will commence to shell the town. Save yourself." "But Will — I must save some clothes, too! How can I go among strangers with a single dress? I *will* get some!" I cried. He smiled and said, "You will run with only what articles you happen to have on." Bang! went the first shell, the people rushed by with screams, and I awakened to tell Miriam what an absurd dream I had had. It happened as Will had said, either that same day or the day after; for the change of clothes we saved apiece were given to Tiche, who lost sight of us and quietly came home when all was over, and the two dirty skirts and old cloak mother saved, after carrying them a mile and a half, I put in the buggy that took her up; so I saved nothing except the bag that was tied under my hoops. Will was right. I saved not even my powder-bag. (Tiche had it in the bundle.) My handkerchief I gave mother before we had walked three squares, and throughout that long fearfully warm day, riding and walking through the fiery sunshine and stifling dust, I had neither to cool or comfort me.

June 19th.

Miriam and I have disgraced ourselves! This morning I was quietly hearing Dellie's lessons, when I was startled by mother's shrieks of "Send for a guard — they've murdered him!" I saw through the window a soldier sitting in the road just opposite, with blood streaming from his hand in a great pool in the dust. I was downstairs in three bounds, and, snatching up some water, ran to where he sat alone, not a creature near, though all the inhabitants of our side of the street were looking on from the balconies, all crying "Murder!" and "Help!" without moving themselves. I poured some water on the man's bloody hand, as he held it streaming with gore up to me, saying, "The man in there did it," meaning the one who keeps the little grog-shop, though it puzzled me at the time to see that all the doors were closed and not a face visible. I had hardly time to speak when Tiche called loudly to me to come away, — she was safe at the front gate, — and looking up, I found myself in a knot of a dozen soldiers, and took her advice and retreated home. It proved to be the guard Miriam had roused. She ran out as I did, and seeing a gentleman, begged him to call the guard for that murdered man. The individual — he must have been a "patriot" — said he did n't know where to find one. She cried out they were at Heroman's;

he said he did n't believe they were. "Go! I tell you!" she screamed at last; but the brave man said he did n't like to, so she ran to the corner and called the soldiers herself. O most brave man! Before we got back from our several expeditions, we heard mother, Lilly, Mrs. Day, all shouting, "Bring in the children! lock the doors!" etc. All for a poor wounded soldier!

We after discovered that the man was drunk, and had cursed the woman of the grog-shop, whereupon her husband had pitched him out in the street, where they found him. They say he hurt his hand against a post; but wood could never have cut deep enough to shed all that gore. I don't care if he was drunk or sober, soldier or officer, Federal or Confederate! If he had been Satan himself lying helpless and bleeding in the street, I would have gone to him! I can't believe it was as criminal as though I had watched quietly from a distance, believing him dying and contenting myself with looking on. Yet it seems it was dreadfully indecorous; Miriam and I did very wrong; we should have shouted murder with the rest of the women and servants. Whereas the man who declined committing himself by calling one soldier to the rescue of another, supposed to be dying, acted most discreetly, and showed his wisdom in the most striking manner.

May I never be discreet, or wise, if this is Christian conduct, or a sample of either! I would rather be a rash, impetuous fool! Charlie says he would not open his mouth to save a dozen from being murdered. I say I am not Stoic enough for that. Lilly agrees with him, Miriam with me; so here we two culprits stand alone before the tribunal of "patriotism." Madame Roland, I take the liberty of altering your words and cry, "O Patriotism! How many base deeds are sanctioned by your name!" Don't I wish I was a heathen! In twenty-four hours the whole country will be down on us.

> O for a pen to paint the slaves
> Whose "country" like a deadly blight
> Closes all hearts when Pity craves
> And turns God's spirit to darkest night!
> May life's patriotic cup for such
> Be filled with glory overmuch;
> And when their spirits go above in pride,
> Spirit of Patriotism, let these valiant abide
> Full in the sight of grand mass-meeting — I don't
> Want you to cuss them,
> But put them where they can hear politics,
> And yet can't discuss them!

(I can't say worse than that!)

June 26th.

Yesterday morning, just as I stepped out of bed I heard the report of four cannon fired in rapid succession, and everybody asked everybody else, "Did you hear that?" so significantly, that I must say my heart beat very rapidly for a few moments, at the thought of another stampede. At half-past six this morning I was wakened by another report, followed by seven others, and heard again the question, "Did you hear *that?*" on a higher key than yesterday. —

It did not take me many minutes to get out of bed, and to slip on a few articles, I confess. My chief desire was to wash my face before running, if they were actually shelling us again. It appears that they were only practicing, however, and no harm was intended. But we are living on such a volcano, that, not knowing what to expect, we are rather nervous.

I am afraid this close confinement will prove too much for me; my long walks are cut off, on account of the soldiers. One month to-morrow since my last visit to the graveyard! That haunts me always; it must be so dreary out there! Here is a sketch of my daily life, enough to finish me off forever, if much longer persisted in.

First, get up a little before seven. After breakfast, which is generally within a few minutes after I get down (it used to be *just* as I got ready, and sometimes before, last winter), I attend to my garden, which consists of two strips of ground the length of the house, in front, where I can find an hour's work in examining and admiring my flowers, replanting those that the cows and horses occasionally (once a day) pull up for me, and in turning the soil over and over again to see which side grows best. O my garden! abode of rare delights! how many pleasant hours I have passed in you, armed with scissors, knife, hoe, or rake, only pausing when Mr. This or Mr. That leaned over the fence to have a talk! — last spring, that was; ever so many are dead now, for all I know, and all off at the war. Now I work for the edification of proper young women, who look in astonishment at me, as they would consider themselves degraded by the pursuit. A delicate pair of hands my flower mania will leave me!

Then I hear Dellie's and Morgan's lessons, after which I open my desk and am lost in the mysteries of Arithmetic, Geography, Blair's Lectures, Noël et Chapsal, Ollendorff, and reading aloud in French and English, besides writing occasionally in each, and sometimes a peep at Lavoisne, until very nearly dinner. The day is not half long enough for me. Many things I would like to study I am forced to give up, for want of leisure to devote to them. But one of these days, I will make up for present deficiencies. I study only what I absolutely love, now; but then, if I can, I will study what I am at present ignorant of, and cultivate a taste for something new.

The few moments before dinner, and all the time after, I devote to writing, sewing, knitting, etc., and if I included darning, repairs, alterations, etc., my list would be tremendous, for I get through with a great deal of sewing. Somewhere in the day, I find half an hour, or more, to spend at the piano. Before sunset I dress, and am free to spend the evening at home, or else walk to Mrs. Brunot's, for it is not safe to go farther than those three squares, away from home. From early twilight until supper, Miriam and I sing with the guitar, generally, and after, sit comfortably under the chandelier and read until about ten. What little reading I do, is almost exclusively done at that time. It sounds woefully little, but my list of books grows to quite a respectable size, in the course of a year.

At ten comes my Bible class for the servants. Lucy, Rose, Nancy, and Dophy assemble in my room, and hear me read the Bible, or stories from the Bible for a while. Then one by one say their prayers — they cannot be persuaded to say them together; Dophy says "she can't say with Rose, 'cause she ain't got no brothers and sisters to pray for," and Lucy has no father or mother, and so they go. All difficulties and grievances during the day are laid before me, and I sit like Moses judging the children of Israel, until I can appease the discord. Sometimes it is not so easy. For instance, that memorable night when I had to work Rose's stubborn heart to a proper pitch of repentance for having stabbed a carving-fork in Lucy's arm in a fit of temper. I don't know that I was ever as much astonished as I was at seeing the dogged, sullen girl throw herself on the floor in a burst of tears, and say if God would forgive her she would never do it again. I was lashing myself internally for not being able to speak as I should, furious at myself for talking so weakly, and lo! here the girl tumbles over wailing and weeping! And Dophy, overcome by her feelings, sobs, "Lucy, I scratched you last week! please forgive me this once!" And amazed and bewildered I look at the touching tableau before me of kissing and reconciliation, for Lucy can bear malice toward no one, and is ready to forgive before others repent, and I look from one to the other, wondering what it was that upset them so completely, for certainly no words of mine caused it. Sometimes Lucy sings a wild hymn, "Did you ever hear the heaven bells ring?" "Come, my loving brothers," "When I put on my starry crown," etc.; and after some such scene as that just described, it is pleasant to hear them going out of the room saying, "Good-night, Miss Sarah!" "God bless Miss Sarah!" and all that.

June 27th.

A proclamation of Van Dorn has just been smuggled into town, that advises all persons living within eight miles of the Mississippi to remove into the interior, as he is determined to defend his department at all hazards to the last extremity. Does not look like the Peace I have been deluding myself with, does it? That means another Exodus. How are we to leave, when we are not allowed to pass the limits of the corporation by the Federals? Where are we to go? We are between the two armies, and here we must remain patiently awaiting the result. Some of these dark nights, bang! we will hear the cannon, and then it will be *sauve qui peut* in a shower of shells. Bah! I don't believe God will suffer that we should be murdered in such a dreadful way! I don't believe He will suffer us to be turned homeless and naked on the world! "Something will turn up" before we are attacked, and we will be spared, I am certain. We can't look forward more than an hour at a time now, sometimes not a minute ahead (witness the shelling frolic), so I must resume my old habit of laying a clean dress on my bed before going to sleep, which I did every night for six weeks before the shelling of Baton Rouge, in order to run respectably, as muslin cross-bar nightgowns are not suitable for day dresses.

June 28th.

I am afraid I shall be nervous when the moment of the bombardment actually arrives. This suspense is not calculated to soothe one's nerves. A few moments since, a salute was fired in honor of General Butler's arrival, when women, children, and servants rushed to the front of the houses, confident of a repetition of the shelling which occurred a month ago to-day. The children have not forgotten the scene, for they all actually howled with fear. Poor little Sarah stopped her screams to say, "Mother, don't you wish we was dogs 'stead o' white folks?" in such piteous accents that we had to laugh. *Don't* I wish I was a dog! Sarah is right. I don't know if I showed my uneasiness a while ago, but certainly my heart has hardly yet ceased beating rather rapidly. If I knew what moment to expect the stampede, I would not mind; but this way — to expect it every instant — it is too much! Again, if I knew where we could go for refuge from the shells! ——

A window banging unexpectedly just then gave

me a curious twinge; not that I thought it was the signal, oh, dear, no! I just thought — what, I wonder? Pshaw! "Picayune Butler's coming, coming" has upset my nervous system. He interrupted me in the middle of my arithmetic; and I have not the energy to resume my studies. I shall try what effect an hour's practice will have on my spirits, and will see that I have a pair of clean stockings in my stampede sack, and that the fastenings of my "running-bag" are safe. Though if I expect to take either, I should keep in harness constantly. How long, O Lord! how long?

June 29th, Sunday.

"Any more, Mr. Lincoln, any more?" Can't you leave our racked homes in repose? We are all wild. Last night, five citizens were arrested, on no charge at all, and carried down to Picayune Butler's ship. What a thrill of terror ran through the whole community! We all felt so helpless, so powerless under the hand of our tyrant, the man who swore to uphold the Constitution and the laws, who is professedly only fighting to give us all Liberty, the birthright of every American, and who, nevertheless, has ground us down to a state where we would not reduce our negroes, who tortures and sneers at us, and rules us with an iron hand! Ah! Liberty! what a humbug! I would rather belong to England or France, than to the North! Bondage, woman that I am, I can never stand! Even now, the Northern papers, distributed among us, taunt us with our subjection and tell us "how coolly Butler will grind them down, paying no regard to their writhing and torture beyond tightening the bonds still more!" Ah, truly! this is the bitterness of slavery, to be insulted and reviled by cowards who are safe at home and enjoy the protection of the laws, while we, captive and overpowered, dare not raise our voices to throw back the insult, and are governed by the despotism of one man, whose word is our law! And that man, they tell us, "is the right man in the right place. *He* will develop a Union sentiment among the people, if the thing can be done!" Come and see if he can! Hear the curse that arises from thousands of hearts at that man's name, and say if he will "speedily bring us to our senses." Will he accomplish it by love, tenderness, mercy, compassion? He might have done it; but did he try? When he came, he assumed his natural rôle as tyrant, and bravely has he acted it through, never once turning aside for Justice or Mercy. . . . This degradation is worse than the bitterness of death!

I see no salvation on either side. No glory awaits the Southern Confederacy, even if it does achieve its independence; it will be a mere speck in the world, with no weight or authority. The North confesses itself lost without us, and has paid an unheard-of ransom to regain us. On the other hand, conquered, what hope is there in this world for us? Broken in health and fortune, reviled, contemned, abused by those who claim already to have subdued us, without a prospect of future support for those few of our brothers who return; outcasts without home or honor, would not death or exile be preferable? Oh, let us abandon our loved home to these implacable enemies, and find refuge elsewhere! Take from us property, everything, only grant us liberty! Is this rather frantic, considering I abhor politics, and women who meddle with them, above all? My opinion has not yet changed; I still feel the same contempt for a woman who would talk at the top of her voice for the edification of Federal officers, as though anxious to receive an invitation requesting her presence at the Garrison. "I can suffer and be still" as far as outward signs are concerned; but as no word of this has passed my lips, I give it vent in writing, which is more lasting than words, partly to relieve my heart, partly to prove to my own satisfaction that I am no coward; for one line of this, surrounded as we are by soldiers, and liable to have our houses searched at any instant, would be a sufficient indictment for high treason.

Under General Williams's rule, I was perfectly satisfied that whatever was done, was done through necessity, and under orders from Headquarters, beyond his control; we all liked him. But now, since Butler's arrival, I believe I am as frantic in secret as the others are openly. I know that war sanctions many hard things, and that both sides practice them; but now we are so completely lost in Louisiana, is it fair to gibe and taunt us with our humiliation? I could stand anything save the cowardly ridicule and triumph of their papers. Honestly, I believe if all vile abusive papers on both sides were suppressed, and some of the fire-eating editors who make a living by lying were soundly cowhided or had their ears clipped, it would do more towards establishing peace, than all the bloodshedding either side can afford. I hope to live to see it, too. Seems to me, more liberty is allowed to the press than would be tolerated in speech. Let us speak as freely as any paper, and see if to-morrow we do not sleep at Fort Jackson!

This morning the excitement is rare; fifteen more citizens were arrested and carried off, and all the rest grew wild with expectation. So great a martyrdom is it considered, that I am sure those who are not arrested will be woefully disappointed. It is ludicrous to see how each man thinks he is the very one they are in search of! We asked a twopenny lawyer, of no more importance in the community than Dophy is, if it was possible he was not arrested. "But I am expecting to be every instant!" So much for his self-assurance! Those arrested have, some, been quietly released (those are so smiling and mysterious that I suspect them), some been obliged to take the oath, some sent to Fort Jackson. Ah, Liberty! What a blessing it is to enjoy thy privileges! If some of these poor men are not taken prisoners, they will die of mortification at the slight.

Our valiant Governor, the brave Moore, has by order of the real Governor, Moïse, made himself visible at some far-distant point, and issued a proclamation, saying, whereas we of Baton Rouge were held forcibly in town, he therefore considered men, women, and children prisoners of war, and as such the Yankees are bound to supply us with all necessaries, and consequently any one sending us aid or comfort or provisions from the country will be severely punished. Only Moore is fool enough for such an order. Held down by the Federals, our paper money so much trash, with hardly any other to buy food and no way of earning it; threatened with starvation and utter ruin, our own friends, by way of making our burden lighter, forbid our receiving the means of prolonging life, and after generously warning us to leave town, which they know is perfectly impossible, prepare to burn it over our heads, and let the women run the same risk as the men. Penned in on one little square mile, here we await our fate like sheep in the slaughter-pen. Our hour may be at hand now, it may be to-night; we have only to wait; the booming of the cannon will announce it to us soon enough.

Of the six sentenced to Fort Jackson, one is the Methodist minister, Mr. Craven. The only charge is, that he was heard to pray for the Confederate States by some officers who passed his house during his family prayers. According to that, which of us would escape unhung? I do not believe there is a woman in the land who closes her eyes before praying for God's blessing on the side on which her brothers are engaged. Are we all to cease? Show me the dungeon deep enough to keep me from praying for them! The man represented that he had a large family totally dependent on him, who must starve. "Let them get up a subscription," was General Butler's humane answer. "I will head it myself." It is useless to say the generous offer was declined.

June 30th.

As a specimen of the humanity of General Butler, let me record a threat of his uttered with all the force and meaning language can convey, and certainly enough to strike terror in the hearts of frail women, since all these men believe him fully equal to carry it into execution; some even believe it will be done. In speaking to Mr. Solomon Benjamin of foreign intervention in our favor, he said, "Let England or France try it, and I'll be —— if I don't arm every negro in the South, and make them cut the throat of every man, woman, and child in it! I'll make them lay the whole country waste with fire and sword, and leave it desolate!" Draw me a finer picture of Coward, Brute, or Bully than that one sentence portrays! O men of the North! you do your noble hearts wrong in sending such ruffians among us as the representatives of a great people! Was ever a more brutal thought uttered in a more brutal way? Mother, like many another, is crazy to go away from here, even to New Orleans; but like the rest, will be obliged to stand and await her fate. I don't believe

Butler would *dare* execute his threat, for at the first attempt, thousands, who are passive now, would cut the brutal heart from his inhuman breast.

Tuesday, July 1st.

I heard such a good joke last night! If I had belonged to the female declaiming club, I fear me I would have resigned instantly through mere terror. (Thank Heaven, I don't!) These officers say the women talk too much, which is undeniable. They then said, they meant to get up a sewing society, and place in it every woman who makes herself conspicuous by her loud talking about them. Fancy what a refinement of torture! But only a few would suffer; the majority would be only too happy to enjoy the usual privilege of sewing societies, slander, abuse, and insinuations. How some would revel in it. The mere threat makes me quake! If I could so far forget my dignity, and my father's name, as to court the notice of gentlemen by contemptible insult, etc., and if I should be ordered to take my seat at the sewing society —! ! ! I would never hold my head up again! Member of a select sewing circle! Fancy me! (I know "there is never any *gossip* in *our* society, though the one over the way gets up dreadful reports"; I have heard all that, but would rather try neither.) Oh, how I would beg and plead! Fifty years at Fort Jackson, good, kind General Butler, rather than half an hour in your sewing society! Gentle, humane ruler, spare me and I split my throat in shouting "Yankee Doodle" and "Hurrah for Lincoln!" Any, every thing, so I am not disgraced! Deliver me from your sewing society, and I'll say and do what you please!

Butler told some of these gentlemen that he had a detective watching almost every house in town, and he knew everything. True or not, it looks suspicious. We are certainly watched. Every evening two men may be seen in the shadow on the other side of the street, standing there until ever so late, sometimes until after we have gone to bed. It may be that, far from home, they are attracted by the bright light and singing, and watch us for their amusement. A few nights ago, so many officers passed and repassed while we were singing on the balcony, that I felt as though our habit of long standing had suddenly become improper. Saturday night, having secured a paper, we were all crowding around, Lilly and I reading every now and then a piece of news from opposite ends of the paper, Charlie, walking on the balcony, found five officers leaning over the fence watching us as we stood under the light, through the open window. Hope they won't elect me to the sewing society!

Thursday night, July 3d.

Another day of sickening suspense. This evening, about three, came the rumor that there was to be an attack on the town to-night, or early in the morning, and we had best be prepared for anything. I can't say I believe it, but in spite of my distrust, I made my preparations. First of all I made a charming improvement in my knapsack, *alias* pillow-case, by sewing a strong black band down each side of the centre from the bottom to the top, when it is carried back and fastened below again, allowing me to pass my arms through, and thus present the appearance of an old peddler. Miriam's I secured also, and tied all our laces in a handkerchief ready to lay it in the last thing.

But the interior of my bag! — what a medley it is! First, I believe, I have secured four underskirts, three chemises, as many pairs of stockings, two under-bodies, the prayer book father gave me, "Tennyson" that Harry gave me when I was fourteen, two unmade muslins, a white mull, English grenadine trimmed with lilac, and a purple linen, and nightgown. Then, I must have Lavinia's daguerreotype, and how could I leave Will's, when perhaps he was dead? Besides, Howell's and Will Carter's were with him, and one single case did not matter. But there was Tom Barker's I would like to keep, and oh! let's take Mr. Stone's! and I can't slight Mr. Dunnington, for these two have been too kind to Jimmy for me to forget; and poor Captain Huger is dead, and I *will* keep his, so they all went together. A box of pens, too, was indispensable, and a case of French note-paper, and a bundle of Harry's letters were added. Miriam insisted on the old diary that preceded this, and found place for it, though I am afraid if she knew what trash she was to carry, she would retract before going farther.

It makes me heartsick to see the utter ruin we will be plunged in if forced to run to-night. Not a hundredth part of what I most value can be saved — if I counted my letters and papers, not a thousandth. But I cannot believe we will run to-night. The soldiers tell whoever questions them that there will be a fight before morning, but I believe it must be to alarm them. Though what looks suspicious is, that the officers said — to whom is not stated — that the ladies must not be uneasy if they heard cannon to-night, as they would probably commence to celebrate the Fourth of July about twelve o'clock. What does it mean? I repeat, I don't believe a word of it; yet I have not yet met the woman or child who is not prepared to fly. Rose knocked at the door just now to show her preparations. Her only thought seems to be mother's silver, so she has quietly taken possession of our shoe-bag, which is a long sack for odds and ends with cases for shoes outside, and has filled it with all the contents of the silver-box; this hung over her arm, and carrying Louis and Sarah, this young Samson says she will be ready to fly.

I don't believe it, yet here I sit, my knapsack serving me for a desk, my seat the chair on which I have carefully spread my clothes in order. At my elbow lies my running- or treasure-bag, surrounded by my cabas filled with hair-pins, starch, and a band I was embroidering, etc.; near it lie our combs, etc., and the whole is crowned by my dagger; — by the way, I must add Miriam's pistol which she has forgotten, though over there lies her knapsack ready, too, with our bonnets and veils.

It is long past eleven, and no sound of the cannon. Bah! I do not expect it. "I'll lay me down and sleep in peace, for Thou only, Lord, makest me to dwell in safety." Good-night! I wake up to-morrow the same as usual, and be disappointed that my trouble was unnecessary.

July 4th.

Here I am, and still alive, having wakened but once in the night, and that only in consequence of Louis and Morgan crying; nothing more alarming than that. I ought to feel foolish; but I do not. I am glad I was prepared, even though there was no occasion for it.

While I was taking my early bath, Lilly came to the bath-house and told me through the weather-boarding of another battle. Stonewall Jackson has surrounded McClellan completely, and victory is again ours. This is said to be the sixth battle he has fought in twenty days, and they say he has won them all. And the Seventh Regiment distinguished itself, and was presented with four cannon on the battlefield in acknowledgment of its gallant conduct! Gibbes belongs to the "ragged howling regiment that rushed on the field yelling like unchained devils and spread a panic through the army," as the Northern papers said, describing the battle of Manassas. Oh, how I hope he has escaped!

And they say "Palmerston has urged the recognition of the Confederacy, and an armed intervention on our side." Would it not be glorious? Oh, for peace, blessed peace, and our brothers once more! Palmerston is said to have painted Butler as the vilest oppressor, and having added he was ashamed to acknowledge him of Anglo-Saxon origin. Perhaps knowing the opinion entertained of him by foreign nations, caused Butler to turn such a somersault. For a few days before his arrival here, we saw a leading article in the leading Union paper of New Orleans, threatening us with the arming of the slaves for our extermination if England interfered, in the same language almost as Butler used when here; three days ago the same paper ridiculed the idea, and said such a brutal, inhuman thing was never for a moment thought of, it was too absurd. And so the world goes! We all turn somersaults occasionally.

And yet, I would rather we would achieve our independence alone, if possible. It would be so much more glorious. And then I would hate to see England conquer the North, even if for our sake; my love for the old Union is still too great to be willing to see it so humiliated. If England would just make Lincoln come to his senses, and put an end to all this confiscation which is sweeping over everything, make him agree to let us alone and behave himself, that will be quite enough. But what a task! If it were put to the vote to-morrow to return free and unmolested to the Union, or stay out, I am sure Union would have the majority; but this way, to think we are to be sent to Fort Jackson and all the other prisons for expressing our ideas, however harmless, to have our houses burned over our heads, and all the prominent men hanged, who would be eager for it? — unless, indeed, it was to escape even the greater horrors of a war of extermination.

July 5th.

. . . .

Think, that since the 28th of May, I have not walked three squares at a time, for my only walks are to Mrs. Brunot's!

It is enough to kill any one; I might as well be at Ship Island, where Butler has sentenced Mrs. Phillips for laughing while the corpse of a Federal officer [1] was passing — at least, that is to be the principal charge, though I hope, for the sake of Butler's soul, that he had better reasons. Shocking as her conduct was, she hardly deserved two years' close confinement in such a dreadful place as that, because she happened to have no sense of delicacy, and no feeling.

"The darkest hour is just before the day"; we have had the blackest night for almost three months, and I don't see the light yet. "Better days are coming —" I am getting skeptical, I fear me.

I look forward to my future life with a shudder. This one cannot last long; I will be "up and doing" before many months are past. Doing what? Why, if

[1] Note by Mrs. Dawson in 1906: DeKay, our relative.

all father left us is lost forever, if we are to be penniless as well as homeless, I'll work for my living. How, I wonder? I will teach. I know I am not capable, but I can do my best. I would rather die than be dependent; I would rather die than teach. There now, you know how I feel! Teaching before dependence, death before teaching. My soul revolts from the drudgery. I never see a governess that my heart does not ache for her. I think of the nameless, numberless insults and trials she is forced to submit to; of the hopeless, thankless task that is imposed on her, to which she is expected to submit without a murmur; of all her griefs and agony shut up in her heart, and I cry Heaven help a governess. My heart bleeds for them and —

1 o'clock P.M.

Thus far had I reached when news came that our forces were attacking the town, and had already driven the pickets in! I am well now.

We all rushed to make preparations instantly. I had just finished washing my hair, before I commenced writing, and had it all streaming around me; but it did not take a minute to thrust it into a loose net. Then we each put on a fresh dress, except myself, as I preferred to have a linen cambric worn several times before, to a clean one not quite so nice, for that can do good service when washed. The excitement is intense; mother is securing a few of father's most valuable papers; Lilly running around after the children, and waiting for Charlie who cannot be found; Miriam, after securing all things needful, has gone downstairs to wait the issue; and I, dressed for instant flight, with my running-bag tied to my waist, and knapsack, bonnet, veil, etc., on the bed, occupy my last few moments at home in this profitable way.

Nobody knows what it is. A regiment has been marched out to meet our troops, some say commanded by Van Dorn, which I doubt. The gunboats are preparing to second them; we hear the Garrison drum and see people running, that is all. We don't know what is coming. I believe it will prove nothing, after all. But —! The gunboat is drawn up so as to command our street here; the guns aimed up the street just below, and if a house falls, ours will be about the first. Well! this time next year, we will know all of which we are now ignorant. That is one consolation! The house will either be down or standing, then.

6 P.M.

We have once more subsided; how foolish all this seems! Miriam and I laughed while preparing, and laughed while unpacking; it is the only way to take such things, and we agree on that, as on most other subjects. "They say" the affair originated from half a dozen shots fired by some Federal soldiers through idleness, whereupon the pickets rushed in screaming Van Dorn was after them at the head of six thousand men. I have my reasons for doubting the story; it must have been something more than that, to spread such a panic; for they certainly had time to ascertain the truth of the attack before they beat the long roll and sent out their troops, for if it had been Van Dorn, he would have been on them before that. Whatever it was, I am glad of the excitement, for it gave me new life for several hours; I was really sick before. Oh, this life! When will it end? Evermore and forevermore shall we live in this suspense? I wish we were in the Sandwich Islands.

July 7th.

As we have no longer a minister — Mr. Gierlow having gone to Europe — and no papers, I am in danger of forgetting the days of the week, as well as those of the month; but I am positive that yesterday was Sunday because I heard the Sunday-School bells, and Friday I am sure was the Fourth, because I heard the national salute fired. I must remember that to find my dates by.

Well, last night being Sunday, a son of Captain Hooper, who died in the Fort Jackson fight, having just come from New Orleans, stopped here on his way to Jackson, to tell us the news, or rather to see Charlie, and told us afterwards. He says a boat from Mobile reached the city Saturday evening, and the captain told Mr. La Noue that he brought an extra from the former place, containing news of McClellan's surrender with his entire army, his being mortally wounded, and the instant departure of a French, and English, man-of-war, from

Hampton Roads, with the news. That revived my spirits considerably — all except McClellan's being wounded; I could dispense with that. But if it were true, and if peace would follow, and the boys come home —! Oh, what bliss! I would die of joy as rapidly as I am pining away with suspense now, I am afraid!

About ten o'clock, as we came up, mother went to the window in the entry to tell the news to Mrs. Day, and while speaking, saw a man creeping by under the window, in the narrow little alley on the side of the house, evidently listening, for he had previously been standing in the shadow of a tree, and left the street to be nearer. When mother ran to give the alarm to Charlie, I looked down, and there the man was, looking up, as I could dimly see, for he crouched down in the shadow of the fence. Presently, stooping still, he ran fast towards the front of the house, making quite a noise in the long tangled grass. When he got near the pepper-bush, he drew himself up to his full height, paused a moment as though listening, and then walked quietly towards the front gate. By that time Charlie reached the front gallery above, and called to him, asking what he wanted. Without answering the man walked steadily out, closed the gate deliberately; then, suddenly remembering drunkenness would be the best excuse, gave a lurch towards the house, walked off perfectly straight in the moonlight, until seeing Dr. Day fastening his gate, he reeled again.

That man was not drunk! Drunken men cannot run crouching, do not shut gates carefully after them, would have no inclination to creep in a dim little alley merely to creep out again. It may have been one of our detectives. Standing in the full moonlight, which was very bright, he certainly looked like a gentleman, for he was dressed in a handsome suit of black. He was no citizen. Form your own conclusions! Well! after all, he heard no treason. Let him play eavesdropper if he finds it consistent with his character as a gentleman.

The captain who brought the extra from Mobile wished to have it reprinted, but it was instantly seized by a Federal officer, who carried it to Butler, who monopolized it; so *that* will never be heard of again; we must wait for other means of information. The young boy who told us, reminds me very much of Jimmy; he is by no means so handsome, but yet there is something that recalls him; and his voice, though more childish, sounds like Jimmy's, too. I had an opportunity of writing to Lydia by him, of which I gladly availed myself, and have just finished a really tremendous epistle.

Wednesday, 9th July.

Poor Miriam! Poor Sarah! they are disgraced again! Last night we were all sitting on the balcony in the moonlight, singing as usual with our guitar. I have been so accustomed to hear father say in the evening, "Come, girls! where is my concert?" and he took so much pleasure in listening, that I could not think singing in the balcony was so very dreadful, since he encouraged us in it. But last night changed all my ideas. We noticed Federals, both officers and soldiers, pass singly, or by twos or threes at different times, but as we were not singing for their benefit, and they were evidently attending to their own affairs, there was no necessity of noticing them at all.

But about half-past nine, after we had sung two or three dozen others, we commenced "Mary of Argyle." As the last word died away, while the chords were still vibrating, came a sound of — clapping hands, in short! Down went every string of the guitar; Charlie cried, "I told you so!" and ordered an immediate retreat; Miriam objected, as undignified, but renounced the guitar; mother sprang to her feet, and closed the front windows in an instant, whereupon, dignified or not, we all evacuated the gallery and fell back into the house. All this was done in a few minutes, and as quietly as possible; and while the gas was being turned off downstairs, Miriam and I flew upstairs, — I confess I was mortified to death, very, very much ashamed, — but we wanted to see the guilty party, for from below they were invisible. We stole out on the front balcony above, and in front of the house that used to be Gibbes's, we beheld one of the culprits. At the sight of the creature, my mortification vanished in intense compassion for his. He was standing under the tree, half in the moonlight, his hands in his pockets, looking at the extinction of light below, with the true state of affairs dawning on his astonished mind, and looking by no means satisfied with himself! Such an abashed creature! He looked just as though he had received a kick, that, conscious of deserving, he dared not return! While he yet gazed on the house in silent amazement and consternation, hands still forlornly searching his pockets, as though for a reason for our behavior, from under the dark shadow of the tree another slowly picked himself up from the ground — hope he was not knocked down by surprise — and joined the first. His hands sought his pockets, too, and, if possible, he looked more mortified than the other. After looking for some time at the house, satisfied that they had put an end to future singing from the gallery, they walked slowly away, turning back every now and then to be certain that it was a fact. If ever I saw two mortified, hangdog-looking men, they were these two as they took their way home. Was it not shocking?

But they could not have meant it merely to be insulting or they would have placed themselves in full view of us, rather than out of sight, under the trees. Perhaps they were thinking of their own homes, instead of us.

July 10th.

A proclamation is out announcing that any one talking about the war, or present state of affairs, will be "summarily" dealt with. Now, seems to me "summarily" is not exactly the word they mean, but still it has an imposing effect. What a sad state their affairs must be in, if they can't bear comment. An officer arrived day before yesterday, bringing the surprising intelligence that McClellan had captured Richmond and fifty thousand prisoners; that is the time *they* talked. But when we received yesterday confirmation of his being finally defeated by our troops, and the capture of his railroad train twelve miles in length, they forbid further mention of the subject. I wonder if they expect to be obeyed? What a stretch of tyranny! O free America! You who uphold free people, free speech, free everything, what a foul blot of despotism rests on a once spotless name! A nation of brave men, who wage war on women and lock them up in prisons for using their woman weapon, the tongue; a nation of free people who advocate despotism; a nation of Brothers who bind the weaker ones hand and foot, and scourge them with military tyrants and other Free, Brotherly institutions; what a picture! Who would not be an American? One consolation is, that this proclamation, and the extraordinary care they take to suppress all news except what they themselves manufacture, proves me our cause is prospering more than they like us to know. I do believe day is about to break!

If our troops are determined to burn our houses over our heads to spite the Yankees, I wish they would hurry and have it over at once. Ten regiments of infantry are stationed at Camp Moore, and Scott's cavalry was expected at Greenwell yesterday, both preparing for an attack on Baton Rouge. If we must be beggars, let it come at once; I can't endure this suspense.

July 11th.

A letter from George this morning! It was written on the 20th of June, and he speaks of being on crutches in consequence of his horse having fallen with him, and injured his knee. Perhaps, then, he was not in the first battle of the 25th? But bah! I know George too well to imagine he would keep quiet at such a moment, if he could possibly stand! I am sure he was there with the rest of the Louisiana regiment. The papers say "the conduct of the First Louisiana is beyond all praise"; of course, George was there!

And Jimmy is with him at Richmond; but whether in the army, or navy, or what rank if in the first, he does not say; he only says he is looking remarkably well. Gibbes he had heard from in a letter dated the 16th, and up to then he was in perfect health. His last letter here was dated 10th of March, so we are thankful enough now. I was so delighted to read the accounts of the "gallant Seventh" in some paper we fortunately procured. At Jackson's address, and presentation of the battery they had so bravely won, I was beside myself with delight; I was thinking that Gibbes, of course, was "the" regiment, had taken the battery with his single sword, and I know not what besides. Strange to say, I have not an idea of the names of the half-dozen battles he was in, in June, but believe that one to be Port Republic.

June 12th [*sic*].

Brother writes that rumors of the capture of Baton Rouge by our troops have made him very uneasy about us; and he wishes us to go down to New Orleans if possible. I wish we could. The impression here, is that an attack is inevitable, and the city papers found it necessary to contradict the rumor of Ruggles having occupied it already. I wish mother would go. I can see no difference there or here, except that there, we will be safe, for a while at least. . . .

I grow desperate when I read these Northern papers reviling and abusing us, reproaching us for being broken and dispersed, taunting us with their victories, sparing no humiliating name in speaking of us, and laughing as to what "we'll see" when we vile rebels are "driven out of Virginia, and the glorious Union firmly established." I can't bear these taunts! I grow sick to read these vile, insulting papers that seem written expressly to goad us into madness! . . . There must be many humane, reasonable men in the North; can they not teach their editors decency in this their hour of triumph?

July 13th, Sunday.

A profitable way to spend such a day! Being forced to dispense with church-going, I have occupied myself in reading a great deal, and writing a little, which latter duty is a favorite task of mine after church on Sundays. But this evening, the mosquitoes are so savage that writing became im-

JAMES MORRIS MORGAN

possible, until Miriam and I instituted a grand extermination process, which we partly accomplished by extraordinary efforts. She lay on the bed with the bar half-drawn over her, and half-looped up, while I was commissioned to fan the wretches from all corners into the pen. It was rather fatiguing, and in spite of the numbers slain, hardly recompensed me for the trouble of hunting them around the room; but still, Miriam says exercise is good for me, and she ought to know.

I have been reading that old disguster, Boswell. Bah! I have no patience with the toady! I suppose "my mind is not yet thoroughly impregnated with the Johnsonian ether," and that is the reason why I cannot appreciate him, or his work. I admire him for his patience and minuteness in compiling such trivial details. He must have been an amiable man, to bear Johnson's brutal, ill-humored remarks; but seems to me if I had not spirit enough to resent the indignity, I would at least not publish it to the world! Briefly, my opinion, which this book has only tended to confirm, is that Boswell was a vain, conceited prig, a fool of a jackanape, an insupportable sycophant, a — whatever mean thing you please; there is no word small enough to suit him. As to Johnson, he is a surly old bear; in short, an old brute of a tyrant. All his knowledge and attainments could not have made me tolerate him, I am sure. I could have no respect for a man who was so coarse in speech and manners, and who eat like an animal.

Fact is, I am not a Boswellian, or a Johnsonian, either. I do not think him such an extraordinary man. I have heard many conversations as worthy of being recorded as nineteen-twentieths of his. In spite of his learning, he was narrow-minded and bigoted, which I despise above all earthly failings. Witness his tirades against Americans, calling us Rascals, Robbers, Pirates, and saying he would like to burn us! Now I have railed at many of these ordinary women here, for using like epithets for the Yankees, and have felt the greatest contempt for their absurd abuse. These poor women do not aspire to Johnsonian wisdom, and their ignorance may serve as an excuse for their narrow-mindedness; but the wondrous Johnson to rave and bellow like any Billingsgate nymph! Bah! He is an old disguster!

July 14th, 3 P.M.

Another pleasant excitement. News has just arrived that Scott's cavalry was having a hard fight with the Yankees eight miles from town. Everybody immediately commenced to pick up stray articles, and get ready to fly, in spite of the intense heat. I am resigned, as I hardly expect a shelling. Another report places the fight fourteen miles from here. A man on horseback came in for reinforcements. Heaven help poor Howell, if it is true. I am beginning to doubt half I hear. People tell me the most extravagant things, and if I am fool enough to believe them and repeat them, I suddenly discover that it is not half so true as it might be, and as they themselves frequently deny having told it, all the odium of "manufacturing" rests on my shoulders, which have not been accustomed to bear lies of any kind. I mean to cease believing anything, unless it rests on the word of some responsible person. By the way — the order I so confidently believed, concerning the proclamation, turns out not quite so bad. I was told women were included, and it extended to private houses as well as public ones, though I fortunately omitted that when I recorded it. When I read it, it said, "All discussions concerning the war are prohibited in bar-rooms, public assemblies, and street corners." As women do not frequent such places, and private houses are not mentioned, I cannot imagine how my informant made the mistake, unless, like me, it was through hearing it repeated. Odious as I thought it then, I think it wise now; for more than one man has lost his life through discussions of the kind.

July 17th, Thursday.

It is decided that I am to go to New Orleans next week. I hardly know which I dislike most, going or staying. I know I shall be dreadfully homesick; but —

Remember — and keep quiet, Sarah, I beg of you. Everything points to an early attack here. Some say this week. The Federals are cutting down all our beautiful woods near the Penitentiary, to throw up breastworks, some say. Cannon are to be planted on the foundation of Mr. Pike's new house; everybody is in a state of expectation. Honestly, if Baton Rouge *has* to be shelled, I shall hate to miss the fun. It will be worth seeing, and I would like to be present, even at the risk of losing my big toe by a shell. But then, by going, I can save many of my clothes, and then Miriam and I can divide when everything is burned — that is one advantage, besides being beneficial by the change of air. *They say* the town is to be attacked to-night. I don't believe a word of it.

Oh, I was so distressed this evening! They tell me Mr. Biddle was killed at Vicksburg. I hope it is not true. Suppose it was a shot from Will's battery?

July 20th, Sunday.

Last night the town was in a dreadful state of excitement. Before sunset a regiment, that had been camped out of town, came in, and pitched their tents around the new theatre, in front of our church. All was commotion and bustle; and as the pickets had been drawn in, and the soldiers talked freely of expecting an attack, everybody believed it, and was consequently in rather an unpleasant state of anticipation. Their cannon were on the commons back of the church, the artillery horses tied to the wheels; while some dozen tents were placed around, filled with men who were ready to harness them at the first alarm. With all these preparations in full view, we went to bed as usual. I did not even take the trouble of gathering my things which I had removed from my "peddler sack"; and slept, satisfied that, if forced to fly, I would lose almost everything in spite of my precaution in making a bag.

Well! night passed, and here is morning, and nothing is heard yet. The attack is delayed until this evening, or to-morrow, they say. Woman though I am, I am by no means as frightened as some of these men are. I can't get excited about it. Perhaps it is because they know the danger, and I do not. But I hate to see *men* uneasy! I have been so accustomed to brave, fearless ones, who would beard the Devil himself, that it gives me a great disgust to see any one less daring than father and the boys.

I have been so busy preparing to go to the city that I think if the frolic should intervene and prevent my departure, I would be disappointed, though I do not want to go. It would be unpleasant, for instance, to pack all I own in my trunk, and just as I place the key in my pocket to hear the shriek of "Van Dorn!" raised again. This time it is to be Ruggles, though. I would not mind if he came before I was packed. Besides, even if I miss the fun here, they say the boats are fired into from Plaquemine; and then I have the pleasure of being in a fight anyhow. Mother is alarmed about that part of my voyage, but Miriam and I persuaded her it is nothing.

If I was a man — oh, would n't I be in Richmond

with the boys! . . . What is the use of all these worthless women, in war times? If they attack, I shall don the breeches, and join the assailants, and fight, though I think they would be hopeless fools to attempt to capture a town they could not hold for ten minutes under the gunboats. How do breeches and coats feel, I wonder? I am actually afraid of them. I kept a suit of Jimmy's hanging in the armoir for six weeks waiting for the Yankees to come, thinking fright would give me courage to try it (what a seeming paradox!), but I never succeeded. Lilly one day insisted on my trying it, and I advanced so far as to lay it on the bed, and then carried my bird out — I was ashamed to let even my canary see me; — but when I took a second look, my courage deserted me, and there ended my first and last attempt at disguise. I have heard so many girls boast of having worn men's clothes; I wonder where they get the courage.

To think half the men in town sat up all night in expectation of a stampede, while we poor women slept serenely! Everybody is digging pits to hide in when the ball opens. The Days have dug a tremendous one; the Wolffs, Sheppers, and some fifty others have taken the same precaution. They may as well dig their graves at once; what if a tremendous shell should burst over them, and bury in the dirt those who were not killed? Oh, no! let me see all the danger, and the way it is coming, at once. To-morrow, — or day after, — in case no unexpected little incident occurs in the interval, I purpose going to New Orleans, taking father's papers and part of Miriam's and mother's valuables for safe-keeping. I hate to go, but they all think I should, as it will be one less to look after if we are shelled — which I doubt. I don't know that I require *much* protection, but I might as well be agreeable and go. Ouf! how I will grow homesick, before I am out of sight!

Midnight.

Here we go, sure enough. At precisely eleven o'clock, while we were enjoying our first dreams, we were startled by the long roll which was beat half a square below us. At first I only repeated "The roll of the drum," without an idea connected with it; but hearing the soldiers running, in another instant I was up, and was putting on my stockings when Miriam ran in, in her nightgown. The children were roused and dressed quickly, and it did not take us many instants to prepare, — the report of two shots, and the tramp of soldiers, cries of "Double-quick," and sound as of cannon moving, rather hastening our movements. Armoirs, bureaus, and everything else were thrown open, and Miriam and I hastily packed our sacks with any articles that came to hand, having previously taken the precaution to put on everything fresh from the armoir. We have saved what we can; but I find myself obliged to leave one of my new muslins I had just finished, as it occupied more room than I can afford, the body of my lovely lilac, and my beauteous white mull. But then, I have saved eight half-made linen chemises! that will be better than the outward show.

Here comes an alarm of fire — at least a dreadful odor of burning cotton which has set everybody wild with fear that conflagration is to be added to these horrors. The cavalry swept past on their way to the river ten minutes ago, and here comes the news that the gunboats are drawing up their anchors and making ready. Well! here an hour has passed; suppose they do not come after all? I have been watching two sentinels at the corner, who are singing and dancing in the gayest way. One reminds me of Gibbes; I have seen him dance that way often. I was glad to see a good-humored man again. I wish I was in bed. I am only sitting up to satisfy my conscience, for I have long since ceased to expect a *real* bombardment. If it must come, let it be now; I am tired of waiting. A crowd of women have sought the protection of the gunboats. I am distressed about the Brunots; suppose they did not hear the noise? O girls! if I was a man, I wonder what would induce me to leave you four lone, unprotected women sleeping in that house, unconscious of all this? Is manhood a dream that is past? Is humanity an idle name? Fatherless, brotherless girls, if I was honored with the title of Man, I do believe I would be fool enough to run around and wake you, at least! Not another word, though. I shall go mad with rage and disgust. I am going to bed. This must be a humbug.

Morgan came running in, once more in his night-gear, begging Lilly to hear his prayers. In answer to her "Why? You have said them to-night!" he says, "Yes! but I've been getting up so often!" Poor child! no wonder he is perplexed!

One hour and a half of this nonsense, and no result known. We are told the firing commenced, and the pickets were driven in, twenty minutes before the long roll beat.

July 21st.

It is impossible to discover the true story of last night's alarm. Some say it was a gang of negroes who attacked the pickets in revenge for having been turned out of the Garrison; others say it was a number of our soldiers who fired from the bushes; and the most amusing story is that they took alarm at an old white horse, which they killed, mistaking him for the Confederates. One regiment has refused to do picket duty; and the story runs among these poor soldiers that our army, which is within a mile, is perfectly overwhelming. The excitement still continues.

I have been writing to the Brunots the news confirming the death of McClellan, the surrender of his army, and the good tidings of our Ram's recent exploits above Vicksburg, and her arriving safely under the guns there. If we could keep all the dispatches that have passed between us since the battle of the forts, what a collection of absurdity and contradiction it would be! "Forts have been taken." "Their ships have passed; forts safe; Yankees at our mercy." "Ships at New Orleans. City to be bombarded in twelve hours." "Forts surrendered." "City under British protection." "No, it is n't." "City surrendered." "Mistake." "Baton Rouge to be burned when Yankee ships come." And so on, sometimes three times a day, each dispatch contradicting the other, and all equally ridiculous.

The crowd here seems to increase. The streets are thronged with the military, and it will soon be impossible to go even to Mrs. Brunot's, which will be a great privation to me. . . . Five thousand are to come next week, and then it will really be impossible to go in the streets.

July 22d, Tuesday.

Another such day, and there is the end of me! Charlie decided to send Lilly and the children into the country early to-morrow morning, and get them safely out of this doomed town. Mother, Miriam, and I were to remain here alone. Take the children away, and I can stand whatever is to come; but this constant alarm, with five babies in the house, is too much for any of us. So we gladly packed their trunks and got them ready, and then news came pouring in.

First a negro man just from the country told Lilly that our soldiers were swarming out there, that he had never seen so many men. Then Dena wrote us that a Mrs. Bryan had received a letter from her son, praying her not to be in Baton Rouge after Wednesday morning, as they were to attack to-morrow. Then a man came to Charlie, and told him that though he was on parole, yet as a Mason he must beg him not to let his wife sleep in town to-night; to get her away before sunset. But it is impossible for her to start before morning. Hearing so many rumors, all pointing to the same time, we began to believe there might be some danger; so I packed all necessary clothing that could be dispensed with now in a large trunk for mother, Miriam, and me, and got it ready to send out in the country to Mrs. Williams. All told, I have but eight dresses left; so I'll have to be particular. I am wealthy, compared to what I would have been Sunday night, for then I had but two in my sack, and now I have my best in the trunk. If the attack comes before the trunk gets off, or if the trunk is lost, we will verily be beggars; for I pack well, and it contains everything of any value in clothing.

The excitement is on the increase, I think. Everybody is crazy to leave town.

Thursday, July 24th.

Yes; that must be the date, for one day and two nights have passed since I was writing here. Where shall I begin the story of my wanderings? I don't know that it has a beginning, it is all so hurried and confused.

But it was Tuesday evening that the Federals were seized with a panic which threw the whole town in alarm. They said our troops were within eight miles, ten thousand in number. The report was even started that the advance guard was skirmishing with the Federals; the shots were heard distinctly, a dozen people were ready to swear. The Yankees struck their tents, galloped with their cannon through the streets with the most terrific din, troops passed at double-quick on their way to the Garrison, everything was confusion. Mr. Tunnard told us yesterday he was present when part of them reached the gate of the Garrison, and saw one of the officers spring forward, waving his sword, and heard him cry, "Trot, men! Gallop, I say! Damn you! *run* in!" — with a perfect yell at the close; whereupon all lookers-on raised a shout of laughter, for the man was frightened out of his wits. A Federal officer told him that their fright was really a disgrace; and if one thousand of our men had come in town, the whole thirty-five hundred would have been at their mercy. Even the naval officers denounce it as a most arrant piece of cowardice; for instead of marching their troops out to meet ours, they all rushed into the Garrison, where, if attacked, their only retreat would have been into the river. The gunboats were ordered into the middle of the stream, in front of the Garrison; and cooped up there, these valiant men awaited the assault in such trepidation that yesterday they freely said the force could be purchased for fifty cents, they are so ashamed of their panic.

Imagine what effect this had on the inhabitants! Soon, an exodus took place, in the direction of the Asylum, and we needs must follow the general example and run, too. In haste we packed a trunk with our remaining clothes, — what we could get in, — and the greatest confusion prevailed for an hour. Beatrice had commenced to cry early in the evening, and redoubled her screams when she saw the preparations; and Louis joining in, they cried in concert until eight o'clock, when we finally got off. What a din! Lilly looked perfectly exhausted; that look on her face made me heartsick. Miriam flew around everywhere; mother always had one more article to find, and the noise was dreadful, when white and black assembled in the hall ready at last. Charlie placed half of the trunks on the dray, leaving the rest for another trip; and we at last started off. Besides the inevitable running-bag, tied to my waist, on this stifling night I had my sunbonnet, veil, comb, toothbrush, cabas filled with dozens of small articles, and dagger to carry; and then my heart failed me when I thought of my guitar, so I caught it up in the case; and remembering father's heavy inkstand, I seized that, too, with two fans. If I was asked what I did with all these things, I could not answer. Certain it is I had every one in my hands, and was not *very* ridiculous to behold.

Seventeen in number, counting white and black, our procession started off, each loaded in their own way. The soldiers did not scruple to laugh at us. Those who were still waiting in front of the churches to be removed laughed heartily, and cried, "Hello! Where are you going? Running? Good-bye!" Fortunately they could not see our faces, for it was very dark. One stopped us under a lamp-post and wanted us to go back. He said he knew we were to be attacked, for the Confederates were within five miles; but we were as safe at home as at the Asylum. He was a very handsome, respectable-looking man, though dirty, as Yankee soldiers always are, and in his shirt-sleeves besides. We thanked him for his kindness, and went on. All stopped at the Brunots', to see that they were ready to fly; but the two parties were so tremendous that we gladly divided, and Miriam and I remained with them until they could get ready, while our detachment went on.

Wagons, carts, every vehicle imaginable, passed on to places of safety, loaded with valuables, while women and children hurried on, on foot. It took the Brunots as long to prepare as it did us. I had to drag Sophie out of her bed, where she threw herself, vowing she would not run; and after an interminable length of time, we were at last ready and started, with the addition of Mrs. Loucks and her sons in our train. The volunteer, whose sole duty seems to be to watch the Brunots, met us as we got out. He stopped as he met the first, looked in silence until Sophie and I passed, and then burst out laughing. No wonder! What a walk it was! Nobody hesitated to laugh, even though they meant to run themselves, and we made fun of each other, too, so our walk was merry enough.

When we reached there, the Asylum was already crowded — at least, it would have been a crowd in any other place, though a mere handful in such a building. The whole house was illuminated, up to the fifth story, and we were most graciously received by the director, who had thrown the whole house open to whoever chose to come, and exerted himself to be accommodating. It looked like a tremendous hotel where every one is at home; not a servant or one of the deaf and dumb children was to be seen; we had all the lower story to ourselves. Was n't it pleasant to unload, and deposit all things in a place of safety! It was a great relief. Then we five girls walked on the splendid balcony which goes around the house until we could no longer walk, when I amused myself by keeping poor Sophie standing, since she would not sit down like a Christian, but insisted on going to bed like a lazy girl, as she is. When I finally let her go, it did not take her many minutes to undress, and soon we were all ready for bed. The Brunots had beds on the parlor floor; across the wide hall, we had a room opposite; and next to ours, Lilly and the children were all sleeping soundly. I ran the blockade of the hall in my nightgown, and had a splendid romp with the girls after rolling Sophie out of bed, and jerking Nettie up. Mother and Mrs. Brunot cried, "Order," laughing, but they came in for their share of the sport, until an admiring crowd of females at the door told us by their amused faces they were enjoying it, too; so I ran the gauntlet again, and got safely through the hall, and after a few more inroads, in one of which Miriam accompanied me, and on which occasion I am sure we were seen in our nightgowns, we finally went to bed. I won't say went to sleep, for I did not pretend to doze. All our side of the house had bars, except me; and the mosquitoes were unendurable; so I watched mother and Miriam in their downy slumbers and lay on my hard bed for hours, fighting the torments with bare arms.

Every now and then I heard a stir among the females above, indicating that some few were anticipating a panic. Once they took a rush from the fourth story, and cried they heard the cannon; twenty guns had been fired, etc. I lay still, determined not to believe it; and presently all subsided. I lay there for hours longer, it seemed, when Nettie at last wandered in disconsolate to find if we were asleep; for with the exception of Sophie, they, too, had been awake all night. I went to the parlor with her, when she, Dena, and I, decided to dress at once and sit on the balcony, since sleep was hopeless. Behold me in a blue muslin flounced to the waist, with a cape, too! What a running costume! Miriam only had time to take off her white dress before starting. All dressed, we went to the northwest corner, as far as possible from the rest of the household, and sat in a splendid breeze for hours. It was better than fighting insatiable mosquitoes; so there we sat talking through the greater part of a night which seemed to have borrowed a few additional hours for our benefit. We'll have no Leap Year in '64; the twenty-four extra hours were crowded in on that occasion, I think.

We discussed our favorite books, characters, authors, repeated scraps here and there of the mock sentimental, talked of how we would one day like to travel, and where we would go; discussed love and marriage, and came to the conclusion neither was the jest it was thought to be. (O wise young women!) Poor Nettie retired in despair, and we two watched alone for hours longer. The sun must have been arrested by some Joshua on the road; could n't make me believe it was doing its duty as usual. We wandered around the balconies, through the grounds in the dim starlight (for it was cloudy), and finally, beholding a faint promise of morning, sat still and waited for the coming of the lazy sun. What was still more aggravating was that every time we looked in at the others showed them sleeping peacefully. Miriam lay her full length with outstretched arms, the picture of repose, looking *so* comfortable! When the sun finally made his appearance (he was out on a spree, I found, for his eyes were not half opened, and he looked dull and heavy as he peeped from behind his bed curtains), others began to stir, and in an hour more, we were ready to leave. Those who had slept, came out with swelled eyes and drowsy looks; while we three, who had been up all night, were perfectly calm, though *rather* pale; but I am seldom otherwise.

Were we not thankful to see home still standing!

I did not feel tired *much*, but somehow, when it struck half-past six, and I found myself alone here (Miriam having stopped at Mrs. Day's), I suddenly found myself divested of my flounces, and most other articles, and involuntarily going towards the bed. I could not sleep, was n't thinking of such a thing; meant to — there was an end of my soliloquy! Where I went, I don't know. As the clock struck eight, I got up as unaccountably, and discovered I had lost all idea of time in sleep. If it had not been for the clock, I should have said I had slept a day and a night, and it was now Thursday morning. A giant refreshed, I rose from my slumbers, took a hasty cup of coffee, and set to work packing Lilly's trunk, for I was crazy to see the children off as soon as possible.

It was no short work, but we all hurried, said good-bye, and saw them go with a feeling of relief. By the experience of the night before, we knew that when the real moment came it would be impossible to get them off in time to escape danger. Poor Lilly! we miss her sadly; but are thankful to know that she is out of danger with her poor little children. She looked heartbroken at the idea of leaving us alone; but then, when one weak woman has five small babies to take care of, is it fair to impose three big ones on her? I'd never stay here, if she sacrificed her children to take care of us who need no protection. I was very lazy after they left; and sat reading until a note was brought from Charlie saying they were safe beyond the lines.

Last night came another alarm. Some fifty cannon were fired somewhere above, reports came that a body of our troops were a few miles out, so a thousand of these men took courage and went out to reconnoitre. Mrs. Brunot and mother insisted on going again to the Asylum for protection against the coming attack, though we at first begged and pleaded to stay at home. But we had to follow, and I don't think any of us were in the best of humors, as we were all conscious of doing a foolish thing.

We were cordially received again, and got quite gay. Sleeping accommodations no better than before, as far as I was concerned. Sophie, Miriam, and I had but one bar between us, so we placed two mattresses side by side, and by dint of chairs and strings, stretched the net as far as possible over them. Those two were well enough; but to my share fell a baby's mattress two feet by four, placed between the wall and the other great bed, with the end of the bar a foot above my face, and one sheet to do the duty of two — however, they had only one, also. Well! I believe I am tall, so my bed did not fit me. As it was two inches higher than theirs, there was no sharing. In spite of a heavy rain that was now pouring, my warm place was intolerable, and the perspiration streamed from my face so as to be disagreeable, to say the least. It drove me to walk in my sleep, I am afraid, for I have an indistinct recollection of finding myself standing at the window trying to breathe. It was a very, very little piece of sleep I got after all, and that little by no means refreshing.

Up at sunrise again, but it took some time to get ready, for I had to get some clothes out of the trunk, to send home. Well, ever since I reached here I have been writing, and I am ashamed to say how long it is. As the time grows more exciting, my book grows shorter, to my great distress. What will I do?

We all vowed that would be the last time we would run until we heard the cannon, or had some better reason than a Yankee panic to believe the Confederates were coming; though if we listened to mother, she would go there every night if this lasted for a whole year. Kind Phillie Nolan wrote insisting on our staying with them on the plantation until it was over, but we cannot do it; the time is too uncertain; if we *knew* it was to come this week, we might stay that long with her; but to go for an indefinite period, Miriam and I would not hear of.

I have kept for the last a piece of news I received with thankfulness, when I finally heard it; for, though known to the whole family and all the town on Tuesday night, no one thought it worth while to tell me until I heard it by accident last evening. It was that a Mr. Bell, writing to his wife, says Gibbes asked him to send word to mother that he, George, and Jimmy were in the fight of the 10th and 11th, and all safe. God be praised!

July 25th.

An old gentleman stopped here just now in a

carriage and asked to see me. Such a sad, sick old man! He said his name was Caldwell, and that passing through East Feliciana, Mrs. Flynn had asked him to deliver a message to us. Had we heard from our brothers? I told him the message from Mr. Bell. He commenced crying. There was one of them, he said, who got hurt. I held my breath and looked at him. He cried more still, and said yes, it was Gibbes — in the hand — not dangerous — but — Here I thought he meant to tell me worse; perhaps he was dead; but I could not speak, so he went on saying Lydia and the General had gone on to Richmond instantly, and had probably reached there before today. He took so long to tell it, and he cried so, that I was alarmed, until I thought perhaps he had lost one of his own sons; but I dared not ask him. Just then one of the horses fell down with sunstroke, and I begged the old gentleman to come in and rest until they could raise the horse; but he said no, he must go on to the river. He looked so sick that I could not help saying he looked too unwell to go beyond, and I wished he would come in. But he burst into tears, saying, "Yes, my child, I am very, very sick, but I must go on." Poor old man, with his snow-white beard!

July 27th.

I have my bird back! As I waked this morning, I heard a well-known chirp in the streets, and called to mother I knew it was Jimmy. Sure enough it *is* my bird. Lucy Daigre has had him ever since the shelling, as a negro caught it that day and gave it to her.

July 29th.

This town, with its ten thousand soldiers, is more quiet than it was with the old population of seven thousand citizens. With this tremendous addition, it is like a graveyard in its quiet, at times. These poor soldiers are dying awfully. Thirteen went yesterday. On Sunday the boats discharged hundreds of sick at our landing. Some lay there all the afternoon in the hot sun, waiting for the wagon to carry them to the hospital, which task occupied the whole evening. In the mean time these poor wretches lay uncovered on the ground, in every stage of sickness. Cousin Will saw one lying dead without a creature by to notice when he died. Another was dying, and muttering to himself as he lay too far gone to brush the flies out of his eyes and mouth, while no one was able to do it for him. Cousin Will helped him, though. Another, a mere skeleton, lay in the agonies of death, too; but he evidently had kind friends, for several were gathered around holding him up, and fanning him, while his son leaned over him crying aloud. Tiche says it was dreadful to hear the poor boy's sobs. All day our *vis-à-vis*, Baumstark, with his several aids, plies his hammer; all day Sunday he made coffins, and says he can't make them fast enough. Think, too, he is by no means the only undertaker here! Oh, I wish these poor men were safe in their own land! It is heartbreaking to see them die here like dogs, with no one to say Godspeed. The Catholic priest went to see some, sometime ago, and going near one who lay in bed, said some kind thing, when the man burst into tears and cried, "Thank God, I have heard *one* kind word before I die!" In a few minutes the poor wretch was dead.

July 31st.

I believe I forgot to mention one little circumstance in my account of that first night at the Deaf and Dumb Asylum, which at the time struck me with extreme disgust. That was seeing more than one man who had no females or babies to look after, who sought there a refuge from the coming attack. At daylight, one dapper young man, in fashionable array, came stepping lightly on the gallery, carrying a neat carpet-bag in his hand. I hardly think he expected to meet two young ladies at that hour; I shall always believe he meant to creep away before any one was up; for he certainly looked embarrassed when we looked up, though he assumed an air of indifference, and passed by bravely swinging his sack — but I think he wanted us to believe he was not ashamed. I dare say it was some little clerk in his holiday attire; but I can't say what contempt I felt for the creature.

Honestly, I believe the women of the South are as brave as the men who are fighting, and certainly braver than the "Home Guard." I have not yet been able to coax myself into being as alarmed as many

I could name are. They say it is because I do not know the danger. *Soit.* I prefer being brave through ignorance, to being afraid in consequence of my knowledge of coming events. Thank Heaven, my brothers are the bravest of the brave! I would despise them if they shrunk back, though Lucifer should dispute the path with them. Well! *All* men are not Morgan boys! They tell me cowards actually exist, though I hope I never met one. The poor men that went to the Asylum for safety might not have what Lavinia calls "a moral backbone." No wonder, then, they tumbled in there! Besides, I am told half the town spent the night on the banks of the river, on that occasion; and perhaps these unfortunates were subject to colds, and preferred the shelter of a good roof. Poor little fellows! How I longed to give them my hoops, corsets, and pretty blue organdie in exchange for their boots and breeches! Only I thought it was dangerous; for suppose the boots had been so used to running that they should prance off with me, too? Why, it would ruin my reputation! Miss Morgan in petticoats is thought to be "as brave as any other man"; but these borrowed articles might make her fly as fast "as any other man," too, if panic is contagious, as the Yankees here have proved. One consolation is, that all who could go with any propriety, and all who were worthy of fighting, among those who believed in the South, are off at the seat of war; it is only trash, and those who are obliged to remain for private reasons, who still remain. Let us count those young individuals as trash, and step over them. Only ask Heaven why you were made with a man's heart, and a female form, and those creatures with beards were made as bewitchingly nervous?

August 2d, Saturday.

I had thought my running days were over; so little did I anticipate another stampede that I did not notice the report of the attack that was prophesied for night before last, and went to bed without gathering my clothes. But to-day comes a hasty note from Charlie, telling us to leave instantly as General Breckinridge is advancing with ten thousand men to attack us, and at 12 M. yesterday was within thirty-four miles. He begged us to leave today; there would be trouble before to-morrow night. It was so earnest, and he asserted all so positively, that we are going to Phillie's this evening to stay a week, as they say eight days will decide. Ah, me! our beautiful town! Still I am skeptical. If it *must be*, pray Heaven that the blow comes now! Nothing can be equal to suspense. These poor men! Are they not dying fast enough? Will Baumstark have orders for an unlimited supply of coffins next week? Only Charlie's family, ours, and the Brunots know it. He enjoined the strictest secrecy, though the Brunots sent to swear Mrs. Loucks in, as she, like ourselves, has no protector. I would like to tell everybody; but it will warn the Federals. I almost wish we, too, had been left in ignorance; it is cruel to keep it to ourselves. I believe the Yankees expect something; "they say" they have armed fifteen hundred negroes. Foes and insurrection in town, assailing friends outside. — Nice time!

Our cavalry has passed the Amite. Poor Charlie has come all the way to the ferry landing on the other side to warn us. If we do not take advantage, it will not be for want of knowing what is to come. How considerate it was in him to come such a long way! I am charmingly excited! If I only had a pair of breeches, my happiness would be complete. Let it come! I lose all, but in Heaven's name let us have it over at once! My heart fails when I look around, but "Spit fire!" and have an end to this at once! Liberty forever, though death be the penalty.

Treason! Here lies my pass at my elbow, in which has been gratuitously inserted that "Parties holding it are considered to give their parole not to give information, countenance, aid, or support to the so-called Confed. S." As I did not apply for it, agree to the stipulation, or think it by any means proper, I don't consider it binding. I could not give my word for doing what my conscience tells me is Right. I cross with this book full of treason. It "countenances" the C. S.; shall I burn it? That is a stupid ruse; they are too wise to *ask* you to subscribe to it, they just append it.

August 3d, Westover.

Enfin nous sommes arrivées! And after what a trip! As we reached the ferry, I discovered I had lost the pass, and had to walk back and search for it, aided by Mr. Tunnard, who met me in my distress, as it has always been his luck to do. But somebody had already adopted the valuable trifle, so I had to rejoin mother and Miriam without it. The guard resolutely refused to let us pass until we got another, so off flew Mr. Tunnard to procure a second — which was vastly agreeable, as I knew he would have to pay twenty-five cents for it, Yankees having come down as low as that, to procure money. But he had gone before we could say anything, and soon returned with the two-bits' worth of leave of absence. Then we crossed the river in a little skiff after sundown, in a most unpleasant state of uncertainty as to whether the carriage was waiting at the landing for us, for I did not know if Phillie had received my note, and there was no place to go if she had not sent for us. However, we found it waiting, and leaving mother and Miriam to pay the ferry, I walked on to put our bundles in the carriage. A man stepped forward, calling me by name and giving me a note from Charlie before I reached it; and as I placed my foot on the step, another came up and told me he had left a letter at home for me at one o'clock. I bowed Yes (it was from Howell; must answer to-morrow). He asked me not to mention it was "him"; a little servant had asked his name, but he told her it was none of her business. I laughed at the refined remark, and said I had not known who it was — he would hardly have been flattered to hear I had not even inquired.

He modestly said that he was afraid I had seen him through the window. Oh, no! I assured him. "Well, please, *any*how, don't say it's me!" he pleaded most grammatically. I answered, smiling, "I did not know who it was then, I know no more now, and if you choose, I shall always remain in ignorance of your identity. "He burst out laughing, and went off with, "Oh, do, Miss Morgan, forget all about me!" as though it was a difficult matter! Who can he be?

We had a delightful drive in the moonlight, though it was rather long; and it was quite late when we drove up to the house, and were most cordially welcomed by the family. We sat up late on the balcony listening for the report of cannon, which, however, did not come. Baton Rouge is to be attacked to-morrow, "they say." Pray Heaven it will all be over by that time! Nobody seems to doubt it, over here. A while ago a long procession of guerrillas passed a short distance from the house, looking for a party of Yankees they heard of in the neighborhood, and waved their hats, for lack of handkerchiefs, to us as we stood on the balcony.

I call this writing under difficulties! Here I am employing my knee as a desk, a position that is not very natural to me, and by no means comfortable. I feel so stupid, from want of sleep last night, that no wonder I am not even respectably bright. I think I shall lay aside this diary with my pen. I have procured a nicer one, so I no longer regret its close. What a stupid thing it is! As I look back, how faintly have

I expressed things that produced the greatest impression on me at the time, and how completely have I omitted the very things I should have recorded! Bah! it is all the same trash! And here is an end of it — for *this* volume, whose stupidity can only be equaled by the one that precedes, and the one that is to follow it. But who expects to be interesting in war times? If I kept a diary of events, it would be one tissue of lies. Think! There was no battle on the 10th or 11th, McClellan is *not* dead, and Gibbes was never wounded! After that, who believes in reliable information? Not I!

BOOK III

WESTOVER,
Monday, August 4th, 1862.

HERE we are at Dr. Nolan's plantation, with Baton Rouge lying just seven miles from us to the east. We can surely hear the cannon from here. They are all so kind to us that I ought to be contented; but still I wish I was once more at home. I suppose it is very unreasonable in me, but I cannot help it. I miss my old desk very much; it is so awkward to write on my knee that I cannot get used to it. Mine is a nice little room upstairs, detached from all the rest, for it is formed by a large dormer window looking to the north, from which I have seen a large number of guerrillas passing and repassing in their rough costumes, constantly. I enjoy the fresh air, and all that, but pleasant as it is, I wish I was at home and all the fuss was over. Virginia Nolan and Miriam are already equipped in their riding costumes, so I must lay this down and get ready to join them in a scamper across the fields. How delighted I will be to get on a horse again.

August 5th.

About half-past nine, as we got up from the breakfast table, a guerrilla told us the ram Arkansas was lying a few miles below, on her way to coöperate with Breckinridge, whose advance guard had already driven the pickets into Baton Rouge. Then we all grew wild with excitement.

Such exclamations! such delight that the dreadful moment had at last arrived! And yet you could see each stop as we rejoiced, to offer up a prayer for the preservation of those who were risking their lives at that moment. Reason, and all else, was thrown aside, and we determined to participate in the danger, if there was any to be incurred. Mother threatened us with shot and shell and bloody murder, but the loud report of half a dozen cannon in slow succession only made us more determined to see the fun, so Lilly Nolan and Miss Walters got on horseback, and Phillie, Ginnie, Miriam, and I started off in the broiling sun, leaving word for the carriage to overtake us. When we once got in, the driver, being as crazy as we, fairly made his horses run along the road to catch a glimpse of our Ram. When, miles below, she came in sight, we could no longer remain in the carriage, but mounted the levee, and ran along on foot until we reached her, when we crossed to the outer levee, and there she lay at our feet.

And nothing in her after all! There lay a heavy, clumsy, rusty, ugly flatboat with a great square box in the centre, while great cannon put their noses out at the sides, and in front. The decks were crowded with men, rough and dirty, jabbering and hastily eating their breakfast. That was the great Arkansas! God bless and protect her, and the brave men she carries.

While there, a young man came up, and in answer to Phillie's inquiries about her father — who, having gone to town yesterday to report, being paroled, had written last night to say no passes were granted to leave town — the young fellow informed her *so* pleasantly that her father was a prisoner, held as hostage for Mr. Castle. Poor Phillie had to cry; so, to be still more agreeable, he told her, Yes, he had been sent to a boat lying at the landing, and ran the greatest risk, as the ram would probably sink the said boat in a few hours. How I hated the fool for his relish of evil tidings!

But never mind our wild expedition, or what came of it. Am I not patient! Ever since I commenced to write, the sound of a furious bombardment has been ringing in my ears; and beyond an occasional run to see the shells fly through the air (their white smoke, rather) I have not said a word of it. The girls have all crowded on the little balcony up here, towards town, and their shrieks of "There it goes!" "Listen!" "Look at them!" rise above the sound of the cannon, and occasionally draw me out, too. But I sit here listening, and wonder which report precedes the knocking down of our home; which shell is killing some one I know and love. Poor Tiche and Dophy! — where are they? And oh, I hope they did not leave my birdie Jimmy to die in his cage. I charged them to let him loose if they could not carry him. Dophy will be so frightened. I hope they are out of danger. Oh, my dear home! shall I ever see you again? And the Brunots! Oh, how I hope they are safe. These loud cannon make me heartsick, and yet I am so excited! How rapidly they answer each other! I am told the attack commenced at five this morning, and lasted three hours. Those girls are shouting that Baton Rouge must be on fire, from the volume of smoke in that direction. How they scream as the balls go up, to show it to each other. I think I'll take a look, too.

We are all going four or five miles through this warm sun to be nearer the scene of action. Any one might know there was no white man on the premises. There is the carriage! Oh, I am *so* seasick! What will I be before we get back?

August 6th.

We six madcaps got in the carriage and buggy, and rode off in search of news. We took a quantity of old linen rags along, and during the whole drive, our fingers were busy making lint. Once we stopped at a neighbor's to gather the news, but that did not interfere with our labors at all. Four miles from here we met a crowd of women flying, and among them recognized Mrs. La Noue and Noémie. A good deal of loud shouting brought them to the carriage in great surprise to see us there. They were running from the plantation where they had taken refuge, as it was not safe from the shells, as the gunboats had proved to them. The reports we had heard in the morning were from shots fired on this side of the river by them, in hopes of hurting a guerrilla or two. Noémie told us that two Western regiments had laid down their arms, and General Williams had been killed by his own men. She looked so delighted, and yet it made me sick to think of his having been butchered so. Phillie leaned out, and asked her, as she asked everybody, if she knew anything about her father. Noémie, in her rapture over that poor man's death, exclaimed, "Don't know a word about him! know Williams was cut to pieces, though!" — and that is all we could learn from her.

We went on until we came in sight of Baton Rouge. There it stood, looking so beautiful against the black, lowering sky that I could not but regret its fate. We could see the Garrison, State House, Asylum, and all that; but the object of the greatest interest to me was the steeple of the Methodist church, for to the right of it lay home. While looking at it, a negro passed who was riding up and down the coast collecting lint, so I gave him all we had made, and commenced some more. Presently, we met Mr. Phillips, to whom Phillie put the same question. "He is on the Laurel Hill a prisoner — Confound that negro! where did he go?" And so on, each answer as far as concerned her, seeming a labor, but the part relating to the servant very hearty. Poor Phillie complained that everybody was selfish — thought only of their own affairs, and did not sympathize with her. "Yes, my dear," I silently assented; for it was *very* true; every one seemed to think of their own interests alone. It was late before we got home, and then we had great fun in watching shells which we could dimly trace against the clouds, falling in what must have been the Garrison. Then came a tremendous fire, above, which *may* have been a boat — I don't know.

I hear a tremendous firing again, and from the two volumes of smoke, should judge it was the Arkansas and the Essex trying their strength at a distance. We are going down to see what's the fun. It would be absurd to record all the rumors that have reached us, since we can rely on none. They say we fought up to nine last night, and occupied the Garrison for five minutes, when the shells forced us to abandon it. Also that four regiments laid down their arms, that the Federals were pursued by our men to the river, driven to the gunboats, and pushed off to prevent the Western men from coming aboard. An eye-witness, from this side, reports that General Williams, "they say," was forcibly held before a cannon and blown to pieces. For the sake of humanity, I hope this is false.

Oh, what a sad day this is for our country! Mother disapproved so of our going to the levee to see the fight, that we consented to remain, though Miriam and Ginnie jumped into the buggy and went off alone. Presently came tidings that all the planters near Baton Rouge were removing their families and negroes, and that the Yankees were to shell the whole coast, from there up to here. Then Phillie,

Lilly (Nolan), and I jumped in — the carriage that was still waiting, and ran after the others to bring them back before they got in danger; but when we reached the end of the long lane, we saw them standing on the high levee, wringing their hands and crying. We sprang out and joined them, and there, way at the bend, lay the Arkansas on fire! All except myself burst into tears and lamentations, and prayed aloud between their sobs. I had no words or tears; I could only look at our sole hope burning, going, and pray silently. Oh, it was so sad! Think, it was our sole dependence! And we five girls looked at her as the smoke rolled over her, watched the flames burst from her decks, and the shells as they exploded one by one beneath the water, coming up in jets of steam. And we watched until down the road we saw crowds of men toiling along toward us. Then we knew they were those who had escaped, and the girls sent up a shriek of pity.

On they came, dirty, half-dressed, some with only their guns, others, a few, with bundles and knapsacks on their backs, grimy and tired, but still laughing. We called to the first, and asked if the boat were really afire; they shouted, "Yes," and went on, talking still. Presently one ran up and told us the story. How yesterday their engine had broken, and how they had labored all day to repair it; how they had succeeded, and had sat by their guns all night; and this morning, as they started to meet the Essex, the other engine had broken; how each officer wrote his opinion that it was impossible to fight her with any hope of success under such circumstances, and advised the Captain to abandon her; how they had resolved to do so, had exchanged shots with the Essex across the point, and the first of the latter (only one, also) had set ours afire, when the men were ordered to take their side arms. They thought it was to board the Essex, assembled together, when the order was given to fire the Arkansas and go ashore, which was done in a few minutes. Several of the crew were around us then, and up and down the road they were scattered still in crowds.

Miriam must have asked the name of some of the officers; for just then she called to me, "He says that is Mr. Read!" I looked at the foot of the levee, and saw two walking together. I hardly recognized the gentleman I was introduced to on the McRae in the one that now stood below me in rough sailor pants, a pair of boots, and a very thin and slazy lisle undershirt. That is all he had on, except an old straw hat, and — yes! he held a primer! I did not think it would be embarrassing to him to meet me under such circumstances; I only thought of Jimmy's friend as escaping from a sad fate; so I rushed down a levee twenty feet high, saying, "O Mr. Read! You won't recognize me, but I am Jimmy's sister!" He blushed modestly, shook my hand as though we were old friends, and assured me he remembered me, was glad to meet me, etc. Then Miriam came down and talked to him, and then we went to the top of the levee where the rest were, and watched the poor Arkansas burn.

By that time the crowd that had gone up the road came back, and we found ourselves in the centre of two hundred men, just we five girls, talking with the officers around us as though they were old friends. You could only *guess* they were officers, for a dirtier, more forlorn set I never saw. Not *dirty* either; they looked clean, considering the work they had been doing. Nobody introduced anybody else; we all felt like brothers and sisters in our common calamity. There was one handsome Kentuckian, whose name I soon found to be Talbot, who looked charmingly picturesque in his coarse cottonade pants, white shirt, straw hat, black hair, beard, and eyes, with rosy cheeks. He was a graduate of the Naval Academy some years ago. Then another jolly-faced young man from the same Academy, pleased me, too. He, the doctor, and the Captain, were the only ones who possessed a coat in the whole crowd, the few who saved theirs carrying them over their arms. Mr. Read more than once blushingly remarked that they were prepared to fight, and hardly expected to meet us; but we pretended to think there was nothing unusual in his dress. I can understand, though, that he should feel rather awkward; I would not like to meet *him*, if I was in the same costume.

They all talked over their loss cheerfully, as far as the loss of money, watches, clothes, were concerned; but they were disheartened about their boat.

One threw himself down near my feet, saying, "*Me voilà.* I have saved my gun, *et puis* the clothes that I stand in!" and laughed as though it were an excellent joke. One who had been on the Merrimac chiefly regretted the loss of the commission appointing him there, though he had not saved a single article. The one with the jolly face told me Will Pinckney was among those attacking Baton Rouge, and assured him he expected to take supper there last night. He thought it would be with us, I know! I hope he is safe!

After a while the men were ordered to march up the lane, to some resting spot it is best not to mention here, and straggled off; but there were many sick among them, one wounded at Vicksburg, and we instantly voted to walk the mile and three quarters home, and give them the carriage and buggy. But long after they left, we stood with our new friends on the levee watching the last of the Arkansas, and saw the Essex, and two gunboats crowded with men, cautiously turn the point, and watch her burn. What made me furious was the thought of the glowing accounts they would give of their "capture of the Arkansas!!!" Capture, and they fired a shot apiece! — for all the firing we heard was the discharge of her guns by the flames. We saw them go back as cautiously, and I was furious, knowing the accounts they would publish of what we ourselves had destroyed. We had seen many shells explode, and one magazine, and would have waited for the other, if the clouds had not threatened rain speedily. But we had to leave her a mere wreck, still burning, and started off on our long walk.

In our hurry, I had brought neither handkerchief nor gloves, but hardly missed either, I was so excited. Mr. Talbot walked home with me, and each of the others with some one else. He had a small bundle and a sword, and the latter I insisted on carrying. It was something, to shoulder a sword made for use rather than for ornament! So I *would* carry it. He said "he would remember who had carried it, and the recollection would give it a new value in his eyes, and I might rest assured it should never be disgraced after *that*," and all that sort of thing, *of course*, as it is usual to say it on such occasions. But I shouldered the sword bravely, determined to show my appreciation of the sacrifice they had made for us, in coming to our rescue on a boat they had every reason to believe was unsafe. I liked Mr. Talbot! He made himself very agreeable in that long walk. He asked permission to send me a trophy from the first action in which he used "that" sword, and *did n't* I say yes! He thought Southern men had every encouragement in the world, from the fact that the ladies welcomed them with great kindness in victory or defeat, insinuating he thought they hardly deserved our compassion after their failure on the Arkansas. But I stoutly denied that it *was* a failure. Had they not done their best? Was it their fault the machinery broke? And in defeat or victory, were they not still fighting for us? Were we the less grateful when they met with reverse? Oh, did n't I laud the Southern men with my whole heart!—and I think he felt better for it, too! Yes! I like him!

We all met at the steps, and water was given to our cavaliers, who certainly enjoyed it. We could not ask them in, as Dr. Nolan is on his parole; but Phillie intimated that if they chose to order, they might do as they pleased, as women could not resist armed men! So they took possession of the sugar-house, and helped themselves to something to eat, and were welcome to do it, since no one could prevent! But they first stood talking on the balcony, gayly, and we parted with many warm wishes on both sides, insisting that, if they assisted at a second attack on Baton Rouge, they must remember our house was at their service, wounded or in health. And they all shook hands with us, and looked pleased, and said "God bless you," and "Good-bye."

Evening.

I heard a while ago, the doctor of the Ram, who brought back the buggy, say the Arkansas's crew were about leaving; so remembering poor Mr. Read had lost everything, mother, suggesting he might need money, gave me twenty dollars to put in his hands, as some slight help towards reaching his destination. Besides, coming from Jimmy's mother, he could not have been hurt. But when I got down, he was far up the lane, walking too fast for me to overtake him; then I tried to catch Mr. Stephenson, to give it to him for me, but failed. Presently, we saw I am afraid to say how many wagons loaded with them, coming from the sugar-house; so Phillie, Lilly, and I snatched up some five bottles of gin, between us, and ran out to give it to them. A rough old sailor received mine with a flood of thanks, and the others gave theirs to those behind. An officer rode up saying, "Ladies, there is no help for it! The Yankee cavalry are after us, and we must fight them in the corn. Take care of yourselves!" We shouted "Yes!" told them to bring in the wounded and we would nurse them. Then the men cried, "God bless you," and we cried, "Hurrah for the Arkansas's crew," and "Fight for us!" Altogether it was a most affecting scene. Phillie, seeing how poorly armed they were, suggested a gun, which I flew after and delivered to a rough old tar. When I got out, the cart then passing held Mr. Talbot, who smiled benignly and waved his hat like the rest. He looked still better in his black coat, but the carts reminded me of what the guillotine days must have been in France. He shouted "Good-bye," we shouted "Come to us, if you are wounded"; he smiled and bowed, and I cried, "*Use* that sword!" — whereupon he sprang to his feet and grasped the hilt as though about to commence. Then came other officers; Mr. Scales, Mr. Barblaud, etc., who smiled recognition, stopped the wagon as Phillie handed up a plate of bread and meat, and talked gayly as they divided it, until the Captain rode up. "On, gentlemen! not a moment to lose!" Then the cart started off, the empty plate was flung overboard, and they rode off waving hats and crying, "God bless you, ladies!" in answer to our repeated offers of taking care of them if they were hurt. And they have gone to meet the Yankees, and I hope they *won't*, for they have worked enough to-day, and from my heart I pray God prosper those brave men!

August 7th.

Last night, shortly after we got in bed, we were roused by loud cannonading towards Baton Rouge, and running out on the small balcony up here, saw the light of a great fire in that direction. From the constant reports, and the explosion of what seemed to be several powder magazines, we imagined it to be either the Garrison or a gunboat. Whatever it was, it was certainly a great fire. We all ran out in our nightgowns, and watched for an hour in the damp air, I without even shoes. We listened to the fight a long while, until the sound ceased, and we went back to bed.

Evening.

I am so disheartened! I have been listening with the others to a man who was telling us about Baton Rouge, until I am heartsick. He says the Yankees have been largely reinforced, and are prepared for another attack which will probably take place to-morrow; that the fight was a dreadful one, we driving them in, and losing twelve hundred, to their fifteen hundred. It must have been awful! And that our troops have resolved to burn the town down, since they cannot hold it under the fire of the gunboats.

August 8th, Friday.

Again last night, about nine, we heard cannon in Baton Rouge, and watched the flashes, which preceded the reports by a minute, at least, for a long time. We must have seen our own firing; perhaps we wanted to find out the batteries of the enemy. It was not the most delightful thing imaginable to watch what might be the downfall of our only home! And then to think each ball might bring death to some one we love! Ah, no! it was not pleasant!

Miriam and I have many friends in Breckinridge's division, I expect, if we could only hear the names of the regiments. The Fourth is certainly there. And poor Will! I wonder if he has had his supper yet? I have been thinking of him ever since Mr. Scales told me he was there, and praying myself sick for his safety and that of the rest. I shut my eyes at every report and say, "Oh, please! poor Will! — and the others, too!" And when I *don't* hear the cannon, I pray, to be in advance of the next.

It is now midday, and again we hear firing; but have yet to learn the true story of the first day's fight. Preserve me from the country in such stirring days! We might as well be in Europe as to have the Mississippi between us and town.

By unanimous consent, the little lane in front of the house has been christened "Guerrilla Lane," and the long one leading to the river, "Arkansas." What an episode that was, in our lives! The officers go by the name of Miriam's, Ginnie's, Sarah's, as though they belonged to each!

Those girls did me the meanest thing imaginable. Mr. Talbot and I were planning a grand combined attack on Baton Rouge, in which he was to command a fleet and attack the town by the river, while I promised to get up a battalion of girls and attack them in the rear. We had settled it all, except the time, when just then all the others stopped talking. I went on: "And now, it is only necessary for you to name the day —" Here the girls commenced to giggle, and the young men tried to suppress a smile; I felt annoyed, but it did not strike me until after they had left, that I had said anything absurd. What evil imaginations they must have, if they could have fancied I meant anything except the battle!

August 9th.

To our great surprise, Charlie came in this morning from the other side. He was in the battle, and General Carter, and dozens of others that we did not think of. See the mountain reduced to a mole-hill! He says, though the fight was desperate, we lost only eighty-five killed, and less than a hundred and fifty wounded! And we had only twenty-five hundred against the Yankees' four thousand five hundred. There is no truth in our having held the Garrison even for a moment, though we drove them down to the river in a panic. The majority ran like fine fellows, but a Maine regiment fought like devils. He says Will and Thompson Bird set fire to the Yankee camp with the greatest alacrity, as though it were rare fun. General Williams was killed as he passed Piper's, by a shot from a window, supposed to have been fired by a citizen. Some one from town told him that the Federals were breaking in the houses, destroying the furniture, and tearing the clothes of the women and children in shreds, like maniacs. O my home! I wonder if they have entered ours? What a jolly time they would have over all the letters I left in my desk! Butler has ordered them to burn Baton Rouge if forced to evacuate it. Looks as though he was not so sure of holding it.

Miss Turner told Miriam that her mother attempted to enter town after the fight to save some things, when the gallant Colonel Dudley put a pistol to her head, called her an old she-devil, and told her he would blow her d—— brains out if she moved a step; that anyhow, none but we d—— women had put the men up to fighting, and we were the ones who were to blame for the fuss. There is no name he did not call us.

August 10th, Sunday.

Is this really Sunday? Never felt less pious, or less seriously disposed! Listen to my story, and though I will, of course, fall far short of the actual terror that reigned, yet it will show it in a lukewarm light, that can at least recall the excitement to me.

To begin, then, last evening, about six o'clock, as we sat reading, sewing, and making lint in the parlor, we heard a tremendous shell whizzing past, which those who watched, said passed not five feet above the house. Of course, there was a slight stir among the unsophisticated; though we, who had passed through bombardments, sieges, and alarms of all kinds, coolly remarked, "a shell," and kept quiet. (The latter class was not very numerous.) It was from one of the three Yankee boats that lay in the river close by (the Essex and two gunboats), which were sweeping teams, provisions, and negroes from all the plantations they stopped at from Baton Rouge up. The negroes, it is stated, are to be armed against us as in town, where all those who manned the cannon on Tuesday were, for the most part, killed; and served them right! Another shell was fired at a carriage containing Mrs. Durald and several children, under pretense of discovering if she was a guerrilla, doubtless. Fortunately, she was not hurt, however.

By the time the little *émeute* had subsided, determined to have a frolic, Miss Walters, Ginnie, and I got on our horses, and rode off down the Arkansas Lane, to have a gallop and a peep at the gunboats from the levee. But mother's entreaties prevented us from going that near, as she cried that it was well known they fired at every horse or vehicle they saw in the road, seeing a thousand guerrillas in every puff of dust, and we were sure to be killed, murdered, and all sorts of bloody deaths awaited us; so to satisfy her, we took the road about a mile from the river, in full view, however. We had not gone very far before we met a Mr. Watson, a plain farmer of the neighborhood, who begged us to go back. "You'll be fired on, ladies, sure! You don't know the danger! Take my advice and go home as quick as possible before they shell you! They shot buggies and carriages, and of course they won't mind *horses* with women! Please go home!" But Ginnie, who had taken a fancy to go on, acted as spokeswoman, and determined to go on in spite of his advice, so, nothing loath to follow her example, we thanked him, and rode on. Another met us; looked doubtful, said it was not so dangerous if the Yankees did not see the dust; but if they did, we would be pretty apt to see a shell soon after. Here was frolic! So we rode on some mile or two beyond, but failing to see anything startling, turned back again.

About two miles from here, we met Mr. Watson coming at full speed. The ladies, he said, had sent him after us in all haste; there was a report that the whole coast was to be shelled; a lady had passed, flying with her children; the carriage was ordered out; they were only waiting for us, to run, too. We did not believe a word of it, and were indignant at their credulity, as well as determined to persuade them to remain where they were, if possible. When told their plan was to run to the house formerly used as a guerrilla camp, we laughed heartily. Suppose the Yankees fired a shell into it to discover its inhabitants? The idea of choosing a spot so well known! And what fun in running to a miserable hole, when we might sleep comfortably here? I am afraid rebellion was in the air. Indeed, an impudent little negro, who threw open the gate for us, interrupted Ginnie in the midst of a tirade with a sly "Here's the beginning of a little fuss!"

We found them all crazy with fear. I did not say much; I was too provoked to trust myself to argue with so many frightened women. I only said I saw no necessity. Ginnie resisted; but finally succumbed. Mr. Watson, whom we had enlisted on our side also, said it was by no means necessary, but if we were determined, we might go to his house, about four miles away, and stay there. It was very small, but we were welcome. We had in the mean time thrown off our riding-skirts, and stood just in our plain dresses, though the others were freshly dressed for an exodus. Before the man left, the carriage came, though by that time we had drawn half the party on our side; we said we would take supper, and decide after, so he went off.

In a few moments a rocket went up from one of the boats, which attracted our attention. Five minutes after, we saw a flash directly before us. "See it? Lightning, I expect," said Phillie. The others all agreed; but I kept quiet, knowing that some, at least, knew what it was as well as I, and determined not to give the alarm — for I was beginning to feel foolish. Before half a minute more came a tearing, hissing sound, a sky-rocket whose music I had heard before. Instantly I remembered my running-bag, and flew upstairs to get it, escaping just in time from the scene which followed on the gallery which was afterwards most humorously described to me. But I was out of hearing of the screams of each (and yet I must have heard them); neither saw Miss Walters tumble against the wall, nor mother turn over her chair, nor the general *mêlée* that followed, in which Mrs. Walters, trying to scale the carriage, was pulled out by Uncle Will, who shouted to his plunging horses first, then to the other unreasoning creatures, "Woa, there! 'T ain't safe! Take to the fields! Take to the woods! Run to the sugar-house! Take to your heels!" in a frenzy of excitement.

I escaped all that, and was putting on my hoops and hastily catching up any article that presented itself to me in my speed, when the shell burst over the roof, and went rolling down on the gallery, according to the account of those then below. Two went far over the house, out of sight. All three were seen by Mr. Watson, who came galloping up in a few moments, crying, "Ladies, for God's sake, leave the house!" Then I heard mother calling, "Sarah! You will be killed! Leave your clothes and run!"— and a hundred ejaculations that came too fast for

T. G. P. A. Morgan — Cr

and packed off to prevent the Western men from coming aboard. An eye-witness, from this side, reports that Gen. Williams "they say" was forcibly held before a cannon and blown to pieces. For the sake of humanity I hope this is false. Ah what a sad day this is for our country!

Mother disapproved so of our going to the levee to see the fight, that we consented to remain, though Miriam and Ginnie jumped in the buggy and went off alone. Presently came tidings that all the planters near Baton R. were removing their families and negroes, and that the Yanks were to shell this whole coast, from there up to here. Then Phillie, Lilly and I jumped in the carriage that was still waiting, and ran after the others to bring them back before they got in danger, but when we reached the end of the long lane, we saw them standing on the high levee, wringing their hands and crying. We sprang out and joined them, and there, way at the bend, lay the Arkansas on fire! All except myself burst into tears and lamentations, and prayed aloud between their sobs. I had no words or tears, I could only

[illegible]

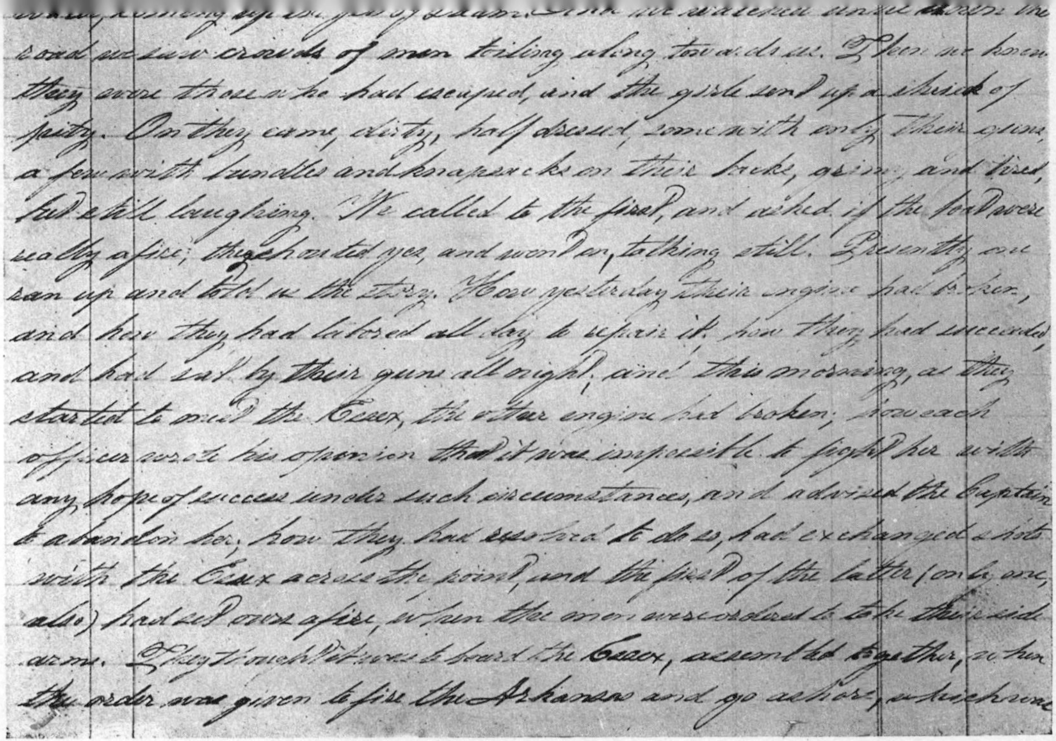
road we saw crowds of men toiling along towards us. When we knew
they were those who had escaped, and the girls sent up a shriek of
pity. On they came, dirty, half dressed, some with only their guns,
a few with bundles and knapsacks on their backs, aching and tired,
but still laughing. We called to the first, and asked if the boat were
really afire; they shouted yes, and went on, talking still. Presently one
ran up and told us the story. How yesterday their engine had broken,
and how they had labored all day to repair it, how they had succeeded,
and had sat by their guns all night, and this morning, as they
started to meet the Essex, the other engine had broken; how each
officer wrote his opinion that it was impossible to fight her with
any hope of success under such circumstances, and advised the Captain
to abandon her, how they had resolved to do so, had exchanged shots
with the Essex across the point, and the first of the latter (only one,
also) had set ours afire, when the men were ordered to take their side
arms. They thought it was to board the Essex, assembled together, when
the order was given to fire the Arkansas and go ashore, which none

FACSIMILE OF A PAGE FROM THE DIARY

me to answer except by an occasional "Coming, if you will send me a candle!" Candle was the same as though I had demanded a hand-grenade, in mother's opinion, for she was sure it would be the signal for a bombardment of my exposed room; so I tossed down my bundles, swept combs and hairpins into my bosom (all points up), and ravished a candle from some one. How quickly I got on, then! I saved the most useless of articles with the greatest zeal, and probably left the most serviceable ones. One single dress did my running-bag contain — a white linen cambric with a tiny pink flower — the one I wore when I told Hal good-bye for the last time. The others I left.

When I got down with my knapsack, mother, Phillie, and Mrs. Walters were —

AT RANDALLSON'S LANDING, August 11th.

I don't mean those ladies were, but that I am at present. I'll account for it after I have disposed of the stampede. Imagine no interruption, and continue — in the carriage urging Uncle Will to hurry on, and I had hardly time to thrust my sack under their feet before they were off. Lilly and Miss Walters were already in the buggy, leaving Ginnie and me to follow on horseback. I ran up after my riding-skirt, which I was surprised to find behind a trunk, and rolled up in it was my running-bag, with all my treasures! I was very much provoked at my carelessness; indeed, I cannot imagine how it got there, for it was the first thing I thought of. When I got back, there was no one to be seen except Ginnie and two negroes who held our horses, and who disappeared the instant we were mounted; with the exception of two women who were running to the woods, we were the only ones on the lot, until Mr. Watson galloped up to urge us on. Again I had to notice this peculiarity about women — that the married ones are invariably the first to fly, in time of danger, and always leave the young ones to take care of themselves. Here were our three matrons, prophesying that the house would be burnt, the Yankees upon us, and all murdered in ten minutes, flying down the Guerrilla Lane, and leaving us to encounter the horrors they foretold, alone.

It was a splendid gallop in the bright moonlight, over the fields, only it was made uncomfortable by the jerking of my running-bag, until I happily thought of turning it before. A hard ride of four miles in about twenty minutes brought us to the house of the man who so kindly offered his hospitality. It was a little hut, about as large as our parlor, and already crowded to overflowing, as he was entertaining three families from Baton Rouge. Can't imagine where he put them, either. But it seems to me the poorer the man, and the smaller the house, the greater the hospitality you meet with. There were so many of us that there was not room on the balcony to turn. The man wanted to prepare supper, but we declined, as Phillie had sent back for ours which we had missed.

I saw another instance of the pleasure the vulgar

take in the horrible. A Mr. Hill, speaking of Dr. Nolan, told Phillie "he had no doubt he had been sent to New Orleans on the Whiteman, that carried General Williams's body; and that every soul had gone down on her." Fortunately, just then the overseer brought a letter from him saying he had gone on another boat, or the man's relish of the distressing might have been gratified.

It was so crowded there that we soon suggested going a short distance beyond, to Mr. Lobdell's, and staying there for the night, as all strenuously objected to our returning home, as there was danger from prowling Yankees. So we mounted again, and after a short ride we reached the house, where all were evidently asleep. But necessity knows no rules; and the driver soon aroused an old gentleman who came out and invited us in. A middle-aged lady met us, and made us perfectly at home by leaving us to take care of ourselves; most people would have thought it indifference; but I knew it was *manque de savoir faire*, merely, and preferred doing as I pleased. If she had been officious, I would have been embarrassed. So we walked in the moonlight, Ginnie and I, while the rest sat in the shade, and all discussed the fun of the evening, those who had been most alarmed laughing loudest. The old gentleman insisted that we girls had been the cause of it all; that our white bodies (I wore a Russian shirt) and black skirts could easily have caused us to be mistaken for men. That, at all events, three or four people on horseback would be a sufficient pretext for firing a shell or two. "In short, young ladies," he said, "there is no doubt in my mind that you were mistaken for guerrillas, and that they only wanted to give you time to reach the woods where they heard they have a camp, before shooting at you. In short, take my advice and never mount a horse again when there is a Yankee in sight." We were highly gratified at being mistaken for them, and pretended to believe it was true. I hardly think he was right, though; it is too preposterous.

Pourtant, Sunday morning the Yankees told a negro they did not mean to touch the house, but were shooting at some guerrillas at a camp just beyond. We know the last guerrilla left the parish five days ago.

Our host insisted on giving us supper, though Phillie represented that ours was on the road; and by eleven o'clock, tired alike of moonlight and fasting, we gladly accepted, and rapidly made the preserves and batter-cakes fly. Ours was a garret room, well finished, abounding in odd closets and corners, with curious dormer windows that were reached by long little corridors. I should have slept well; but I lay awake all night. Mother and I occupied a narrow single bed, with a bar of the thickest, heaviest material imaginable. Suffocation awaited me inside, gnats and mosquitoes outside. In order to be strictly impartial, I lay awake to divide my time equally between the two attractions, and think I succeeded pretty well. So I spent the night on the extreme edge of the bed, never turning over, but fanning mother constantly. I was not sorry when daybreak appeared, but dressed and ascended the observatory to get a breath of air.

Below me, I beheld four wagons loaded with the young Mrs. Lobdell's baggage. The Yankees had visited them in the evening, swept off everything they could lay their hands on, and with a sick child she was obliged to leave her house in the night and fly to her father-in-law. I wondered at their allowing her four wagons of trunks and bundles; it was very kind. If I were a Federal, I think it would kill me to hear the whisper of "Hide the silver" wherever I came. Their having frequently relieved families of such trifles, along with negroes, teams, etc., has put others on their guard now. As I sat in the parlor in the early morning, Mrs. Walters *en blouse volante* and all *échevelée*, came in to tell me of Mr. Lobdell's misfortunes. "They took his negroes [right hand up]; his teams [left hand up]; his preserves [both hands clutching her hair]; they swept off everything, except four old women who could not walk! they told him if he did n't come report himself, they'd come fetch him in three days! They beggared him!" [Both eyes rolling like a ship in a storm.] I could not help laughing. Mr. Bird sat on the gallery, and had been served in the same way, with the addition of a pair of handcuffs for a little while. It was not a laughing matter; but the old lady made it comical by her gestures.

When we suggested returning, there was another difficulty. All said it was madness; that the Yankees would sack the house and burn it over our heads; we would be insulted, etc. I said no one yet had ever said an impudent thing to me, and Yankees certainly would not attempt it; but the old gentleman told me I did not know what I was talking about; so I hushed, but determined to return. Ginnie and I sat an hour on horseback waiting for the others to settle what they would do; and after having half-roasted ourselves in the sun, they finally agreed to go, too, and we set off in a gallop which we never broke until we reached the house, which to our great delight we found standing, and not infested with Yankees.

Linwood, August 12th.

Another resting-place! Out of reach of shells for the first time since last April! For how long, I wonder? For wherever we go, we bring shells and Yankees. Would not be surprised at a visit from them out here, now!

Let me take up the thread of that never-ending story, and account for my present position. It all seems tame now; but it was very exciting at the time.

As soon as I threw down bonnet and gloves, I commenced writing; but before I had halfway finished, mother, who had been holding a consultation downstairs, ran up to say the overseer had advised us all to leave, as the place was not safe; and that

I must pack up instantly, as, unless we got off before the Essex came up, it would be impossible to leave at all. All was commotion; every one flew to pack up. Phillie determined to go to her friends at Grosse Tête, and insisted on carrying us off with her. But I determined to reach Miriam and Lilly if possible, rather than put the Federal army between us. All *en déshabillé*, I commenced to pack our trunk, but had scarcely put an article in when they cried the Essex was rounding the point, and our last opportunity passing away. Then I flew; and by the time the boat got opposite to us, the trunk was locked, and I sat on it, completely dressed, waiting for the wagon. We had then to wait for the boat to get out of sight, to avoid a broadside; so it was half-past ten before we set off, fortified by several glasses of buttermilk apiece.

All went in the carriage except Ginnie, Lilly (Nolan), and me, and we perched on the baggage in the wagon. Such stifling heat! The wagon jarred dreadfully, and seated at the extreme end, on a wooden trunk traversed by narrow slats, Ginnie and I were jolted until we lost our breath, all down Arkansas Lane, when we changed for the front part. I shall never forget the heat of that day.

Four miles beyond, the carriage stopped at some house, and, still determined to get over the river, I stepped into the little cart that held our trunks, drove up to the side of it, and insisted on mother's getting in, rather than going the other way with

Phillie. I had a slight discussion, and overcame mother's reluctance to Phillie's objections with some difficulty; but finally prevailed on the former to get into the cart, and jolted off amid a shower of reproaches, regrets, and good-byes. I knew I was right, though; and the idea reconciled me to the heat, dust, jarring, and gunboat that was coming up behind us.

Six miles more brought us to Mr. Cain's, where we arrived at two o'clock, tired, dirty, and almost unrecognizable. We were received with the greatest cordiality in spite of that. Mother knew both him and his wife, but though I had never seen either, the latter kissed me as affectionately as though we had known each other. It was impossible to cross when the gunboat was in sight, so they made us stay with them until the next morning. A bath and clean clothes soon made me quite presentable, and I really enjoyed the kindness we met with, in spite of a "tearing" headache, and a distended feeling about the eyes as though I never meant to close them again — the consequence of my vigil, I presume. O those dear, kind people! I shall not soon forget them. Mr. Cain told mother he believed he would keep me; at all events, he would make an exchange, and give her his only son in my place. I told him I was willing, as mother thought much more of her sons than of her daughters.

I forgot to say that we met General Allen's partner a mile or two from Dr. Nolan's, who told us it was a wise move; that he had intended recommending it.

All he owned had been carried off, his plantation stripped. He said he had no doubt that all the coast would be ravaged, and they had promised to burn his and many other houses; and Dr. Nolan's—though it might *possibly* be spared in consideration of his being a prisoner, and his daughter being unprotected — would most probably suffer with the rest, but even if spared, it was no place for women. He offered to take charge of us all, and send the furniture into the interior before the Yankees should land, which Phillie gladly accepted.

What a splendid rest I had at Mrs. Cain's! I was not conscious of being alive until I awaked abruptly in the early morning, with a confused sense of having dreamed something very pleasant.

Mr. Cain accompanied us to the ferry some miles above, riding by the buggy; and leaving us under care of Mr. Randallson, after seeing us in the large flat, took his leave. After an hour spent at the hotel after landing on this side, we procured a conveyance and came on to Mr. Elder's, where we astonished Lilly by our unexpected appearance very much. Miriam had gone over to spend the day with her, so we were all together, and talked over our adventures with the greatest glee. After dinner Miriam and I came over here to see them all, leaving the others to follow later. I was very glad to see Helen Carter once more. If I was not, I hope I may live in Yankee-land! — and I can't invoke a more dreadful punishment than that.

Well! here we are, and Heaven only knows our next move. But we must settle on some spot, which seems impossible in the present state of affairs, when no lodgings are to be found. I feel like a homeless beggar. Will Pinckney told them here that he doubted if our house were still standing, as the fight occurred just back of it, and every volley directed towards it. He says he thought of it every time the cannon was fired, knowing where the shot would go.

August 13th.

I am in despair. Miss Jones, who has just made her escape from town, brings a most dreadful account. She, with seventy-five others, took refuge at Dr. Enders's, more than a mile and a half below town, at Hall's. It was there we sent the two trunks containing father's papers and our clothing and silver. Hearing that guerrillas had been there, the Yankees went down, shelled the house in the night, turning all those women and children out, who barely escaped with their clothing, and let the soldiers loose on it. They destroyed everything they could lay their hands on, if it could not be carried off; broke open armoirs, trunks, sacked the house, and left it one scene of devastation and ruin. They even stole Miss Jones's braid! She got here with nothing but the clothes she wore.

This is a dreadful blow to me. Yesterday, I thought myself beggared when I heard that our house was probably burnt, remembering all the clothing, books, furniture, etc., that it contained; but I consoled myself with the recollection of a large trunk packed in the most scientific style, containing quantities of nightgowns, skirts, chemises, dresses, cloaks, — in short, our very best, — which was in safety. Winter had no terrors when I thought of the nice warm clothes; I only wished I had a few of the organdie dresses I had packed up before wearing. And now? It is all gone, silver, father's law papers, without which we are beggars, and clothing! Nothing left!

I could stand that. But as each little article of Harry's came up before me (I had put many in the trunk), I lost heart. . . . They may clothe their negro women with my clothes, since they only steal for them; but to take things so sacred to me! O my God, teach me to forgive them!

Poor Miss Jones! They went into her clothes-bag and took out articles which were certainly of no service to them, for mere deviltry. There are so many sufferers in this case that it makes it still worse. The plantation just below was served in the same way; whole families fired into before they knew of the intention of the Yankees; was it not fine sport? I have always been an advocate of peace — if we could name the conditions *ourselves* — but I say, War to the death! I would give my life to be able to take arms against the vandals who are laying waste our fair land! I suppose it is because I have no longer anything to lose that I am desperate. Before,

I always opposed the burning of Baton Rouge, as a useless piece of barbarism in turning out five thousand women and children on the charity of the world. But I noticed that those who had no interest there warmly advocated it. Lilly Nolan cried loudly for it; thought it only just; but the first shell that whistled over her father's house made her crazy with rage. The brutes! the beasts! how cruel! wicked! etc. It was too near home for her, then. There is the greatest difference between *my* property and *yours*. I notice that the further I get from town, the more ardent are the people to have it burned. It recalls very forcibly Thackeray's cut in "The Virginians," when speaking of the determination of the Rebels to burn the cities: he says he observed that all those who were most eager to burn New York were inhabitants of Boston; while those who were most zealous to burn Boston had all their property in New York. It is true all the world over. And I am afraid I am becoming indifferent about the fate of our town. Anything, so it is speedily settled! Tell me it would be of service to the Confederacy, and I would set fire to my home—if still standing—willingly! But would it?

August 17th.

Another Sunday. Strange that the time, which should seem so endless, flies so rapidly! Miriam complains that Sunday comes every day; but though that seems a little too much, I insist that it comes twice a week. Let time fly, though; for each day brings us so much nearer our destiny, which I long to know.

Thursday, we heard from a lady just from town that our house was standing the day before, which somewhat consoled us for the loss of our silver and clothing; but yesterday came the tidings of new afflictions. I declare we have acted out the first chapter of Job, all except that verse about the death of his sons and daughters. God shield us from that! I do not mind the rest. "While he was yet speaking, another came in and said, 'Thy brethren and kinsmen gathered together to wrest thine abode from the hand of the Philistines which pressed sore upon thee; when lo! the Philistines sallied forth with fire and sword, and laid thine habitation waste and desolate, and I only am escaped to tell thee.'" Yes! the Yankees, fearing the Confederates might slip in unseen, resolved to have full view of their movements, so put the torch to all eastward, from Colonel Matta's to the Advocate. That would lay open a fine tract of country, alone; but unfortunately, it is said that once started, it was not so easy to control the flames, which spread considerably beyond their appointed limits. Some say it went as far as Florida Street; if so, we are lost, as that is a half-square below us. For several days the fire has been burning, but very little can be learned of the particulars. I am sorry for Colonel Matta. Such a fine brown stone front, the finest in town. Poor Minna! poverty will hardly agree with her. As for our home, I hope against hope. I will not believe it is burnt, until somebody declares having been present on that occasion. Yet so many frame houses on that square must have readily caught fire from the sparks.

Wicked as it may seem, I would rather have all I own burned, than in the possession of the negroes. Fancy my magenta organdie on a dark beauty! Bah! I think the sight would enrage me! Miss Jones's trials are enough to drive her crazy. She had the pleasure of having four officers in her house, men who sported epaulets and red sashes, accompanied by a negro woman, at whose disposal all articles were placed. The worthy companion of these "gentlemen" walked around selecting things with the most natural airs and graces. "*This*," she would say, "we *must* have. And some of these books, you know; and all the preserves, and these chairs and tables, and all the clothes, of course; and yes! the rest of these things." So she would go on, the "gentlemen" assuring her she had only to choose what she wanted, and that they would have them removed immediately. Madame thought they really must have the wine, and those handsome cut-glass goblets. I hardly think I could have endured such a scene; to see all I owned given to negroes, without even an accusation being brought against me of disloyalty.[1] One officer departed with a fine velvet cloak on his arm; another took such a bundle of Miss Jones's clothes,

[1] The Act of July 16th, 1862, authorized the confiscation of property only in the cases of rebels whose disloyalty was established. — W. D.

that he had to have it lifted by some one else on his horse, and rode off holding it with difficulty. This I heard from herself, yesterday, as I spent the day with Lilly and mother at Mr. Elder's, where she is now staying. Can anything more disgraceful be imagined? They all console me by saying there is no one in Baton Rouge who could possibly wear my dresses without adding a considerable piece to the belt. But that is nonsense. Another pull at the corset strings would bring them easily to the size I have been reduced by nature and bones. Besides, O horror! Suppose, instead, they should let in a piece of another color? That would annihilate me! Pshaw! I do not care for the dresses, if they had only left me those little articles of father's and Harry's. But that is hard to forgive.

August 19th.

Yesterday, two Colonels, Shields and Breaux, both of whom distinguished themselves in the battle of Baton Rouge, dined here. Their personal appearance was by no means calculated to fill me with awe, or even to give one an idea of their rank; for their dress consisted of merely cottonade pants, flannel shirts, and extremely short jackets (which, however, is rapidly becoming the uniform of the Confederate States).

. . . .

Just three lines back, three soldiers came in to ask for molasses. I was alone downstairs, and the nervous trepidation with which I received the dirty, coarsely clad strangers, who, however, looked as though they might be gentlemen, has raised a laugh against me from the others who looked down from a place of safety. I don't know what I did that was out of the way. I felt odd receiving them as though it was my home, and having to answer their questions about buying, by means of acting as telegraph between them and Mrs. Carter. I confess to that. But I know I talked reasonably about the other subjects. Playing hostess in a strange house! Of course, it was uncomfortable! and to add to my embarrassment, the handsomest one offered to pay for the milk he had just drunk! Fancy my feelings, as I hastened to assure him that General Carter never received money for such things, and from a soldier, besides, it was not to be thought of! He turned to the other, saying, "In Mississippi we don't meet with such people! Miss, they don't hesitate to charge four bits a canteen for milk. They take all they can. They are not like you Louisianians." I was surprised to hear him say it of his own State, but told him we thought here we could not do enough for them.

August 20th.

Last evening, after hard labor at pulling molasses candy, needing some relaxation after our severe exertions, we determined to have some fun, though the sun was just setting in clouds as watery as New Orleans milk, and promised an early twilight. All day it had been drizzling, but that was nothing; so

Anna Badger, Miriam, and I set off, through the mud, to get up the little cart to ride in, followed by cries from the elder ladies of "Girls! Soap is a dollar and a half a bar! Starch a dollar a pound! Take up those skirts!" We had all started stiff and clean, and it did seem a pity to let them drag; so up they went — you can imagine how high when I tell you my answer to Anna's question as to whether hers were in danger of touching the mud, was, "Not unless you sit down."

The only animal we could discover that was not employed was a poor old pony, most appropriately called "Tom Thumb," and him we seized instantly, together with a man to harness him. We accompanied him from the stable to the quarter where the cart was, through mud and water, urging him on with shouts and cries, and laughing until we could laugh no longer, at the appearance of each. The cart had been hauling wood, but that was nothing to us. In we tumbled, and with a driver as diminutive as the horse, started off for Mr. Elder's, where we picked up all the children to be found, and went on. All told, we were twelve, drawn by that poor horse, who seemed at each step about to undergo the ham process, and leave us his hind quarters, while he escaped with the fore ones and harness. I dare say we never enjoyed a carriage as much, though each was holding a muddy child. Riding was very fine; but soon came the question, "How shall we turn?" — which was not so easily solved, for neither horse nor boy understood it in the least. Every effort to describe a circle brought us the length of the cart farther up the road, and we promised fair to reach Bayou Sara before morning, at that rate. At last, after fruitless efforts to dodge under the harness and escape, pony came to a standstill, and could not be induced to move. The children took advantage of the pause to tumble out, but we sat still. Bogged, and it was very dark already! Would n't we get it when we got home! Anna groaned, "Uncle Albert!" Miriam laughed, "the General!" I sighed, "Mrs. Carter!" We knew what we deserved; and darker and darker it grew, and pony still inflexible! At last we beheld a buggy on a road near by and in answer to Morgan's shouts of "Uncle! Uncle! come turn our cart!" a gentleman jumped out and in an instant performed the Herculean task. Pony found motion so agreeable that it was with the greatest difficulty we prevailed on him to stop while we fished seven children out of the mud, as they pursued his flying hoofs. Once more at Mr. Elder's, we pitched them out without ceremony, and drove home as fast as possible, trying to fancy what punishment we would receive for being out so late.

Miriam suggested, as the most horrible one, being sent to bed supperless; Anna's terror was the General's displeasure; I suggested being deprived of rides in future; when all agreed that mine was the most severe yet. So as we drove around the circle, those two set up what was meant for a hearty laugh to show "they were not afraid," which, however, sounded rather shaky to me. I don't think any of us felt like facing the elders; Miriam suggested anticipating our fate by retiring voluntarily to bed; Anna thought we had best run up and change our shoes, anyway; but at last, with her dare-devil laugh, Miriam sauntered into the room, where they all were, followed by us, and thrusting her wet feet into the fire that was kindled to drive away the damp (followed also by us), commenced a laughable account of our fun — in which we, of course, followed, too. If I had fancied we were to escape scot free, we would most surely have got a scolding. It is almost an inducement to hope always for the — worst! The General did not mention the hour! did not prohibit future rides!

While we were yet toasting, a negro came in with what seemed a bank-note, and asked his master to see how much it was, as one of the women had sold some of her watermelons to the three soldiers of the morning, who had given that to her for a dollar. The General opened it. It was a pass! So vanish all faith in human nature! They looked so honest! I could never have believed it of them! But it looked so much like the "shinplasters" we are forced to use, that no wonder they made the mistake. To discover who had played so mean a trick on the poor old woman, the General asked me if I could decipher the name. I threw myself on my knees by the hearth, and by the flickering light read "S. Kimes. By order of C! H!! Luzenberg! ! ! Provost Marshal! ! ! ! Onolona, Miss.," with a gasp of astonishment that raised a burst of laughter against me. Thought he was taken prisoner long ago! At all events, I did n't know he had turned banker, or that his valuable autograph was worth a dollar!

August 21st.

Miriam and mother are going to Baton Rouge in a few hours, to see if anything can be saved from the general wreck. From the reports of the removal of the Penitentiary machinery, State Library, Washington Statue, etc., we presume that that part of the town yet standing is to be burnt like the rest. I think, though, that mother has delayed too long. However, I dreamed last night that we had saved a great deal, in trunks; and my dreams sometimes come true. Waking with that impression, I was surprised, a few hours after, to hear mother's sudden determination. But I also dreamed I was about to marry a Federal officer! That was in consequence of having answered the question, whether I would do so, with an emphatic "Yes! if I loved him," which will probably ruin my reputation as a patriot in this parish. Bah! I am no bigot! — or fool either. . . .

August 23d.

Yesterday Anna and I spent the day with Lilly, and the rain in the evening obliged us to stay all night. Dr. Perkins stopped there, and repeated the same old stories we have been hearing, about the powder placed under the State House and Garrison, to blow them up, if forced to evacuate the town. He confirms the story about all the convicts being set free, and the town being pillaged by the negroes and the rest of the Yankees. He says his own slaves told him they were allowed to enter the houses and help themselves, and what they did not want the Yankees either destroyed on the spot, or had it carried to the Garrison and burned. They also bragged of having stopped ladies on the street, cut their necklaces from their necks, and stripped the rings from their fingers, without hesitation. It may be that they were just bragging to look great in the eyes of their masters; I hope so, for Heaven help them if they fall into the hands of the Confederates, if it is true.

I could not record all the stories of wanton destruction that reached us. I would rather not believe that the Federal Government could be so disgraced by its own soldiers. Dr. Day says they left nothing at all in his house, and carried everything off from Dr. Enders's. He does not believe we have a single article left in ours. I hope they spared Miriam's piano. But they say the soldiers had so many that they offered them for sale at five dollars apiece! We heard that the town had been completely evacuated, and all had gone to New Orleans except three gunboats that were preparing to shell, before leaving.

This morning Withers's battery passed Mr. Elder's on their way to Port Hudson, and stopped to get water. There were several buckets served by several servants; but I took possession of one, to their great amusement. What a profusion of thanks over a can of water! It made me smile, and they smiled to see my work, so it was all very funny. It was astonishing to see the number of Yankee canteens in the possession of our men. Almost all those who fought at Baton Rouge are provided with them. In their canvas and wire cases, with neat stoppers, they are easily distinguished from our rough, flat, tin ones. I declare I felt ever so important in my new situation as waiting-maid!

There is very little we would not do for our soldiers, though. There is mother, for instance, who got on her knees to bathe the face and hands of a fever-struck soldier of the Arkansas, while the girls held the plates of those who were too weak to hold them and eat at the same time. Blessed is the Confederate soldier who has even toothache, when there are women near! What sympathies and remedies are volunteered! I always laugh, as I did then, when I think of the supposed wounded man those girls discovered on that memorable Arkansas day. I must first acknowledge that it was my fault; for seized with compassion for a man supported by two others who headed the procession, I cried, "Oh, look! he is wounded!" "Oh, poor fellow!" screamed the others, while tears and exclamations flowed abundantly, until one of the men, smiling humorously, cried out, "Nothing the matter with him!" and on nearer view, I perceived it was laziness, or perhaps something else, and was forced to laugh at the streaming eyes of those tender-hearted girls.

August 24th, Sunday.

Soon after dinner yesterday two soldiers stopped here, and requested permission to remain all night. The word "soldier" was enough for us; and without even seeing them, Anna and I gladly surrendered our room, and said we would sleep in Mrs. Badger's, instead. However, I had no curiosity to see the heroes, and remained up here reading until the bell summoned me to supper, when I took my seat without looking at them, as no introduction was possible, from their having refrained from giving their names.

Presently I heard the words, "That retreat from Norfolk was badly conducted." I looked up, and saw before me a rather good-looking man covered with the greatest profusion of gold cloth and buttons, for which I intuitively despised him. The impulse seized me, so I spoke. "Were you there?" "No; but near by. I was there with the First Louisiana for 'most a year." "Do you know George Morgan?" "Know George? Yes, indeed! You are his sister." This was an assertion; but I bowed assent, and he went on, "Thought so, from the resemblance. I remember seeing you ten years ago, when you were a very little girl. I used to be at your house with the boys; we were schoolmates." I remarked that I had no recollection of him. "Of course not," he said, but did not inform me of his name. He talked very familiarly of the boys, and said he had met them all at Richmond. Next he astounded me by saying he was a citizen of Baton Rouge, though he had been almost four years in New York before the war broke out. He was going to town to look after the " property," hearing his father had gone to France. An inhabitant of that city, who was so familiar with my brothers and me, and with whom I was not acquainted! Here was a riddle to solve. Let us see who among our acquaintances had gone to France. I could think of none. I made up my mind to find out his name if I had to ask it.

All through supper he talked, and when, in country style, the gentlemen left us at table, I found the curiosity of the others was even more excited than mine. I was determined to know who he was, then.

In the parlor, he made some remark about never having been in ladies' society the whole time he was in Virginia. I expressed my surprise, as George often wrote of the pleasant young ladies he met everywhere. "Oh, yes!" said monsieur, "but it is impossible to do your duty as an officer, and be a lady's man; so I devoted myself to my military profession exclusively." "Insufferable puppy!" I said to myself. Then he told me of how his father thought he was dead, and asked if I had heard of his rallying twenty men at Manassas, and charging a Federal regiment, which instantly broke? I honestly told him, "No." "Iagoo, the great boaster," I decided. Abruptly he said there were very few nice young ladies in Baton Rouge. "Probably so, in *his* circle," I thought, while I dryly remarked, "Indeed?" "Oh, yes!" and still more abruptly he said, "Ain't you the youngest? — Yes! I thought so! I remember you when you were a wee thing, so high," placing his hand at a most insultingly short distance from the floor. "Really I must ask your name," I said. He hesitated a moment and then said in a low tone, "De J——." "De —— What?" I absurdly asked, thinking I was mistaken. "A—— de J——" he repeated. I bowed slightly to express my satisfaction, said, "Anna, we must retire," and with a good-night to my newly discovered gentleman, went upstairs.

He is the one I heard George speak of last December when he was here, as having been court-martialed, and shot, according to the universal belief in the army; that was the only time I had ever heard his name, though I was quite familiar with the cart of De J—— *père*, as it perambulated the streets. My first impressions are seldom erroneous. From the first, I knew that man's respectability was derived from his buttons. That is why he took such pride in them, and contemplated them with such satisfaction. They lent him social backbone enough to converse so familiarly with me; without the effulgence of that splendid gold, which he hoped would dazzle my eye to his real position, he would have hardly dared to "remember me when I was a wee thing, so high." Is he the only man whose coat alone entitles him to respectability? He may be colonel, for all I know; but still, he is A—— de J—— to me. He talked brave enough to be general.

This morning I met him with a cordial "Good-morning, Mr. de J——," anxious to atone for several "snubs" I had given him, long before I knew his name, last night; you see I could afford to be patronizing now. But the name probably, and the fluency with which I pronounced it, proved too much for him, and after "Good-morning, Miss Morgan," he did not venture a word. We knew each other then; his name was no longer a secret.

August 25th. About 12 at night.

Sleep is impossible after all that I have heard, so, after vainly endeavoring to follow the example of the rest, and sleep like a Stoic, I have lighted my candle and take to this to induce drowsiness.

Just after supper, when Anna and I were sitting with Mrs. Carter in her room, I talking as usual of home, and saying I would be perfectly happy if mother would decide to remain in Baton Rouge and brave the occasional shellings, I heard a well-known voice take up some sentence of mine from a dark part of the room, and with a cry of surprise, I was hugging Miriam until she was breathless. Such a forlorn creature! — so dirty, tired, and fatigued, as to be hardly recognizable. We thrust her into a chair, and made her speak. She had just come with Charlie, who went after them yesterday; and had left mother and the servants at a kind friend's, on the road. I never heard such a story as she told. I was heartsick; but I laughed until Mrs. Badger grew furious with me and the Yankees, and abused me for not abusing them.

She says when she entered the house, she burst into tears at the desolation. It was one scene of ruin. Libraries emptied, china smashed, sideboards split open with axes, three cedar chests cut open, plundered, and set up on end; all parlor ornaments carried off — even the alabaster Apollo and Diana that Hal valued so much. Her piano, dragged to the centre of the parlor, had been abandoned as too heavy to carry off; her desk lay open with all letters and notes well thumbed and scattered around, while Will's last letter to her was open on the floor, with the Yankee stamp of dirty fingers. Mother's portrait half-cut from its frame stood on the floor. Margret, who was present at the sacking, told how she had saved father's. It seems that those who wrought destruction in our house were all officers. One jumped on the sofa to cut the picture down (Miriam saw the prints of his muddy feet) when Margret cried, "For God's sake, gentlemen, let it be! I'll help you to anything here. He's dead, and the young ladies would rather see the house burn than lose it!" "I'll blow your damned brains out," was the "gentleman's" answer as he put a pistol to her head, which a brother officer dashed away, and the picture was abandoned for finer sport. All the others were cut up in shreds.

Upstairs was the finest fun. Mother's beautiful mahogany armoir, whose single door was an extremely fine mirror, was entered by crashing through the glass, when it was emptied of every article, and the shelves half-split, and half-thrust back crooked. Letters, labeled by the boys "Private," were strewn over the floor; they opened every armoir and drawer, collected every rag to be found and littered the whole house with them, until the wonder was, where so many rags had been found. Father's armoir was relieved of everything; Gibbes's handsome Damascus sword with the silver scabbard included. All his clothes, George's, Hal's, Jimmy's, were appropriated. They entered my room, broke that fine mirror for sport, pulled down the rods from the bed, and with them pulverized my toilet set, taking also all Lydia's china ornaments I had packed in the wash-stand. The débris filled my basin, and ornamented my bed. My desk was broken open. Over it was spread all my letters, and private papers, a diary I kept when twelve years old, and sundry tokens of dried roses, etc., which must have been *very* funny, they all being labeled with the donor's name, and the occasion. Fool! how I writhe when I think of all they saw; the invitations to buggy rides, concerts, "Compliments of," etc. —! Lilly's sewing-machine had disappeared; but as mother's was too heavy to move, they merely smashed the needles.

In the pillaging of the armoirs, they seized a pink

SARAH FOWLER
Sully's portrait of Mrs. Morgan

flounced muslin of Miriam's, which one officer placed on the end of a bayonet, and paraded round with, followed by the others who slashed it with their swords crying, "I have stuck the damned Secesh! that's the time I cut her!" and continued their sport until the rags could no longer be pierced. One seized my bonnet, with which he decked himself, and ran in the streets. Indeed, all who found such, rushed frantically around town, by way of frolicking, with the things on their heads. They say no frenzy could surpass it. Another snatched one of my calico dresses, and a pair of vases that mother had when she was married, and was about to decamp when a Mrs. Jones jerked them away, and carried them to her boarding-house, and returned them to mother the other day. Blessed be Heaven! I have a calico dress! Our clothes were used for the vilest purposes, and spread in every corner — at least those few that were not stolen.

Aunt Barker's Charles tried his best to defend the property. "Ain't you 'shamed to destroy all dis here, that belongs to a poor widow lady who's got two daughters to support?" he asked of an officer who was foremost in the destruction. "Poor? Damn them! I don't know when I have seen a house furnished like this! Look at that furniture! *They* poor!" was the retort, and thereupon the work went bravely on, of making us poor, indeed.

It would have fared badly with us had we been there. The servants say they broke into the house crying, "Where are those damned Secesh women? We know they are hid in here, and we'll make them dance for hiding from Federal officers!" And they could not be convinced that we were not there, until they had searched the very garret. Wonder what they would have done? Charles caught a Captain Clark in the streets, when the work was almost over, and begged him to put an end to it. The gentleman went readily, but though the devastation was quite evident, no one was to be seen, and he was about to leave, when, insisting that there was some one there, Charles drew him into my room, dived under the bed, and drew from thence a Yankee captain, by one leg, followed by a lieutenant, each with a bundle of the boys' clothes, which they instantly dropped, protesting they were only looking around the house. The gentleman captain carried them off to their superior.

Ours was the most shockingly treated house in the whole town. We have the misfortune to be equally feared by both sides, because we will blackguard neither. So the Yankees selected the only house in town that sheltered three forlorn women, to wreak their vengeance on. From far and near, strangers and friends flocked in to see the ravages committed. Crowds rushed in before, crowds came in after, Miriam and mother arrived, all apologizing for the intrusion, but saying they had heard it was a sight never before seen. So they let them examine to their hearts' content; and Miriam says the sympathy of all was extraordinary. A strange gentleman picked up a piece of mother's mirror, which was as thick as his finger, saying, "Madame, I should like to keep this as a memento. I am about to travel through Mississippi, and having seen what a splendid piece of furniture this was, and the state your house is left in, should like to show this as a specimen of Yankee vandalism."

William Waller flew to our home to try to save it; but was too late. They say he burst into tears as he looked around. While on his kind errand, another band of Yankees burst into his house and left not one article of clothing to him, except the suit he had on. The whole talk is about our dreadful treatment at the Yankees' hands. Dr. Day, and Dr. Enders, in spite of the assertions of the former, lost nothing.

Well! I am beggared! Strange to say, I don't feel it. Perhaps it is the satisfaction of knowing my fate that makes me so cheerful that Mrs. Carter envied my stoicism, while Mrs. Badger felt like beating me because I did not agree that there was no such thing as a gentleman in the Yankee army. I know Major Drum for one, and that Captain Clark must be two, and Mr. Biddle is three, and General Williams — God bless him, wherever he is! for he certainly acted like a Christian. The Yankees boasted loudly that if it had not been for him, the work would have been done long ago.

And now, I am determined to see my home, before Yankee shells complete the work that Yankee axes spared. So by sunrise, I shall post over to Mr. Elder's, and insist on Charlie taking me to town with him. I hardly think it is many hours off. I feel so settled, so calm! Just as though I never meant to sleep again. If I only had a desk, — a luxury I have not enjoyed since I left home, — I could write for hours still, without being sleepy; but this curved attitude is hard on my stiff back, so good-night, while I lie down to gain strength for a sight they say will make me faint with distress. *Nous verrons!* If I say I Won't, I know I'll not cry. The Brunots lost nothing at all from their house, thank Heaven for the mercy! Only they lost all their money in their flight. On the door, on their return, they found written, "Ladies, I have done my best for you," signed by a Yankee soldier, who they suppose to be the one who has made it a habit of continually passing their house.

Forgot to say Miriam recovered my guitar from the Asylum, our large trunk and father's papers (untouched) from Dr. Enders's, and with her piano, the two portraits, a few mattresses (all that is left of housekeeping affairs), and father's law books, carried them out of town. For which I say in all humility, Blessed be God who has spared us so much.

Thursday, August 28th.

I am satisfied. I have seen my home again. Tuesday I was up at sunrise, and my few preparations were soon completed, and before any one was awake,

I walked over to Mr. Elder's, through mud and dew, to meet Charlie. Fortunate was it for me that I started so early; for I found him hastily eating his breakfast, and ready to leave. He was very much opposed to my going; and for some time I was afraid he would force me to remain; but at last he consented, — perhaps because I did not insist, — and with wet feet and without a particle of breakfast, I at length found myself in the buggy on the road home. The ride afforded me a series of surprises. Half the time I found myself halfway out of the little low-necked buggy when I thought I was safely in; and the other half, I was surprised to find myself really in when I thought I was wholly out. And so on, for mile after mile, over muddy roads, until we came to a most terrific cross-road, where we were obliged to pass, and which is best undescribed. Four miles from town we stopped at Mrs. Brown's to see mother, and after a few moments' talk, went on our road.

I saw the first Yankee camp that Will Pinckney and Colonel Bird had set fire to the day of the battle. Such a shocking sight of charred wood, burnt clothes, tents, and all imaginable articles strewn around, I had never before seen. I should have been very much excited, entering the town by the route our soldiers took; but I was not. It all seemed tame and familiar. I could hardly fancy I stood on the very spot where the severest struggle had taken place. The next turn of the road brought us to two graves, one on each side of the road, the resting-place of two who fell that day. They were merely left in the ditch where they fell, and earth from the side was pulled over them. When Miriam passed, parts of their coats were sticking out of the grave; but some kind hand had scattered fresh earth over them when I saw them. Beyond, the sight became more common. I was told that their hands and feet were visible from many. And one poor fellow lay unburied, just as he had fallen, with his horse across him, and both skeletons. That sight I was spared, as the road near which he was lying was blocked up by trees, so we were forced to go through the woods, to enter, instead of passing by, the Catholic graveyard. In the woods, we passed another camp our men destroyed, while the torn branches above testified to the number of shells our men had braved to do the work. Next to Mr. Barbee's were the remains of a third camp that was burned; and a few more steps made me suddenly hold my breath, for just before us lay a dead horse with the flesh still hanging, which was hardly endurable. Close by lay a skeleton, — whether of man or horse, I did not wait to see. Not a human being appeared until we reached the Penitentiary, which was occupied by our men. After that, I saw crowds of wagons moving furniture out, but not a creature that I knew. Just back of our house was all that remained of a nice brick cottage — namely, four crumbling walls. The offense was that the husband was fighting for the Confederates; so the wife was made to suffer, and is now homeless, like many thousands besides. It really seems as though God wanted to spare our homes. The frame dwellings adjoining were not touched, even. The town was hardly recognizable, and required some skill to avoid the corners blocked up by trees, so as to get in at all.

Our house could not be reached by the front, so we left the buggy in the back yard, and running through the lot without stopping to examine the storeroom and servants' rooms that opened wide, I went through the alley and entered by the front door.

Fortunate was it for this record that I undertook to describe the sacking only from Miriam's account. If I had waited until now, it would never have been mentioned; for as I looked around, to attempt such a thing seemed absurd. I stood in the parlor in silent amazement; and in answer to Charlie's "Well?" I could only laugh. It was so hard to realize. As I looked for each well-known article, I could hardly believe that Abraham Lincoln's officers had really come so low down as to steal in such a wholesale manner. The *papier-maché* workbox Miriam had given me was gone. The baby sacque I was crocheting, with all knitting needles and wools, gone also. Of all the beautiful engravings of Annapolis that Will Pinckney had sent me, there remained a single one. Gentlemen, my name is written on each! Not a book remained in the parlor, except "Idyls of the King," that contained my name also, and which, together with the door-plate, was the only case in which the name of Morgan was spared. They must have thought we were related to John Morgan, and wreaked their vengeance on us for that reason. Thanks for the honor, but there is not the slightest connection! Where they did not carry off articles bearing our name, they cut it off, as in the visiting-cards, and left only the first name. Every book of any value or interest, except Hume and Gibbon, was "borrowed" permanently. I regretted Macaulay more than all the rest. Brother's splendid French histories went, too; all except "L'Histoire de la Bastille." However, as they spared father's law libraries (all except one volume they used to support a flour barrel with, while they emptied it near the parlor door), we ought to be thankful.

The dining-room was *very* funny. I looked around for the cut-glass celery and preserve dishes that were to be part of my "dot," as mother always said, together with the champagne glasses that had figured on the table the day that I was born; but there remained nothing. There was plenty of split-up furniture, though. I stood in mother's room before the shattered armoir, which I could hardly believe the same that I had smoothed my hair before, as I left home three weeks previously. Father's was split across, and the lock torn off, and in the place of the hundreds of articles it contained, I saw two bonnets at the sight of which I actually sat down to laugh.

One was mother's velvet, which looked very much like a football in its present condition. Mine was not to be found, as the officers forgot to return it. Wonder who has my imperial? I know they never saw a handsomer one, with its black velvet, purple silk, and ostrich feathers.

I went to my room. Gone was my small paradise! Had this shocking place ever been habitable? The tall mirror squinted at me from a thousand broken angles. It looked so knowing! I tried to fancy the Yankee officers being dragged from under my bed by the leg, thanks to Charles; but it seemed too absurd; so I let them alone. My desk! What a sight! The central part I had kept as a little curiosity shop with all my little trinkets and keepsakes of which a large proportion were from my gentlemen friends; I looked for all I had left, found only a piece of the McRae, which, as it was labeled in full, I was surprised they had spared. Precious letters I found under heaps of broken china and rags; all my notes were gone, with many letters. I looked for a letter of poor ——, in cipher, with the key attached, and name signed in plain hand. I knew it would hardly be agreeable to him to have it read, and it certainly would be unpleasant to me to have it published; but I could not find it. Miriam thinks she saw something answering the description, somewhere, though.

Bah! What is the use of describing such a scene?[1]

[1] In her book, *From Flag to Flag*, Mrs. Eliza McHatton Ripley gives a vivid description of Judge Morgan's house as she herself saw it after the sacking. — W. D.

Many suffered along with us, though none so severely. Indeed, the Yankees cursed loudly at those who did not leave anything worth stealing. They cannot complain of us, on that score. All our handsome Brussels carpets, together with Lydia's fur, were taken, too. What did they not take? In the garret, in its darkest corner, a whole gilt-edged china set of Lydia's had been overlooked; so I set to work and packed it up, while Charlie packed her furniture in a wagon, to send to her father.

It was now three o'clock; and with my light linen dress thrown off, I was standing over a barrel putting in cups and saucers as fast as I could wrap them in the rags that covered the floor, when Mr. Larguier sent me a nice little dinner. I had been so many hours without eating — nineteen, I think, during three of which I had slept — that I had lost all appetite; but nevertheless I ate it, to show my appreciation. If I should hereafter think that the quantity of rags was exaggerated, let me here state that, after I had packed the barrel and china with them, it made no perceptible diminution of the pile.

As soon as I had finished my task, Charlie was ready to leave again; so I left town without seeing, or hearing, any one, or any thing, except what lay in my path. As we drove out of the gate, I begged Charlie to let me get my bird, as I heard Charles Barker had him. A man was dispatched, and in a few minutes returned with my Jimmy. I have since heard that Tiche deserted him the day of the battle, as I so much feared she would; and that Charles found him late in the evening and took charge of him. With my pet once more with me, we drove off again. I cast many a longing look at the grave-yard; but knowing Charlie did not want to stop, I said nothing, though I had been there but once in three months, and that once, six weeks ago. I could see where the fence had been thrown down by our soldiers as they charged the Federals, but it was now replaced, though many a picket was gone. Once more I stopped at Mrs. Brown's, while Charlie went on to Clinton, leaving me to drive mother here in the morning. Early yesterday, after seeing Miriam's piano and the mattresses packed up and on the road, we started off in the buggy, and after a tedious ride through a melting sun, arrived here about three o'clock, having again missed my dinner, which I kept a profound secret until supper-time.

By next Ash Wednesday, I will have learned how to fast without getting sick! Though very tired, I sat sewing until after sunset, dictating a page and a half to Anna, who was writing to Howell.

August 29, CLINTON, LA.

Noah's *duck* has found another resting-place! Yesterday I was interrupted while writing, to pack up for another move, it being impossible to find a boarding-house in the neighborhood. We heard of some about here, and Charlie had engaged a house for his family, where the servants were already settled, so I hurried off to my task. No easy one, either, considering the heat and length of time allowed. This time I ate dinner as I packed, again. About four, finding Miriam did not come to Mr. Elder's as she promised, I started over to General Carter's with her clothes, and found her just getting into the buggy to ride over, as I arrived warm, tired, hardly able to stand. After taking her over, the General sent the buggy back for Mrs. Carter and myself, and soon we were all assembled waiting for the cars. At last, determining to wait for them near the track, we started off again, General Carter driving me in his buggy. I love General Carter. Again, after so many kind invitations, he told me he was sorry we would not remain with him; if we were content, he would be only too happy to have us with him; and spoke so kindly that I felt as though I had a Yankee ball in my throat. I was disposed to be melancholy anyway; I could not say many words without choking. I was going from the kindest of friends to a country where I had none at all; so could not feel very gay. As we reached the track, the cars came shrieking along. There was a pause, a scuffle, during which the General placed me and my bird in a seat, while Lilly, Charlie, Miriam, mother, five children, and two servants, with all the baggage, were thrown aboard some way, when with a shriek and a jerk we were off again, without a chance of saying good-bye, even.

I enjoyed that ride. It had but one fault; and that

was, that it came to an end. I would have wished it to spin along until the war was over, or we in a settled home. But it ended at last, to Jimmy's great relief, for he was too frightened to move even, and only ventured a timid chirp if the car stopped, as if to ask, "Is it over?" Nothing occurred of any interest except once a little boy sent us slightly off the track, by meddling with the brakes.

Landed at sunset, it is hard to fancy a more forlorn crew, while waiting at the depot to get the baggage off before coming to the house. We burst out laughing as we looked at each lengthened face. Such a procession through the straggling village has hardly been seen before. How we laughed at our forlorn plight as we trudged through the hilly streets, — they have no pavements here, — looking like emigrants from the Ould Counthry, as we have watched them in New Orleans!

At the house we found Tiche laid up. The loaded wagon, with its baggage, four mules, three grown servants, and four children, was precipitated from a bridge twenty-five feet high, by the breaking of the before-mentioned causeway, and landed with the whole concern in deep water below. Wonderful to relate, not a life was lost! The mattress on which the negroes remained seated floated them off into shallow water. The only one hurt was Tiche, who had her leg severely sprained. The baggage was afterwards fished out, rather wet. In the mud next morning (it happened late at night), Dophy found a tiny fancy bottle that she had secreted from the Yankees; a present from Clemmy Luzenberg, it was, and one of two things left in my curiosity shop by the Yankees.

After seeing everything in, we started off for the hotel, where we arrived after dark, rather tired, I think. Not a comfortable house, either, unless you call a bare, unfurnished, dirty room without shutter or anything else, comfortable; particularly when you are to sleep on the floor with four children and three grown people, and a servant. After breakfast we came here until we can find a place to settle in, which Mr. Marsden has promised to attend to for us. It is rather rough housekeeping yet, but Lilly has not yet got settled. Our dinner was rather primitive. There was a knife and fork to carve the meat, and then it was finished with spoons. I sat on the floor with my plate, and a piece of cornbread (flour not to be bought at any price) and ate with my fingers — a new experience. I found that water can be drunk out of a cup!

Ouf! I am tired!

August 30th.

Still no prospect of a lodging; so here we remain. I never before lived in a house without a balcony, and have only now found out how inconvenient it is. The whole establishment consists of two rooms on each side of a passage as wide as the front door; and as it has a very low ceiling, with no opening, and no shade near, it is decidedly the warmest spot I ever inhabited. We all sleep on the floor and keep our clothes in our trunks — except Lilly, who has an armoir without doors. Knives and forks for dinner to-day, though the table still consists of a single plank. The house really has a suffocating effect on me, there is such a close look about it. The front is fully a foot below the level of the street, while quite a flight of steps leads from the back door to the yard. In fact, the whole town consists of abrupt little mounds. It is rather a pretty place; but Heaven save me from the misery of living in it! Miriam is crazy to remain — even advocates that dirty, bare, shutterless boarding-house where we passed the first night, from what attraction I cannot imagine. I am just as anxious to get into the country. I would hate the dull round of this little place; I prefer solitude where I can do as I please without being observed. Here we are as well known by people we never before heard of as though we were fellow-citizens.

September 1st, Monday.

I woke up this morning and, to my great surprise, find that summer has already passed away, and that we have already entered the first month of fall. Where has the summer gone to? Since the taking of Fort Jackson, the days have gone by like a dream. I had hardly realized spring, when now I find it is autumn. I am content to let the time fly, though, as every day brings us nearer Peace — or something else.

How shockingly I write! Will I ever again have a desk or a table to write on? At present, my seat is a mattress, and my knee my desk; and that is about the only one I have had since the 2d of August. This is the dreariest day I have seen for some time. Outside, it has been raining since daybreak, and inside, no one feels especially bright or cheerful. I sometimes wish mother would carry out her threat and brave the occasional shellings at Baton Rouge. I would dare anything, to be at home again. I know that the Yankees have left us little besides the bare house; but I would be grateful for the mere shelter of the roof. I often fancy how we will miss little articles that we thought necessary to our comfort before, when we return. . . . And the shoes I paid five dollars for, and wore a single time? I am wishing I had them now that I am almost barefooted, and cannot find a pair in the whole country. . . . Would it not be curious, if one of these days while traveling in the North (if I ever travel again), I should find some well-loved object figuring in a strange house as a "trophy of the battle of Baton Rouge"? I should have to seek for them in some very low house, perhaps; respectable people had very little to do with such disgraceful work, I fancy. Suppose I should see father's cigar-stand, for instance, or Miriam's little statues? I wonder if the people would have the conscience to offer to return them? A young lady, passing by one of the pillaged houses, expressed her surprise at seeing an armoir full of women's and children's clothes being emptied, and the contents tied up in sheets. "What can you do with such things?" she asked a soldier who seemed more zealous than the rest. "Ain't I got a wife and four children in the North?" was the answer. So we, who have hardly clothes enough for our own use, are stripped to supply Northerners!

One would think that I had no theme save the wreck of our house, if they read this. But I take it all out in here. I believe I must be made of wood, or some other tough material, not to feel it more. I sometimes ask myself if it is because I did not care for home, that I take it so quietly now. But I know that is not it. I was wild about it before I knew what had happened; since I learned all, few are the words that have escaped my lips concerning it. Perhaps it is because I have the satisfaction of knowing what all women crave for — the Worst. Indeed it is a consolation in such days as these when truth concerning either side is difficult to discover. The certainty of anything, fortune or misfortune, is comfort to me. I really feel sorry for the others who suffered; but it does not strike me that sympathy is necessary in our case.

Mrs. Flynn came to Lilly's room, when she heard of it, well prepared for sympathy, with a large handkerchief and a profusion of tears, when she was horrified to find both her and Miriam laughing over the latter's description of some comical scene that met her sight in one of the rooms. Seems to me that tears on all occasions come in as the fortieth article, to the articles of belief of some people.

September 3d.

Political news it would be absurd to record; for our information is more than limited, being frequently represented by a blank. Of the thirteen battles that Gibbes has fought in, I know the names of four only: Bull Run, Stonebridge, Port Republic, and Cedar Run. Think of all I have yet to hear! To-day comes the news of another grand affair, the defeat of McClellan, Pope, and Burnside combined. If I dared believe it! But accounts are too meagre as yet. Both Gibbes and George were in it, if there *was* a fight, and perhaps Jimmy, too. Well! I must wait in patience. We have lost so much already that God will surely spare those three to us. Oh! if they come again, if we can meet once more, what will the troubles of the last six months signify? If I dared hope that next summer would bring us Peace! I always prophesy it just six months off; but do I believe it?

Indeed, I don't know what will become of us if it is delayed much longer. If we could only get home, it would be another thing; but boarding, how long will mother's two hundred and fifty last? And that is all the money she has. As to the claims, amounting to a small fortune, she might as well burn them. They will never be paid. But if we get home, what will we do for bedding? The Yankees did not leave us a single comfort, and only two old bars and a pair of ragged sheets, which articles are not to be replaced at any price in the Confederacy, so we must go without. How glad I am that we gave all our blankets to our soldiers last summer! So much saved from the Yankees!

Poor Lavinia! She fancies us comfortably settled at home; I dare say she spends all her time in picturing to herself what we may be doing, and recalling each piece of furniture the rooms contained. Wonder if she would not be shocked if the real scene were suddenly revealed to her, and she should see the desolated house and see us fugitives in a strange town. Wonder how the cry of "Where are those three damned Secesh women?" would have struck her, had she heard the strange oaths and seen the eager search which followed? I dare say it would have frightened her more than it did me when I was told of it. William Waller says it is God's mercy that we had escaped already, for we certainly would have suffered. I hardly think we could have been harmed, though, and shall always regret that we did not return immediately after the battle. It took them from that day to the evacuation to finish the work; and I rather think that our presence would have protected the house.

Our servants they kindly made free, and told them they must follow them (the officers). Margret was boasting the other day of her answer, "I don't want to be any free-er than I is now — I'll stay with my mistress," when Tiche shrewdly remarked, "Pshaw! Don't you know that if I had gone, you'd have followed me?" The conduct of all our servants is beyond praise. Five thousand negroes followed their Yankee brothers from the town and neighborhood; but ours remained. During the fight, or flight, rather, a fleeing officer stopped to throw a musket in Charles Barker's hands, and bade him fight for his liberty. Charles drew himself up, saying, "I am only a slave, but I am a Secesh nigger, and won't fight in such a d—— crew!" Exit Yankee, continuing his flight down to the riverside.

September 4th.

I hear to-day that the Brunots have returned to Baton Rouge, determined to await the grand finale there. They, and two other families, alone remain. With these exceptions, and a few Dutch and Irish who cannot leave, the town is perfectly deserted by all except the Confederate soldiers. I wish I was with them! If all chance of finding lodgings here is lost, and mother remains with Lilly, as she sometimes seems more than half inclined, and Miriam goes to Linwood, as she frequently threatens, I believe I will take a notion, too, and go to Mrs. Brunot! I would rather be there, in all the uncertainty, expecting to be shelled or burnt out every hour, than here. Ouf! what a country! Next time I go shopping, I mean to ask some clerk, out of curiosity, what they *do* sell in Clinton. The following is a list of a few of the articles that shopkeepers actually laugh at you if you ask for: Glasses, flour, soap, starch, coffee, candles, matches, shoes, combs, guitar-strings, bird-seed,—in short, everything that I have heretofore considered as necessary to existence. If any one had told me I could have lived off of cornbread, a few months ago, I would have been incredulous; now I believe it, and return an inward grace for the blessing at every mouthful. I have not tasted a piece of wheatbread since I left home, and shall hardly taste it again until the war is over.

I do not like this small burg. It is very straggling and pretty, but I would rather not inhabit it. We are as well known here as though we carried our cards on our faces, and it is peculiarly disagreeable to me to overhear myself spoken about, by people I don't know, as "There goes Miss Morgan," as that young man, for instance, remarked this morning to a crowd, just as I passed. It is not polite, to say the least.

Will Carter was here this morning and told me he saw Theodore Pinckney in the streets. I suppose he is on his way home, and think he will be a little disappointed in not finding us at Linwood as he expects, and still more so to hear he passed through the very town where we were staying, without knowing it.

Beech Grove,
September 6th, Saturday.

Another perch for Noah's duck! Where will I be in a week or two from this? I shall make a mark, twenty pages from here, and see where I shall be when I reach it. Here, most probably; but oh, if I could then be at home! General Carter, who spent the evening with us day before yesterday, remarked that the first thing he heard as he reached town was that all the gentlemen and ladies of Clinton were hunting for country lodgings for us. It was pretty much the case. The General was as kind as ever, bless his gray head! and made us promise to go back to Linwood with him when he passes back next week. This is the way we keep the promise—coming out here.

Early yesterday morning we received a note from Eliza Haynes, one of our indefatigable agents, saying her grandmother, Mrs. McCay, had consented to receive us, and would come for us in the evening. Immediately my packing task was begun. But imagine my disappointment, just as I had finished one trunk, to hear mother announce her determination to let us go alone, while she remained with Lilly! Prayers, entreaties, tears, arguments, all failed; and we were forced to submit. So with a heart fuller than I can express, I repacked the trunk with Miriam's and my clothing, and got ready to depart. In the evening the carriage drove up to the door with Eliza and her grandmother, and with a hasty and rather choky good-bye to Lilly and mother, we were hurried in, and in another moment were off.

I fancied the house would be north of Clinton, so of course the horses took the road south. Then I decided on a white cottage to the left of the road, and about two miles out, found that it was to the right, not painted, and no cottage at all, but a nondescript building, besides. "'T was ever thus from childhood's hour!" When did I ever fancy anything exactly as it was? But the appearance does not affect the house, which is really very comfortable, though apparently unfinished. The same objection might be made to it that I made to Mrs. Moore's, for there is not a shutter on the place. But fine shade trees take their place, and here I do not feel the want of them so much, as our room is in the back of the house, to the west, where the rising sun cannot salute my nose as it did at Mrs. Moore's. As to what effect the setting sun has, I must wait for the evening to decide, though I always enjoy that. At Greenwell, we used to walk a mile away from home to see the sun set in an open field.

I find Mrs. McCay an excellent, plain old lady, with neither airs nor pretentions, and very kindhearted. Here she lives alone, with the exception of an orphan girl called Jane, whose position, half-menial, half-equal, it would be hard to define. Poor girl! the name of orphan alone was enough to make me sorry for her. She must be "Friday's child"! she is so "ready and willing." Eliza, who it seems stays a great deal with her grandmother, is one of the brightest little girls I have seen for a long while. She sings and plays on the piano with a style and assurance that I can only mutely covet. Why cannot I have the confidence I see all others possess? She took me to the gin-house last evening, though I could not see much, as it was almost sunset when we arrived. An early tea, and singing, and music after, completed our evening, and then we were shown to our room.

Mrs. McCay has only room for us two, so it is fortunate that mother would not come. She says she wants us to spend a few days with her, to see if we like it, or if we will be willing to be separated from mother. In the mean time, we can look around for lodgings in a larger and more comfortable place where we can be together. She tells such stories about the house Lilly lives in, of its age, and unhealthiness, that I am frightened about mother. She says she will die if she stays there this month. Miriam and Eliza have gone to town to see them, and are then going to Mrs. George's to see if she can accommodate us.

I wanted to have a splendid dream last night, but failed. It was pleasant, though, to dream of welcoming George and Gibbes back. Jimmy I could not see; and George was in deep mourning. I dreamed of fainting when I saw him (a novel sensation, since I never experienced it awake), but I speedily came to, and insisted on his "pulling Henry Walsh's red hair for his insolence," which he promised to do instantly. How absurd! Dreams! dreams! That pathetic "Miss Sarah, do you ever dream?" comes vividly back to me sometimes. Dream? Don't I!

not the dreams that he meant; but royal, purple dreams, that De Quincey could not purchase with his opium; dreams that I would not forego for all the inducements that could be offered. I go to sleep, and pay a visit to heaven or fairyland. I have white wings, and with another, float in rosy clouds, and look down on the moving world; or I have the power to raise myself in the air without wings, and silently float wherever I will, loving all things and feeling that God loves me. I have heard Paul preach to the people, while I stood on a fearful rock above. I have been to strange lands and great cities; I have talked with people I have never beheld. Charlotte Brontë has spent a week with me — in my dreams — and together we have talked of her sad life. Shakespeare and I have discussed his works, seated tête-à-tête over a small table. He pointed out the character of each of his heroines, explaining what I could not understand when awake; and closed the lecture with "You have the tenderest heart I have ever read, or sung of" — which compliment, considering it as original with him, rather than myself, waked me up with surprise.

CLINTON, September 9th, Tuesday.

Back again! For how long, I know not. At sunset Saturday, Eliza and Miriam returned to Mrs. McCay's with Nannie Davidson. Mother had proved obdurate and refused to leave Clinton; so they had all gone on, and spent the day with Mrs.

Haynes instead of going to Mrs. George's. After my quiet, solitary day, I was glad to see them again, particularly as they brought confirmation of the great victory in Virginia. It is said the enemy were cut off from Washington, and that we were pursuing them. O my brothers! If God will only spare them! I envy Lydia who is so near them, and knows all, and can take care of them if they are hurt. It will be several days at least, before we can hear from them, if we hear at all; for Jimmy has never yet written a line, and George has written but once since the taking of the forts, and that was before the battle of Chickahominy. We can only wait patiently. Perhaps General Carter will bring us news.

Mrs. Haynes sent a very pressing invitation for us to spend the next day with her, so, although it was Sunday, we went. I am becoming dreadfully irreligious. I have not been to church since Mr. Gierlow went to Europe last July. It is perfectly shocking; but the Yankees have kept me running until all pious dispositions have been shaken out of me; so they are to blame. Like heathens, we called on Miss Comstock as we passed through town, and spent an hour with her. Landed at Mr. Haynes's, we had ample time to look around before he and his wife got back from church. Here again I found what seems to be the prevailing style of the country, wide-spread doors and windows, with neither blinds nor shade trees to keep off the glare of the sun. The dining-room was a wide hall, where the rising sun shone in your face at breakfast, and at dinner, being directly overhead, seemed to shine in at both ends at once. A splendid arrangement for a Fire Worshiper; but I happened to be born in America, instead of Persia, so fail to appreciate it.

September 10th.

Yesterday I was interrupted to undertake a very important task. The evening before, mother and Lilly happened to be in a store where two officers were buying materials for making shirts, and volunteered to make them for them, which offer they gladly accepted, though neither party knew the other. They saw that they were friends of Charlie, so had no scruples about offering their services; the gentlemen saw that they were ladies, and very kind ones, besides, so made no difficulty about accepting. Lilly undertook one of purple merino, and I took a dark blue one. Miriam nominally helped her; but her very sore finger did not allow her to do much. Mother slightly assisted me; but I think Lilly and I had the best of the task. All day we worked, and when evening came, continued sewing by the light of these miserable home-made candles. Even then we could not finish, but had to get up early this morning, as the gentlemen were to leave for Port Hudson at nine o'clock. We finished in good time, and their appearance recompensed us for our trouble. Lilly's was trimmed with folds of blue from mine, around collar, cuffs, pockets, and down the front band; while mine was pronounced a *chef d'œuvre*, trimmed with bias folds of tiny red and black plaid. With their fresh colors and shining pearl buttons, they were really very pretty. We sent word that we would be happy to make as many as they chose for themselves or their friends, and the eldest, with many fears that it was an "imposition" and we were "too good," and much more of the same kind, left another one with Charlie for us. We cannot do too much, or even enough, for our soldiers. I believe that is the universal sentiment of the women of the South.

Well, but how did we get back here? I hardly know. It seems to me we are being swayed by some kind of destiny which impels us here or there, with neither rhyme nor reason, and whether we will or no. Such homeless, aimless, purposeless, wandering individuals are rarely seen. From one hour to another, we do not know what is to become of us. We talk vaguely of going home "when the Yankees go away." When will that be? One day there is not a boat in sight; the next, two or three stand off from shore to see what is being done, ready, at the first sight of warlike preparation, to burn the town down. It is particularly unsafe since the news from Virginia, when the gunboats started from Bayou Goula, shelling the coast at random, and destroying everything that was within reach, report says. Of course, we cannot return to our homes when commissioned officers are playing the part of pirates, burning, plundering, and destroying at will, with neither law nor reason. Donaldsonville they burned before I left Baton Rouge, because some fool fired a shotgun at a gunboat some miles above; Bayou Sara they burned while we were at General Carter's, for some equally reasonable excuse. The fate of Baton Rouge hangs on a still more slender thread. I would give worlds if it were all over.

At Mrs. Haynes's we remained all night, as she sent the carriage back without consulting us. Monday we came to town and spent the day with Lilly. How it was, I can't say; but we came to the conclusion that it was best to quit our then residence, and either go back to Linwood or to a Mrs. Somebody who offered to take us as boarders. We went back to Mrs. McCay's, to tell her of our determination, and in the morning took leave of her and came back home.

We hear so much news, piece by piece, that one would imagine some definite result would follow, and bring us Peace before long. The Virginia news, after being so great and cheering, has suddenly ceased to come. No one knows the final result. The last report was that we held Arlington Heights. Why not Washington, consequently? Cincinnati (at last accounts) lay at our mercy. From Covington, Kirby Smith had sent over a demand for its surrender in two hours. Would it not be glorious to avenge New Orleans by such a blow? But since last night the telegraph is silent.

News has just come of some nice little affair

between our militia in Opelousas and the Yankees from New Orleans, in which we gave them a good thrashing, besides capturing arms, prisoners, and ammunition. "It never rains but it pours" is George's favorite proverb. With it comes the "rumor" that the Yankees are preparing to evacuate the city. If it could be! Oh, if God would only send them back to their own country, and leave ours in peace! I wish them no greater punishment than that they may be returned to their own homes, with the disgrace of their outrages here ever before their eyes. That would kill an honest man, I am sure.

Sunday, September 14th, 1862.

I have been so busy making Lieutenant Bourge's shirt that I have not had time to write, besides having very little to write about. So my industry saved my paper and spared these pages a vast amount of trash. I would not let any one touch Lieutenant Bourge's shirt except myself; and last evening, when I held it up completed, the loud praises it received satisfied me it would answer. Miriam and Miss Ripley declared it the prettiest ever made. It is dark purple merino. The bosom I tucked with pleats a quarter of an inch deep, all the way up to the collar, and stitched a narrow crimson silk braid up the centre to hold it in its place. Around the collar, cuffs, pockets, and band down the front, the red cord runs, forming a charming contrast to the dark foundation. Indeed, I devoted the sole article the Yankees let fall from my two workboxes — a bunch of soutache — to the work. Large white pearl buttons completed the description, and my shirt is really as quiet, subdued, and pretty a one as I ever saw. I should first hear the opinion of the owner, though. If he does not agree with all the others, I shall say he has no taste.

I got a long sweet letter from Sophie on Friday that made me happy for the whole day. They were about leaving for Alexandria. I was glad to hear they would be out of danger, but still I was sorry they were going so far away. I have been laying a hundred wild schemes to reach Baton Rouge and spend a day or two with them, which is impossible now. Sophie writes just as she talks — and that means remarkably well, so I can at least have the pleasure of corresponding. At Dr. Carnal's they will be out of the reach of all harm and danger; so I ought to rejoice. There is one thing in which Sophie and I agree, and that is in making Stonewall Jackson our hero. Talk of Beauregard! he never had my adoration; but Stonewall is the greatest man of the age, decidedly.

Still no authentic reports of the late battles in Virginia. I say late, referring to those fought two weeks ago. From the Federal accounts, glowing as they usually are, I should gather the idea that their rout was complete. I cannot imagine why we can hear nothing more from our own side. . . .

I think my first act on my return home will be to take a cup of coffee and a piece of bread, two luxuries of which I have been deprived for a long while. Miriam vows to devour an unheard-of number of biscuits, too. How many articles we considered as absolutely necessary, before, have we now been obliged to dispense with! Nine months of the year I reveled in ice, thought it impossible to drink water without it. Since last November, I have tasted it but once, and that once by accident. And oh, yes! I caught some hail-stones one day at Linwood! Ice-cream, lemonade, and sponge cake was my chief diet; it was a year last July since I tasted the two first, and one since I have seen the last. Bread I believed necessary to life; vegetables, senseless. The former I never see, and I have been forced into cultivating at least a toleration of the latter. Snap beans I can actually swallow, sweet potatoes I really like, and one day at Dr. Nolan's I "bolted" a mouthful of tomatoes, and afterwards kept my seat with the heroism of a martyr. These are the minor trials of war. If that were all — if coarse, distasteful food were the only inconvenience!

When I think of what Lavinia must suffer so far from us, and in such ignorance of our condition, our trials seem nothing in comparison to hers. And think how uneasy Brother must be, hearing of the battle, and not knowing where we fled to! For he has not heard of us for almost two months. In return we are uneasy about him and Sister. If New Orleans is attacked, what will become of them with all those children?

Tuesday, September 16th.

Yesterday Miriam determined to go to Linwood, and consequently I had a severe task of trunk-packing, one of my greatest delights, however. I hate to see any one pack loosely or in a slovenly manner. Perhaps that is the reason I never let any one do it if I am able to stand. This morning was appointed as our day for leaving, but I persuaded her to wait until to-morrow, in hope that either the General, or news from Virginia, would arrive this evening. Bless this village! It is the meanest place for news that I ever was in. Not a word can be gathered, except what is false or unfounded; and they are even tired of that, in the last few days.

Talk of Baton Rouge turning Yankee, as the report went here! Of the three or four there who took the oath, not one can be compared to some loyal citizens of this small burg. Why, I talked to two gentlemen yesterday who, if it were not for the disgrace and danger incurred by bearing the name, I should style Union men, and talked or rather listened to them, until my spirits were reduced to the lowest ebb. People were shocked at our daring to believe there lived gentlemen and Christians in the North — I mean those wild fanatics, who could only take in one idea at a time, and rarely divested their brains of that one to make room for a newer one, were shocked at our belief; but if they could converse with a few here, that I could point out, our gnat of common sense would be swallowed by this behemoth of heterodoxy.

This morning Mrs. Bar, Miss Bernard, and a Miss Mud came to town and surprised us by a most unexpected visit. They spent the day with us, and have just now driven off on their return home, through this drizzly, misting evening. A while ago a large cavalry company passed, at the corner, on their way from Port Hudson to Camp Moore, the report is. They raised their hats to us, seeing us at the gate, and we waved our handkerchiefs in return, each with a silent "God bless you," I am sure.

As though to prove my charge unjust, news comes pouring in. Note we a few items, to see how many will prove false. First, we have taken Baltimore without firing a gun; Maryland has risen *en masse* to join our troops; Longstreet and Lee are marching on Washington from the rear; the Louisiana troops are ordered home to defend their own State — thank God! if it will only bring the boys back! Then comes tidings of nine gunboats at Baton Rouge; Ponchatoula on the railroad taken by Yankees; Camp Moore and three batteries, ditto. Not so cheering! If that is so, Clinton lies within reach, being thirty-five miles off.

Leaving much the most valuable portion of our clothing here, the Yankees will probably appropriate what little they spared us and leave us fairly destitute; for we take only summer clothes to Linwood. I have plenty of underclothes, but the other day, when I unpacked the large trunk from Dr. Enders's, I found I had just two dresses for winter; a handsome blue silk I bought just two years ago last spring, and one heavy blue merino that does not fit me. What an outfit for winter! Miriam has two poplins and a black silk, and mother a wine-colored merino, only. But each of us is blessed with a warm cloak, and are correspondingly grateful. I was confident I had saved my green, dark blue, and brown silk dresses, but the Yankees saved them instead, for me, or their suffering sweethearts, rather. On the other hand, taking so many necessary articles to Linwood, the risk of losing them is the same. An attack on Port Hudson is apprehended, and if it falls, General Carter's house will be decidedly unsafe from Yankee vengeance. The probability is that it will burn, as they have been daily expecting ever since the Yankees occupied Baton Rouge. The risk seems equal, either way. Go or stay, the danger seems the same. Shall we go, then, for variety, or die here of stagnation while waiting for the Yankees to make up their minds? I would rather be at neither place, just now; in fact I could hardly name the place I should like to be in now, unless it were Europe or the Sandwich Islands; but I love Linwood and its dear inhabitants, and under other circumstances should be only too happy to be there. I was regretting the other day that our life was now so monotonous; almost longed for the daily alarms we had when under Yankee rule in Baton Rouge. Stirring times are probably ahead.

LINWOOD,
September 17th, Wednesday.

Still floating about! This morning after breakfast, General Carter made his appearance, and in answer to his question as to whether we were ready to leave with him, Miriam replied, "Yes, indeed!" heartily, glad to get away from Clinton, where I have detained her ever since the day Theodore returned home, to her great disgust. As our trunk was already packed, it did not take many minutes to get ready; and in a little while, with a protracted good-bye, we were on our way to the depot, which we reached some time before the cars started. Though glad to leave Clinton, I was sorry to part with mother. For ten days she has been unable to walk, with a sore on her leg below the knee; and I want to believe she will miss me while I am away. I could not leave my bird in that close, ill-ventilated house. He has never sung since I recovered him; and I attribute his ill health or low spirits to that unhealthy place, and thought Linwood might be beneficial to him, too; so brought him with me, to see what effect a breath of pure air might have.

We were the only ladies on the cars, except Mrs. Brown, who got off halfway; but in spite of that, had a very pleasant ride, as we had very agreeable company. The train only stopped thirteen times in the twenty miles. Five times to clear the brushwood from the telegraph lines, once running back a mile to pick up a passenger, and so on, to the great indignation of many of the passengers aboard, who would occasionally cry out, "Hello! if this is the 'clearing-up' train, we had better send for a hand-car!" "What the devil 's the matter now?" until the General gravely assured them that it was an old habit of this very accommodating train, which in summer-time stopped whenever the passengers wished to pick blackberries on the road.

Many soldiers were aboard on their way to Port Hudson, to rejoin their companies. One gallant one offered me a drink of water from his canteen, which I accepted out of mere curiosity to see what water from such a source tasted of. To my great surprise, I found it tasted just like any other. The General introduced a Mr. Crawford to us, who took the seat next to me, as the one next to Miriam was already occupied, and proved a very pleasant and talkative *compagnon de voyage*. General Carter's query as to my industry since he had seen me, brought my acknowledgment of having made two shirts, one of which I sent yesterday. Who to? was the next question. I gave the name, adding that I did not know the gentleman, and he was under the impression that it was made by mother. "I'll see that he is undeceived!" cried the General. "Hanged if I don't tell him!" "Thirtieth Louisiana, you say?" queried Mr. Crawford. "That is the very one I am going to! I will tell him myself!" So my two zealous champions went on, the General ending with "See to it, Crawford; Mrs. Morgan shall not have the credit!" as though there was any great merit in sewing for one's countrymen! Our new acquaintance handed me from the cars as we reached Linwood, and stood talking while the accommodating train slowly rolled out its freight. He told me he was going to send me a tiny sack of coffee, which proposition, as it did not meet with the slightest encouragement, will of course never be thought of again.

I noticed, too, on the train, one of the Arkansas's crew. The same who, though scarcely able to stand on a severely wounded foot, made such a fuss about riding in a carriage while "real ladies" had to walk. Of course he did not recognize us, any more than we would have known him if Dr. Brown had not pointed him out. I hear all of them are at Port Hudson. Anna told me, as we got here, that Dr. Addison (the one I disliked because he was so scrupulously neat while the others were dressed, or rather undressed, for working) was here yesterday, and inquired for the Miss Morgans, saying they were the most charming young ladies he had ever met. On what he founded his opinion, or how he happened to inquire for us in this part of the country, I cannot imagine.

The General brings news of the boys from Jackson. He there met an officer who left Stonewall Jackson's command on the 2d inst., and says Gibbes was unhurt, God be praised! Another saw George a week ago in Richmond, still lame, as the cap of his knee had slipped in that fall last spring. Of Jimmy we hear not a word, not even as to where he is. It seems as though we are destined never to hear again.

September 20th, Saturday.

General Carter has just received a letter from Lydia, which contains what to me is the most melancholy intelligence — the news of the death of Eugene Fowler,[1] who was killed on the 22d of August, in some battle or skirmish in Virginia. Poor Eugene! . . . Does it not seem that this war will sweep off all who are nearest and dearest, as well as most worthy of life, leaving only those you least care for, unharmed?

September 21st.

After supper last night, by way of variety, Anna, Miriam, and I came up to our room, and after undressing, commenced popping corn and making candy in the fireplace. We had scarcely commenced when three officers were announced, who found their way to the house to get some supper, they having very little chance of reaching Clinton before morning, as the cars had run off the track. Of course, we could not appear; and they brought bad luck with them, for our corn would not pop, and our candy burned, while to add to our distress the odor of broiled chicken and hot biscuit was wafted upstairs, after a while, in the most provoking way. In vain we sent the most pathetic appeals by each serv-

[1] A cousin.

ant, for a biscuit apiece, after our hard work. Mrs. Carter was obdurate until, tired out with our messages, she at last sent us an empty jelly-cup, a shred of chip beef, two polished drumsticks, and half a biscuit divided in three. With that bountiful repast we were forced to be content and go to bed.

At sunrise this morning, Mrs. Carter left to go down to her father in Iberville, to see her stepmother who is expected to die. Scarcely had she gone when six more officers and soldiers came in from the still stationary cars to get their breakfast. We heard that Mr. Marsden, too, was down there, so the General sent him a nice breakfast, and I sent my love with it; but he had already breakfasted at Mr. Elder's. As soon as they left, we prepared for church, and just as we were ready, Captain Brown and Mr. Addison were announced. The Doctor greeted us with an elegant bow, but they did not remain long, as we were about going out.

. . . .

Many officers were in church, and as I passed out, Colonel Breaux joined me, and escorted Miriam and me to the carriage, where we stood talking some time under the trees before getting in. He gave us a most pressing invitation to name a day to visit the camp that he might "have the pleasure of showing us the fortifications," and we said we would beg the General's permission to do so. Charming Colonel Breaux! Like all nice men, he is married, of course. He and another officer drove just behind our carriage in coming home, until we came to the fork of the road. Then, leaning from their buggy, both gentlemen bowed profoundly, which we as cordially returned. Two more behind followed their example, and to our great surprise, ten, who were seated in a small wagon drawn by two diminutive mules, bowed also, and, not content with that, rose to their feet as the distance between the two roads increased, and raised their caps, though in the most respectful silence. Rather queer; and I would have said impertinent had they been any others than Confederates fighting for us, who, of course, are privileged people.

September 24th.

Yesterday the General saluted us with "Young ladies, if you will ride in a Confederate carriage, you may go to dress parade this evening." Now, in present phraseology, "Confederate" means anything that is rough, unfinished, unfashionable, or poor. You hear of Confederate dresses, which means last year's. Confederate bridle means a rope halter. Confederate silver, a tin cup or spoon. Confederate flour is corn meal, etc. In this case the Confederate carriage is a Jersey wagon with four seats, a top of hickory slats covered with leather, and the whole drawn by mules. We accepted gladly, partly for the ride and sight, partly to show we were not ashamed of a very comfortable conveyance; so with Mrs. Badger as chaperon, we went off in grand style. I must say I felt rather abashed and wished myself at home as we drove into town, and had the gaze of a whole regiment riveted on us. But soon the men fell in line, and I did not feel so painfully conspicuous. I was amused at a contrast near by, too. There was but one carriage present, besides ours, though there were half a dozen ladies on horseback. This carriage was a very fine one, and in it sat three of the ugliest, dowdiest, worst dressed females I ever saw. We three girls sat in our rough carriage as comfortable as could be, dressed — well, we could not have been dressed better —and looking our very best. *Sans mentir*, I think the Confederates were much the most respectable.

And what a sad sight the Fourth Louisiana was, that was then parading! Men that had fought at Shiloh and Baton Rouge were barefooted. Rags was their only uniform, for very few possessed a complete suit, and those few wore all varieties of colors and cuts. Hats could be seen of every style and shape, from the first ever invented down to the last one purchased evidently some time since. Yet he who had no shoes looked as happy as he who had, and he who had a cap had something to toss up, that's all.

Four or five that we knew gathered around our vehicle and talked to us. Mr. Heuston told me he heard I had been thrown, severely injured, had a narrow escape, etc. Was not thrown! Saddle turned. A few steps off we recognized Mr. Scales. He would stare very hard at us, and if we turned towards him, would look quickly the other way as though afraid to meet our gaze. Presently he gave us an opportunity, and we bowed. He came forward eagerly, blushing deeply, and looking very much pleased, and shook hands with us, and remained some time talking. He said he had not heard of our arrival, but would call as soon as possible. Mr. Talbot had joined Breckinridge.

Having seen the last of that parade, he invited us to see that of his sailors, which was next; but it was too far; so we turned off to see Colonel Breaux's, a mile away. His, the Thirtieth Louisiana, is a beautiful encampment on a large open common. Parade was almost over as we reached there, and soon the Colonel came to meet us. I did not look at the drill. I was watching the hundreds of tents — it looked like a great many — and was wondering how men could live in such places, and was trying to fancy what George's or Gibbes's looked like. It was pleasant to watch the barefoot soldiers race around like boys let loose from school, tossing caps and chips at two old gray geese that flew in circles around the encampment, just as though they had never had more earnest work. One gray-headed man stood in the door of his tent, while a black-headed young one danced before him, to his own whistle, with his arms akimbo. Altogether it was a very pretty picture; but poor men! how can they be happy in these tents?

Sarah Morgan. X.

September 26th, Friday.

My mark finds me at Linwood, though I had not the slightest idea that it would. Wonder where twenty pages beyond will find me? At home, I hope and pray, though I am as happy here as I could possibly be in any place on earth.

Stirring news from our armies comes pouring in. Sunday, Colonel Breaux told me of Wool's defeat, and the great number of prisoners, cannon, and the large supplies of stores and ammunition that we had captured. Then Tuesday we heard of three great battles in Maryland, the third one still continuing; but no particulars of any of them. Yesterday came tidings of our having recrossed the Potomac, and to-day we hear that McClellan's army has been cut to pieces; but whether it is the same old fight or a new one, I cannot as yet learn; for reliable information is not easily obtained in America at this period.

Did I ever record how little truth there was in any of that last Clinton news? It speaks for itself, though. Not a boat lay at Baton Rouge; Camp Moore was not even threatened; Ponchatoula Station was burned, but the one battery was retaken by our men the same night.

But still these false reports cannot equal the Yankees'. Take, for instance, the report of the Captain of the Essex. I give General Carter as my authority. The Captain reports having been fired on by a battery of thirty-six large guns, at Port

LINWOOD

Hudson, some weeks ago, when he opened fire and silenced them, one after the other, from the first to the last. Not a shot from the "rebel" batteries reached them, and not a casualty on their side occurred. But the loss of the Confederates must have been awful. He came within — I forget how many — yards from the shore, and there was not a live man to be seen. He did not mention if there were any dead ones! Now for the other side. There were but four guns mounted there at the time. Shot and shell from those four certainly reached something, for one was seen to enter a porthole, from whence issued frightful shrieks soon after, and it is well known that the Essex is so badly injured by "something" as to be in a sinking condition, and only kept afloat by a gunboat lashed on either side. If she is uninjured, why did she not return and burn Natchez as she announced? In leaving Port Hudson, where "not a live man was to be seen" (nor a dead one to be found), she stopped at Mr. Babin's, just below Dr. Nolan's, where she remained the rest of the day. After she left, being curious to discover the reason of her short stay, Mr. Babin walked to the place where she had been, and discovered sixteen fresh graves on the bank. If they buried them as they did at Baton Rouge and Vicksburg, four in a grave, how many would they be? But granting there were but sixteen, would that prove the veracity of the Captain? Poor man! Perhaps he is related to Pope, and cannot help himself.

September 27th.

I often wonder how lies first came into the world, and whether those who originate them do not believe them as firmly as any one else would believe truth. Lying seems to be the common creed of children and servants.

Anna told me of having heard Lennice telling the other servants that she knew there were spirits, because I often talked to them. Every morning and evening I walked to the graveyard with a basket of flowers, and would sit by father's and Harry's graves and call their spirits to me; and they would all fly to me, and talk and sing with me for hours until I would tell them good-bye and go home, when they would go away too. I suppose the ignorant girl, having foundation enough from my frequent visits there, which were most often alone, made up the rest to account for my never seeming to like company out there. The fervent "Good Lord" with which the tale was received by the other servants, and the full credence they gave it, might have proved unpleasant if further circulated; and I believe some members of the family found it necessary to put an end to it at once.

And speaking of the graveyard recalls something I heard for the first time last night. Miriam was telling me that Tiche had asked if we knew that Mr. Sparks had visited Harry's grave? That he had got a basket of flowers from the Davidsons, and had made their driver carry it for him. And the man had told her that, after filling the vases with roses, and spreading them over the grave, he had thrown himself on it with a shriek of despair, calling on Harry to forgive him; that it was only because forced by his father that he had killed him; and calling on God to prove that he would give his life gladly to recall Harry's. The man thought him a raving maniac and fled in terror. Miriam asked Fanny if it was true, and she said yes; she had gathered the flowers for him herself.

I saw them there, but little knew whose hand had brought them. I perceived at once that they were not mine, and touched even to tears by so silent an offering from an unknown person, I said, "It is some woman's work; God bless the hand that laid them there." I cannot say how much that little tribute affected me. And, Mr. Sparks, I do not retract the blessing now. No! "God have mercy on him!" has been my prayer ever since I knew what an awful loss you had caused us. God knows that I never even desired this revenge — remorse standing over his grave. It has ever been, "God pity and forgive!" — never yet for an instant, "God pursue and avenge!"

September 28th.

We were roused up at four o'clock last night by the arrival of Lydia and Eugene Carter,[1] the first from Virginia and the second from Tennessee; and,

[1] Lydia, daughter of General Carter and wife of Captain Thomas Gibbes Morgan; Eugene, eldest son of General Carter, and husband of Helen mentioned in the Diary.

of course, there was very little sleep for any of us, so anxious were we to hear the news they brought. First I learned that Gibbes was safe up to the 17th; that George, in spite of the advice of his surgeon, had rejoined Stonewall Jackson in Maryland; and Jimmy was midshipman on the ironclad Palmetto State at Charleston. How thankful I was to hear that much, I need not say. Lydia said they all three looked remarkably well; Jimmy handsomer than ever. After that, news of all kinds came indiscriminately. The boys were very anxious about us, but had no idea of our misfortunes or whereabouts. They believed us still in Baton Rouge, and feared we had been there during the battle. Lydia only heard of our house having been plundered when she reached Alabama, so of course they are still ignorant of it. They were all very homesick, but said that we were their only trouble.

A few of the C——s' stories had reached them through brother officers; and George swore to make himself understood by those ladies if he ever saw them again. A gentleman from Cooper's Wells told Lydia that they never tired of repeating their stories to every new arrival; and no man was suffered to depart without having heard a few. If a gentleman friend of ours or the boys inquired if they knew the Miss Morgans of Baton Rouge, "Oh, yes!" would be the answer, "intimately! But you know they have turned Yankee. Received Federal officers every day, and placed all their property under Yankee protection. I" (or "my sister," as it happened who was retailing the lie, meaning Mrs. S——) "slept in their house when it was surrounded by a Yankee guard. Oh, they are perfectly in favor of the Yankees," and so on. Think of a common, low soldier who stopped for buttermilk somewhere where Anna was, introducing the subject. "It is all false!" Anna interrupted. The man answered, "Oh, Miss! you don't suppose we believe it? We would not believe such stories of any young ladies, much less these; for if they are true, their conduct must have been perfectly disgraceful. But though we know these stories to be lies, it does not prevent their being discussed in camp." . . .

Lydia saw Mr. McG——, too, at Lynchburg, who sent me his "regards." Poor fellow! He says he still has "dreams"! He told her a few, but she says they were chiefly about meeting me at a ball, when I always treated him with the most freezing coldness. The same old nightmare. How often he has told me of that same dream, that tormented him eighteen months ago. He says he often thinks of me now — and he still "dreams" of me! "Dreams are baseless fabrics whose timbers are mere moonbeams." Apply your own proverb! . . .

A clatter of hoofs down the road! And bent over the window-sill which is my desk, my fingers are not presentable with the splattering of this vile pen in consequence of my position. Two hours yet before sundown, so of course I am not dressed. They come nearer still. Now I see them! Dr. Addison and Mr. M——! I shall not hurry my toilet for them. It will take some time to comb my hair, too. Wish I could remain up here!

Tuesday, September 30th.

It required very little persuasion to induce those gentlemen to stay to supper, the other evening, and it was quite late before they took their leave. Dr. Addison I was very much pleased with, and so were all the rest. Mr. M——, none of us fell desperately in love with. He is too nonchalant and indifferent, besides having a most peculiar pronunciation which grated harshly on my ears, and that no orthography could fully express. "Garb," for instance, was distorted into "gairb," "yard" into "yaird," "Airkansas," and all such words that I can only imitate by a violent dislocation of my lower jaw that puts Anna into convulsions of laughter — only she would laugh the same if it was *not* funny. This Kentuckian pronunciation grates "hairshly" on my Southern ears. Miriam addressed herself exclusively to the Doctor, so I was obliged to confine my attention entirely to neglected Mr. M——, in which pious duty I was ably and charitably seconded by the General. Speaking of the bravery and daring displayed by the Southern soldiers during this war, Mr. M—— mentioned the dangerous spot he had seen us in the first day we went down to the "Airkansas" and said that, lying directly across the point from the Essex, they expected every instant to see one of her shells explode among us, and were very uneasy about our position, as we did not seem to know the danger. I asked him if he had observed anything peculiar among the dozen planters and overseers standing a short distance from us, when the Captain sent us word that our position was a very dangerous one, as they expected the Essex to open fire every instant, and we had best stand below the levee, higher up, where we would be safe from shells. "I noticed that before any of you understood your position, every man had disappeared as though by magic." Now I had noticed that myself. When I turned, under shelter of the levee, our gallant planters were galloping off in the distance. While Ginnie and I looked and laughed, we suddenly found ourselves the sole objects on the horizon; the other girls were in the road below, going carelessly toward the carriage; so we followed, having lost sight of the brave representatives of Southern chivalry, being the last to leave the supposed field of danger. To my former remark, let me add that there is only one set who take better care for their safety than married women; and that set is composed exclusively of the "Home Guard." Timid girls, either through ignorance or fun, compose the majority of the brave "men" that the volunteer service has not absorbed.

October 1st, Wednesday.

Just after sunset yesterday, Anna and I were walking down the road towards the sugar-house, she reading occasionally from Abbott's "Napoleon," and then pausing for me to explain the *very* difficult passages she could not understand, when we suddenly became aware of the approach of a horse, and raising our bowed heads, beheld Colonel Breaux and another before us, to our infinite surprise and astonishment. The Colonel sprang from his horse and advanced on foot; his companion slowly followed his example, and was introduced as Captain Morrison. We adjourned our historical fit for some future period, and walked home with the gentlemen. Miriam did not get back from her excursion to the cane-patch until it was quite late; when after sitting down a few moments, she ran upstairs to change her dress. She had just put it on an hour before, but nothing would do but she must dress up fine; so she put on her handsomest organdie. In vain I pointed to my simple pink muslin with a white body that I had worn all day, and begged she would not make the contrast between us more striking than ever, as I felt I could not change it without exciting remark. She was obdurate; dressed herself in gorgeous array, and, as usual, I looked like her lady's maid.

Colonel Breaux paid my hair the most extravagant compliments. He said he could not say his prayers for looking at it in church, Sunday before last. Perhaps that is the reason St. Paul said a woman should not worship in church with her head uncovered! But as the Yankees stole my bonnet, I am reduced to wearing my black straw walking-hat with its curled brim, trimmed in black ribbon with golden sheaves of wheat. Two years ago this fall, father threw me a banknote at table, and I purchased this with it. Now it is my only headgear, except a sunbonnet. Before leaving, which was not until quite late, this evening was named for our ride to the fortifications, to our infinite delight, as we have dreamed and talked of nothing else for a week. . . .

A dispatch just received from Gibbes, from Mobile, on his way home. I am so happy! But what can bring him? I fear ——

Lydia has gone to Clinton to meet him at Lilly's.

October 2d, Thursday.

With what extraordinary care we prepared for our ride yesterday! One would have thought that some great event was about to take place. But in spite of our long toilet, we stood ready equipped almost an hour before Colonel Breaux arrived. I was standing in a novel place — upon the bannisters looking over the fields to see if he was coming — and, not seeing him, made some impatient exclamation, when lo! he appeared before me, having only been concealed by the wood-pile, and O my prophetic soul! Captain Morrison was by his side!

There was quite a cavalcade of us: Mr. Carter and his wife, Mrs. Badger and Mrs. Worley, in two buggies; the three boys, who, of course, followed on horseback, and the two gentlemen, Miriam, Anna, and I, riding also. It was really a very pretty sight, when Captain Morrison and I, who took the lead going, would reach the top of one of the steep hills and look down on the procession in the hollow below. Fortunately it was a very cloudy evening; for, starting at four, it would have been very unpleasant to ride that distance with the sun in our faces.

As we reached the town we heard the loud report of two cannon which caused the elder ladies to halt and suggest the propriety of a return. But if it was a gunboat, that was the very thing I was anxious to see; so we hurried on to the batteries. It proved to be only practicing, however. At the first one we stopped at, the crew of the Arkansas were drilling. After stopping a while there, we followed the river to see the batteries below. It was delightful to ride on the edge of a high bluff with the muddy Mississippi below, until you fancied what would be the probable sensation if the horse should plunge down into the waters; then it ceased to be so pleasant. The great, strong animal I rode could have carried me over without a protest on my part; for the ridiculous bit in his mouth was by no means suited to his strength; and it would require a more powerful arm than mine to supply the deficiency. Miriam had generously sacrificed her own comfort to give him to me; and rode fiery Joe instead of her favorite. But it was by no means a comfort to me. Then Anna was not reconciled to her pony while I was on such a fine horse, until I proposed an exchange, and gladly dismounted near an old mill two miles and a half below Port Hudson, as we returned home.

In leaving the town, we lost sight of the buggies, as there was no carriage road that might follow the bluff; and though there was one just back, we never saw our buggies again. Once, following a crescent, far below us lay the water battery concealed by the trees that grew by the water's edge, looking, from where we stood, like quite a formidable precipice. Then still beyond, after leaving the river, we passed through a camp where the soldiers divided their attention equally between eating their supper and staring at us in the most profound silence. Then, through an old gate, down a steep hill, past a long line of rifle-pits, a winding road, and another camp where more men stared and cooked their supper, we came to the last battery but one, which lay so far below that it was too late to visit it. We returned highly delighted with what we had seen and our pleasant ride. It was late when we got back, as altogether our ride had been some fifteen miles in length. As soon as we could exchange our habits for our evening dresses, we rejoined our guests at the supper-table, where none of us wanted for an appetite except poor Captain Morrison, who could not be tempted by the dishes we so much relished. After supper, Colonel Breaux and I got into a discussion, rather, *he* talked, while I listened with eyes and ears, with all my soul. . . . What would I not give for such knowledge! He knows everything, and can express it all in the clearest, purest language, though he says he could not speak a word of English at fourteen!

The discussion commenced by some remark I made about physiognomy; he took it up, and passed on to phrenology — in which he is no great believer. From there he touched on the mind, and I listened, entranced, to him. Presently he asserted that I possessed reasoning faculties, which I fear me I very rudely denied. You see, every moment the painful conviction of my ignorance grew more painful still, until it was most humiliating; and I repelled it rather as a mockery. He described for my benefit the process of reasoning, the art of thinking. I listened more attentively still, resolving to profit by his words. . . . Then he turned the conversation on quite another theme. Health was the subject. He delicately alluded to my fragile appearance, and spoke of the necessity of a strong constitution to sustain a vigorous mind. If the mind prevailed over the weak body, in its turn it became affected by decay, and would eventually lose its powers. It was applicable to all cases; he did not mean that I was sickly, but that my appearance bespoke one who had not been used to the exercise that was most necessary for me. Horseback rides, walks, fresh air were necessary to preserve health. No man had greater disgust for a freckled face than he; but a fair face could be preserved by the most ordinary precautions and even improved by such exercise. He illustrated my case by showing the difference between the flower growing in the sunshine and that growing in a cellar. Father's own illustration and very words, when he so often tried to impress on me the necessity of gaining a more robust frame than nature had bestowed! And a letter he had made Hal write me, showing the danger of such neglect, rose before me. I forgot Colonel Breaux; I remembered only the ardent desire of those two, who seemed to speak to me through his lips. It produced its effect. I felt the guilt I had incurred by not making greater efforts to gain a more robust frame; and putting on my sunbonnet as I arose from the breakfast-table this morning, I took my seat here on the wide balcony where I have remained seated on the floor ever since, with a chair for a desk, trying to drink an extra amount of fresh air.

I was sorry when Colonel Breaux arose to take his leave. As he took my hand, I said earnestly, "Thank you for giving me something to think about." He looked gratified, made some pleasant remark, and after talking a while longer, said good-night again and rode off. While undressing, Miriam and I spoke of nothing else. And when I lay down, and looked in my own heart and saw my shocking ignorance and pitiful inferiority so painfully evident even to my own eyes, I actually cried. Why was I denied the education that would enable me to be the equal of such a man as Colonel Breaux and the others? He says the woman's mind is the same as the man's, originally; it is only education that creates the difference. Why was I denied that education? Who is to blame? Have I exerted fully the natural desire To Know that is implanted in all hearts? Have I done myself injustice in my self-taught ignorance, or has injustice been done to me? Where is the fault, I cried. Have I labored to improve the few opportunities thrown in my path, to the best of my ability? "Answer for yourself. With the exception of ten short months at school, where you learned nothing except arithmetic, you have been your own teacher, your own scholar, all your life, after you were taught by mother the elements of reading and writing. Give an account of your charge. What do you know?" Nothing! except that I am a fool! and I buried my face in the sheet; I did not like even the darkness to see me in my humiliation.

October 4th, Saturday.

While Anna and Miriam went out riding last evening, just as I put down my pen, I went out for a solitary walk down the road that Gibbes would have to pass; but saw nothing of the carriage. When I got back, they told me he was wounded. My fears were well founded, then. With what anxiety we waited for his coming it would be impossible to describe. Every wagon rattling through the fields made us stop and listen; every canestalk waving in the moonlight brought us to our feet.

At last, after supper, far off in the clear light we

saw the carriage. I could not sit still. I walked down the steps and stood under the tree in front, followed by Anna. I did not like her to stand nearer the spot where it would stop than I, even. All the rest remained on the balcony. We did not know how serious the wound might be; we must be careful. Eugene Carter advised caution for more reasons than one. "Look out!" he cried; "suppose it should be Colonel Breaux?" "Then I am afraid the Colonel will get a kiss," I answered nervously, shuffling from one foot to the other. "But suppose it is Mr. M——?" he persisted. "Oh, thank you for the caution! I will look carefully before I greet him!" I returned, moving to the other side, for nearer around the circle moved the carriage. I heard his voice.

"O Gibbes, where is it?" "Left shoulder; mere scratch," he answered. The carriage stopped, "Gibbes! Gibbes!" I cried. "My darling!" and he had his great strong arm around me; the left was hanging in a sling. Slowly the others moved down the steps towards him. What a meeting! My heart was in my throat, I was so happy. Every one caught the well hand and kissed him again and again, and every one shrunk from that left side. I had almost forgotten my "gear Lygia" in my excitement. We followed him on the balcony and put him in a chair near the steps. I pulled off his hat and coat, and knelt in front of him with my arm across his lap, to get near enough. Miriam stood on the steps with his arm around her shoulder, and Lydia near. The others stood around; altogether, it was a happy group that performed in the tableau of "The Soldier's Return." Presently the negroes gathered too. "How is you, Mass' Gibbes?" in all imaginable keys and accents was heard, while the Captain shook hands with each and inquired into their own state of health.

But even wounded soldiers can eat; so supper was again prepared. I am afraid it gave me too much pleasure to cut up his food. It was very agreeable to butter his cornbread, carve his mutton, and spread his preserves; but I doubt whether it could be so pleasant to a strong man, accustomed to do such small services for himself. We listened to him talk, but though it was evident from his slow, deliberate speech, so different from his ordinary habit, that he was suffering, yet I felt impatient when he was interrupted by any commonplace observation by one of us. I wanted to learn something of his exploits. Much knowledge I obtained! He was wounded at Sharpsburg on the 17th September, at nine in the morning. That is all the information I got concerning himself. One would imagine that the seventeen months that have elapsed since we last met had been passed in a prolonged picnic. Concerning others, he was quite communicative. Father Hubert told him he had seen George in the battle, and he had come out safe. Gibbes did not even know that he was in it, until then. Our army, having accomplished its object, recrossed the Potomac, after what was decidedly a drawn battle. Both sides suffered severely.

Hardly an officer on either side escaped unhurt. Mr. McGimsey is wounded, and Major Herron reported killed. I expect the list will contain the names of many friends when it comes.

I have just come from seeing Gibbes's wound dressed. If that is a scratch, Heaven defend me from wounds! A minié ball struck his left shoulder strap, which caused it to glance, thereby saving the bone. Just above, in the fleshy part, it tore the flesh off in a strip three inches and a half by two. Such a great raw, green, pulpy wound, bound around by a heavy red ridge of flesh! Mrs. Badger, who dressed it, turned sick; Miriam turned away groaning; servants exclaimed with horror; it was the first experience of any, except Mrs. Badger, in wounds. I wanted to try my nerves; so I held the towel around his body and kept the flies off while it was being washed. He talked all the time, ridiculing the groans of sympathy over a "scratch," and oh, how I loved him for his fortitude! It is so offensive that the water trickling on my dress has obliged me to change it.

October 6th.

Last night, I actually drew from Gibbes the outlines of Jackson's campaign. He told me of some heroic deeds of his fellow soldiers; but of his own, not a word. I have seen his name too often in the papers, to believe that he has no deeds of his own to relate, if he only would.

October 9th, Thursday.

It is astonishing what a quantity of fresh air has been consumed by me since I formed that wise resolution. The supply must be largely increased, to keep up with the demand; perhaps that is the cause of all these clouds and showers; I must be making a severe drain on the economy of heaven. From breakfast to dinner I remain on the balcony, and read aloud several chapters of the "Mémoires" of Dumas, by way of practice. A dictionary lies by me, and I suffer no word to pass without a perfect definition. Then comes my French grammar, which I study while knitting or sewing, which takes very nearly until dinner-time. After that, I do as I please, either reading or talking, until sunset when we can ride or walk; the walk being always sweetened with sugar-cane. The evening we always spend on the balcony. Is that *grand air* enough? *O mon teint! je serai joliment brune!*

We three girls occupy the same room, since Gibbes's arrival, and have ever so much fun and not half enough sleep. I believe the other two complain of me as the cause; but I plead not guilty. I never was known to laugh aloud, no matter how intense might have been my mirth; "it won't come," as Gibbes murmured last night while reading aloud Artemus Ward's last letter, when we discovered it was suppressed laughter, rather than suppressed pain, that caused him to writhe so. On the other hand, Anna and Miriam laugh as loud and lustily as daughters of the Titans — if the respectable gentlemen had daughters. I confess to doing more than half the talking, but as to the laugh that follows, not a bit. Last night I thought they would go wild, and I too laughed myself into silent convulsions, when I recited an early effusion of my poetic muse for their edification. Miriam made the bedstead prance, fairly, while Anna's laugh sounded like a bull of Bashan with his head in a bolster case.

Saturday, October 11th.

Miriam went off to Clinton before daylight yesterday, with Mr. Carter and Mrs. Worley. She would not let me go for fear mother should keep us. At midnight they got back last night, tired, sleepy, and half-frozen, for our first touch of cool weather came in a strong north wind in the evening which grew stronger and stronger through the night, and they had worn only muslin dresses. I shall never cease to regret that I did not go too. Miriam says mother is looking very sad. Sad, and I am trying to forget all our troubles, and am so happy here! O mother, how selfish it was to leave you! I ask myself whether it were best to stay there where we would only be miserable without adding anything to your comfort or pleasure, or to be here, careless and happy while you are in that horrid hole so sad and lonesome. According to my theory, Miriam would remind me that I say it is better to have three miserable persons than two happy ones whose happiness occasions the misery of the third. That is my doctrine only in peculiar cases; it cannot be applied to this one. I say that if, for example, Miriam and I should love the same person, while that person loved only me, rather than make her unhappy by seeing me marry him, I would prefer making both him and myself miserable, by remaining single. She says "Fudge!" which means, I suppose, nonsense. But our happiness here does not occasion mother's unhappiness. She would rather see us enjoying ourselves here than moping there. One proof is, that she did not suggest our return. She longs to get home, but cannot leave poor Lilly alone, for Charlie is in Granada. Oh, how willingly I would return to the old wreck of our home! All its desolation could not be half so unendurable as Clinton. But Lilly cannot be left. Poor Lilly! When I look at her sad young face, my heart bleeds for her. With five helpless little children to care for, is she not to be pitied? I think that such a charge, in such dreadful days, would kill me. How patiently she bears it!

Thursday, October 16th.

It seems an age since I have opened this book. How the time has passed since, I have but a vague idea, beyond that it has passed very pleasantly. . . . Once since, I have been with Mrs. Badger to a Mr Powell, who has started quite an extensive shoemaking establishment, in the vain attempt to get something to cover my naked feet. I am so much in need that I have been obliged to borrow Lydia's shoes every time I have been out since she returned. This was my second visit there, and I have no greater satisfaction than I had at first. He got my measure, I got his promise, and that is the end of it, thus far. His son, a young man of about twenty-four, had the cap of his knee shot off at Baton Rouge. Ever since he has been lying on his couch, unable to stand; and the probability is that he will never stand again. Instead of going out to the manufactory, Mrs. Badger has each time stopped at the house to see his mother (who, by the way, kissed me and called me "Sissie," to my great amusement) and there I have seen this poor young man. He seems so patient and resigned that it is really edifying to be with him. He is very communicative, too, and seems to enjoy company, no matter if he does say "her'n" and "his'n." Wonder why he does n't say "*shisen*" too? The girls are highly amused at the description I give of my new acquaintance, but still more so at Mrs. Badger's account of the friendship of this poor young cripple, and his enjoyment of my visits. Of course it is only her own version, as she is very fond of jokes of all kinds.

Night before last Lydia got playing the piano for me in the darkened parlor, and the old tunes from her dear little fingers sent me off in a sea of dreams. She too caught the vision, and launched off in a well-remembered quadrille. The same scene flashed on us, and at each note, almost, we would recall a little circumstance, charming to us, but unintelligible to Anna, who occupied the other side. Together we talked over the *dramatis personæ.* Mrs. Morgan, Jr., in dark blue silk with black flounces, a crimson chenille net on her black hair, sits at the piano in her own parlor. On the Brussels carpet stands, among others, Her Majesty, Queen Miriam, in a lilac silk, with bare neck and arms save for the protection afforded by a bertha of *appliqué* lace trimmed with pink ribbon, with hair *à la* madonna, and fastened low on her neck. Is she not handsome as she stands fronting the folding doors, her hand in tall Mr. Trezevant's, just as she commences to dance, with the tip of her black bottine just showing? Vis-à-vis stands pretty Sophie, with her large, graceful mouth smiling and showing her pretty teeth to the best advantage. A low neck and short-sleeved green and white poplin is her dress, while her black hair, combed off from her forehead carelessly, is caught by a comb at the back and falls in curls on her shoulders. A prettier picture could not be wished for, as she looks around with sparkling eyes, eager for the dance to begin. There stands calm Dena in snuff-colored silk, looking so immeasurably the superior of her partner, who, I fancy, rather feels that she is the better man of the two, from his nervous way of shifting from one foot to the other, without saying a word to her. Nettie, in lilac and white, stands by the mantel laughing undisguisedly at her partner, rather than with him, yet so good-humoredly that he cannot take offense, but rather laughs with her. Lackadaisical Gertrude, whose face is so perfect in the daytime, looks pale and insipid by gaslight, and timidly walks through the dance. Stout, good-natured Minna smiles and laughs, never quite completing a sentence, partly from embarrassment, partly because she hardly knows how; but still so sweet and amiable that one cannot find fault with her for so trifling a misfortune. At this point, Lydia suggests, "And Sarah, do you forget her?" I laugh; how could I forget? There she stands in a light blue silk checked in tiny squares, with little flounces up to her knee. Her dress fits well, and she wears very pretty sleeves and collar of *appliqué*. Lydia asks if that is all, and how she looks. The same old song, I answer. She is looking at Miriam just now; you would hardly notice her, but certainly her hair is well combed. That is all you can say for her. Who is she dancing with? A youth fond of "dreams"; futile ones, at that, I laughingly reply. He must be relating one just now, for there is a very perceptible curl on her upper lip, and she is looking at him as though she thought she was the tallest. Lydia dashes off into a lively jig. "Ladies to the right!" I cried. She laughed too, well knowing that that part of the dance was invariably repeated a dozen times at least. She looked slyly up: "I am thinking of how many hands I saw squeezed," she said. I am afraid it did happen, once or twice.

Eighteen months ago! What a change! One who was prominent on such occasions — Mr. Sparks — they tell me is dead. May God have mercy on his soul, in the name of Jesus Christ! I did not ask even this revenge.

October 18th, Saturday.

Last night mother arrived from Clinton with Gibbes and Lydia, who had gone there the day before to get her to go to Baton Rouge.

CLINTON,
October 19th, Sunday.

What an unexpected change! I am surprised myself! Yesterday as the Baton Rouge party were about leaving, Miriam thought Lilly would be lonesome alone here with her sick baby, and decided that we should leave by the cars, and stay with her until mother returned. There was no time to lose; so dressing in haste, we persuaded Anna to accompany us, and in a few moments stood ready. We walked down to the overseer's house to wait for the cars, and passed the time most agreeably in eating sugar-cane, having brought a little negro expressly to cut it for us and carry our carpet-bag. Three young ladies, who expected to be gone from Saturday until Wednesday, having but one carpet-bag between them! Can it be credited? But, then, we knew we had clothes here, and depended upon them for supplies, when we now find they are in the trunk and mother has the key.

We walked aboard alone, in the crowded train, and found ourselves in the only car reserved for ladies, which was already filled with a large party returning from Port Hudson, consisting of the fastest set of girls that I have seen for some time. Anna and I had to content ourselves with a seat on a small box between the benches, while Miriam was established on the only vacant one, with a sick soldier lying at her feet. The fast girls talked as loud as possible and laughed in a corresponding style in spite of the sick man. They must have been on a picnic, from the way they talked. One in a short dress complained that she had not seen her sweetheart. A pert little miss of thirteen cried, "You can bet your head I never went to any place where I did not see one of *my* sweethearts." One of about seventeen, a perfect beauty, declared she would die of thirst. "So will I! and I don't want to die before I get a husband!" exclaimed her vis-à-vis. They evidently expected to produce an impression on us. At every "brilliant" remark ("stupid" understood), they looked at us to see what we thought. All of them sat with bare heads in the strong light, an unfailing proof of *la basse classe* on steamers and cars. Every time my veil blew aside, they made no difficulty about scanning my features as though they thought it might be agreeable. I must confess I was equally impolite in regard to the Beauty; but then her loveliness was an excuse, and my veil sheltered me, besides. While this young

Psyche was fascinating me, with her perfect face and innocent expression, one of her companions made a remark — one that I dare say is made every day, and that I never imagined could be turned into harm. My Beauty uttered a prolonged "Oh!" of horror, and burst out laughing, followed by all the others. My disgust was unspeakable. Mock modesty is always evident. A modest girl could not have noticed the "catch"; the immodest, on the lookout for such an opportunity, was the only one who could have perceived it. Well! after all, no one can be perfect; this may be the single stain on my Beauty, though I confess I would rather have any other failing than this, almost.

Putting this aside, I hardly know which I was most amused by: the giddy, lively girls to my right, or the two ladies to my left who were as cross and ill-natured as two old cats and railed unmercifully at the silly creatures behind them, and carried their spite so far as to refuse to drink because the conductor (the husband of one of them) gave the young ladies water before passing it to their two elders. Did n't the poor man get it! She would n't taste a drop of that nasty dirty drippings, that she would n't! Might have had the decency to attend to his kinsfolks, before them creatures! And why did n't he wait on those two young ladies behind her? He did ask them? Well, ask them again! they must want some! Poor Henpecked meekly passed the can again, to be again civilly declined.

I confess the "drippings" were too much for me also, though I did not give it as my excuse. Mrs. Hen recommenced her pecking; poor Mr. Hen at last surlily rejoined, "For Heaven's sake, don't make a fuss in the cars," with an emphasis on the last word that showed he was accustomed to it at home, at least. With my veil down, I leaned against the window, and remembering Colonel Breaux's remarks two nights before concerning cross people, I played his "little philosopher" for the remainder of the journey.

At sunset we walked in at Lilly's gate, and astonished her by standing before her as she sat alone with her poor sick little Beatrice in her arms. . . .

Wednesday, 22d October, LINWOOD.

We left Clinton this morning, and have just now arrived by the cars. Charlie came in last evening, to our great surprise, so we did not scruple to leave Lilly. . . .

The Baton Rouge party returned late this evening. In spite of all preparation, Gibbes was horrified at the appearance of home.

Friday, October 24th.

A letter from Jimmy, the first we have received since New Orleans fell. It was dated the 10th inst., and he spoke of being on the eve of running the blockade, and going to Liverpool "to represent our unfortunate navy," as he says, though I am at loss to imagine what he can mean. He speaks of a kind friend, a Mr. George Trenholm,[1] whose kindness has been perfectly extraordinary. He has befriended him in every way.

Charlie has just come by the railroad, bringing other letters from him, to mother and Lilly. In mother's is his last good-bye on the 12th. Again Mr. Trenholm is the theme. I could not help crying over my dear little brother's manly, affectionate letter. He says he is sure God will still care for him, He has raised him up friends wherever he has been. He says he lost all his clothing in going to Charleston. There, among other kind people, he met this gentleman, who carried him to his house, where he has kept him ever since, treating him like his son, and forced him to accept a magnificent outfit as a present from him. He procured the appointment which sends Jimmy abroad (I wish Jimmy had been more explicit concerning it; we hardly know what it is, or how long it will keep him). The money he received to pay Jimmy's passage (received from the Government) he in turn obliged Jimmy to accept, as he sails in one of Mr. Trenholm's steamers; and not satisfied with that, gives him *carte blanche* on his house in England, to be filled up with any amount he chooses to name.

Mother went back to Clinton with Charlie that

[1] Secretary of the Treasury of the Confederate States. Later, Colonel James Morris Morgan ("Jimmy" in the Diary), married Mr. Trenholm's daughter Helen, whose portrait appears on an issue of Confederate bank notes.

evening, to my great distress; for she hates that odious place as much as I.

I know the life will kill her if it lasts six months longer. How happy I would be, if it were not for the thought of her uncomfortable position there! Lilly agrees with me that, once out of it, she never wishes to see the vile place again. Margret says that when the Lord had finished all the world and all the people, he had some scraps left, and just thought he'd "batch up" Clinton with them. Perhaps she is right.

Sunday, 26th October.

This place is completely overrun by soldiers passing and repassing. Friday night five stayed here, last night two more, and another has just gone. One, last night, a bashful Tennesseean, had never tasted sugar-cane. We were sitting around a blazing fire, enjoying it hugely, when in answer to our repeated invitations to help himself, he confessed he had never eaten it. Once instructed, though, he got on remarkably well, and ate it in a civilized manner, considering it was a first attempt.

Everything points to a speedy attack on Port Hudson. Rumors reach us from New Orleans of extensive preparations by land and water, and of the determination to burn Clinton as soon as they reach it, in revenge for the looms that were carried from Baton Rouge there, and which can soon be put in working order to supply our soldiers, negroes, and ourselves with necessary clothing. Of two evils, if

Baton Rouge is to be overrun by Yankees, and Clinton burned, I would rather await them at home.

Sunday, November 2d.

Yesterday was a day of novel sensations to me. First came a letter from mother announcing her determination to return home, and telling us to be ready next week. Poor mother! she wrote drearily enough of the hardships we would be obliged to undergo in the dismantled house, and of the new experience that lay before us; but *n'importe!* I am ready to follow her to Yankeeland, or any other place she chooses to go. It is selfish for me to be so happy here while she leads such a distasteful life in Clinton. In her postscript, though, she said she would wait a few days longer to see about the grand battle which is supposed to be impending; so our stay will be indefinitely prolonged. How thankful I am that we will really get back, though! I hardly believe it possible, however; it is too good to be believed.

The nightmare of a probable stay in Clinton being removed, I got in what the boys call a "perfect gale," and sang all my old songs with a greater relish than I have experienced for many a long month. My heart was open to every one. So forgiving and amiable did I feel that I went downstairs to see Will Carter! I made him so angry last Tuesday that he went home in a fit of sullen rage. It seems that some time ago, some one, he said, told him such a joke on me that he had laughed all night at it. Mortified beyond all expression at the thought of having had my name mentioned between two men, I, who have thus far fancied myself secure from all remarks good, bad, or indifferent (of men), I refused to have anything to say to him until he should either explain me the joke, or, in case it was not fit to be repeated to me, until he apologized for the insult. He took two minutes to make up a lie. This was the joke, he said. Our *milkman* had said that that Sarah Morgan was the proudest girl he ever saw; that she walked the streets as though the earth was not good enough for her. My milkman making his remarks! I confess I was perfectly aghast with surprise, and did not conceal my contempt for the remark, or his authority either. But one can't fight one's milkman! I did not care for what he or any of that class could say; I was surprised to find that they thought at all! But I resented it as an insult as coming from Mr. Carter, until with tears in his eyes fairly, and in all humility, he swore that, if it had been anything that could reflect on me in the slightest degree, he would thrash the next man who mentioned my name. I was not uneasy about a milkman's remarks, so I let it pass, after making him acknowledge that he had told me a falsehood concerning the remark which had been made. But I kept my revenge. I had but to cry "Milk!" in his hearing to make him turn crimson with rage. At last he told me that the less I said on the subject, the better it would be for me. I could not agree. "Milk" I insisted was a delightful beverage. I had always been under the impression that we owned a cow, until he had informed me it was a milkman, but was perfectly indifferent to the animal so I got the milk. With some such allusion, I could make him mad in an instant. Either a guilty conscience, or the real joke, grated harshly on him, and I possessed the power of making it still worse. Tuesday I pressed it too far. He was furious, and all the family warned me that I was making a dangerous enemy.

Yesterday he came back in a good humor, and found me in unimpaired spirits. I had not talked even of "curds," though I had given him several hard cuts on other subjects, when an accident happened which frightened all malicious fun out of me. We were about going out after cane, and Miriam had already pulled on one of her buckskin gloves, dubbed "old sweety" from the quantity of cane-juice they contain, when Mr. Carter slipped on its mate, and held it tauntingly out to her. She tapped it with a case-knife she held, when a stream of blood shot up through the glove. A vein was cut and was bleeding profusely.

He laughed, but panic seized the women. Some brought a basin, some stood around. I ran after cobwebs, while Helen Carter held the vein and Miriam stood in silent horror, too frightened to move. It was, indeed, alarming, for no one seemed to know what to do, and the blood flowed rapidly.

Presently he turned a dreadful color, and stopped laughing. I brought a chair, while the others thrust him into it. His face grew more deathlike, his mouth trembled, his eyes rolled, his head dropped. I comprehended that these must be symptoms of fainting, a phenomenon I had never beheld. I rushed after water, and Lydia after cologne. Between us, it passed away; but for those few moments I thought it was all over with him, and trembled for Miriam. Presently he laughed again and said, "Helen, if I die, take all my negroes and money and prosecute those two girls! Don't let them escape!" Then, seeing my long face, he commenced teasing me. "Don't ever pretend you don't care for me again! Here you have been unmerciful to me for months, hurting more than this cut, never sparing me once, and the moment I get scratched, it's 'O Mr. Carter!' and you fly around like wild and wait on me!" In vain I represented that I would have done the same for his old lame dog, and that I did not like him a bit better; he would not believe it, but persisted that I was a humbug and that I liked him in spite of my protestations. As long as he was in danger of bleeding to death, I let him have his way; and, frightened out of teasing, spared him for the rest of the evening.

Just at what would have been twilight but for the moonshine, when he went home after the blood was stanched and the hand tightly bound, a carriage drove up to the house, and Colonel Allen was announced. I can't say I was ever more disappointed. I had fancied him tall, handsome, and elegant; I had heard of him as a perfect fascinator, a woman-killer. Lo! a wee little man is carried in, in the arms of two others, — wounded in both legs at Baton Rouge, he has never yet been able to stand. . . . He was accompanied by a Mr. Bradford, whose assiduous attentions and boundless admiration for the Colonel struck me as unusual. . . . I had not observed him otherwise, until the General whispered, "Do you know that that is the brother of your old sweetheart?" Though the appellation was by no means merited, I recognized the one he meant. Brother to our Mr. Bradford of eighteen months ago! My astonishment was unbounded, and I alluded to it immediately. He said it was so; that his brother had often spoken to him of us, and the pleasant evenings he had spent at home.

November 4th, 1862.

O what a glorious time we had yesterday! First, there were those two gentlemen to be entertained all day, which was rather a stretch, I confess, so I stole away for a while. Then I got the sweetest letter from Miss Trenholm, enclosing Jimmy's photograph, and she praised him so that I was in a damp state of happiness and flew around showing my picture to everybody, Mr. Bradford included, who pronounced him a noble boy, and admired him to my satisfaction. Then came a letter from Lilly, saying mother had decided to remain in Clinton, and wanted us to join her there. O my prophetic soul! My heart went below zero! Then Colonel Allen sent to Port Hudson for the band to serenade us, and raised my spirits in anticipation of the treat. While performing my toilet in the evening, Waller Fowler arrived, on his way to Vicksburg, bringing a letter to Miriam from Major Drum! Heaven only knows how it got here! Such a dear, kind letter, dated 6th of August, only! Affairs were very different then, and he said that Lavinia's distress about us was such that he must try to send her nearer to us. And such an unexpected piece of news! Oh, my heart fails me! I cannot fancy Lavinia a mother.

Slowly I dressed myself, and still more slowly I combed Anna. I could think of nothing else until I heard Miriam and Mr. Bradford call us to take a walk, when we hurried down to them. A race down to the railroad, a merry talk standing on the track mingled with shouts of laughter in which I tried to drown fears for Lavinia, made the early sunset clouds pass away sooner than usual, to us, and moonlight warned us to return. Mrs. Worley passed us in her buggy, coming to stay all night; and half-way a servant met us, saying two soldiers had come to call on us. Once there, I was surprised to find that one was Frank Enders, the one I least expected to see. The other was a Mr. Harold. I need not describe him, beyond this slight indication of his style. Before half an hour was over, he remarked to Anna that I was a *very* handsome girl, and addressed me as — *Miss Sally!* That is sufficient.

Then Will Carter came in, and joined our circle. His first aside was, "If you only knew how much I liked you last night, you would never be cruel to me again. Why, I thought you the greatest girl in the world! Please let's part friends to-night again!" I would not promise, for I knew I would tease him yet; and at supper, when I insisted on his taking a glass of milk, his face turned so red that Mrs. Carter pinched my arm blue, and refused to help me to preserves because I was making Will *mad!* But Waller helped me, and I drank my own milk to Mr. Carter's health with my sweetest smile. "Confound that milkman! I wish he had cut his throat before I stumbled over him," he exclaimed after tea. But I had more amusing game than to make him angry then; I wanted to laugh to get rid of the phantom that pursued me, Lavinia.

The evening passed off very pleasantly; I think there were some eighteen of us in the parlor. About ten the General went to the sugar-house (he commenced grinding yesterday) and whispered to me to bring the young people down presently. Mr. Bradford and I succeeded in moving them, and we three girls retired to change our pretty dresses for plain ones, and get shawls and *nuages*, for our warm week had suddenly passed away, and it was quite cold out. Some of the gentlemen remarked that very few young ladies would have the courage to change pretty evening dresses for calico, after appearing to such advantage. Many would prefer wearing such dresses, however inappropriate, to the sugar-mill. With his droll gravity, Gibbes answered, "Oh, our girls don't want to be stuck up!"

There was quite a string of us as we straggled out in the beautiful moonlight, with only Mrs. Badger as an escort. Mr. Enders and I had a gay walk of it, and when we all met at the furnace, we stopped and warmed ourselves, and had a laugh before going in. Inside, it was lighted up with Confederate gas, in other words, pine torches, which shed a delightful light, neither too much nor too little, over the different rooms. We tried each by turns. The row of bubbling kettles with the dusky negroes bending over in the steam, and lightly turning their paddles in the foamy syrup, the whole under the influence of torchlight, was very interesting; but then, Mr. Enders and I found a place more pleasant still. It was in the first purgery, standing at the mouth of the shoot through which the liquid sugar runs into the car; and taking the place of the car as soon as it was run off to the coolers, each armed with a paddle, scraped the colon up and had our own fun while eating. Then running along the little railroad to where the others stood in the second room over the vats, and racing back again all together to eat sugar-cane and cut up generally around our first pine torch, we had really a gay time.

Presently "Puss wants a corner" was suggested, and all flew up to the second staging, under the cane-carrier and by the engine. Such racing for corners! Such scuffles among the gentlemen! Such confusion among the girls when, springing forward for a place, we would find it already occupied! All dignity was discarded. We laughed and ran as loud and fast as any children, and the General enjoyed our fun as much as we, and encouraged us in our pranks. Waller surpassed himself, Mr. Bradford carried all by storm, Mr. Enders looked like a schoolboy on a frolic, Mr. Carter looked sullen and tried lazily not to mar the sport completely, while Mr. Harold looked timidly foolish and half afraid of our wild sport. Mrs. Badger laughed, the General roared, Anna flew around like a balloon, Miriam fairly danced around with fun and frolic, while I laughed so that it was an exertion to change corners. Then forfeits followed, with the usual absurd formalities in which Mr. Bradford sentenced himself unconsciously to ride a barrel, Miriam to make him a love speech going home, Mr. Enders to kiss my hand, and I to make him (Mr. Enders) a declaration, which I instantly did, in French, whereby I suffered no inconvenience, as Miriam alone comprehended. Then came more sugar-cane and talk in the purgery, and we were horrified when Mrs. Badger announced that it was twelve o'clock, and gave orders to retire.

O the pleasant walk home! Then, of course, followed a last good-night on the balcony, while the two young men mounted their horses and Frank Enders vowed to slip off every time he had a chance and come out to see us. Then there was a grand proposition for a ride to Port Hudson on horseback, and in order to secure a pledge that we would pass by General Beale's headquarters, Mr. Enders wrapped my *nuage* around his throat, declaring that I would be obliged to stop there for it, though, if prevented, he would certainly be obliged to bring it back himself. This morning, however, the married ladies made so much difficulty about who should go, and how, that we were forced to abandon it, much as we would have enjoyed it.

I am afraid to say how late it was when we got to bed. I know it was almost ten when we left the breakfast-table this morning, so I suppose it must have been quite late before we retired. To Colonel Allen's, as well as to our own great disappointment, the band could not come on account of sickness.

November 6th.

We three girls fancied a walk last evening, and immediately after dinner prepared to walk to Mrs. Breaux's, only a mile, and get her to come to the sugar-house. But as we put on our bonnets, Captain Bradford, brother of the one who left in the morning, was announced, and our expedition had to be abandoned. This is the third of the five brothers that I have met, and if it were not for the peculiarity in their voices, I should say that there was not the most distant relationship existing between them. This one is very handsome, quiet, and what Dickens calls "in a high-shouldered state of deportment." He looks like a moss-covered stone wall, a slumbering volcano, a — what you please, so it suggests anything unexpected and dangerous to stumble over. A man of indomitable will and intense feeling, I am sure. I should not like to rouse his temper, or give him cause to hate me. A trip to the sugar-house followed, as a matter of course, and we showed him around, and told him of the fun we had those two nights, and taught him how to use a paddle like a Christian. We remained there until supper-time, when we adjourned to the house, where we spent the remainder of the evening very pleasantly. At least I suppose he found it so, for it was ten o'clock before he left.

. . . .

Just now I was startled by a pistol shot. Threatening to shoot her, Mr. Carter playfully aimed Miriam's pistol at her, and before he could take fair aim, one barrel went off, the shot grazing her arm and passing through the armoir just behind. Of course, there was great consternation. Those two seem doomed to kill each other. She had played him the same trick before. He swore that he would have killed himself with the other shot if she had been hurt; but what good would that do her?

Sunday, November 9th.

I hardly know how these last days have passed. I have an indistinct recollection of rides in cane-wagons to the most distant field, coming back perched on the top of the cane singing, "Dye my petticoats," to the great amusement of the General who followed on horseback. Anna and Miriam, comfortably reposing in corners, were too busy to join in, as their whole time and attention were entirely devoted to the consumption of cane. It was only by singing rough impromptus on Mr. Harold and Captain Bradford that I roused them from their task long enough to join in a chorus of "Forty Thousand Chinese." I would not have changed my perch, four mules, and black driver, for Queen Victoria's coach and six.

And to think old Abe wants to deprive us of all that fun! No more cotton, sugar-cane, or rice! No more old black aunties or uncles! No more rides in mule teams, no more songs in the cane-field, no more steaming kettles, no more black faces and shining teeth around the furnace fires! If Lincoln could spend the grinding season on a plantation, he would recall his proclamation. As it is, he has only proved himself a fool, without injuring us. Why, last evening I took old Wilson's place at the bagasse shoot, and kept the rollers free from cane until I had thrown down enough to fill several carts, and had my hands as black as his. What cruelty to slaves! And black Frank thinks me cruel, too, when he meets me with a patronizing grin, and shows me the nicest vats of candy, and peels cane for me. Oh! very cruel! And so does Jules, when he wipes the handle of his paddle on his apron, to give "Mamselle" a chance to skim the kettles and learn how to work! Yes! and so do all the rest who meet us with a courtesy and "Howd'y, young Missus!" Last night we girls sat on the wood just in front of the furnace — rather Miriam and Anna did, while I sat in their laps — and with some twenty of all ages crowded around, we sang away to their great amusement. Poor oppressed devils! Why did you not chunk us with the burning logs instead of looking happy, and laughing like fools? Really, some good old Abolitionist is needed here, to tell them how miserable they are. Can't Mass' Abe spare a few to enlighten his brethren?

November 10th, Monday.

In spite of its being Sunday, no sooner was dinner concluded yesterday than we adjourned, as usual, to the sugar-house to see how much damage we could do. Each took from a negro his long paddle, and for more than half an hour skimmed the kettles industriously, to the amazement of half a dozen strange soldiers who came to see the extraordinary process of sugar-making. At one time the two boys taking possession of the two other paddles, not a negro was at the kettles, but stood inspecting our work. The hardest part we found to be discharging the batteries, which none of us could do without their assistance.

We had no sooner relinquished our paddles than some one announced two gentlemen at the house. While we were discussing the possibility of changing our dresses before being seen, enter Mr. Enders and Gibbes Morgan[1] of Fenner's battery. No retreat being possible, we looked charmed and self-possessed in spite of plain calicoes and sticky hands. . . . Mr. Enders very conveniently forgot to bring my *nuage*. He says he started expressly to do so, but reflecting that I might then have no inducement to pay that visit to Port Hudson, he left it for another time. . . . We arranged a visit to Gibbes, and Mr. Enders made me promise to call at General Beale's headquarters for a pass. "They will want you to go to the Provost Marshal's for it, but you just come to General Beale's, and send a courier for me, and I will bring it myself!" — and half in fun, half in earnest, I promised.

November 12th, Wednesday.

Once more a cripple and consigned to my bed, for how long, Heaven only knows. This is written while in a horizontal position, reposing on my right arm, which is almost numb from having supported me for some sixteen hours without turning over. Let me see if I can remember how it happened.

Last evening we started out to see Gibbes, just Miriam and Anna in one buggy, and Mrs. Badger and I in the other. Gibbes proper, that is, the Cap-

[1] H. Gibbes Morgan, a cousin.

tain, and the General both approved, but neither could accompany us. It is useless to say how much I objected to going without a gentleman. Indeed, when we reached the road which formed the fourth side of the square formed by Colonel Breaux's, Captain Bradford's, and Captain Fenner's camps, I thought I should die of terror on finding myself in such a crowd of soldiers on parade. My thick veil alone consoled me, but I made a vow that I would not go through it again, not if I never saw Gibbes, Jr., again on earth.

His camp lay far off from the road, so that we had to drive out to it between the other two, and asked a soldier to tell him that we were there. Presently he came up, looking so pleased that I was almost glad that we had come; and then Captain Fenner appeared, looking charmed, and Lieutenant Harris, who looked more alarmed and timid than I. Captain Fenner exerted himself to entertain us, and seeing how frightened I was, assured me that it was an everyday occurrence for young ladies to visit them in parties without gentlemen, and that it was done all through the Confederacy; which, however, did not comfort me for the hundreds of eyes that were looking at us as our small party stood out in front of the encampment around a cannon. I think he can throw more expression into his eyes than any one I ever saw. Miriam suggested sending Gibbes to the Provost to get our pass in order to avoid the crowd that might be there. Eager to leave the present one for a more retired spot, I exclaimed, "Oh, no! let us go ourselves! We can't get in a worse crowd!" I meant a *greater;* but Captain Fenner looked so comically at me that I could scarcely laugh out an apology, while he laughed so that I am sure he did not listen to me. What a comical mouth! I liked him *very* much, this time. He promised to come out to-day or to-morrow, and have a game of "Puss wants a corner" in the sugar-house. But now I can't join in, though it was to me the promise was made.

But to the catastrophe at once.

As we left, we insisted on taking Gibbes to get our pass, and made him get into Miriam's buggy, where there was space for him to kneel and drive. I was to carry out my promise to Mr. Enders. We had to pass just by the camp of the First Alabama, Colonel Steadman's, where the whole regiment was on parade. We had not gone thirty yards beyond them when a gun was discharged. The horse instantly ran off. I don't believe there could be two cooler individuals than Mrs. Badger and I were. I had every confidence in her being able to hold him so long as the bridle lasted. I had heard that there was more danger in jumping at such moments than in remaining quiet, so I sat still. There was nothing to hold to, as it was a no-top, or what I call a "low-neck," buggy; so my hands rested quietly in my lap. Presently I saw the left rein snap close to the horse's mouth. I knew all was over then, but did not utter a word. Death seemed inevitable, and I thought it was as well to take it coolly. The horse turned abruptly; I felt that something impelled me out, followed the impulse, saw Mrs. Badger's white cape fluttering above me, received a blow on the extremity of my spine that I thought would kill me before I reached the ground, landing, however, on my left hip, and quietly reclining on my left elbow, with my face to an upset buggy whose wheels spun around in empty air. I heard a rush as of horses; I saw men galloping up; I would have given worlds to spring to my feet, or even to see if they were exposed; but found I could not move. I had no more power over my limbs than if they were iron; only the intense pain told me I was still alive. I was perfectly conscious, but unable to move. My only wonder was why Miriam, who was in front, did not come to me.

My arm was giving away. Dimly, as through a haze, or dream, I saw a soldier bending over me, trying to raise me. The horse he had sprung from rushed up to his master, and reared up over me. I saw the iron hoofs shining above my body; death was certain this time, but I could not move. He raised his arm and struck him, and obedient to the blow the animal turned aside and let his feet fall without crushing me. Mrs. Carter, when she heard it described, offered a fabulous sum for a correct drawing of that most interesting tableau, the gallant Alabamian supporting a helpless form on one arm, while he reined in a fiery charger with the other. I was not aware of the romance; I was conscious only of the unpleasant situation.

Dozens crowded around, and if I had been a girl for display, here was an opportunity, for thirty pair of soldier arms were stretched out to hold me. "No! Gibbes! Gibbes!" I whispered, and had the satisfaction of being transferred from a stranger's to my cousin's arms. Gibbes trembled more than I, but with both arms clasped around me, held me up. But for that I would have returned to my original horizontal position. "Send for the doctor!" cried one. "A surgeon, quick!" cried another. "Tell them no!" I motioned. I was conscious of a clatter of hoofs and cloud of dust. One performed a feat never heard of before. He brought a glass of water at full gallop which I instantly drained by way of acknowledgment. I think I felt the unpleasant situation more than the pain. Not being accustomed to being the centre of attraction, I was by no means pleased with the novel experience. Miriam held my hand, and questioned me with a voice tremulous with fear and laughter. Anna convulsively sobbed or giggled some question. I felt the ridiculous position as much as they. Laughing was agony, but I had to do it to give them an excuse, which they readily seized to give vent to their feelings, and encouraged by seeing it, several gold-band officers joined in, constantly endeavoring to apologize or check themselves with a "Really, Miss, it may seem unfeeling, but it is impossible" — the rest was lost in a gasp, and a wrestle between politeness and the desire to laugh.

I don't know what I was thinking of, but I certainly paid very little attention to what was going on. I only wanted to get home, away from all those eyes; and my most earnest wish made me forget them. The first remark I heard was my young Alabamian crying, "It is the most beautiful somerset I ever saw! Indeed, it could not be more gracefully done! Your feet did not show!" Naïf, but it was just what I wanted to know, and dared not ask. Some one ran up, and asked who was hurt, and I heard another reply, "I am afraid the young lady is seriously injured, only she won't acknowledge it. It is worth while looking at her. She is the coolest, most dignified girl you ever saw"; and another was added to the already too numerous audience. Poor Mrs. Badger, having suffered only from torn clothing, received very little sympathy, while I got more than my share. I really believe that the blow I received was from her two hundred and forty pound body, though the Alabamian declares he saw the overturning buggy strike me as I fell.

To her and others I am indebted for the repetition of many a remark that escaped me. One bold soldier boy exclaimed, "Madame, we are all warriors, but we can't equal that! It is braver than any man!" I had to laugh occasionally to keep my spirits up, but Miriam ordered me to quit, saying that I would go off in hysterics. I had previously repeatedly declared to the Doctor that I was not hurt, and seeing him idle, and hearing Miriam's remark, the Alabamian — I am told — cried, "O Doctor! Doctor! can't you do something? Is she going to have hysterics?" "Really," said the Doctor, "the young lady objects to being examined; but as far as I can judge, she has no limbs broken." Everybody ordered me to confess at once my injury; but how was I to inform a whole crowd that I had probably broken the tip of my backbone, and could not possibly sit down? So I adhered to my first affirmation, and made no objection when they piled the cushions up and made Gibbes put me down; for I knew he must be tired.

I am told I remained there an hour. I know they talked to me, and that I answered; but have not an idea of the subject. A gentleman brought a buggy, and offered to drive me home; but a Captain Lenair insisted on running after the ambulance. Arrived there, Mr. Enders says he rushed in, crying, "For God's sake, General Beale, lend me the ambulance! There is a dreadful accident, and I am afraid the young lady will die!" Coming back he exclaimed, "By Jove! boys, if you want to see a sight, run down and see her hair! The prettiest auburn (?) you ever looked at, and sweeps the ground! I would n't mind such a fall if I had such hair to show. Come look at it, do!" Mr. Enders says he was sure that it was I, as soon as hair was mentioned, and started out as soon as he had finished a duty he had to perform. My garter, a purple silk ribbon, lay in the centre of the ring. By the respectful silence observed, I saw they recognized its use, so, unwilling to leave such a relic behind, I asked aloud for my "ribbon," whereupon Anna says the officers pinched each other and smiled. Up came the ambulance, and I was in imminent danger of being carried to it, when with a desperate effort I regained my feet with Gibbes's help, and reached it without other assistance. Beyond, I could do no more.

Captain Lenair got inside, and several others lifted me up to him, and I sank motionless on the floor. All bade me good-bye, and my little Alabamian assured me that he was proud of having been the first to assist me. President Miller whispered to Mrs. Badger for permission to accompany us, which she readily granted, and raising me on the seat, he insisted on putting his arm around me to hold me up. It was useless to decline. "Now, Miss Morgan, I assure you I am an old married man! I know you are suffering! Let me have my way!" and the kind old gentleman held me so comfortably, and broke the force of so many jolts, that I was forced to submit and acknowledge that had it not been for him I could not have endured the rough road. At the gate that leads to General Beale's headquarters, I saw half a dozen figures standing. One was Frank Enders, who hailed the driver. "Hush!" said one I recognized as Captain Lenair. "The young lady is in there, and the Provost, too!"

"I don't care if it is Jeff Davis, I'll find out if she is hurt!" he answered. Miriam and Anna recognized him, as they followed behind us, and called to him. Without more ado, he jumped into their buggy, finding them alone, and drove them home. He asked me something as he passed, but I could not answer.

The road was dreadful. Once the driver mistook it and drove us within two steps of an embankment six feet high, but discovered the mistake before the horses went over.

What I most dreaded was explanations when we should arrive. Miriam stepped out an instant before, and I heard her telling the accident. Then everybody, big and little, white and black, gathered around the ambulance. The Provost thought himself privileged to carry me, Gibbes insisted on trying it with his one arm, when the General picked me up and landed me on the gallery. He wanted me to lie down in old Mrs. Carter's room, but confident that once there I could not get up, and feeling that perhaps the gentlemen would take advantage of its being on the ground floor to suggest calling on me, I struggled upstairs with Helen's assistance. A dozen hands undressed me, and laid me on my face in bed, which position I have occupied up to the present, 3 P.M. . . . Unable to turn, all night I lay awake, lying on my face, the least comfortable of positions; but though the slightest motion tortured me, I had to laugh as we talked it over.

Of course, this has been written in scratches, and

in my same position, which will account for many blots. This morning I was interrupted by mother's unexpected arrival, she having come with Dellie and Morgan to spend the day. Of course, she is horrified at the accident of that "unfortunate Sarah"!

Saturday, November 15th.

I think I grow no better rapidly. Fortunately on Wednesday night they succeeded in turning me over; for my poor elbows, having lost all their skin, were completely used up. Now, if I go slowly and carefully, I can turn myself at the cost of some little suffering. . . .

Yesterday Colonel Steadman, of the First Alabama, called with his father. He sent me many messages of condolence, and the rather unpleasant advice to be cupped and scarified. His profession was that of a physician before he became colonel. His surgeon, whose name is Madding, told him he was satisfied that I was seriously injured, though I had not complained. The Colonel is the same who called when we were in Clinton. They readily accepted our invitation to dinner, and remained until late in the afternoon, when Captain Bradford came in. More messages of condolence and sympathy upstairs, which produced no visible effect on my spine, though very comforting to the spirit.

November 16th.

I was interrupted yesterday morning by Mrs.

Badger, who wished to apply a few dry cups to my back, to which I quietly submitted, and was unable to move afterwards without pain, as a reward for my patience. But towards sunset came two dear letters that made me forget what I had suffered, one from George, and one from Jimmy, dated Bermudas. For the first time I know what my dear little brother suffered during those long months when we could not hear if he were dead or alive. He kept the secret until he no longer needed either friends or money; and now he tells it with a simplicity that made me cry fit to break my heart when I was left alone in the twilight with no one to see. . . . George comforts me with hopes of Peace, and a speedy return. If it could only be! . . .

This morning the boom of Yankee guns reached my ears; a sound I had hoped never to hear again. It is only those poor devils (I can afford to pity them in their fallen state) banging away at some treasonable sugar-houses that are disobedient enough to grind cane on the other side of the river. I hear that one is at Mrs. Cain's. The sound made my heart throb. What if the fight should come off before I can walk? It takes three people to raise me whenever it is necessary for me to move; I am worse than helpless.

Tuesday, November 18th.

A note just came from mother, telling me that the most awful Yankees were coming to burn Linwood and take Port Hudson, and so this evening I must walk down to the cars with a chair to rest in until they came, and must certainly be in Clinton to-night. Delightful arrangement! I wrote to ask if she knew that my legs were of no more service to me than to her? Dr. Dortch has again been murdering me . . . says perhaps I can stand by Sunday. If the Yankees come before —

Friday night, November 21st.

Lying on my face, as it were, with my poor elbows for a support, I try to pass away these lonely hours. For with the exception of old Mrs. Carter, who is downstairs, and the General, who is elsewhere, Anna and I are the only white people on the place. The cause of this heartless desertion is a grand display of *tableaux vivants* at Jackson, for the benefit of the Soldiers' Hospital, and of course it would be sinful to stay away, particularly as Anna is a great deal better, and I need no care. . . .

Thursday, December 4th.[1]

It would be only the absurd tableaux I agreed to, with plenty of fun, and nothing more. So I tried to be merry and content, and so I should have been, for there was plenty to talk about, and every one

[1] A page is here torn from the Diary. It evidently related the beginning of an incident of which my sister and I have often heard our mother tell: how, after the Jackson tableaux, our aunt Miriam laughingly staked herself in a game of cards with Will Carter — and lost. The sequel follows, the scene at the house of his uncle, General Carter, beginning in the middle of a sentence. — W. D.

was so solicitous for my comfort; and there was Mr. Enders who would wheel my chair for me wherever I wished it, and was as kind and attentive as a brother. Surely my first trip should have been a gay one! Miriam sat down by the piano, Mr. Enders drew me by her, and we three sang until dark together. A Mr. Morse, his wife, and mother, who are spending a week here, were our audience. The first two retired at candle-light, while the latter, present at the play the night before, remained to the last. But while we sang, every noise at the parlor door caused us to turn with the apprehension of we hardly knew what. A dozen times Mr. Enders consulted his watch, and telegraphed his fears to me, though I persisted in thinking it only the fun that had been intended.

Half-past six came, and with it, Mrs. Worley. Now, she knew better. For Dr. Dortch had come to see me, and was guiding me in my game of euchre in which I was not even as wise as my partner, Mr. Enders, when her note came. Instantly we put down our cards, while Miriam begged him to write and tell her the true story. He wrote and we all read it. Not only that, but Miriam added a postscript which I think was this, word for word: "Mrs. Worley, it is only a bet at cards, intended as the merest joke. There is not a word of truth in it, and I will consider it the greatest favor if you will contradict the report whenever you may hear it!" Explicit enough, one would think; but still she came, and sent word into the parlor that one of the ladies present when Will made the announcement had sent her contribution to the evening's fun. It turned out to be a complete bridal suit, worn by the lady a year ago! That was too serious a jest. Miriam went into the other room to speak to Mrs. Worley, who, cold as an icicle, refused to receive or make explanation, beyond "I won't kiss you; this is too cruel." There was nothing to do; she returned laughing, but certainly feeling herself the injured one, and so she was.

In fifteen minutes, another stir. I held my breath with expectation. Lydia introduced — Mr. G——. Ten miles he had ridden through mud and water that freezing evening, at Will Carter's request, to perform the ceremony between him and Miriam. Lydia laughed until she could hardly introduce him. He, hat in hand, bowed around the convulsed circle with a countenance shining with the most sublimely vacant expression. O that man's idiotic face, and solemn, portentous look, brought a writhe even to my trembling lips! Mr. Enders would have given one an excellent idea of the effect produced by a real old piney-woods chill; he shook as with suppressed laughter. But when the tremendous preacher (tremendous because composed of gigantic Nothing) turned his lugubrious face towards Mrs. Morse, and addressed her as Mrs. Morgan under the impression that she had come down to see her daughter married, Miriam's risibles could no longer stand it, and she flew from the room in time to avoid a disgraceful explosion.

I was growing frightened. Mr. Enders was leaning over my chair, and involuntarily it burst from me with a groan, "For God's sake, help me save her!" "Hush! Lie back in your chair! I will!" he whispered. "But for the love of Heaven, save my sister!" "I'll do what you will, if you will only keep still and not hurt yourself. I'll do my best." It was all whispered, that the minister and Mrs. Morse might not hear. "If it were your sister, what would you do?" "My God! I'd meet him on the front gallery and kick him out! Then I'd know one of us must die to-morrow!" "But under the circumstances it is impossible for Gibbes to act!" I urged, while we agreed that it was the most unwarrantable piece of insolence ever perpetrated. While we talked, Gibbes had seized Miriam and, without interfering or advising further, advised her to keep her room and not meet Will.

But I skipped the most important part. She came back when she had recovered her composure, and sat by me. Mr. Enders, when I asked what was best to do, whispered that to spare Will's feelings, and avoid a most painful scene, as well as to show that she had no serious intentions whatever, she should see that the minister was put in full possession of the facts before it went any farther. He felt keenly his unpleasant situation, and it was only our earnest request that induced him to remain, or give his advice. Who should explain? Certainly not the General. He thought the joke carried too far, and retired to his room before Mr. G—— came. How take part against his own nephew? Not Gibbes either, for he had gone upstairs too worried and annoyed to talk to any one; besides, it was his wife's cousin. Who then? Miriam is one woman in a thousand. Rising, she crossed the room slowly and as dignified as though she only meant to warm herself. I think I see her before me now, as she stood before the fire, facing Mr. G——, looking so handsome and stylish in her black grenadine with the pale-green trimming, telling her story. Plainly, earnestly, distinctly, without hurry or embarrassment, in the neatest, prettiest, most admirable speech I ever heard, she told everything just as it was. Bravo for Miriam! There lives not the woman in this State who could do so painful a thing in such a beautiful way. I felt like hugging her. Oh, it was magnificent! He heard her in surprise, but when once satisfied of its truth, he said, "Well, Miss Morgan, when you stand on the floor, when I ask if you will, it is your privilege to answer, 'No.'" Miriam is not one to do so cruel a thing; she is too noble to deceive him so far and wound him so cruelly before all, when he believed himself so near happiness. She said that it was mockery, she would not suffer him to believe for an instant that she meant to marry him; if he believed it, he was deceiving himself wilfully, for he already knew that she had told him it could never be. He agreed to take it only as a jest, promised that he would not feel hurt; and with the most admirable tact, Miriam, the trump (I have been playing euchre, excuse me), settled the minister, and the wedding, by her splendid behavior, with no trouble.

A rapid step was heard in the hall; the bridegroom had come! I know he must have killed his horse. He certainly did not leave his house before one o'clock; it is twenty miles by the road to Clinton; he went there, procured his license, and was here at seven, in full costume. He bounded upstairs to meet the bride-elect.

I can fancy him going to Clinton, doubting, fearing, believing against all evidence, yet trembling; securing the license at last, persuading himself that she would not dare refuse when the deeds were recorded in court, and he held them in his hand; — and very few women would have been brave enough, too; he did not know My Miriam! I can fancy the poor horse lashed through the heavy mire, tired, foaming, panting, while his strong arm urged it on, with whip and spur; I can hear the exulting beating of his heart, that wild refrain that was raging as his death-knell — "Mine! Mine at last!" I could hear it, I say. It rung in my ears all night. He held her in his power; she must be his; hastily, yet carefully he performs his toilet; I dare say he stopped to think which cravat she liked best. "Mine! Mine!" the song is ringing in every stroke of his throbbing breast. Mount! Mount! Two miles fly past. He sweeps through the moonlight like Death riding on a pale horse; yonder shine lights in the parlor; and that above; is it hers? He throws himself from his horse; his hour has come, hers too; with the license and minister, his own adoration — and she must love him too! — he will win! Show him the way to her! She is his forever now! His? My God! had I not reason to cry, "In God's name, save her, Frank!" He reaches Mrs. Carter's room, and triumphantly throws the license on her table. He is ready now; where is his bride?

Some one meets him. "Will!"

The story is told; she is not to be won by force; she has appealed to the minister; he has carried the jest too far. The strong man reels; he falls on the bed in his bridal array in agony too great for tears. I dare not ask what followed; they tell me it was awful. What madness and folly, to dream of forcing her to marry him! Why, if she had loved him, the high-handed proceeding would have roused the lion of her spirit! He is no mate for her. He has but one thought, and at last words come. "Miriam! Miriam! Call her, for the love of God!" One word! one look! Oh, she will take pity on him in his misery. Let her come for one instant! she cannot be so cruel! she will marry him if only to save him from death, or worse! And fortunate it was that he was not armed, one of the two would have died; perhaps both. The heartbroken prayer goes on. The exulting "Mine! Mine!" has changed to the groan of despair, "Miriam! for the love of God! come to me!"

And where is the bride? Gibbes has her caged in the next room, this one where I am now lying. He has advised her not to appear; to go to bed and say no more. Sent to bed like a baby on her wedding night! She says that she laughed aloud when the door closed on her. She laughing in here, he groaning in there, it is to be hoped they each drowned the voice of the other. . . . The minister said good-night. He disclaimed all feeling of pique; he felt chiefly for the young lady — and the disappointed groom. (Ouf!) I sent to ask Will to come to me alone for a moment; no, he could not see me; write to him.

Slowly, as though an aged, infirm, tottering man, we heard him descending the steps. How different from the step that carried him up! We, conscience-stricken, sat within, with doors closed. He was off. He has again mounted his horse, and the broken-hearted man, hardly less cruel than the expectant bridegroom, dashes the rowel in his side and disappears like a whirlwind.

. . . .

I can fancy mother's and Lilly's agony, when they hear of the wedding. All Clinton knew it last night, and if they did, too, I know there was as little sleep for them as for us. I know mother shrieked, "My child! My child!" while Lilly cried. How could he believe she meant to marry him, without even sending word to mother when he was going to the very town? Bah! What a jolly go if those two got hysterics about the supposed Moral Suicide! Glad I was not at the tea-party! Well, fearing the effect of such a shock in mother's nervous state, Gibbes advised Miriam to go on the cars this evening, and convince her that it had not occurred, court records and licenses and minister to the contrary notwithstanding; so my duck, my angel, she whom I call my Peri with the singed wings (children who play in the fire must expect to be burned), set off on her pious errand, without the protecting arm of her bridegroom.

Sunday, 7th December.

I have had a shock! While writing alone here (almost all have gone to church), I heard a step ascending the stair. What, I asked, if it should be Will? Then I blamed myself for supposing such a thing possible. Slowly it came nearer and nearer, I raised my head, and was greeted with a ghastly smile. I held out my hand. "Will!" "Sarah!" (Misery discards ceremony.) He stood before me the most woebegone, heartbroken man I ever saw.

With a forced laugh he said, "Where is my bride? Pshaw! I know she has gone to Clinton! I have come to talk to *you*. Was n't it a merry wedding?" The hollow laugh rang again. I tried to jest, but failed. "Sit down and let me talk to you," I said. He was in a wayward humor; cut to the heart, ready to submit to a touch of silk, or to resist a grasp of iron. This was the man I had to deal with, and get from him something he clung to as to — not his life, but — Miriam. And I know so little how to act in such a case, know so little about dealing gently with wild natures!

He alarmed me at first. His forced laugh ceased; he said that he meant to keep that license always. It was a joke on him yesterday, but with that in his possession, the tables would be turned on her. He would show it to her occasionally. It should keep her from marrying any one else. I said that it would be demanded, though; he must deliver it. The very devil shot in his eye as he exclaimed fiercely, "If any one dares demand it, I'll die before giving it up! If God Almighty came, I'd say no! I'll die with it first!" O merciful Father, I thought; what misery is to come of this jest. He must relinquish it. Gibbes will force him into it, or die in the attempt; George would come from Virginia. . . . Jimmy would cross the seas. . . . And I was alone in here to deal with such a spirit!

I commenced gently. Would he do Miriam such a wrong? It was no wrong, he said; let him follow his own will. "You profess to love her?" I asked. "Profess? Great God! how can you? I adore her! I tell you that, in spite of all this, I love her not more — that is impossible, — but as much as ever! Look at my face and ask that!" burst from him with the wildest impulse. "Very well. This girl you *love*, then, you mean to make miserable. You stand forever between her and her happiness, because you love her! Is this love?" He was sullenly silent. I went on: "Not only her happiness, but her honor is concerned. You who love her so, do her this foul injury." "Would it affect her reputation?" he asked. "Ask yourself! Is it quite right that you should hold in your hands the evidence that she is Mrs. Carter, when you know she is not, and never will be? Is it quite honorable?" "In God's name, would it injure Miriam? I'd rather die than grieve her."

My iron was melted, but too hot to handle; I put it on one side, satisfied that I and I only had saved Miriam from injury and three brothers from bloodshed, by using his insane love as a lever. It does not look as hard here as it was in reality; but it was of the hardest struggles I ever had — indeed, it was desperate. I had touched the right key, and satisfied of success, turned the subject to let him believe he was following his own suggestions. When I told him he must free Miriam from all blame, that I had encouraged the jest against her repeated remonstrances, and was alone to blame, he generously took it on himself. "I was so crazy about her," he said, "that I would have done it anyhow. I would have run any risk for the faintest chance of obtaining her"; and much more to the same purpose that, though very generous in him, did not satisfy my conscience. But he surprised me by saying that he was satisfied that if I had been in my room, and he had walked into the parlor with the license, she would have married him. What infatuation! He says, though, that I only prevented it; that my influence, by my mere presence, is stronger than his words. I don't say that is so; but if I helped save her, thank Heaven!

It is impossible to say one half that passed, but he showed me his determination to act just as he has heretofore, and take it all as a joke, that no blame might be attached to her. "Besides, I'd rather die than not see her; I laugh, but you don't know what I suffer!" Poor fellow! I saw it in his swimming eyes.

At last he got up to go before they returned from church. "Beg her to meet me as she always has. I told Mrs. Worley that she must treat her just the same, because I love her so. And — say I go to Clinton to-morrow to have that record effaced, and deliver up the license. I would not grieve her; indeed, I love her too well." His voice trembled as well as his lips. He took my hand, saying, "You are hard on me. I could make her happy, I know, because I worship her so. I have been crazy about her for three years; you can't call it a mere fancy. Why are you against me? But God bless you! Good-bye!" And he was gone.

Why? O Will, because I love my sister too much to see her miserable merely to make you happy!

Friday, 12th December.

My cripple friend that I mentioned so far back continues to send me the most affecting messages.

"He is really wretched about me; never was more distressed; thinks of nothing else"; and so on through the whole list. To cap the climax, he sends me word that he can now walk on crutches, and the first time he can venture in a buggy, means to call on me. *Que le ciel m'en préserve!* What could we talk about? "His'n" and "her'n" several misfortunes? That's too bad! Every one teases me unmercifully about my new conquest. I can't help but be amused; and yet, beware, young girls, of expressing sympathy, even for soldiers! There is no knowing what effect it may produce.

Sunday, December 14th.

Yesterday evening, some time before sunset, Mr. Enders was announced, to our great surprise, as we knew he had been in Clinton all the week, having been transferred there instead of to Jackson, as he threatened. He was the most miserable, unhappy creature one could possibly imagine; even too melancholy for me to laugh at him, which expresses the last degree of wretchedness. To all our questions, he had but one answer, that he had had the most dreadful attack of "blues" ever since he was here Sunday; that he had waited every evening at the cars, expecting us, and at last, seeing that we had no intention of coming, he could no longer stand the temptation, so got permission to come down for a day to Port Hudson so he could come out to see us. . . . Before we could fairly get him cheerful, Will Carter and Ned Badger, who returned only this week from Kentucky, entered. Will was in a bad humor, and wanted to vent it on us; so after waiting some time, he proposed that the two young men should go with him, pocketing at the same moment the cards which had won Miriam and saying they would have a nice game together, and just the rarest old whiskey! He looked around to see the effect produced. We girls did not move, but Mr. Enders said he must really return immediately to Port Hudson, and start for Clinton from there in the night. Will thought it would be such a triumph over us to carry him off, that he insisted. They'd have a fine time! cure the blues! etc. Ned was more than willing; and at last Mr. Enders said, Well! he felt just so desperate that he did not care what he did; he believed he would go. I saw he was in a reckless humor, and that Will knew it, too, and I promised to make at least an effort to save him.

Miriam spoke to him apart, but he said he had promised now; he must go. Will ran down triumphant to mount his horse, calling him to follow. All ran out to see him off, when Frank came back to tell me good-bye. I seized the opportunity, and did n't I plead! I told him I would not ask him to stay here, though he knew we would be happy to have him stay; and begged him to go back to the camp, and leave Will alone. . . . I suggested other resources; talked of his mother whom he idolizes, pleaded like a grandmother; and just as I wound up, came Will's voice from below, "Why the devil don't you come, Enders? Hurry!" He moved a step, looked at me; I dropped my head without a word. Here I must confess to the most consummate piece of acting; I am sorry, but as long as it saved him from doing what I knew he would have cause to regret, I am not ashamed of having tried it. Will called impatiently again, as he stood hesitating before me; I did not say, "Stay," I just gave the faintest sigh imaginable. . . . He went down and told Will he would not go! Of course, Will went off in a rage with us.

Friday, December 26th, 1862.

Monday Dr. Woods and Mr. Van Ingen stopped, just from their regiment in Kentucky and on their way home, and I begged so hard to see the Doctor, and promised so faithfully to retire if I suffered too much, that Mrs. Badger yielded, like an angel, and I carried my point. The Doctor! We looked in vain at each other; I for my dandy friend in irreproachable broadcloth, immaculate shirt bosoms and perfect boots; he for the brusque, impulsive girl who in ordinary circumstances would have run dancing into the parlor, would have given him half-glad, half-indifferent greeting, and then found either occasion to laugh at him or would have turned elsewhere for amusement. We looked, I say, in vain. Before me stood my pattern of neatness in a rough uniform of brown homespun. A dark flannel shirt replaced the snowy cambric one, and there was neither cravat nor collar to mark the boundary line between his dark face and the still darker material. And the dear little boots! O ye gods and little fishes! they were clumsy, and mud-spattered! If my mouth twitched with laughter as I silently commented, the Doctor's did not! I, who always danced on my way, came in lying back on my pillows, and wheeled in by a servant. The Doctor's sympathy was really touching, and poor consolation he gave when he heard the story. "You will recover, to a certain extent; but will feel it more or less all your life."

. . . .

I am the ruin of all these puns; the gentlemen will hate me; I must learn to ignore their conundrums until they answer them themselves, and to wait patiently for the pun instead of catching it and laughing before it is half-spoken. Why can't I do as the others do? There was Mr. Van Ingen with his constant stream of them, that I anticipated several times. He said to me, "If I were asked what town in Louisiana I would rather be in this evening, what would my answer be?" I should have looked perfectly innocent, and politely inquisitive; but I did neither. I saw the answer instantly, and laughed. "Ah, you have guessed! I can see it in your eyes!" he said. Of course I had, but I told him I was afraid to say it, for fear he might think I was flattering myself. Then we both laughed. The place he referred to was *Bayou, Sarah*. . . .

Yesterday, being a beautiful day, I was carried down in honor of Christmas, to meet Captain Fenner and Mr. Duggan who were to dine with us. The cars had brought Miriam a beautiful little set of collars and cuffs from Dellie, and the oddest, sweetest little set for me, from Morgan, for our Christmas gift. It is all Lilly. . . .

We had an exquisite Christmas gift the night before, a magnificent serenade, a compliment from Colonel Breaux. It very singularly happened that Miriam, Anna, and Ned Badger were sitting up in the parlor, watching alone for Christmas, when the band burst forth at the steps, and startled them into a stampede upstairs. But Gibbes, who came with the serenaders, caught them and brought them back into the parlor, where there were only *eight* gentlemen; and in this novel, unheard-of style, only these two girls, with Gibbes to play propriety, entertained all these people at midnight while the band played without. . . .

I commenced writing to-day expressly to speak of our pleasant Christmas; yet it seems as though I would write about anything except that, since I have not come to it yet. Perhaps it is because I feel I could not do it justice. At least, I can say who was there. At sunset came Captain Bradford and Mr. Conn, the first stalking in with all the assurance which a handsome face and fine person can lend, the second following with all the timidity of a first appearance. . . . Again, after a long pause, the door swung open, and enter Mr. Halsey, who bows and takes the seat on the other side of me, and Mr. Bradford, of Colonel Allen memory, once more returned to his regiment, who laughs, shakes hands all around, and looks as happy as a schoolboy just come home for the holidays, who has never-ending visions of plumcakes, puddings, and other sweet things. While all goes on merrily, another rap comes, and enter Santa Claus, dressed in the old uniform of the Mexican War, with a tremendous cocked hat, and preposterous beard of false hair, which effectually conceal the face, and but for the mass of tangled short curls no one could guess that the individual was Bud. It was a device of the General's, which took us all by surprise. Santa Claus passes slowly around the circle, and pausing before each lady, draws from his basket a cake which he presents with a bow, while to each gentleman he presents a wineglass replenished from a most suspicious-looking black bottle which also reposes there. Leaving us all wonder and laughter, Santa Claus retires with a basket much lighter than it had been at his entrance. . . . Then follow refreshments, and more and more talk and laughter, until the clock strikes twelve, when all these ghosts bid a hearty good-night and retire.

January 1st, Thursday, 1863.

1863! Why I have hardly become accustomed to writing '62 yet! Where has this year gone? With all its troubles and anxieties, it is the shortest I ever spent! '61 and '62 together would hardly seem three hundred and sixty-five days to me. Well, let time fly. Every hour brings us nearer our freedom, and we are two years nearer peace now than we were when South Carolina seceded. That is *one* consolation. . . .

I learn, to my unspeakable grief, that the State House is burned down.

Sunday, January 4th.

One just from Baton Rouge tells us that my presentiment about our house is verified; Yankees do inhabit it, a Yankee colonel and his wife. They say they look strangely at home on our front gallery, pacing up and down. . . . And a stranger and a Yankee occupies our father's place at the table where he presided for thirty-one years. . . . And the old lamp that lighted up so many eager, laughing faces around the dear old table night after night; that with its great beaming eye watched us one by one as we grew up and left our home; that witnessed every parting and every meeting; by which we sang, read, talked, danced, and made merry; the lamp that Hal asked for as soon as he beheld the glittering chandeliers of the new innovation, gas; the lamp that all agreed should go to me among other treasures, and be cased in glass to commemorate the old days, — our old lamp has passed into the hands of strangers who neither know nor care for its history. And mother's bed (which, with the table and father's little ebony stand, alone remained uninjured) belongs now to a Yankee woman! Father prized his ebony table. He said he meant to have a gold plate placed in its centre, with an inscription,

ANTE-BELLUM HOME OF JUDGE THOMAS GIBBES MORGAN,
ON CHURCH STREET, BATON ROUGE, LA.

and I meant to have it done myself when he died so soon after. A Yankee now sips his tea over it, just where some beau or beauty of the days of Charles II may have rested a laced sleeve or dimpled arm. . . .[1]

Give the devil his due. Bless Yankees for one thing; they say they tried hard to save our State House.

[1] This "little ebony table" — which happened to be mahogany so darkened with age as to be recognized only by an expert many years after the war — and a mahogany rocking-chair are the two pieces of furniture which survived the sacking of Judge Morgan's house and remain to his descendants to-day. Such other furniture as could be utilized was appropriated by negroes. — W. D.

BOOK IV

From my sick bed, this 15th day of January, 1863.
LINWOOD, Thursday.

AM I not glad to get another blank book! On Sunday my old one gave out, to my unspeakable distress, and I would have been *désolée* if I had not had three or four letters to answer, as writing is my chief occupation during my tedious illness. O that unfortunate trip to Port Hudson! Have I not cause to remember and regret it? Two months last Sunday since I have been lying here a cripple, and I am not yet able to take a step. However, on Monday mother sent Dr. Woods as my fourth physician, and I have made up my mind that either he or Nature will effect a cure before long. Wonder how it feels to walk? It makes me weary to see others try it; I always fear that the exertion must be very painful — an absurd idea which I endeavor to keep to myself. . . .

Monday, January 19th.

That blessed Mr. Halsey like an angel of mercy sent me "Kate Coventry" yesterday, just when I was pining for a *bonne bouche* of some kind, I did not care what, whether a stick of candy or an equally palatable book. It is delightful to have one's wishes realized as soon as they are made. I think it rather caused me to relent towards Mr. Halsey; I did not feel half so belligerent as I did just the Sunday before. At all events, *I felt well enough to go down in the evening when he called again,* though I had been too indisposed to do so on a previous occasion. (O Sarah!)

Wheeled into the parlor, there I beheld not my friend alone, but several other individuals whose presence rather startled me. I found myself undergoing the terrors of an introduction to a Colonel Locke, and to my unspeakable surprise, Major Buckner was claiming the privilege of shaking hands with me, and Colonel Steadman was on the other side, and—*was* that Mr. Halsey? O never! The Mr. Halsey I knew was shockingly careless of his dress, never had his hair smooth; let his beard grow as it would, and wore a most ferocious slouched hat. This one had taken more than one look at the glass, a thing I should have imagined the other incapable of doing. He had bestowed the greatest care and attention on his dress, had brought his beard within reasonable limits, had combed his hair with the greatest precision, and held lightly in one hand an elegant little cap that I am sure must be provokingly becoming. Why, he was handsome! *Ah ça!* some mistake, surely, I cried to myself. *My* Mr. Halsey was not, certainly! "If it be I, as I hope it may be, I've a little dog at home who will surely know me," I kept repeating. I resolved to test the little dog's sagacity, so I pretended to know this apparition, and thanked him for the pleasure he had afforded me by sending me "Kate Coventry."

He looked conscious and pleased! The "little dog" had found out his identity! I was more puzzled than ever. How account for this wondrous change? . . . But metaphorphosed "John" talked! He was expatiating at a most extraordinary rate, and had been doing so for an hour after supper, when Gibbes drew his chair near me (Gibbes likes to hear what visitors say to his little sister); whereupon timid Mr. Halsey drew his slightly back, and very soon after asked for his horse. O Gibbes! you wretch! what an amusing tête-à-tête you spoiled, you innocent! And the General, of course, only waited for his exit before beginning to tease me unmercifully. I must put an end to this; they shall not bring such unjust charges against him. Yet how am I to make them see reason?

Night.

I am more pleased to-night than I could well express. I have been talking to an old and dear friend, no other than Will Pinckney! His arrival was as unexpected as it was agreeable. The cry of "Here comes Will Pinckney" sent me back to August, '60, when the words were always the forerunner of fun and frolic. . . . He told me what he called his secrets; of how he had been treated by the War Department (which has, indeed, behaved shockingly towards the Colonel).

Thursday, 22d January.

What a rush of visitors last night! One would imagine they had all come by appointment, expressly to have an impromptu dance, which they certainly enjoyed, by the way. There was little Captain C——, the Susceptible and Simple, who so innocently says "I seen" and "I done it," without the faintest suspicion of the peculiarity, and looks so sweet, and guileless, and amiable, and soft, that I can't help wondering if he would be sticky if I touch him. Indeed, I think his hands stick, at least; for when he told me good-bye, it was with the greatest difficulty that I extracted mine from his grasp (he having forgotten to return it during a long farewell address), and even when I succeeded in recovering it, by being almost rude, it was not released without a *very* sensible pressure from the *putty*, or whatever it is that is so tenacious. I am afraid it is rather a habit of his, which has lost all force or meaning by being too frequently repeated. Then there was a horrid little wretch, vulgar and underbred (to my idea), to whom I was introduced as Mr. G——. . . . But here is Lieutenant Dupré, whom I have not yet introduced, though we have met before. Tall, good-looking, a fine form, and not a sparkling face, I am inclined to believe that his chief merit lies in his legs. Certainly when he dances he puts his best foot forward, and knows it, too. Miriam, who adores dancing, is flirting openly with this divinity of the "Deux Temps" and polka, and skims around with his arm about her (position sanctified by the lively air Lydia is dashing off on the piano) with a grace and lightness only equaled by his own. And Lieutenant Duggan, with his good, honest, clever face which so unmistakably proclaims him "Tom," we know already, so no further description is needed. Captain Fenner, too, is well known, with his short, though graceful figure, his good-humored, intelligent face, irresistible imperial, and that roguish expression about that large mouth which displays such handsome teeth, and seems to say, "Don't trust me too far."

Little Captain C—— tells me a long story about how Colonel Steadman had come to him and asked if he believed it possible that Miss Morgan had put her life and happiness in the hands of a homœopathic physician; how he considered her fate sealed; and what a shame it was to trifle with such a sad affair, at my age, too, ruined for life! It was dreadful! Too sad! Hereupon, as continuing the story, he remarks that being asked his opinion by the Colonel, he agreed perfectly and thought with him it was an appalling sacrifice, and oh, all sorts of things! Anything, just to make me miserable and unhappy!

Well, what is written will come to pass. First comes a doctor with a butchering apparatus who cups and bleeds me unmercifully, says I'll walk ten days after, and exit. Enter another. Croton oil and strychnine pills, that'll set me up in two weeks. And exit. Enter a third. Sounds my bones and pinches them from my head to my heels. Tells of the probability of a splinter of bone knocked off my left hip, the possibility of paralysis in the leg, the certainty of a seriously injured spine, and the necessity for the most violent counter-irritants. Follow blisters which sicken even disinterested people to look at, and a trifle of suffering which I come very near acknowledging to myself. Enter the fourth. Inhuman butchery! wonder they did not kill you! Take three drops a day out of this tiny bottle, and presto! in two weeks you are walking! A fifth, in the character of a friend, says, "My dear young lady, if you do, your case is hopeless." What wonder that I am puzzled? A wiser head would be confused. I want to believe all, but how is it possible? "What will be, will be."

. . . .

Bon ! here comes a note from Mr. Halsey! *Ah ça !* Lend him "Zaidee"? Certainly! Here is a postscript three times the length of the note; *voyons*. Will Miss Sarah make the annotations he requested, in "Kate Coventry"? He is anxious to have the lady's opinion on the questions of taste and propriety which so frequently occur in the book. . . . I'll not attempt such a display; yet there are several passages I am dying to mark. One in particular, speaking of the peculiarities of men, of how they are always more at ease when they have their hands employed, drawing confidence and conversation from a paper-knife and book to tumble, a pair of scissors and a thread to snip, or even from imbibing the head of a cane, I am anxious to call his attention to. If I dared add to the list, "or a cord and tassel to play with"! This nervous Mr. Halsey is wearing out my pretty blue tassel that Frank admires so much; he says he can talk better when he dangles it. Think the hint might save it in the future!

Friday night, January 23d.

I am particularly happy to-day, for we have just heard from Brother for the first time since last July. And he is well, and happy, and wants us to come to him in New Orleans so he can take care of us, and no longer be so anxious for our safety. If we only could! — To be sure the letter is from a gentleman who is just out of the city, who says he writes at Brother's earnest request; still it is something to hear, even indirectly. One hundred and fifty dollars he encloses with the request that mother will draw for any amount she wishes. Dear Brother, money is the least thing we need; first of all, we are dying for want of a home. If we could only see ours once more!

During this time we have heard incidentally of Brother; of his having taken the oath of allegiance — which I am confident he did not do until Butler's October decree — of his being a prominent Union man, of his being a candidate for the Federal Congress, and of his withdrawal; and finally of his having gone to New York and Washington, from which places he only returned a few weeks since. That is all we ever heard. A very few people have been insolent enough to say to me, "Your brother is as good a Yankee as any." My blood boils as I answer, "Let him be President Lincoln if he will, and I would love him the same." And so I would. Politics cannot come between me and my father's son. What he thinks right, is right, for him, though not for me. If he is for the Union, it is because he believes it to be in the right, and I honor him for acting from conviction, rather than from dread of public opinion. If he were to take up the sword against us to-morrow, Miriam and I, at least, would say, "If he thinks it his duty, he is right; we will not forget he is our father's child." And we will not. From that sad day when the sun was setting for the first time on our father's grave, when the great, strong man sobbed in agony at the thought of what we had lost, and taking us both on his lap put his arms around us and said, "Dear little sisters, don't cry; I will be father and brother, too, now," he has been both. He respects our opinions, we shall respect his. I confess myself a rebel, body and soul. *Confess?* I glory in it! Am proud of being one; would not forego the title for any other earthly one!

Though none could regret the dismemberment of our old Union more than I did at the time, though I acknowledge that there never was a more unnecessary war than this in the beginning, yet once in earnest, from the secession of Louisiana I date my change of sentiment. I have never since then looked back; forward, forward! is the cry; and as the Federal States sink each day in more appalling folly and disgrace, I grow prouder still of my own country and rejoice that we can no longer be confounded with a nation which shows so little fortitude in calamity, so little magnanimity in its hour of triumph. Yes! I am glad we are two distinct tribes! I am proud of my country; only wish I could fight in the ranks with our brave soldiers, to prove my enthusiasm; would think death, mutilation, glorious in such a cause; cry, "War to all eternity before we submit." But if I can't fight, being unfortunately a woman, which I now regret for the first time in my life, at least I can help in other ways. What fingers can do in knitting and sewing for them, I have done with the most intense delight; what words of encouragement and praise could accomplish, I have tried on more than one bold soldier boy, and not altogether in vain; I have lost my home and all its dear contents for our Southern Rights, have stood on its deserted hearthstone and looked at the ruin of all I loved—without a murmur, almost glad of the sacrifice if it would contribute its mite towards the salvation of the Confederacy. And so it did, indirectly; for the battle of Baton Rouge which made the Yankees, drunk with rage, commit outrages in our homes that civilized Indians would blush to perpetrate, forced them to abandon the town as untenable, whereby we were enabled to fortify Port Hudson here, which now defies their strength. True they have reoccupied our town; that Yankees live in our house; but if our generals said burn the whole concern, would I not put the torch to our home readily, though I love its bare skeleton still? Indeed I would, though I know what it is to be without one. Don't Lilly and mother live in a wretched cabin in vile Clinton while strangers rest under our father's roof? Yankees, I owe you one for that!

Well! I boast myself Rebel, sing "Dixie," shout Southern Rights, pray for God's blessing on our cause, without ceasing, and would not live in this country if by any possible calamity we should be conquered; I am only a woman, and that is the way I feel. Brother may differ. What then? Shall I respect, love him less? No! God bless him! Union or Secession, he is always my dear, dear Brother, and tortures could not make me change my opinion.

Friday, January 30th.

A whole week has passed since I opened this book, a week certainly not spent in idleness, if not a very interesting one. For I have kept my room almost all the time, leaving Miriam and Anna to entertain their guests alone. Even when Mr. Halsey called on Sunday, I declined going down. Why, I wonder? I felt better than usual, was in a splendid humor for talking, yet — my excuses took my place, and I lay quietly in bed, dreaming by the firelight, and singing hymns to myself. Once in a while the thought would occur to me, "Why don't I go down?" But it was always answered with a wry face, and the hymn went on. Yet I knew he had come expecting to see me.

On the table near me stood a bunch of snowdrops that Miriam had culled for her *beloved* Captain Bradford. An idea struck me so suddenly that my voice died instantly. The spirit of mischief had taken possession of me. Laughing to myself, I caught them up, drew three long bright hairs from my head — they looked right gold-y in the firelight — and tied them around the flowers — I thought I should never get to the end while wrapping them. Thus secured, a servant carried them into the parlor with "Miss Sarah's compliments to Mr. Halsey." Poor Miriam's cry of surprise at finding her flowers thus appropriated, reached my ears and caused me to laugh again. It *was* rather cool! But then it was better fun than going down. And then did n't it flatter his vanity! O men! you vain creatures! A woman would receive a whole bunch of hair and forty thousand bouquets, without having her head turned; while you — Well! I heard enough from Miriam to amuse me, at all events.

And a day or two after, Captain Bradford had a long story to tell her — what he called a good joke on Mr. Halsey. Of how he had found him kissing three long bright hairs in rapture, and on asking where he got them, received as an answer — "From the God-*blessedest* little angel that ever wore long hair!" This *blessedest* little angel did not intend it as a souvenir, and is consequently annoyed about stories of three hairs, intended as a string and nothing more, being wrapped in tissue paper and treasured up — so goes the tale — instead of being thrown into the fire as I certainly expected.

. . . .

Last night Anna and Miriam sat on my bed at twilight, playing cards while I tried my guitar, when Captain C——, Major Spratley, and Lieutenant Dupré were announced. Quick, down went the cards as they sprang to their feet to throw off their neat calicoes. Where was Miriam's comb, and grenadine, and collar, and belt? Good gracious! where was her buckle? On the bureau, mantel, washstand, or under them? "Please move a moment, Anna!" In such a hurry, do! There was Anna, "Wait! I'm in a hurry, too! Where is that pomatum? You Malvina! if you don't help me, I'll — There! take that, Miss! Now fly around!" Malvina, with a faint, dingy pink suddenly brought out on her pale sea-green face, did fly around, while I, hushing my guitar in the tumult, watch each running over the other, in silent amazement, wondering if order can come out of such confusion, and if the people downstairs were worth all that trouble.

When I finally made my appearance in the parlor, it was with the conviction that I would have a dreadfully stupid time, and Captain C—— too. However, though at first I had both, soon only the last was left me. Some one suggested calling the Spirits, which game I had imagined "played out" long ago; and we derived a great deal of amusement from it. Six of us around a small table invoked them with the usual ceremony. There was certainly no trick played; every finger was above the board, and all feet sufficiently far from the single leg to insure fair play. Every rap seemed to come exactly from the centre of the table, and was painfully distinct though not loud. When asked if there was a writing medium present, it indicated Captain C——. I observed that he seemed averse to trying it, but yielded at length and took the pencil in his hand.

Our first question, of course, was, How long before Peace? Nine months was written. Which foreign nation would recognize us first? France, then England, in eight months. Who was Miriam to marry? Captain of a battery. "Who?" we all shouted. "Captain C. E. Fenner"[1] was written again. When? In ten months. I believe Captain C—— to be honest about it. He seemed to have no control over his hand, and his arm trembled until it became exceedingly painful. Of course, I do not actually believe in Spiritualism; but there is certainly something in it one cannot understand; and Mrs. Badger's experience is enough to convert one, alone. Each was startled in turn by extraordinary revelations concerning themselves. Gibbes was to be transferred to the Trans-Mississippi Department,[2] George would come home, and all the gentlemen had the name and address of future sweethearts written in full. The question was asked, "Who will Sarah Morgan fall in love with?" Every eye was on the

[1] Note by Mrs. Dawson in 1896: wrong — she married Lieutenant Dupré.

[2] Note by Mrs. Dawson: he was transferred in his coffin.

pencil as a capital "H" was traced. As the "a" followed, I confess to a decided disgust at the Spirits, and was about to beg it might be discontinued when the rest followed rapidly until in three separate lines appeared, "Has not seen him yet" (here came an exclamation of surprise from Lydia and Miriam, who knew how true it was, and even Gibbes looked astonished). "Captain, in Virginia. Captain Charles Lewis."[1] A perfect buzz of comments followed; every one asked every one else if they knew any one by that name, and every one said no. Gibbes was decidedly more interested than I. That odd "Has not seen him yet," expressing so exactly the fact that I pride myself upon, carried conviction in the truth of Spirits, *almost*. "Who will she marry?" asked Gibbes. (He has a pet belief, in which I encourage him, that I will never marry.) Again came the name as distinctly as before, of Captain Charles Lewis. "When will she marry him?" "In June, 1864," was the answer. I was to meet him in New Orleans. November followed, after a period.

Of course, the Spirits produced some slight commotion which made the time pass pleasantly until Miriam began to waltz with her Monsieur Deux Temps. Then Captain C—— told me why he had been unwilling to try it; of how his father believed so strongly in it that he had very nearly been made

[1] Captain F. W. Dawson, whom Sarah Morgan eventually married, was at that time a captain in Virginia, and she had not yet seen him.

crazy by it, and how he had sworn to abandon the practice of consulting them, seeing the effect produced. He did not believe in Spirits himself; but could not account for the influence he was under, when he saw his hand involuntarily write things he was totally unconscious of, himself. However, he proposed that we two should have a private consultation with them, which I opened by asking when I should again see my home. I know he did not know anything about it; but on the paper appeared — "Five months have gone — five months more." It is *just* five months since I did see home. I think it was the 26th of August that Charlie took me there. He asked if he should ever marry. "Never. You will be jilted by the lady you love in Missouri, Miss Christina P——." I pointed it out to him, as he happened to be looking at me when it was written. It surprised him into saying, "Why, I'm engaged to her!" I asked whose spirit was communicating with us. He was watching the dance when his hand wrote, "John C——." I laughed and asked if there was such a person, pointing to the name. He looked actually sick as he said, "Yes, my brother; he is dead." I had not the heart to talk of Spirits again; so we took to writing poetry together, every alternate line falling to my lot. It made an odd jingle, the sentimental first line being turned to broad farce by my absurd second one.

February 5th, Thursday night.

A letter from Lavinia has come to me all the way from California. How happy it made me, though written so long ago! Only the 30th of June! Lavinia has changed, changed. There is a sad, worn-out tone in every line; it sounds old, as though she had lived years and years ago and was writing as though she were dead and buried long since. Lavinia, whose letters used to keep me in sunshine for weeks at a time! Well! no wonder she is sad. All these dreary years from home, with so faint a hope of ever again seeing it, and all these sorrows and troubles that have befallen us, combined, are not calculated to make her happy. But I wish she had kept her cheerful heart. Well, perhaps it is easier for us to be cheerful and happy, knowing the full extent of our calamities, than it is for her, knowing so little and having just cause to fear so much. Courage! Better days are coming! And then I'll have many a funny tale to tell her of the days when the Yankees kept us on the *qui vive*, or made us run for our lives. It will "tell" merrily; be almost as lively as those running days were. One of my chief regrets over my helplessness is that I will not be able to run in the next stampede. I used to enjoy it. Oh, the days gone by, the dreary days, when, cut off from our own people, and surrounded by Yankees, we used to catch up any crumb of news favorable to our side that was smuggled into town, and the Brunots and I would write each other little dispatches of consolation and send them by little negroes! Those were dismal days. Yet how my spirits would rise when the long roll would beat, and we would prepare for flight!

Monday, February 9th, 1863. Night.

A letter from my dear little Jimmy! How glad I am, words could not express. This is the first since he arrived in England, and now we know what has become of him at last. While awaiting the completion of the ironclad gunboat to which he has been appointed, like a trump he has put himself to school, and studies hard, which is evident from the great improvement he already exhibits in his letter. . . .

My delight at hearing from Jimmy is overcast by the bad news Lilly sends of mother's health. I have been unhappy about her for a long while; her health has been wretched for three months; so bad, that during all my long illness she has never been with me after the third day. I was never separated from mother for so long before; and I am homesick, and heartsick about her. Only twenty miles apart, and she with a shocking bone felon in her hand and that dreadful cough, unable to come to me, whilst I am lying helpless here, as unable to get to her. I feel right desperate about it. This evening Lilly writes of her having chills and fevers, and looking very, *very* badly. So Miriam started off instantly to see her. My poor mother! She will die if she stays in Clinton, I know she will!

Wednesday, February 18th.

Gibbes has gone back to his regiment. I can't say how dreary I felt when he came to tell me good-bye. I did not mean to cry; but how could I help it when he put his arms around me? . . .

Sunday, February 22d, 1863.

Mother has come to me! O how glad I was to see her this morning! And the Georgia project, which I dared not speak of for fear it should be mere talk and nothing more, is a reality. — Yes! we are actually going! I can hardly believe that such good fortune as getting out of that wretched Clinton really awaits us. Perhaps I shall not like Augusta either; a stranger in a strange city is not usually enchanted with everything one beholds; but still — a change of scene — a new country — new people — it is worth while! Shall we *really* go? Will some page in this book actually record "Augusta, Georgia"? No! I dare not believe it! Yet the mere thought has given me strength within the last two weeks to attempt to walk. Learning to walk at my age! Is it not amusing? But the smallest baby knows more about it than I did at first. Of course, I knew one foot was to be put before the other; but the question was how it was to be done when they would not go? I have conquered that difficulty, however, and can now walk almost two yards, if some one holds me fast.

Sunset. Will [Pinckney] has this instant left. Ever since dinner he has been vehemently opposing the Georgia move, insisting that it will cost me my life, by rendering me a confirmed cripple. He says *he* could take care of me, but no one else can, so I must not be moved. I am afraid his arguments have about shaken mother's resolution. Pshaw! it will do me good! I must go. It will not do to remain here. Twenty-seven thousand Yankees are preparing to march on Port Hudson, and this place will certainly be either occupied by them, or burned. To go to Clinton is to throw myself in their hands, so why not one grand move to Augusta?

Monday, February 23d.

Here goes! News has been received that the Yankees are already packed, ready to march against us at any hour. If I was up and well, how my heart would swell with exultation. As it is, it throbs so with excitement that I can scarcely lie still. Hope amounts almost to presumption at Port Hudson. They are confident that our fifteen thousand can repulse twice the number. Great God! — I say it with all reverence — if we could defeat them! *If* we could scatter, capture, annihilate them! My heart beats but one prayer — Victory! I shall grow wild repeating it. In the mean time, though, Linwood is in danger. This dear place, my second home; its loved inhabitants; think of their being in such peril! Oh, I shall cry heartily if harm comes to them! But I must leave before. No use of leaving my bones for the Yankees to pick; better sing "Dixie" in Georgia.

To-morrow, consequently, I go to that earthly paradise, Clinton, thence to be re-shipped (so goes the *present* programme) to Augusta in three days. And no time for adieux! Wonder who will be surprised, who vexed, and who will cry over the unforeseen separation? Not a single "good-bye"! Nothing — except an old brass button that Mr. Halsey gave me as a souvenir in case he should be killed in the coming assault. It is too bad. Ah! Destiny! Destiny! Where do you take us? During these two trying years, I have learned to feel myself a mere puppet in the hands of a Something that takes me here to-day, to-morrow there, always unexpectedly, and generally very unwillingly, but at last leads me somewhere or other, right side up with care, after a thousand troubles and distresses. The hand of Destiny is on me now; where will it lead me?

Tuesday [February] 24th.

Meeting Miriam by mere accident on the road last evening and hearing of our surprising journey to Georgia, Mr. Halsey came to spend a last evening with us, and say good-bye. What a deluge of regrets, hopes, fears, etc. Perfectly overwhelming. Why had I not told him of it the night before? All our friends would be so disappointed at not having an opportunity of saying good-bye. If the Yankees would only postpone their attack so he might accompany us! But no matter; he would come on in two months, and meet us there. And would we not write to him?

Thank you! Miriam may, but I shall hardly do so! We had such a pleasant evening together, talking over our trip. Then we had a dozen songs on the guitar, gay, sad, and sentimental; then he gave me a sprig of jessamine as a keepsake, and I ripped open my celebrated "running-bag" to get a real *for true* silver five cents — a perfect curiosity in these days — which I gave him in exchange, and which he promised to wear on his watch-chain. He and Miriam amused themselves examining the contents of my sack and laughing at my treasures, the wretches! Then came — good-bye. I think he was sorry to see us go. Well! he ought to miss us! Ah! these farewells! To-day I bid adieu to Linwood. "It may be for years, and it may be forever!" *This* good-bye will cost me a sigh.

Wednesday, February 25th.

Here we are still, in spite of our expectations. Difficulty on difficulty arose, and an hour before the cars came, it was settled that mother should go to Clinton and make the necessary arrangements, and leave us to follow in a day or two. Two days more! Miriam no more objected than I did, so mother went alone. Poor Miriam went to bed soon after, *very* ill. So ill that she lay groaning in bed at dusk, when a stir was heard in the hall below, and Colonel Steadman, Major Spratley, and Mr. Dupré were announced. Presto! up she sprang, and flew about in the most frantic style, emptying the trunk on the floor to get her prettiest dress, and acting as though she had never heard of pains and groans. When we leave, how much I shall miss the fun of seeing her and Anna running over each other in their excitement of dressing for their favorites. Anna's first exclamation was, "Ain't you glad you did n't go!" and certainly we were not sorry, from mere compassion; for what would she have done with all three? If I laughed at their extra touches to their dresses, it did not prevent me from bestowing unusual attention on my own. And by way of bravado, when I was carried down, I insisted on Mrs. Badger lending me her arm, to let me walk into the parlor and prove to Colonel Steadman that in spite of his prophecies I was able to take a few steps at least.

. . . .

His last words, "You *won't* go, will you? Think once more!" sent me upstairs wondering, thinking, undecided, and unsatisfied, hardly knowing what to do, or what to say. Every time I tried to sleep, those calm, deep, honest gray eyes started up before my closed ones, and that earnest "You *won't* go, will you? Think once more!" rang in my ears like a solemn warning. Hopes of seeing Georgia grew rather faint, that night. Is it lawful to risk my life? But is it not better to lose it while believing that I have still a chance of saving it by going, than to await certain death calmly and unresisting in Clinton? I'd rather die struggling for this life, this beautiful, loved, blessed life that God has given me!

March 10th, Tuesday.

. . . .

I had so many nice things to say — which now, alas, are knocked forever from my head — when news came that the Yankees were advancing on us, and were already within fifteen miles. The panic which followed reminded me forcibly of our running days in Baton Rouge. Each one rapidly threw into trunks all clothing worth saving, with silver and valuables, to send to the upper plantation. I sprang up, determined to leave instantly for Clinton so mother would not be alarmed for our safety; but before I got halfway dressed, Helen Carter came in, and insisted on my remaining, declaring that my sickness and inability to move would prove a protection to the house, and save it from being burned over their heads. Put on that plea, though I have no faith in melting the bowels of compassion of a Yankee, myself, I consented to remain, as Miriam urgently represented the dangers awaiting Clinton. So she tossed all we owned into our trunk to send to mother as hostage of our return, and it is now awaiting the cars. My earthly possessions are all reposing by me on the bed at this instant, consisting of my guitar, a change of clothes, running-bag, cabas, and this book. For in spite of their entreaties, I would not send it to Clinton, expecting those already there to meet with a fiery death — though I would like to preserve those of the most exciting year of my life. They tell me that this will be read aloud to me to torment me, but I am determined to burn it if there is any danger of that. Why, I would die without some means of expressing my feelings in the stirring hours so rapidly approaching. I shall keep it by me.

Such bustle and confusion! Every one hurried, anxious, excited, whispering, packing trunks, sending them off; wondering negroes looking on in amazement until ordered to mount the carts waiting at the door, which are to carry them too away. How disappointed the Yankees will be at finding only white girls instead of their dear sisters and brothers whom they love so tenderly! Sorry for their disappointment!

"They say" they are advancing in overwhelming numbers. That is nothing, so long as God helps us, and from our very souls we pray His blessing on us in this our hour of need. For myself, I cannot yet fully believe they are coming. It would be a relief to have it over. I have taken the responsibility of Lydia's jewelry on my shoulders, and hope to be able to save it in the rush which will take place. Down at the cars Miriam met Frank Enders, going to Clinton in charge of a car full of Yankees, — deserters, who came into our lines. He thinks, just as I do, that our trunks are safer here than there. Now that they are all off, we all agree that it was the most foolish thing we could have done. These Yankees interfere with all our arrangements.

I am almost ashamed to confess what an absurdly

selfish thought occurred to me a while ago. I was lamenting to myself all the troubles that surround us, the dangers and difficulties that perplex us, thinking of the probable fate that might befall some of our brave friends and defenders in Port Hudson, when I thought, too, of the fun we would miss. Horrid, was it not? But worse than that, I was longing for something to read, when I remembered Frank told me he had sent to Alexandria for Bulwer's "Strange Story" for me, and then I unconsciously said, "How I wish it would get here before the Yankees!" I am *very* anxious to read it, but confess I am ashamed of having thought of it at such a crisis. So I toss up the farthing Frank gave me for a keepsake the other day, and say I'll try in future to think less of my own comfort and pleasure.

Poor Mr. Halsey! What a sad fate the pets he procures for me meet! He stopped here just now on his way somewhere, and sent me a curious bundle with a strange story, by Miriam. It seems he got a little flying-squirrel for me to play with (must know my partiality for pets), and last night, while attempting to tame him, the little creature bit his finger, whereupon he naturally let him fall on the ground, (Temper!) which put a period to his existence. He had the nerve to skin him after the foul murder, and sent all that remains of him out to me to prove his original intention. The softest, longest, prettiest fur, and such a duck of a tail! Poor little animal could n't have been larger than my fist. Wonder if its spirit will meet with that of the little bird which flew heavenward with all that pink ribbon and my letter from Mr. Halsey?

Saturday, March 14th.
5 o'clock, P.M.

They are coming! The Yankees are coming at last! For four or five hours the sound of their cannon has assailed our ears. There! — that one shook my bed! Oh, they are coming! God grant us the victory! They are now within four miles of us, on the big road to Baton Rouge. On the road from town to Clinton, we have been fighting since daylight at Readbridge, and have been repulsed. Fifteen gunboats have passed Vicksburg, they say. It will be an awful fight. No matter! With God's help we'll conquer yet! Again! — the report comes nearer. Oh, they *are* coming! Coming to defeat, I pray God.

Only we seven women remain in the house. The General left this morning, to our unspeakable relief. They would hang him, we fear, if they should find him here. Mass' Gene has gone to his company; we are left alone here to meet them. If they *will* burn the house, they will have to burn me in it. For I cannot walk, and I know they shall not carry me. I'm resigned. If I *should* burn, I have friends and brothers enough to avenge me. Create *such* a consternation! Better than being thrown from a buggy — only I'd not survive to hear of it!

Letter from Lilly to-day has distressed me beyond measure. Starvation which threatened them seems actually at their door. With more money than they could use in ordinary times, they can find nothing to purchase. Not a scrap of meat in the house for a week. No pork, no potatoes, fresh meat obtained *once* as a favor, and poultry and flour articles unheard of. Besides that, Tiche crippled, and Margret very ill, while Liddy has run off to the Yankees. Heaven only knows what will become of them. The other day we were getting ready to go to them (Thursday) when the General disapproved of my running such a risk, saying he'd call it a d—— piece of nonsense, if I asked what he thought; so we remained. They will certainly starve soon enough without our help; and yet — I feel we should all be together still. That last superfluous word is the refrain of Gibbes's song that is ringing in my ears, and that I am chanting in a kind of ecstasy of excitement: —

"Then let the cannon boom as it will,
We'll be gay and happy still!"

And we will be happy in spite of Yankee guns! Only — my dear This, That, and the Other, at Port Hudson, how I pray for your safety! God spare our brave soldiers, and lead them to victory! I write, touch my guitar, talk, pick lint, and pray so rapidly that it is hard to say which is my occupation. I sent Frank some lint the other day, and a bundle of it for Mr. Halsey is by me. Hope neither will need it! But to my work again!

Half-past One o'clock, A.M.

It has come at last! What an awful sound! I thought I had heard a bombardment before; but Baton Rouge was child's play compared to this. At half-past eleven came the first gun — at least the first *I* heard, and I hardly think it could have commenced many moments before. Instantly I had my hand on Miriam, and at my first exclamation, Mrs. Badger and Anna answered. All three sprang to their feet to dress, while all four of us prayed aloud. Such an incessant roar! And at every report the house shaking so, and we thinking of our dear soldiers, the dead and dying, and crying aloud for God's blessing on them, and defeat and overthrow to their enemies. That dreadful roar! I can't think fast enough. They are too quick to be counted. We have all been in Mrs. Carter's room, from the last window of which we can see the incessant flash of the guns and the great shooting stars of flame, which must be the hot shot of the enemy. There is a burning house in the distance, the second one we have seen to-night. For Yankees can't prosper unless they are pillaging honest people. Already they have stripped all on their road of cattle, mules, and negroes.

Gathered in a knot within and without the window, we six women up here watched in the faint starlight the flashes from the guns, and silently wondered which of our friends were lying stiff and dead, and then, shuddering at the thought, betook ourselves to silent prayer. I think we know what it is to "wrestle with God in prayer"; we had but one thought. Yet for women, we took it almost too coolly. No tears, no cries, no fear, though for the first five minutes everybody's teeth chattered violently. Mrs. Carter had her husband in Fenner's battery, the hottest place if they are attacked by the land force, and yet to my unspeakable relief she betrayed no more emotion than we who had only friends there. We know absolutely nothing; when does one ever know anything in the country? But we presume that this is an engagement between our batteries and the gunboats attempting to run the blockade.

Firing has slackened considerably. All are to lie down already dressed; but being in my nightgown from necessity, I shall go to sleep, though we may expect at any instant to hear the tramp of Yankee cavalry in the yard.

Sunday, March 15th.

To my unspeakable surprise, I waked up this morning and found myself alive. Once satisfied of that, and assuring myself of intense silence in the place of the great guns which rocked me to sleep about half-past two this morning, I began to doubt that I had heard any disturbance in the night, and to believe I had written a dream within a dream, and that no bombardment had occurred; but all corroborate my statement, so it must be true, and this portentous silence is only the calm before the storm. I am half afraid the land force won't attack.

We can beat them if they do; but suppose they lay siege to Port Hudson and starve us out? That is the only way they can conquer.

We hear nothing still that is reliable.

Just before daylight there was a terrific explosion which electrified every one save myself. I was sleeping so soundly that I did not hear anything of it, though Mrs. Badger says that when she sprang up and called me, I talked very rationally about it, and asked what it could possibly be. Thought that I had ceased talking in my sleep. Miriam was quite eloquent in her dreams before the attack, crying aloud, "See! See! What do I behold?" as though she were witnessing a rehearsal of the scene to follow.

Later. Dr. Kennedy has just passed through, and was within the fortifications last night; brings news which is perhaps reliable, as it was obtained from Gardiner. It was, as we presumed, the batteries and gunboats. One we sunk; another, the Mississippi, we disabled so that the Yankees had to abandon and set fire to her, thirty-nine prisoners falling into our hands. It was her magazine that exploded this morning. Two other boats succeeded in passing, though badly crippled. Our batteries fired gallantly. Hurrah! for Colonel Steadman! I know his was by no means the least efficient!

Clinton, they say, will inevitably be sacked. Alas, for mother and Lilly! What can we do? The whole country is at the mercy of the Yankees as long as Gardiner keeps within the fortifications. Six miles below here they entered Mr. Newport's, pulled the pillow-cases from the beds, stuffed them with his clothes, and helped themselves generally. What can we expect here? To tell the truth, I should be disappointed if they did not even look in at us, on their marauding expedition.

March 17th.

On dit the Yankees have gone back to Baton Rouge, hearing we had sixty thousand men coming down after them. I believe I am positively disappointed! I did want to see them soundly thrashed! The light we thought was another burning house was that of the Mississippi. They say the shrieks of the men when our hot shells fell among them, and after they were left by their companions to burn, were perfectly appalling.

Another letter from Lilly has distressed me beyond measure. She says the one chicken and two dozen eggs Miriam and I succeeded in buying from the negroes by prayers and entreaties, saved them from actual hunger; and for two days they had been living on one egg apiece and some cornbread and syrup. Great heavens! has it come to this? Nothing to be bought in that abominable place for love or money. Where the next meal comes from, nobody knows.

Wednesday, March 25th.

Early last evening the tremendous clatter of a sword that made such unnecessary noise that one might imagine the owner thereof had betaken himself to the favorite pastime of his childhood, and was prancing in on his murderous weapon, having mistaken it for his war steed, announced the arrival of Captain Bradford, who with two friends came to say adieu. Those vile Yankees have been threatening Ponchatoula, and his battery, with a regiment of infantry, was on its way there to drive them back. The Captain sent me word of the distressing departure, with many assurances that he would take care of "my" John.

Scarcely had he departed, when lo! John arrives, and speaks for himself. Yes! he is going! Only a moment to say good-bye . . . sunset approaches. Well! he must say good-bye now! Chorus of young ladies: "Oh, will you not spend the evening with us? You can easily overtake the battery later." Chorus of married ladies: "You must not think of going. Here is a comfortable room at your service, and after an early breakfast you can be on the road as soon as the others." No necessity for prayers; he readily consents. And yet, as the evening wore on, when we laughed loudest I could not help but think of poor little Mrs. McPhaul sitting alone and crying over her brother's departure, fancying his precious bones lying on the damp ground with only the soldier's roof — the blue vault of heaven — above, while two miles away he sat in a comfortable parlor amusing himself.

About sunrise, while the most delightful dreams floated through my brain, a little voice roused me exclaiming, "Sady! Sady! John Hawsey say so! Say give Sady!" I opened my eyes to see little Gibbes standing by me, trying to lay some flowers on my cheek, his little face sparkling with delight at his own importance. A half-opened rosebud with the faintest blush of pink on its creamy leaves — a pink, and a piece of arbor vitæ, all sprinkled with dew, this was my bouquet. The servant explained that Mr. Halsey had just left, and sent me that with his last good-bye. And he has gone! "And now there's nothing left but weeping! His face I ne'er shall see, and naught is left to me, save" — putting away my book and all recollections of nonsense. So here goes!

Tuesday, March 31st.

"To be, or not to be; that's the question." Whether 't is nobler in the Confederacy to suffer the pangs of unappeasable hunger and never-ending trouble, or to take passage to a Yankee port, and there remaining, end them. Which is best? I am so near daft that I cannot pretend to say; I only know that I shudder at the thought of going to New Orleans, and that my heart fails me when I think of the probable consequence to mother if I allow a mere outward sign of patriotism to overbalance what should be my first consideration — her health. For Clinton is growing no better rapidly. To be hungry is there an everyday occurrence. For ten days, mother writes, they have lived off just hominy enough to keep their bodies and souls from parting, without being able to procure another article — not even a potato. Mother is not in a condition to stand such privation; day by day she grows weaker on her new regimen; I am satisfied that two months more of danger, difficulties, perplexities, and starvation will lay her in her grave. The latter alone is enough to put a speedy end to her days. Lilly has been obliged to put her children to bed to make them forget they were supperless, and when she followed their example, could not sleep herself, for very hunger.

We have tried in vain to find another home in the Confederacy. After three days spent in searching Augusta, Gibbes wrote that it was impossible to find a vacant room for us, as the city was already crowded with refugees. A kind Providence must have destined that disappointment in order to save my life, if there is any reason for Colonel Steadman's fears. We next wrote to Mobile, Brandon, and even that horrid little Liberty, besides making inquiries of every one we met, while Charlie, too, was endeavoring to find a place, and everywhere received the same answer — not a vacant room, and provisions hardly to be obtained at all.

The question has now resolved itself to whether we shall see mother die for want of food in Clinton, or, by sacrificing an outward show of patriotism (the inward sentiment cannot be changed), go with her to New Orleans, as Brother begs in the few letters he contrives to smuggle through. It looks simple enough. Ought not mother's life to be our first consideration? Undoubtedly! But suppose we could preserve her life and our free sentiments at the same time? If we could only find a resting-place in the Confederacy! This, though, is impossible. But to go to New Orleans; to cease singing "Dixie"; to be obliged to keep your sentiments to yourself — for I would not wound Brother by any Ultra-Secession speech, and such could do me no good and only injure him — *if* he is as friendly with the Federals as they say he is; to listen to the scurrilous abuse heaped on those fighting for our homes and liberties, among them my three brothers — could I endure it? I fear not. Even if I did not go crazy, I would grow so restless, homesick, and miserable, that I would pray for even Clinton again. Oh, I don't, don't want to go! If mother would only go alone, and leave us with Lilly! But she is as anxious to obtain Dr. Stone's advice for me as we are to secure her a comfortable home; and I won't go anywhere without Miriam, so we must all go together. Yet there is no disguising the fact that such a move will place us in a very doubtful position to both friends and enemies. However, all our friends here warmly advocate the move, and Will Pinckney and Frank both promised to knock down any one who shrugged their shoulders and said anything about it. But what would the boys say? The fear of displeasing them is my chief distress. George writes in the greatest distress about my prolonged illness, and his alarm about my condition. "Of one thing I am sure," he writes, "and that is that she deserves to recover; for a better little sister never lived." God bless him! My eyes grew right moist over those few words. Loving words bring tears to them sooner than angry ones. Would he object to such a step when he knows that the very medicines necessary for my recovery are not to be procured in the whole country? Would he rather have mother dead and me a cripple, in the Confederacy, than both well, out of it? I feel that if we go we are wrong; but I am satisfied that it is worse to stay. It is a distressing dilemma to be placed in, as we are certain to be blamed whichever course we pursue. But I don't want to go to New Orleans!

Before I had time to lay down my pen this evening, General Gardiner and Major Wilson were announced; and I had to perform a hasty toilette before being presentable. The first remark of the General was that my face recalled many pleasant recollections; that he had known my family very well, but that time was probably beyond my recollection; and he went on talking about father and Lavinia, until I felt quite comfortable, with this utter stranger. . . . I would prefer his speaking of "our" recent success at Port Hudson to "my"; for we each, man, woman, and child, feel that we share the glory of sinking the gunboats and sending Banks back to Baton Rouge without venturing on an attack; and it seemed odd to hear any one assume the responsibility of the whole affair and say "my success" so unconsciously. But this may be the privilege of generals. I am no judge, as this is the first Confederate general I have had the pleasure of seeing. Wish it had been old Stonewall! I grow enthusiastic every time I think of the dear old fellow!

I am indebted to General Gardiner for a great piece of kindness, though. I was telling him of how many enemies he had made among the ladies by his strict regulations that now rendered it almost impossible for the gentlemen to obtain permission to call on them, when he told me if I would signify to my friends to mention when they applied that their visit was to be here, and not elsewhere, that he would answer for their having a pass whenever they called for one. *Merci àu compliment; mais c'est trop tard, Monsieur!*

Tuesday, April 7th.

I believe that it is *for true* that we are to leave for New Orleans, via Clinton and Ponchatoula, this evening. Clinton, at least, I am sure of. Lilly came down for me yesterday, and according to the present programme, though I will not answer for it in an hour from now, we leave Linwood this evening, and Clinton on Thursday. I am almost indifferent about our destination; my chief anxiety is to have some definite plans decided on, which seems perfectly impossible from the number of times they are changed a day. The uncertainty is really affecting my spine, and causing me to grow alarmingly thin....

JUDGE THOMAS GIBBES MORGAN

Wednesday, CLINTON, April 8th, 1863.

Our last adieux are said, and Linwood is left behind, "it may be for years, and it may be forever." My last hours were spent lying on the sofa on the gallery, with Lydia at my feet, Helen Carter sitting on the floor at my side, while all the rest were gathered around me as I played for the *last time* "the centre of attraction." I grew almost lachrymose as I bid a last adieu to the bed where I have spent so many months, as they carried me downstairs. Wonder if it will not miss me? It must have been at least five before the cars returned. Mrs. Carter grew quite pathetic as they approached, while poor little Lydia, with streaming eyes and choking sobs, clung first to Miriam and then to me, as though we parted to meet only in eternity. All except her mother started in a run for the big gate, while I was carried to the buggy through the group of servants gathered to say good-bye, when the General drove me off rapidly.

What a delightful sensation is motion, after five months' inaction! The last time I was in a vehicle was the night General Beale's ambulance brought me to Linwood a helpless bundle, last November. It seemed to me yesterday that I could again feel the kind gentleman's arm supporting me, and his wondering, sympathetic tone as he repeated every half-mile, "Really, Miss Morgan, you are *very* patient and uncomplaining!" Good, kind President Miller! As though all the trouble was not his, just then! But stopping at the gate roused me from my short reverie, and I opened my eyes to find myself stationary, and in full view of a train of cars loaded with soldiers, literally covered with them; for they covered the roof, as well as filled the interior, while half a dozen open cars held them, seated one above the other in miniature pyramids, and even the engine was graced by their presence. Abashed with finding myself confronted with so many people, my sensation became decidedly alarming as a dozen rude voices cried, "Go on! we won't stop!" and a chorus of the opposition cried, "Yes, we will!" "No!" "Yes!" they cried in turn, and as the General stood me on the ground (I would have walked if it had been my last attempt in life), I paused irresolute, not knowing whether to advance or retreat before the storm. I must say they are the only rude soldiers I have yet seen in Confederate uniforms. But as I walked slowly, clinging to the General's arm, half from fear, and half from weakness, they ceased the unnecessary dispute, and remained so quiet that I was more frightened still, and actually forgot to say good-bye to Mrs. Carter and Mrs. Worley as they stood by the road. How both the General and I escaped being hurt as he raised me on the platform, every one is at a loss to account for. I experienced only what may be called slight pain, in comparison to what I *have* felt; but really fear that the exertion has disabled him for to-day. It must have been very severe. Some officers led me to my seat, Lilly, Miriam, and Anna got in, the General kissed us heartily, with damp eyes and kind wishes; the cars gave a whistle, and I put my head out of the window to see Mrs. Carter industriously applying white cambric to her face, which occupation she relinquished to call out last good-byes; another whistle and a jerk, and we were off, leaving her and Mrs. Worley, surrounded by children and servants, using their handkerchiefs to wipe tears and wave farewell, while the General waved his hat for good-bye. Then green hedges rapidly changing took their place, and Linwood was out of sight before we had ceased saying and thinking, God bless the kind hearts we had left behind. Can I ever forget the kindness we have met among them?

To see green trees and wild flowers once more, after such an illness, is a pleasure that only those long deprived of such beauties by a similar misfortune can fully appreciate.

It was a relief to discover that what I had thought shocking rudeness in the soldiers had not been reserved for me alone. For every time we stopped, the same cry of "No waiting for slow people" was raised, varied by constant expostulations with the engine for drinking ponds dry, and mild suggestions as to taking the road the other side of the fence, which would no doubt prove smoother than the track. These Arkansas troops have acquired a reputation for roughness and ignorance which they seem to cultivate as assiduously as most people would their virtues. But rudeness does not affect their fighting qualities.

MADISONVILLE, Sunday, April 12th, 1863.

We arrived here about five last evening, and, strange to say, the journey, fatiguing as it was, has not altogether disabled me. But I must go back to Clinton to account for this new change. It would never do to take more than a hundred miles at a single jump without speaking of the incidents by the way. Numerous and pleasant as they were, some way they have unaccountably paled; and things that seemed so extremely amusing, and afforded me so much pleasure during these four days, now seem to be absurd trifles half forgotten.

I now remember lying in state on Lilly's bed Wednesday, talking to Mrs. Badger (who had been several days in town), Anna, Sarah Ripley, and the others, when Frank suddenly bolted in, just from Port Hudson, to say another good-bye, though I told him good-bye at Linwood Sunday. Presently the General entered, just from Linwood, to see us off; then Mr. Marston and his daughter, and Mr. Neafus, all as kind as possible, until a perfect levee was assembled, which I, lying all dressed with a shawl thrown over me, enjoyed all the more as I could take my ease, and have my fun at the same time. Frank, sitting by my pillow, talked dolorously of how much he would miss us, and threatened to be taken prisoner before long in order to see us again.

. . . .

When we were finally left alone, I fancy there was very little sleep in the house. As to me, I lay by Lilly wide awake, thinking how lonely she would be without us, and perfectly *désolée* at the idea of leaving the Confederacy (the dear gray coats included); so when it was almost sunrise there was no necessity of rousing me to dress, as I was only too glad to leave my sleepless bed. Before I got dressed, Anna, her mother, and Sarah Ripley came in again; then Miss Comstock; and just as I had put the last touch to my dress, the gentlemen of the night before entered, and we had almost an hour and a half's respite before the carriage, less punctual than we, drove to the door.

The General picked me up in his arms and carried me once more to the carriage. Then the servants had to say good-bye; then Lilly, very quiet, very red, and dissolved in tears, clung to me almost without a word, hardly able to speak, whilst I, distressed and grieved as I was, had not a tear in my eyes — nothing but a great lump in my throat that I tried to choke down in order to talk to Frank, who stood at the window by me, after she left. . . . How the distance lengthens between us! I raise up from my pillows and find myself at Camp Moore at four o'clock. Forty miles are passed over; good-bye, Frank!

From Camp Moore we had to go three miles back, to find Captain Gilman's house where we were expected. The gentleman is a friend of Gibbes, though I had never seen any of them before. Such a delightful place, with everything looking so new, and cool, and such a hospitable hostess that I thought everything charming in spite of my fatigue. I had hardly a moment to look around; for immediately we were shown to our rooms, and in a very few minutes Miriam had me undressed and in bed, the most delightful spot in the world to me just then. While congratulating myself on having escaped death on the roadside, I opened my eyes to behold a tray brought to my bedside with a variety of refreshments. Coffee! Bread! Loaf-sugar! Preserves! I opened my mouth to make an exclamation at the singular optical illusion, but wisely forbore speaking, and shut it with some of the unheard-of delicacies instead. . . .

Early next morning the same routine was gone through as Thursday morning. Again the carriage drove to the door, and we were whisked off to Camp Moore, where the engine stood snorting with impatience to hurry us off to Ponchatoula. . . . Soon we were steaming down the track, I reclining on my pillows in an interesting state of invalidism, sadly abashed now and then at the courteous, wondering gaze of the soldiers who were aboard. Having very little idea of the geography of that part of the country, and knowing we were to take a carriage from some point this side of Ponchatoula, fancying how surprised Mr. Halsey would be to hear we had passed him on the way, I took a card from my traveling-case, and wrote a few words for "good-bye," as we could not see him again. I sealed it up, and put it in my pocket to send to the first post-office we passed.

About twelve o'clock we stopped at Hammond, which was our place to disembark. Mother sent out to hire a negro to carry me off the platform; and while waiting in great perplexity, a young officer who had just seated himself before me, got up and asked if he could assist her, seizing an arm full of cloaks as he spoke. I got up and walked to the door to appear independent and make believe I was not the one, when mother begged him not to trouble himself; she wanted a man to assist her daughter who was sick. Calling a friend, the gentleman kindly loaded him with the cloaks, etc., while he hurried out after me. I was looking ruefully at the impracticable step which separated me from the platform. The question of how I was to carry out my independent notions began to perplex me. "Allow me to assist you," said a voice at my elbow. I turned and beheld the handsome officer. "Thank you; I think I can get down alone." "Pray allow me to lift you over this place." "Much obliged, but your arm will suffice." "Sarah, let the gentleman carry you! You know you cannot walk!" said my very improper mother. I respectfully declined the renewed offer. "Don't pay any attention to her. Pick her up, just as you would a child," said my incorrigible mother. The gentleman turned very red, while Miriam asserts I turned extremely white. The next thing I knew, by passing his arm around my waist, or taking me by my arms — I was so frightened that I have but a confused idea of it — I was lifted over the intervening gulf and landed on the platform!

Hammond boasts of four houses. One, a shoe manufactory, stood about twenty or thirty yards off, and there the gentleman proposed to conduct me. Again he insisted on carrying me; and resolutely refusing, I pronounced myself fully equal to the walk, and accepting his proffered arm, walked off with dignity and self-possession. He must have fancied that the injury was in my hand; for holding my arm so that my entire weight must have been thrown on him, not satisfied with that support, with his other hand he held mine *so* respectfully and so carefully that I could not but smile as it struck me, which, by the way, *was not until I reached the house!*

Discovering that he belonged to Colonel Simonton's command, I asked him to take Mr. Halsey the note I had written an hour before. He pronounced himself delighted to be of the slightest service, and seeing that we were strangers, traveling unprotected, asked if we had secured a conveyance to take us beyond. We told him no. He modestly suggested that some gentleman might attend to it for us. He would be happy to do anything in his power. I thought again of Mr. Halsey, and said if he would mention we were in Hammond, he would be kind enough to see to it for us. "May I ask your name?" he asked, evidently surprised to find himself asking a question he was dying to know. I gave him my card, whereupon mother asked *his* name, which he told us was Howard. We had been talking for some ten minutes, when feeling rather uncomfortable at being obliged to look up at such a tall man from my low seat, to relieve my neck as well as to shade my face from any further scrutiny, I put down my head while I was still speaking. Instantly, so quietly, naturally, and unobtrusively did he stoop down by me, on one knee so that his face was in full view of mine, that the action did not seem to me either singular or impertinent —in fact, I did not think of it until mother spoke of it after he left. After a few moments it must have struck him; for he got up and made his parting bow, departing, as I afterwards heard, to question Tiche as to how I had been hurt, and declaring that it was a dreadful calamity to happen to so "lovely" a young lady.

Monday, April 13th.

Having nothing to do, I may as well go on with the history of our wanderings. When the cars were moving off with the handsome Mr. Howard, mother turned to a gentleman who seemed to own the place, and asked to be shown the hotel. He went out, and presently returning with a chair and two negroes, quietly said he would take us to his own house; the hotel was not comfortable. And, without listening to remonstrances, led the way to a beautiful little cottage, where he introduced his wife, Mrs. Cate, who received us most charmingly, and had me in bed before five minutes had elapsed. I don't know how any one can believe the whole world so wicked; for my part I have met none but the kindest people imaginable; I don't know any wicked ones.

Before half an hour had passed, a visitor was announced; so I gathered up my weary bones, and with scarcely a peep at the glass, walked to the parlor. I commenced laughing before I got there, and the visitor smiled most absurdly, too; for it was — Mr. Halsey! It seemed so queer to meet in this part of the world that we laughed again after shaking hands. It *was* odd. I was thinking how much amused the General would be to hear of it; for he had made a bet that we would meet when I asserted that we would not.

After the first few remarks, he told me of how he had heard of our arrival. A gentleman had walked into camp, asking if a Mr. Halsey was there. He signified that he was the gentleman, whereupon the other drew out my note, saying a young lady on the cars had requested him to deliver it. Instantly recognizing the chirography, he asked where I was. "Hammond. This is her name," replied the other, extending to him my card. Thinking, as he modestly confessed, that I had intended it only for him, Mr. Halsey coolly put it into his pocket, and called for his horse. Mr. Howard lingered still, apparently having something to say, which he found difficult to put in words. At last, as the other prepared to ride off, with a tremendous effort he managed to say, "The young lady's card is mine. If it is all the same to you, I should like to have it returned." Apologizing for the mistake, Mr. Halsey returned it, feeling rather foolish, I should imagine, and rode on to the village, leaving, as he avers, Mr. Howard looking enviously after the lucky dog who was going to see *such* a young lady.

He told me something that slightly disgusted me with Captain Bradford. It was that when he reached the bivouac the next morning after leaving Linwood, the Captain had put him under arrest for having stayed there all night. It was too mean, considering that it is more than probable that he himself remained at Mrs. Fluker's. We discovered, too, that we had missed two letters Mr. Halsey had written us, which, *of course*, is a great disappointment. One, written to both, the other, a short note of ten pages, for me, which I am sure was worth reading.

It was not until after sunset that we exhausted all topics of conversation, and Mr. Halsey took his leave, promising to see us in the morning.

And, to be sure, as soon as I was dressed on Saturday, he again made his appearance, followed soon after by the carriage. Taking a cordial leave of Mrs. Cate, with many thanks for her hospitality, we entered our conveyance, and with Mr. Halsey riding by the side of the carriage, went on our way. He was to accompany us only as far as Ponchatoula — some six miles; but the turning-point in his journey seemed to be an undetermined spot; for mile after mile rolled away — rather the wheels rolled over them — and still he rode by us, talking through the window, and the sprays of wild flowers he would pick for me from time to time were growing to quite a bouquet, when he proposed an exchange with the farmer who was driving us, and, giving him his horse, took the reins himself.

I think Miriam and I will always remember that ride. The laughter, the conversation, the songs with the murmuring accompaniment of the wheels, and a thousand incidents pleasant to remember though foolish to speak of, will always form a delightful tableau in our recollections. I have but one disagreeable impression to remember in connection with the trip, and that occurred at a farmhouse two miles from here, where we stopped to get strawberries. I preferred remaining in the carriage, to the trouble of getting out; so all went in, Mr. Halsey dividing his time equally between Miriam in the house and me in the carriage, supplying me with violets and *pensées* one moment, and the next showing me the most tempting strawberries at the most provoking distance, assuring me they were exquisite. The individual to whom the carriage belonged, who had given up the reins to Mr. Halsey, and who, no doubt, was respectable enough for his class in his part of the country, would allow no one to bring me my strawberries, reserving the honor for himself. Presently he appeared with a large saucer of them covered with cream. I was naturally thankful, but would have preferred his returning to the house after he had fulfilled his mission. Instead, he had the audacity to express his admiration of my personal appearance; without a pause gave me a short sketch of his history, informed me he was a widower, and *very* anxious to marry again, and finally, — Lares and Penates of the house of Morgan ap Kerrig, veil your affronted brows! You will scarcely credit that the creature had the insolence to say that — he would marry me tomorrow, if he could, and think himself blessed; for the jewel of the soul must be equal to the casket that contained it! Yes! this brute of a man had the unparalleled audacity to speak to me in such a way! Just then, mother, remembering her invalid, came to the gallery and asked how I was enjoying my lunch. "I'm courting her!" cried the wretch. "Glad she did not go in! Swear she's the prettiest girl I *ever* saw!" At that moment Mr. Halsey came sauntering out with a handful of violets for me, and, turning my shoulder to the creature, I entered into a lively discussion with him, and at last had the satisfaction of seeing the wretch enter the house.

A drive through the straggling, half-deserted town brought us here to Mrs. Greyson's, a large, old-fashioned-looking house so close to the Tchefuncta (I think that is the name of the river) that I could throw a stone in it from my bed, almost.

Mrs. Greyson herself would require two or three pages to do her justice. Fancy the daughter of Sir Francis Searle, the widow of General Greyson, the belle of New Orleans in her young days, settled down into a hotel-keeper on a small scale, with stately ladies and gentlemen looking down in solemn surprise at her boarders from their rich portrait frames on the parlor wall! Fallen greatness always gives me an uncomfortable thrill. Yet here was the heiress of these shadows on the wall, gay, talkative, bustling, active; with a word of caution, or a word of advice to all; polite, attentive, agreeable to her guests, quarreling and exacting with her servants, grasping and avaricious with all; singing a piece from "Norma" in a voice, about the size of a thread No. 150, that showed traces of former excellence; or cheapening a bushel of corn meal with equal volubility. What a character! Full of little secrets and mysteries. "Now, my dear, I don't ask you to tell a *story*, you know; but if the others ask you if you knew it, just look surprised and say, 'Oh, dear me, when did it happen?' 'Cause I promised not to tell; only you are such favorites that I could not help it, and it would not do to acknowledge it. And if any one asks you if I put these candles in here, just say you brought them with you, that's a love, because they will be jealous, as I only allow them lamps." Eccentric Mrs. Greyson! Many an hour's amusement did she afford me.[1]

[1] This paragraph, which occurs retrospectively in the Diary under

A ride of twenty-six miles bolt upright in the carriage, over such bad roads, had almost used me up; I retired to bed in a state of collapse, leaving Miriam to entertain Mr. Halsey alone. After supper, though, I managed to put on my prettiest dress, and be carried down to the parlor where I rejoined the rest. Several strange ladies were present, one of whom has since afforded me a hearty laugh. She was a horrid-looking woman, and ten minutes after I entered, crossing the room with a most laughable look of vulgarity attempting to ape righteous scorn, jerked some articles of personal property from the table and retired with the sweep of a small hurricane. I thought her an eccentric female; but what was my amazement yesterday to hear that she sought Mrs. Greyson, told her it was impossible for her to stay among so many elegantly dressed ladies, and that she preferred keeping her room. Next day, she told her that she was entirely too attentive to us, and rather than be neglected in that way for other people, would leave the house, which she did instantly.

There was a singular assembly of odd characters in the parlor Saturday night, six of whom looked as though they were but so many reflections of the same individual in different glasses, and the seventh differed from the rest only in playing exquisitely on the banjo — "Too well to be a gentleman," I fear. These were soldiers, come to "call" on us. Half an

date of New Orleans, Sunday, May 24th, 1863, is inserted here for the sake of clearness. — W. D.

hour after we arrived, a dozen of them took possession of the bench on the bank of the river, one with his banjo who played and sang delightfully. Old Mrs. Greyson, who is rather eccentric, called, "Ah, Mr. J——! Have you heard already of the arrival of the young ladies? You never serenaded *me!*" The young man naturally looked foolish; so she went out and asked him to come around after dark and play for the young ladies. So after a while he came, "bringing six devils yet worse than himself," as the old Scriptural phrase has it, all of whom sat on the same side of the room, and looked at us steadily when they thought we were not looking. All had the same voice, the same bow, the same manner — that is to say none at all of the latter; one introduced an agreeable variety, saying as he bowed to each separately, "Happy to make your acquaintance, ma'am." Mr. Halsey just managed to keep his face straight, while I longed for a Dickens to put them all together and make one amusing picture out of the seven. I troubled myself very little about them, preferring Mr. Halsey's company, not knowing when we would meet again. It would not have been quite fair to leave him to himself after he had ridden such a distance for us; so I generously left the seven to Miriam, content with one, and rather think I had the best of the bargain. The one with the banjo suggested that we should sing for them before he played for us, so Miriam played on the piano, and sang with me on the guitar half a dozen songs, and then the other commenced. I don't know when I have been more amused. There was an odd, piney-woods dash about him that was exceedingly diverting, and he went through comic, sentimental, and original songs with an air that showed his whole heart was in it. Judging from the number of youth too timid to venture in, who peeped at us from the windows, I should say that young ladies are curiosities just now in Madisonville.

Tuesday, April 14th.

Ah! another delightful glimpse of society has been offered to our charmed view. Such a treat has not often fallen to our lot. Good Mrs. Greyson, in her anxiety to make all around her happy, determined we should have a dance. I should say "Miriam"; for Mrs. Bull and Mrs. Ivy never indulge in such amusements, and I can't; so it must have been for Miriam alone. Such a crew! The two ladies above mentioned and I almost laughed ourselves into hysterics. Poor Miriam, with a tall, slender Texan who looked as though he had chopped wood all his life, moved through the dance like the lady in "Comus"; only, now and then a burst of laughter at the odd mistakes threatened to overcome her dignity. We who were fortunately exempt from the ordeal, laughed unrestrainedly at the mêlée. One danced entirely with his arms; his feet had very little to do with the time. One hopped through with a most dolorous expression of intense absorption in the arduous task. Another never changed a benign smile that had appeared on entering, but preserved it unimpaired through every accident. One female, apparently of the tender age of thirty, wore a yellow muslin, with her hair combed rigidly *à la chinoise*, and tightly fastened at the back of her head in a knot whose circumference must have been fully equal to that of a dollar. In addition to other charms, she bore her neck and chin in a very peculiar manner, as though she were looking over the fence, Mr. Christmas remarked. Mr. Christmas had ridden all the way from Ponchatoula to see us, and if it had not been for him, Mr. Worthington, and Dr. Capdevielle, who came in after a while, I think I should have expired, and even Miriam would have given up in despair. The Doctor was an old friend of Harry's, though we never met him before.

Thursday, April 16th.

Mr. Halsey brought us each a little tortoise-shell ring he had made for us by his camp-fire, as a keepsake, and of course we promised to wear them for him, particularly as they make our hands look as white as possible. Towards sunset, in spite of prayers and entreaties from Miriam, who insisted that I was too feeble to attempt it, I insisted on walking out to the bench by the river to enjoy the cool breeze; and was rather glad I had come, when soon after Dr. Capdevielle made his appearance, with two beautiful bouquets which he presented with his French bow to us; and introducing his friend, Mr. Miltonberger, entered into one of those lively discussions about nothing which Frenchmen know how to make so interesting. . . .

No sooner had they left than, to our infinite surprise, the immortal seven of Saturday night walked in. Wonder what fun they find in coming? I see none. For we rarely trouble ourselves about their presence; there are but two I have addressed as yet; one because I am forced to say yes or no to his remarks, and the other because I like his banjo, which he brought again, and feel obliged to talk occasionally since he is so accommodating, and affords me the greatest amusement with his comic songs. I was about retiring unceremoniously about twelve o'clock, completely worn out, when they finally bethought themselves of saying good-night, and saved me the necessity of being rude. Wonder if that is all the fun they have? I should say it was rather dry. It is mean to laugh at them, though; their obliging dispositions should save them from our ridicule. Last evening Mr. Halsey succeeded in procuring a large skiff, whereupon four or five of them offered to row, and took us 'way down the Tchefuncta through the most charming scenery to a spot where Echo answered us in the most remarkable way; her distinct utterance was really charming. Not being aware of the secret, I thought the first answer to the halloo was from pickets. Mr. Halsey has a magnificent voice; and the echoes came back so full and rich that soon we appointed him speaker by mutual consent, and were more than repaid by the delightful sounds that came from the woods. The last ray of the sun on the smooth waters; the soldiers resting on their oars while we tuned the guitar and sang in the still evening, until twilight, slowly closing over, warned us to return, forms another of those pictures indescribable though never to be forgotten.

BONFOUCA, Saturday, April 18th.

When I paused on Thursday to rest a few moments, how little idea I had that the rest I was taking would soon be required for another journey!

It was agreed among us, with our fellow travelers, Mrs. Bull and Mrs. Ivy, whom we met at Mrs. Greyson's, endeavoring to reach the city like ourselves, that we would wait there until we could receive our passports from General Pemberton. When this journey was first seriously contemplated, Miriam wrote to Colonel Szymanski representing mother's state of health and my unfortunate condition, the necessity of medical advice for both, and the impossibility of remaining in famishing Clinton, and asked him to apply to the General for a pass to go to Brother. The Colonel sent word through Eugene La Noue that we should obtain it in a few days, and advised us to go by way of Ponchatoula. Tired of delay, and hearing that we could pass as readily on General Gardiner's order, we obtained one and started off without waiting for the other. The first news on arriving at Madisonville was that no one should pass except on General Pemberton's order.

Pleasant intelligence for those who had come that far without! The other two ladies were in the same dilemma. They were told that they should have a pass if they would wait. Waiting at the expense of four dollars a day for each, — Mrs. Ivy with two very sick babies, Mrs. Bull with all her property in New Orleans at stake, Tiche with her broken foot, mother with a powerless hand, and I with an injured spine, — was anything but agreeable under the circumstances; though nothing could be more pleasant, apart from this sense of restriction, than our stay at Madisonville. General Pemberton took his leisure about the affair, which is not surprising, as our Generals have more weighty matters than women's passports to attend to. Still, pleased as we were with our residence there, it was necessary to get on as soon as possible. So as I rested from labors about one o'clock on Thursday, Mrs. Bull came in to suggest a new plan to mother. It was to leave immediately for a plantation called Bonfouca, thirty miles off, where schooners came twice a week, and where we would be allowed to embark without a pass. Carriages that had just brought a party of ladies from Mandeville were waiting on the other side of the river, which could take us off immediately, for there was not a moment to lose.

Instantly we resolved to hazard the undertaking.

About three we got into the large scow to cross the Tchefuncta, in a party numbering five ladies, four children, and four servants. One of the devoted pickets, after setting me carefully in the most comfortable place, asked permission to accompany me as far as the carriage; he was sure he could assist me more carefully than the drivers. And without further parley, he followed. Before we turned the point, Mr. Worthington[1] . . . the dim distance, rowing up the stream in the direction of Madisonville. What if he had perceived us, and was hastening after us, deeming it his duty to arrest us for trying to get away without General Pemberton's order? As the idea was suggested, there was rather a nervous set of ladies on board. The half-mile that we had to go before reaching our landing-place was passed over in nervous apprehension. At last the spot was reached. Mr. Worthington had not appeared, and we reached *terra firma* without being "nabbed," as we confidently expected. The obliging picket put me into the carriage, bade me a most friendly adieu, and returned to the village, leaving us with every prospect of getting off without serious difficulty, in spite of our serious apprehensions.

With two little children and Tiche with me, our carriage started off some time before the others. Two or three miles from our starting-point, I perceived three gentlemen riding towards us, one of whom I instantly recognized as Dr. Capdevielle. Instantly I stopped the carriage to speak to him. His look of astonishment when satisfied of my identity rather

[1] The torn edge of a page has obliterated several words, which might, to judge by the context, have been "was seen in."

amused me; but my amusement was changed to a slight feeling of disappointment when he commenced talking. Was it possible I was leaving Madison? Oh, how distressed he was! He was promising himself so much pleasure! And to leave so unexpectedly! He had just come with his friends from — somewhere. They had planned a surprise party at Mrs. Greyson's for us that evening, and had been after the supper they had procured — somewhere, as I before observed, and were just now returning. And now we were deserting them! He had invited Monsieur Berger, Monsieur Pollock, Monsieur —— *Mais enfin des Messieurs!* he exclaimed with a comical emphasis and smile that brought vivid recollections of the other party before my eyes, by force of contrast, I suppose. And was n't I sorry we had left! We fairly condoled with each other. Twenty minutes had elapsed before I had so far recovered from the disappointment as to bethink myself of the propriety of continuing my journey. And then with the assurance of being mutually *désolé*, we parted with a hearty good-bye, and he rode on to rejoin his companions, while I went the way he had come.

Two miles beyond, I met three others of the six gentlemen he had mentioned, riding in a little dog-cart which contained champagne baskets in which the supper was evidently packed, each gentleman elegantly dressed, holding between them a little basket of bouquets that my prophetic soul told me was intended for Miriam and me. I was not personally acquainted with the gentlemen, or I should have told them of the disappointment that awaited them. It *must* have been a disappointment!

In the midst of profound reflections about fate, vanity of human wishes and calculations, friendships formed on the roadside in the journey through life (or from Clinton), I raised my eyes to behold Lake Ponchartrain, and to find myself in Mandeville, just seven miles from the Tchefuncta. Looking at the dreary expanse of water, which suggested loneliness and desolation, first recalled my own situation to me. Here I was in this straggling place, with Tiche, a cripple like myself, and two little children under my care, without an idea of where we were to go. Any one as timid and dependent as I to be placed in such a position as pioneer to such a tremendous company would feel rather forlorn. But some step had to be taken, so I consulted the driver as to where we could obtain board, and followed his suggestion. One house after the other we stopped at, and with my veil down and my heart beating as though I were soliciting charity, or some other unpleasant favor, I tried to engage rooms for the company, without success. At last we were directed to a Frenchman, who after the usual assurance of "nothing to eat" (which we afterwards found to be only too true), consented to receive us. "Taking possession" seemed to me such a dreadful responsibility that for some time I remained in the carriage, afraid to get out before the others arrived. But there was still no sign of them;

so I gathered my children and Tiche, and prepared to dismount with the Frenchman's assistance.

I have read descriptions of such houses and people, but I have not often seen them. The man and his wife were perfect specimens of the low Canadian, speaking only French. No sooner had they discovered that I was "blessée," as they supposed, than each seized an arm and with overwhelming exclamations of sympathy, halfway dragged me into the room, where they thrust me into a chair. Their family seemed to consist only of cats and dogs who seemed to agree most harmoniously, and each of whom conceived the liveliest affection for us. As we were leaving Mrs. Greyson's, a stranger just from the city, brought to our room a paper of ham, tongue, and biscuits for "the sick young lady" (Heaven only knows how she heard of her), saying she had just traveled the road herself, and knew I would find nothing to eat; so she would insist on putting this in our basket. It was done in a manner that put all refusal out of the question; so it had to be accepted. I was feeding little Jenny Ivy and Minna Bull on this lunch for want of something else to do, when the affection of the cats and dogs became overpowering. Six of them jumped at us, licked Jenny's face, eat Minna's ham, and what with sundry kicks and slaps I had exercise enough to last a week, and was rapidly losing all my strength, when the woman came to my rescue and called her pets off just as the rest of the party drove up to find me almost exhausted.

Such a bedroom! There was a narrow single bed in which mother, Jenny, and I slept, a decrepit table on which stood a diseased mirror, a broken lounge without a bottom, and a pine armoir filled with — corn! In the centre stood the chief ornament, a huge pile of dirt, near which Miriam's mattress was placed, while the sail of a boat flanked it in on the other side, arranged as a bed for Tiche. The accommodations in the other bedroom were far inferior to ours. Then the mosquitoes swarmed like pandemonium on a spree, and there was but one bar in the house, which the man declared should be only for me. I would rather have been devoured by the insects than enjoy comforts denied to the others; so I made up my mind it should be the last time.

Our supper was rare. "Nothing like it was ever seen in Paris," as McClellan would say. It consisted of one egg apiece, with a small spoonful of rice. A feast, you see! Price, one dollar each, besides the dollar paid for the privilege of sleeping among dirt, dogs, and fleas.

Sunday, April 19th.

Friday morning we arose and prepared to resume our journey for Bonfouca, twenty-three miles away. The man walked in very unceremoniously to get corn from the armoir as we got up, throwing open the windows and performing sundry little offices usually reserved for *femmes-de-chambre;* but with that exception everything went on very well. Breakfast being a luxury not to be procured, we got into the carriages before sunrise, and left this romantic abode of dogs and contentment. Again our road lay through piney woods, so much like that from Hammond to Ponchatoula that involuntarily I found myself looking through the window to see if Mr. Halsey was there. It lacked only his presence to make the scene all in all the same. But alas! this time the driver picked me wild flowers, and brought us haws. Mr. Halsey, in blissful ignorance of our departure, was many and many a mile away. The drive was not half as amusing. The horse would not suffer any one except Miriam to drive, and at last refused to move until the driver got down and ran along by the carriage. Every time the poor boy attempted to occupy his seat, the obstinate animal would come to a dead stop and refuse to go until he dismounted again. I am sure that he walked nineteen miles out of the twenty-three, out of complaisance to the ungrateful brute.

All equally fatigued and warm, we reached this place about twelve o'clock. Mrs. Bull had arrived before us; and as the carriage stopped, her girl Delia came to the gate the personification of despair, crying, "You can't get out, ladies. They say we can't stop here; we must go right back." The panic which ensued is indescribable. Go back when we were almost at our journey's end, after all the money we had spent, the fatigue we had undergone, to be turned back all the way to Clinton, perhaps! "With my sick babies!" cried Mrs. Ivy. "With my sick child!" cried mother. "Never! You may turn me out of your house, but we will die in the woods first! To go back is to kill my daughter and these babies!" This was to the overseer who came to the carriage. "Madam, I have orders to allow no one to pass who has not written permission. Lieutenant Worthington sent the order two days ago; and I am liable to imprisonment if I harbor those who have no passport," the man explained. "But we have General Gardiner's order," I expostulated. "Then you shall certainly pass; but these ladies cannot. I can't turn you away, though; you shall all come in and stay until something can be determined on."

This much granted was an unlooked-for blessing. He showed us the way to a large unfurnished house, one room of which contained a bed with one naked mattress, which was to be our apartment. Mrs. Bull sat down in a calm, dignified state of despair; little Mrs. Ivy dissolved in tears; we all felt equally disconsolate; the prospect of getting off was not so pleasant when we thought we should be obliged to leave them behind. Our common misfortunes had endeared us to each other, strangers as we were a week ago. So we all lamented together, a perfect *Jérémiade* of despair. The overseer is very tender-hearted; he condoled, comforted, and finally determined that if there was any way of getting them off, they should go. A glimpse of sunshine returned to our lowering sky, and cheerfulness reigned once more, to be violently dethroned some hours later. Three of the Madisonville pickets were announced approaching the house. Of course, they were coming after us! Oh, that vile Mr. Worthington! We always *did* hate him! There was such a sneaky look about him. Hypocrite! we always felt we should hate him! Oh, the wretch! "I won't go back!" cried mother. "I shall not," said quiet Mrs. Bull. "He shall pay my expenses if he insists on taking me back!" exclaimed Mrs. Ivy. "Spent all my money! Mrs. Bull, you have none to lend me, remember, and Mrs. Morgan *shan't!* Oh, that Worthington! Let's make him pay for all!" We smothered our laughter to sit trembling within as the pickets stepped on the gallery. I believe we commenced praying. Just think! Thus far, our journey has cost mother two hundred and twenty dollars. It would cost the same to get back to blessed Clinton, and fancy our spending that sum to settle there again! Besides, we gave away all our clothes to our suffering friends; and what would we do there now?

After half an hour of painful suspense, we discovered that it would have been as well to spare poor Mr. Worthington; for the pickets were not after us, but had come to escort Mrs. R——, a woman who was taking the body of her son, who was killed at Murfreesboro, to the city for interment. Poor woman! she rode all this distance sitting on her child's coffin. Her husband was one of those who with B—— stole that large sum of money from father which came so near ruining him. She speaks of her husband as of a departed saint. I dare say she believes him innocent of the theft in spite of his public confession. The grave has wiped out even the disgrace of the penitentiary where he expiated his offense. . . . When I told Tiche who the woman was, she clasped her hands, saying, "The Lord is good! Years and years master suffered while she grew rich, and now *her* time comes! The Lord don't forget!" I can't feel that way. It is well for the narrow-minded to look for God's judgment on us for our sins; but mine is a more liberal faith. God afflicted her for some wise purpose; but if I thought it was to avenge father, I should be afraid of her. As it is, I can be sorry, oh, *so* sorry for her!

As usual I find myself taken care of at the expense of the others. There are but two bars on the place; one, the overseer said, should be for me, the other for the children. Sheets were scarce, covers scarcer still. Tired of being spoiled in this way, I insisted on being allowed to sleep on a mattress on the floor, after a vigorous skirmish with mother and Miriam, in which I came off victorious. For a bar, I impressed Miriam's grenadine dress, which she fastened to the doorknob and let fall over me à la Victoria tester arrangement. To my share fell a double blanket, which, as Tiche had no cover, I unfolded, and as she used the foot of my bed for a pillow, gave her the other end of it, thus (tell it not in Yankeeland, for it will never be credited) actually sleeping under the same bedclothes with our black, shiny negro nurse! We are grateful, though, even for these discomforts;

it might have been so much worse! Indeed, I fear that our fellow travelers do not fare as well. Those who have sheets have no bars; those who have blankets have no sheets; and one woman who has recently joined us has nothing except a mattress which is to do the duty of all three. But then, we got bread! Real, pure, wheat bread! And coffee! None of your potato, burnt sugar, and parched corn abomination, but the unadulterated berry! I can't enjoy it fully, though; every mouthful is cloyed with the recollection that Lilly and her children have none.

As usual, as Mrs. Greyson says, the flowers follow us; yesterday I received three bouquets, and Miriam got one too. In this out-of-the-way place such offerings are unexpected; and these were doubly gratifying coming from people one is not accustomed to receiving them from. For instance, the first was from the overseer, the second from a servant, and the third from a poor boy for whom we have subscribed to pay his passage to the city.

Wednesday, April 22d,
NEW ORLEANS.

Yesterday we arrived; I thought we should never get here. Monday we had almost given up in despair, believing the schooner would never return. But in the evening, when all were gathered in our room discussing our hopes and fears, a sail was perceived at the mouth of the bayou, whereupon every one rushed out to see the boat land. I believe that I have not mentioned that this Bonfouca is on a bayou of the same name that runs within a few yards of this house. It is an Indian name signifying Winding River, which struck us as very appropriate when we watched the schooner sailing now to the left, now to the right, apparently through the green fields; for the high grass hid the course of the stream so that the faintest line was not perceptible, except just in front of the house. All was now bustle and confusion, packing, dressing, and writing last words to our friends at home, until half-past eleven, when we embarked.

This is my first experience of schooners, and I don't care if I never behold another. The cabin where Mr. Kennedy immediately carried me, was just the size of my bed at home (in the days I had a home) and just high enough to stand in. On each side of the short ladder, there was a mattress two feet wide. One of them Mrs. R—— had possession of already, the other was reserved for me. I gave the lower part of mine to Minna and Jennie, who spent the rest of the night fighting each other and kicking me.

Just before twelve we "weighed anchor" and I went on deck to take a last look at Dixie with the rest of the party. Every heart was full. Each left brothers, sisters, husband, children, or dear friends behind. We sang, "Farewell dear land," with a slight quaver in our voices, looked at the beautiful starlight shining on the last boundary of our glorious land, and, fervently and silently praying, passed out of sight.

God bless you, all you dear ones we have left in our beloved country! God bless and prosper you, and grant you the victory in the name of Jesus Christ.

I returned to my mattress, and this is the way we spent the night.

Mrs. R——, rocking and moaning as she sat up in bed, whined out her various ills with a minute description of each, ceasing the recital only to talk of her son's body which lay on deck. (Yesterday morning she was sitting crying on his coffin while a strange woman sat on its head eating her bread and cheese.) Mrs. Bull, one of the most intelligent and refined ladies I have yet met, who is perfectly devoted to me, sat by me, laughing and talking, trying her best to make every one comfortable and happy in her unobtrusive way. Mother talked to Mrs. R—— and cried at the thought of leaving her children fighting and suffering. The space between the two beds was occupied by three Irishwomen and Mrs. Ivy's two babies. The babies had commenced screaming as they were brought into the pen, at which I was not surprised. Having pitched their voices on the proper key, they never ceased shrieking, kicking, crying, throwing up, and going through the whole list of baby performances. The nurses scolded with shrill voices above the bedlam that had hushed even Mrs. R——'s complaints; Jennie and Minna quarreled, kicked, and cried; and as an aggravation to the previous discomforts, a broad-shouldered, perspiring

Irishwoman sat just by my head, bracing herself against my pillow in the most unpleasant style. I endured it without flinching until about half-past three, when the condensed odor of a dozen different people and children became unendurable, and I staggered up on deck where Miriam and Mrs. Ivy had been wise enough to remain without venturing below. They laid me on a bench in the stern, rolled me up in shawls to keep off the heavy dew, and there I remained until daylight with them, as wide awake as ever.

At daylight there was a universal smoothing of heads, and straightening of dresses, besides arrangements made for the inspection of baggage. Being unwilling for any Christian to see such a book as this, I passed a piece of tape through the centre leaves, and made Miriam tie it under her hoops. At sunrise we were in sight of the houses at the lake end. It seemed as though we would never reach land.

I forgot to speak of our alarm as we got in the lake. No sooner had we fairly left the bayou than the sky suddenly became threatening. The captain shook his head and spoke of a very ugly night for the lake, which sent everybody's heart to their throats, and alarmed us immeasurably. We got talking of the sailor's superstition of crossing the water with a corpse, until we persuaded ourselves that it was more than probable we would founder in the coming storm. But the severest storm we met was the one in the cabin; and all night the only wind was a head breeze, and the spicy gale from below.

When we at last entered the canal, I beheld the animal now so long unseen, the Yankee. In their dark blue uniforms, they stood around, but I thought of the dear gray coats, and even the pickets of Madisonville seemed nobler and greater men than these. Immediately a guard was placed on board, we whispering before he came, "Our dear Confederates, God bless them."

We had agreed among ourselves that come what would, we would preserve our dignity and self-respect, and do anything rather than create a scene among such people. It is well that we agreed. So we whispered quietly among ourselves, exhorting each other to pay no attention to the remarks the Yankees made about us as we passed, and acting the martyr to perfection, until we came to Hickock's Landing. Here there was a group of twenty Yankees. Two officers came up and asked us for papers; we said we had none. In five minutes one came back, and asked if we had taken the oath. No; we had never taken *any*. He then took down our names. Mother was alone in the coop. He asked if there was not another. The schooner had fifteen passengers, and we had given only fourteen names. Mother then came up and gave her name, going back soon after.

While one went after our passes, others came to examine our baggage. I could not but smile as an unfortunate young man got on his knees before our trunk and respectfully handled our dirty petticoats and stockings. "You have gone through it before," he said. "Of course, the Confederates searched it." — "Indeed, they did not touch it!" I exclaimed. "They never think of doing such work." — "Miss, it is more mortifying to me than it can be to you," he answered. And I saw he was actually blushing. He did his work as delicately as possible, and when he returned the keys, asked if we had letters. I opened my box and put them into his hand. One came near getting me into serious trouble. It was sent by some one I never saw, with the assurance that it contained nothing objectionable. I gave it sealed to the man, who opened it, when it proved to be rather disagreeable, I judged from his language. He told me his captain must see it before he could let me have it, and carried it off. Presently he came back and told me it could not be returned. I told him to burn it then, as I neither knew the writer, the contents, nor those it was written to. "I may save you some difficulty if I destroy it," he remarked, whereupon he tore it up and flung it into the canal. I have since found I had cause to be grateful; for just after came an officer to see the young lady who brought that letter. I showed the pieces in the water, saying the young man had torn it up, which seemed to annoy him; it was to be sent to headquarters, he said.

Then came a bundle of papers on board carried by another, who standing in front of us, cried in a startling way, "Sarah Morgan!" — "Here" (very quietly). — "Stand up!" — "I cannot" (firmly). — "Why not?" — "Unable" (decisively). After this brief dialogue, he went on with the others until all were standing except myself, when he delivered to each a strip of paper that informed the people that Miss, or Mrs. So-and-So had taken and subscribed the oath as Citizen of the United States. I thought that was all, and rejoiced at our escape. But after another pause he uncovered his head and told us to hold up our right hands. Half-crying, I covered my face with mine and prayed breathlessly for the boys and the Confederacy, so that I heard not a word he was saying until the question, "So help you God?" struck my ear. I shuddered and prayed harder. There came an awful pause in which not a lip was moved. Each felt as though in a nightmare, until, throwing down his blank book, the officer pronounced it "All right!" Strange to say, I experienced no change. I prayed as hard as ever for the boys and our country, and felt no nasty or disagreeable feeling which would have announced the process of turning Yankee.

Then it was that mother commenced. He turned to the mouth of the diminutive cave, and asked if she was ready to take the oath. "I suppose I *have* to, since I belong to you," she replied. "No, madam, you are not obliged; we force no one. Can you state your objections?" "Yes, I have three sons fighting against you, and you have robbed me, beggared me!"

she exclaimed, launching into a speech in which Heaven knows *what* she did not say; there was little she left out, from her despoiled house to her sore hand, both of which she attributed to the at first amiable man, who was rapidly losing all patience. Faint with hunger, dizzy with sleeplessness, she had wrought on her own feelings until her nerves were beyond control. She was determined to carry it out, and crying and sobbing went through with it.

I neither spoke nor moved. . . . The officer walked off angrily and sent for a guard to have mother taken before General Bowens. Once through her speech, mother yielded to the entreaties of the ladies and professed herself ready to take the oath, since she was obliged to. "Madam, I did not invite you to come," said the polite officer, who refused to administer the oath; and putting several soldiers on board, ordered them to keep all on board until one could report to General Bowens. Mother retired to the cabin, while we still kept our seats above.

Oh, that monotonous, never-ending canal! We thought it would go on forever. At last we came to the basin in the centre of the city. Here was a position for ladies! Sitting like Irish emigrants on their earthly possessions, and coming in a schooner to New Orleans, which a year ago would have filled us with horror. Again the landing was reached, and again we were boarded by officers. I don't know how they knew of the difficulty mother had made, but they certainly did, and ordered that none should leave until the General's will was made known.

Mrs. Bull and Mrs. Ivy, after a long delay and many representations, at last prepared to leave. I was sitting in the spot I had occupied ever since before daylight, with nothing to support me above my hips. All of us had fasted since an early and light supper the night before; none had slept. I was growing so weak from these three causes, and the burning sun (for it was now twelve), that I could hardly speak when they came to tell me good-bye. Alarmed at my appearance, Mrs. Bull entreated the officer to allow me to leave the boat. No, he said; it was impossible; we should remain on board until General Bowens could come. We may get an answer in half an hour, or we may not get it for some time; and there we must stay until it came. "But this young lady has been ill for months; she is perfectly exhausted, and will faint if she is not removed immediately," pleaded Mrs. Bull. She did not know my powers of control. Faint! I would have expired silently first! The officer said those were his orders; I could not leave. "Do you think you are performing your duty as a gentleman and a Christian? This young lady has obtained her pass already, without the slightest difficulty," she persisted. Still he said he was acting according to orders. Not to be baffled, she begged that she might be allowed to take me to Brother, telling him who he was, while our trunk, Miriam, Tiche, and mother would remain as hostages. Then he gave a reluctant consent on condition I left my number, so he could go after me when I was wanted.

I don't know what good came of the consent, for there I was to remain until something, I don't know what, happened. I only know I was growing deathly sick and faint, and could hardly hold myself up, when some time after Mrs. Bull and Mrs. Ivy left (under the impression that I was to go immediately), a gentleman in citizen's clothes came to me and said he had obtained permission for me to wait General Bowens's orders in his office, a few steps from the schooner. Thankful for so much, I accepted his arm and slowly dragged myself along to the first shelter I had seen that day. By some wonderful condescension Miriam and mother were allowed to follow; and with the guard at the door, we waited there for half an hour more until our sentence could be received.

Miriam had written a line to Brother as soon as possible, telling him of the situation, and while we were waiting in this office, I half dead with fatigue, a carriage dashed up to the door, and out of it stepped Brother. I felt that all our troubles were over then. He looked so glad to see us that it seemed a pity to tell the disagreeable story that yet remained to be told. But once heard, he made all go right in a few moments. He got into the carriage with mother, to take her to General Bowens, while we got into another to come to the house. I saw no more of the guard or officer.

When we arrived, Sister was too astonished to speak. She did not believe we would come when it was ordered that all should take the oath on entering. If we had only realized it I don't think we would, either.

In half an hour mother got back. Supported by Brother's presence, she had managed to hold up her right hand and say "Yes" to the oath — which was more than any of us had done.

. . . .

Brother found an officer at the door who had been ordered (before he took mother to the General) to arrest her and confine her in the Custom-House. I suppose Miriam and I would have shared the imprisonment with her. But Brother has a way of making all these things right; and the man was sent back without accomplishing his mission.

Sunday, April 26th.

I am getting well! Bless the Lord, O my soul! Life, health, and happiness dawn on my trembling view again! . . . Dr. Stone came to see me a few hours after I arrived; two days after, he called again; this morning I walked out to meet him when he was announced, and he asked me how my sister was. When I told him I was myself, "God bless my soul! You don't say so!" he exclaimed, evidently astonished at the resurrection.

Thursday, April 30th.

Was not the recollection of this day bitter enough to me already? I did not think it could be more so.

Yet behold me crying as I have not cried for many and many a day. Not for Harry; I dare not cry for him. I feel a deathlike quiet when I think of him; a fear that even a deep-drawn breath would wake him in his grave. And as dearly as I love you, O Hal, I don't want you in this dreary world again. . . .

Talk of the Revocation of the Edict of Nantes! Talk of Louis XIV! Of — pshaw! my head is in such a whirl that history gets all mixed up, and all parallels seem weak and moderate in comparison to this infamous outrage. To-day, thousands of families, from the most respectable down to the least, all who have had the firmness to register themselves enemies to the United States, are ordered to leave the city before the fifteenth of May. Think of the thousands, perfectly destitute, who can hardly afford to buy their daily bread even here, sent to the Confederacy, where it is neither to be earned nor bought, without money, friends, or a home. Hundreds have comfortable homes here, which will be confiscated to enrich those who drive them out. "It is an ill wind that blows no one good." Such dismal faces as one meets everywhere! Each looks heartbroken. Homeless, friendless, beggars, is written in every eye. Brother's face is too unhappy to make it pleasant to look at him. True, he is safe; but hundreds of his friends are going forth destitute, leaving happy homes behind, not knowing where the crust of bread for famishing children is to come from to-morrow. He went to General Bowens and asked if it were possible that women and children were included in the order. Yes, he said; they should all go, and go in the Confederacy. They should not be allowed to go elsewhere. Penned up like sheep to starve! That's the idea! With the addition of forty thousand mouths to feed, they think they can invoke famine to their aid, seeing that their negro brothers don't help them much in the task of subjugating us.

. . . .

Don't care who knows I smuggled in a dozen letters! Wish I had had more!

June 9th, Tuesday.

My dear Brother, who is always seeking to make somebody happy, arranged a dinner-party at the lake for us Saturday. There was quite a number of us, as, besides ourselves and the five children, we had Mrs. Price and her children, Mrs. Bull, and three nurses. . . . There are no Southern young men left in town, and those who remain would hardly be received with civility by Miriam and myself. Of the Yankees, Brother has so much consideration for us that he has never invited one to his house since we have been here, though he has many friends among them who visited here before our arrival. Such delicacy of feeling we fully appreciate, knowing how very few men of such a hospitable nature would be capable of such a sacrifice. Thinking we need company, Brother frequently invites what he calls "a safe old Secessionist" (an old bachelor of fifty-three who was wounded at Shiloh) to dine with us; thinking it a fair compromise between the stay-at-home youth and Yankees, neither of whom this extremely young man could be confounded with.

Sunday, June 14th.

The excitement about Port Hudson and Vicksburg is intense. When I heard on Friday that the last attack was being made on the former place, I took to my prayers with a delirium of fervor. If I was a man, if I had the blessed privilege of fighting, I would be on the breastworks, or perchance on the water batteries under Colonel Steadman's command. But as I was unfortunately born a woman, I stay home and pray with heart and soul. That is all I can do; but I do it with a will. In my excitement, I was wishing that I was a Catholic, that I might make a vow for the preservation of Port Hudson, when a brilliant idea struck me. It was this: though vows are peculiar to Catholics, mosquitoes are common to all sects. From that arose this heroic scheme: I said, "Hear me, Miriam, thou who knowest I have slept undisturbed but three nights out of seventeen, four hours out of each of the other fourteen having been spent in destroying my insatiable foe. Thou seest that nightly vigils are torturing me pale and weak, thou knowest what unspeakable affection I have for the youth yclept by the ancients Morpheus. Yet listen to my vow: If Port Hudson holds out, if our dear people are victorious, I offer up myself on the altar of my country to mosquitoes, and never again will I murmur at their depredations and voracity."

Talk of pilgrimages, and the ordinary vow of wearing only the Virgin's colors (the most becoming in the world); there never was one of greater heroism or more sublime self-sacrifice than this. And as if to prove my sincerity, they have been worse than ever these last two nights. But as yet I have not murmured; for the Yankees, who swore to enter Port Hudson before last Monday night, have not yet fulfilled their promise, and we hold it still. *Vivent* vows and mosquitoes, and forever may our flag wave over the entrenchments! We will conquer yet, with God's blessing!

A week or ten days ago came a letter from Lydia, who is placed within the lines by this recent raid. She writes that the sugar-house and quarters have been seized for Yankee hospitals, that they have been robbed of their clothing, and that they are in pursuit of the General, who I pray Heaven may escape them. She wrote for clothing, provisions, and a servant, and after we had procured them all, and were ready to send them, we discovered that they would not be allowed to pass; so I hardly know what the poor child will do unless she accepts Brother's invitation to come down to him immediately, if she thinks it right.

June 17th.

I must write something somewhere, I don't care if dinner is ready, and Brother's "safe old Secesh" downstairs! Lydia has another boy! Letter has just come, and I am demented about my new godchild! There now! feel better!

One more word — it shall be called "Howell." Dear, blessed little baby! how I shall love it!

Sunday, June 21st.

How about that oath of allegiance? is what I frequently ask myself, and always an uneasy qualm of conscience troubles me. Guilty or not guilty of perjury? According to the law of God in the abstract, and of nations, Yes; according to my conscience, Jeff Davis, and the peculiar position I was placed in, No. Which is it? Had I had any idea that such a pledge would be exacted, would I have been willing to come? Never! The thought would have horrified me. The reality was never placed before me until we reached Bonfouca. There I was terrified at the prospect; but seeing how impossible it would be to go back, I placed all my hopes in some miracle that was to intervene to prevent such a crime, and confidently believed my ill health or something else would save me, while all the rest of the party declared they would think it nothing, and take forty oaths a day, if necessary. A forced oath, all men agree, is not binding. The Yankees lay particular stress on this being voluntary, and insist that no one is solicited to take it except of their own free will. Yet look at the scene that followed, when mother showed herself unwilling! Think of being ordered to the Custom-House as a prisoner for saying she supposed she would *have* to! *That's* liberty! that is free will! It is entirely optional; you have only to take it quietly or go to jail.

That is freedom enough, certainly! There was not even that choice left to me. I told the officer who took down my name that I was unwilling to take the oath, and asked if there was no escaping it. "None whatever" was his reply "You have it to do, and there is no getting out of it." His rude tone frightened me into half-crying; but for all that, as he said, I had it to do. If perjury it is, which will God punish: me, who was unwilling to commit the crime, or the man who forced me to it?

Friday, June 26th.

O praise the Lord, O my soul! Here is good news enough to make me happy for a month! Brother is so good about that! Every time he hears good news on our side, he tells it just as though it was on his side, instead of on ours; while all bad news for us he carefully avoids mentioning, unless we question him. So to-day he brought in a budget for us.

Lee has crossed the Potomac on his way to Washington with one hundred and sixty thousand men. Gibbes and George are with him. Magruder is marching on Fort Jackson, to attack it in the rear. One or two of our English ironclads are reported at the mouth of the river, and Farragut has gone down to capture them. O Jimmy! Jimmy! suppose he should be on one of them? We don't know the name of his ship, and it makes us so anxious for him, during these months that we have heard nothing of his whereabouts.

It is so delightful to see these frightened Yankees! One has only to walk downtown to be satisfied of the alarm that reigns. Yesterday came the tidings of the capture of Brashere City by our troops, and that a brigade was fifteen miles above here, coming down to the city. Men congregated at corners whispering cautiously. These were evidently Confederates who had taken the oath. Solitary Yankees straggled along with the most lugubrious faces, troubling no one. We walked down to Blineau's with Mrs. Price, and over our ice-cream she introduced her husband, who is a true blue Union man, though she, like ourselves, is a rank Rebel. Mr. Price, on the eve of making an immense fortune, was perfectly disconsolate at the news. Every one was to be ruined; starvation would follow if the Confederates entered; there was never a more dismal, unhappy creature. Enchanted at the news, I naturally asked if it were reliable. "Perfectly! Why, to prove how true, standing at the door of this salon five minutes ago, I saw two young ladies pass with Confederate flags, which they flirted in the face of some Federal officers, unrebuked!" Verily, thought I, something is about to happen! Two days ago the girls who were "unrebuked" this evening would have found themselves in jail instead.

July 10th.

Shall I cry, faint, scream, or go off in hysterics? Tell me which, quickly; for to doubt this news is fine and imprisonment, and if I really believe it I would certainly give way to my feelings and commit some vagaries of the kind. My resolution is formed! I will do neither; I won't gratify the Yankees so much. I have been banging at the piano until my fingers are weary, and singing "The Secret through Life to be Happy" until my voice is cracked; I'll stand on my head if necessary, to prove my indifference; but I'll never believe this is true until it is confirmed by stronger authority.

Day before yesterday came tidings that Vicksburg had fallen on the 4th inst. The "Era" poured out extras, and sundry little popguns fizzled out salutes. All who doubted the truth of the report and were brave enough to say so were fined or imprisoned; it has become a penal offense to doubt what the "Era" says; so quite a number of arrests were made. This morning it was followed up by the announcement of the capture of Port Hudson. The guns are pealing for true, and the Yankees at headquarters may be seen skipping like lambs, for very joy. And I still disbelieve! Skeptic! The first thing I know that "Era" man will be coming here to convert me! But I don't, can't, won't believe it! *If* it is true, — but I find consolation in this faith: it is either true, or not true, — if it is true, it is all for the best, and if it is *not* true, it is better still. Whichever it is, is for some wise purpose; so it does not matter, so we wait, pray, and believe.

5 o'clock, P.M.

I don't believe it? What am I crying about then? It seems so hard! How the mighty are fallen! Port Hudson gone! Brother believes it. That is enough for me. God bless him! I cry hourly. He is so good and considerate. He told me, "Name your friends, and what can be done for them shall be attended to. The prisoners will be sent here. Maybe I cannot do much; but food and clothing you shall have in abundance for them when they arrive." God bless him for his kindness!

O dear, noble men! I am afraid to meet them; I should do something foolish; best take my cry out in private now. May the Lord look down in pity on us! Port Hudson does not matter so much; but these brave, noble creatures! The "Era" says they had devoured their last mule before they surrendered.

Saturday, July 10th, 10 o'clock P.M.

I preach patience; but how about practice? I am exasperated! there is the simple fact. And is it not enough? What a scene I have just witnessed! A motley crew of thousands of low people of all colors parading the streets with flags, torches, music, and all other accompaniments, shouting, screaming, exulting over the fall of Port Hudson and Vicksburg. The "Era" will call it an enthusiastic demonstration of the loyal citizens of the city; we who saw it from upper balconies know of what rank these "citizens" were. We saw crowds of soldiers mixed up with the lowest rabble in the town, workingmen in dirty clothes, newsboys, ragged children, negroes, and even *women* walking in the procession, while swarms of negroes and low white women elbowed each other in a dense mass on the pavement. To see such creatures exulting over our misfortune was enough to make one scream with rage. One of their dozen transparencies was inscribed with "A dead Confederacy." Fools! The flames are smouldering! They will burst out presently and consume you! More than half, much more, were negroes. As they passed here they raised a yell of "Down with the rebels!" that made us gnash our teeth in silence. The Devil possessed me. "O Miriam, help me pray the dear Lord that their flag may burn!" I whispered as the torches danced around it. And we did pray earnestly—so earnestly that Miriam's eyes were tightly screwed up; but it must have been a wicked prayer, for it was not answered.

Dr. S—— has out a magnificent display of black cotton grammatically inscribed with "Port Hudson and Vicksburg *is* ours," garnished with a luminous row of tapers, and, drunk on two bits' worth of lager beer, he has been shrieking out all Union songs he can think of with his horrid children until my tympanum is perfectly cracked. Miriam wants to offer him an extra bottle of lager for the two places of which he claims the monopoly. He would sell his creed for less. Miriam is dying to ask him what he has done with the Confederate uniform he sported before the Yankees came. His son says they are all Union men over there, and will "lemonate" (illuminate) to-night. A starving seamstress opposite has stuck six tallow candles in her window; better put them in her stomach!

And I won't believe Vicksburg has surrendered! Port Hudson I am sure has fallen. Alas, for all hopes of serving the brave creatures! the rumor is that they have been released on parole. Happily for them; but if it *must* go, what a blessed privilege it would have been to aid or comfort them!

Wednesday, July 15th.

It is but too true; both have fallen. All Port Hudson privates have been paroled, and the officers sent here for exchange. Aye! Aye! I know some privates I would rather see than the officers! As yet, only ten that we know have arrived. All are confined in the Custom-House. Last evening crowds surrounded the place. We did something dreadful, Ada Peirce, Miriam, and I. We went down to the confectionery; and unable to resist the temptation, made a détour by the Custom-House in hope of seeing one of our poor dear half-starved mule and rat fed defenders. The crowd had passed away then; but what was our horror when we emerged from the river side of the building and turned into Canal, to find the whole front of the pavement lined with Yankees! Our folly struck us so forcibly that we were almost paralyzed with fear. However, that did not prevent us from endeavoring to hurry past, though I felt as though walking in a nightmare. Ada was brave enough to look up at a window where several of our prisoners were standing, and kept urging us to do likewise. "Look! He knows you, Sarah! He has called another to see you! They both recognize you! Oh, look, please, and tell me who they are! They are watching you still!" she would exclaim. But if my own dear brother stood there, I could not have raised my eyes; we only hurried on faster, with a hundred Yankees eyes fixed on our flying steps.

My friend Colonel Steadman was one of the commissioners for arranging the terms of the capitulation, I see. He has not yet arrived.

. . . .

Dreadful news has come of the defeat of Lee at Gettysburg. Think I believe it all? He may have been defeated; but not one of these reports of total overthrow and rout do I credit. Yankees jubilant, Southerners dismal. Brother, with principles on one side and brothers on the other, is correspondingly distracted.

Saturday, July 18th.

It may be wrong; I feel very contrite; but still I cannot help thinking it is an error on the right side. It began by Miriam sending Mr. Conn a box of cigars when she was on Canal the other day, with a note saying we would be delighted to assist him in any way. Poor creature! He wrote an answer which breathed desolation and humility, under his present situation, in every line. The cigars, an unexpected kindness, had touched a tender cord evidently. He said he had no friends, and would be grateful for our assistance.

But before his answer arrived, yesterday morning I took it into my head that Colonel Steadman was also at the Custom-House, though his arrival had not been announced, the Yankees declining to publish any more names to avoid the excitement that follows. So Miriam and I prepared a lunch of chicken, soup, wine, preserves, sardines, and cakes, to send to him. And, fool-like, I sent a note with it. It only contained the same offer of assistance; and I would not object to the town crier's reading it; but it upset Brother's ideas of decorum completely. He said nothing to Miriam's, because that was first offense; but yesterday he met Edmond, who was carrying the basket, and he could not stand the sight of another note. I wish he had read it! But he said he would not assume such a right. So he came home very much annoyed, and spoke to Miriam about it. Fortunately for my peace of mind, I was swimming in the bathtub in blissful unconsciousness, else I should have drowned myself. He said, "I want you both to understand that you shall have everything you want for the prisoners. Subscribe any sum of money, purchase any quantity of clothing, send all the food you please, but, for God's sake, don't write to them! In such a place every man knows the other has received a letter, and none know what it contains. I cannot have my sisters' names in everybody's mouth. Never do it again!" All as kind and as considerate for us as ever, and a necessary caution; I love him the better for it; but I was dismayed for having rendered the reproof necessary. For three hours I made the most hideous faces at myself and groaned aloud over Brother's displeasure. He is so good that I would rather bite my tongue off than give him a moment's pain. Just now I went to him, unable to keep silence any longer, and told him how distressed I was to have displeased him about that note. "Don't think any more about it, only don't do it again, dear," was his answer. I was so grateful to him for his gentleness that I was almost hurried into a story. I began, "It is the first time —" when I caught myself and said boldly, "No, it is not. Colonel Steadman has written to me before, and I have replied. But I promise to you it shall not occur again if I can avoid it." He was satisfied with the acknowledgment, and I was more than gratified with his kindness. Yet the error *must* have been on the right side!

Colonel Steadman wrote back his thanks by Edmond, with heartfelt gratitude for finding such friends in his adversity, and touching acknowledgments of the acceptable nature of the lunch. His brother and Colonel Lock were wounded, though recovering, and he was anxious to know if I had yet recovered. And that was all, except that he hoped we would come to see him, and his thanks to Brother for his kind message. Brother had sent him word by one of the prisoners that though he was not acquainted with him, yet as his sisters' friend he would be happy to assist him if he needed money or clothing. There was no harm in either note, and though I would not do it again, I am almost glad I let him know he still had friends before Brother asked me not to write.

And as yet we can't see them. A man was bayoneted yesterday for waving to them, even. It only makes us the more eager to see them. We did see some. Walking on Rampart Street with the Peirces yesterday, in front of a splendid private house, we saw sentinels stationed. Upon inquiry we learned that General Gardiner and a dozen others were confined there. Ada and Miriam went wild. If it had not been for dignified Marie, and that model of propriety, Sarah, there is no knowing but what they would have carried the house by storm. We got them by without seeing a gray coat, when they vowed to pass back, declaring that the street was not respectable on the block above. We had to follow. So! there they all stood on the balcony above. We thought we recognized General Gardiner, Major Wilson, Major Spratley, and Mr. Dupré. Miriam was sure she did; but even when I put on a bold face, and tried to look, something kept me from seeing; so I had all the appearance of staring, without deriving the slightest benefit from it. Wonder what makes me such a fool?

Mr. Conn writes that Captain Bradford is wounded, but does not say whether he is here.

Thursday, July 23d.

It is bad policy to keep us from seeing the prisoners; it just sets us wild about them. Put a creature you don't care for in the least, in a situation that commands sympathy, and nine out of ten girls will fall desperately in love. Here are brave, self-sacrificing, noble men who have fought heroically for us, and have been forced to surrender by unpropitious fate, confined in a city peopled by their friends and kindred, and as totally isolated from them as though they inhabited the Dry Tortugas! Ladies are naturally hero-worshipers. We are dying to show these unfortunates that we are as proud of their bravery as though it had led to victory instead of defeat. Banks wills that they remain in privacy. Consequently our vivid imaginations are constantly occupied in depicting their sufferings, privations, heroism, and manifold virtues, until they have almost become as demigods to us. Even horrid little Captain C—— has a share of my sympathy in his misfortune! Fancy what must be my feelings where those I consider as gentlemen are concerned! It is all I can do to avoid a most tender compassion for a very few select ones. Miriam and I are looked on with envy by other young ladies because some twenty or thirty of our acquaintance have already arrived. To know a Port Hudson defender is considered as the greatest distinction one need desire. If they would only let us see the prisoners once to sympathize with, and offer to assist them, we would never care to call on them again until they are liberated. But this is aggravating. Of what benefit is it to send them lunch after lunch, when they seldom receive it? Colonel Steadman and six others, I am sure, did not receive theirs on Sunday. We sent with the baskets a number of cravats and some handkerchiefs I had embroidered for the Colonel.

Brother should forbid those gentlemen writing, too. Already a dozen notes have been received from them, and what can we do? We can't tell them not to. Miriam received a letter from Major Spratley this morning, raving about the kindness of the ladies of New Orleans, full of hope of future successes, and vows to help deliver the noble ladies from the hands of their oppressors, etc. It is a wonder that such a patriotic effusion could be smuggled out. He kindly assures us that not only those of our acquaintance there, but all their brother officers, would be more than happy to see us in their prison. Position of affairs rather reversed since we last met!

BOOK V

NEW ORLEANS, August, 1863.
Friday, 14th.

DOOMED to be bored! To-night Miriam drags me to a *soirée musicale*, and in the midst of my toilet, I sit down with bare shoulders to scratch a dozen lines in my new treasure which has been by me for three days, untouched. I don't know what tempts me to do it except perversity; for I have nothing to say.

I was in hopes that I would never have occasion to refer to the disagreeable subject that occupied the last pages of my old journal, but the hope proves fallacious, and wherever I turn, the same subject is renewed. So there is no longer any reason in waiting until all mention can be avoided. Yesterday a little, sly, snaky creature asked me if I knew "the Hero of Port Hudson." "Yes," I said briefly. "Unmistakable! I see it in your face!" she remarked. "See what?" "That you betray yourself. Do you know that every one believes that you are engaged to him?" In surprise I said no; such a thing had never been mentioned before me until then. "Well! they say so, and add, too, that you are to be married as soon as the war is over." "'They' are paying me an undeserved compliment," I returned. Where could such a report have originated? Not certainly from him, and not, most assuredly, from me. Where does

Dame rumor spring from? He is a stranger here, and I have never mentioned his name except to the Peirces, who would no more report such a thing than I would myself. I won't mind it if it does not reach his ears; but what assurance have I that it will not? That would be unpleasant! Why can't "they say" let everybody settle their own affairs?

Here comes Miriam after me! What a bore! What a bore! And she looks as though it was a pleasure to go out! How I hate it!

Glancing up the page, the date strikes my eye. What tempted me to begin it Friday? My dear Ada would shiver and declare the blank pages were reserved for some very painful, awful, uncomfortable record, or that "something" would happen before the end of it. Nothing very exciting can happen, except the restoration of peace; and to bring that about, I would make a vow to write only on Fridays.

Sunday, 16th.

Coming out of church this morning with Miriam, a young lady ran up with an important air, as though about to create a sensation. "I have a message for you both," she said, fixing her eyes on mine as though she sought something in them. "I visit the prisoners frequently, you know, and day before yesterday Captain Steadman requested me to beg you to call, that he will not take a refusal, but entreated you to come, if it were only once." The fates must be against me; I had almost forgotten his existence, and having received the same message frequently from another, I thoughtlessly said, "You mean *Colonel*, do you not?" Fortunately Miriam asked the same question at the instant that I was beginning to believe I had done something very foolish. The lady looked at me with her calm, scrutinizing, disagreeable smile — a smile that had all the unpleasant insinuations eyes and lips can convey, a smile that looked like "I have your secret — you can't deceive *me*" — and said with her piercing gaze, "No, *not* the Colonel. He was very ill that day (did you know it?) and could not see us. This was *really* the Captain." "He is very kind," I stammered, and suggested to Miriam that we had better pass on. The lady was still eyeing me inquisitively. Decidedly, this is unpleasant to have the reputation of being engaged to a man that every girl is crazy to win! If one only cared for him, it would not be so unpleasant; but under the circumstances, — *ah ça!* why don't they make him over to the young lady whose father openly avows he would be charmed to have him for a son-in-law? This report has cost me more than one impertinent stare. The young ladies think it a very enviable position. Let some of them usurp it, then!

So the young lady, not having finished her examination, proposed to accompany us part of the way. As a recompense, we were regaled with charming little anecdotes about herself, and her visits. How she had sent a delightful little custard to the Colonel (here was a side glance at my demure face) and had carried an autographic album in her last visit, and had insisted on their inscribing their names, and writing a verse or so. "How interesting!" was my mental comment. "Can a man respect a woman who thrusts him her album, begging for a compliment the first time they meet? What fools they must think us, if they take such as these for specimens of the genus!"

Did we know Captain Lanier? Know him, no! but how vividly his face comes before me when I look back to that grand smash-up at Port Hudson, when his face was the last I saw before being thrown, and the first I recognized when I roused myself from my stupor and found myself in the arms of the young Alabamian. At the sound of his name, I fairly saw the last ray of sunset flashing over his handsome face, as I saw it then. No, I did not know him. He had spoken to me, begging to be allowed to hold me, and I had answered, entreating him not to touch me, and that was all I knew of him; but she did not wait for the reply. She hurried on to say that she had sent him a bouquet, with a piece of poetry, and that he had been heard to exclaim, "How beautiful!" on reading it. "And do you know," she continued, with an air that was meant to be charmingly naïf, but which was not very successful, as naïveté at twenty-nine is rather flat, "I am *so* much afraid he thinks it original! I forgot to put quotation marks, and it would be *so* funny in him to make the mistake! For you know I have not much of the — of that sort of thing about me — I am not a poet — poetess, author, you know." Said Miriam in her blandest tone, without a touch of sarcasm in her voice, "Oh, if he has ever seen you, the mistake is natural!" If I had spoken, my voice would have carried a sting in it. So I waited until I could calmly say, "You know him well, of course." "No, I never saw him before!" she answered with a new outburst of naïveté.

Monday, August 24th.

A letter from Captain Bradford to Miriam. My poor Adonis, that I used to ridicule so unmercifully, what misfortunes have befallen him! He writes that during the siege at Port Hudson he had the top of his ear shot off (wonder if he lost any of that beautiful golden fleece yclept his hair?), and had the cap of his knee removed by a shell, besides a third wound he does not specify. Fortunately he is with kind friends. And he gives news of Lydia, most acceptable since such a time has elapsed since we heard from her. . . . He says, "Tell Miss Sarah that the last I saw of John, he was crossing the Mississippi in a skiff, his parole in his pocket, his sweet little sister by his side," (O you wretch! at it again!) "and Somebody else in his heart." How considerate to volunteer the last statement! Then followed half a page of commendation for his bravery, daring, and skill during the siege (the only kind word he ever spoke of him, I dare say), all looking as though I was to take it as an especial compliment to myself, and was expected to look foolish, blush, and say "Thanky" for it. As though I care!

Monday night.

I consider myself outrageously imposed upon! I am so indignant that I have spent a whole evening making faces at myself. "Please, Miss Sarah, look natural!" William petitions. "I never saw you look cross before." Good reason! I never had more cause! However, I stop in the midst of a hideous grimace, and join in a game of hide the switch with the children to forget my annoyance.

Of course a woman is at the bottom of it. Last night while Ada and Marie were here, a young lady whose name I decline to reveal for the sake of the sex, stopped at the door with an English officer, and asked to see me in the entry. I had met her once before. Remember this, for that is the chief cause of my anger. Of course they were invited in; but she declined, saying she had but a moment, and had a message to deliver to me alone, so led me apart. "Of course you know who it is from?" she began. I told a deliberate falsehood, and said no, though I guessed instantly. She told me the name then. She had visited the prison the day before, and there had met the individual whose name, joined to mine, has given me more trouble and annoyance during the last few months than it would be possible to mention. "And our entire conversation was about you," she said, as though to flatter my vanity immensely. He told her then that he had written repeatedly to me, without receiving an answer, and at last had written again, in which he had used some expressions which he feared had offended my reserved disposition. Something had made me angry, for without returning letter or message to say I was not displeased, I had maintained a resolute silence, which had given him more pain and uneasiness than he could say. That during all this time he had had no opportunity of explaining it to me, and that now he begged her to tell me that he would not offend me for worlds — that he admired me more than any one he had ever met, that he could not help saying what he did, but was distressed at offending me, etc. The longest explanation! And she was directed to beg me to explain my silence, and let him know if I was really offended, and also leave no entreaty or argument untried to induce me to visit the prison; he *must* see me.

As to visiting the prison, I told her that was impossible. (O how glad I am that I never did!) But as to the letters, told her "to assure him that I had not thought of them in that light, and had passed over the expressions he referred to as idle words it would be ridiculous to take offense at; and that my only reason for persevering in this silence had been that Brother disapproved of my writing to gentlemen, and I had promised that I would not write to him. That I had feared he would misconstrue my silence, and had wished to explain it to him, but I had no means of doing so except by breaking my promise; and so had preferred leaving all explanation to time, and some future opportunity."

"But you did not mean to pain him, did you?" the dear little creature coaxingly lisped, standing on tiptoe to kiss me as she spoke. I assured her that I had not. "He has been dangerously ill," she continued, apologizingly, "and sickness has made him more morbid and more unhappy about it than he would otherwise have been. It has distressed him a great deal."

I felt awkwardly. How was it that this girl, meeting him for the first and only time in her life, had contrived to learn so much that she had no right to know, and appeared here as mediator between two who were strangers to her, so far usurping a place she was not entitled to, as to apologize to *me* for his sensitiveness, and to entreat me to tell him he had not forfeited my esteem, as though *she* was his most intimate friend, and I a passing acquaintance? Failing to comprehend it, I deferred it to a leisure moment to think over, and in the mean time exerted myself to be affable.

I can't say half she spoke of, but as she was going she said, "Then will you give me permission to say as many sweet things for you as I can think of? I'm going there to-morrow." I told her I would be afraid to give her *carte blanche* on such a subject; but that she would really oblige me by explaining about the letters. She promised, and after another kiss, and a few whispered words, left me.

Maybe she exaggerated, though! Uncharitable as the supposition was, it was a consolation. I was unwilling to believe that any one who professed to esteem me would make me the subject of conversation with a stranger—and such a conversation! So my comfort was only in hoping that she had related a combination of truth and fiction, and that he had not been guilty of such folly.

Presently it grew clearer to me. I must be growing in wickedness, to fathom that of others, I who so short a time ago disbelieved in the very existence of such a thing. I remembered having heard that the young lady and her family were extremely anxious to form his acquaintance, and that her cousin had coolly informed Ada that she had selected him among all others, and meant to have him for a "beau" as soon as she could be introduced to him; I remembered that the young lady herself had been very anxious to discover whether the reputation common report had given me had any foundation.

As soon as we were alone, I told mother of our conversation in the entry, and said, "And now I am certain that this girl has made use of my name to become acquainted with him."

Thursday, 10th September.

O my prophetic soul! part of your forebodings are already verified! And in what an unpleasant way!

Day before yesterday an English officer, not the one who came here, but one totally unknown to me, said at Mrs. Peirce's he was going to visit the Confederate prisoners. He was asked if he knew any. Slightly, he said; but he was going this time by request; he had any quantity of messages to deliver to Colonel —— from Miss Sarah Morgan. "How can that be possible, since you are not acquainted with her?" Ada demanded. He had the impudence to say that the young lady I have already mentioned had requested him to deliver them for her, since she found it impossible. Fortunately for me, I have two friends left. Feeling the indelicacy of the thing, and knowing that there must be some mistake that might lead to unpleasant consequences, Ada and Marie, my good angels, insisted on hearing the messages. At first he refused, saying that they were entrusted to him confidentially; but being assured that they were really intimate with me, whereas the other was a perfect stranger, and that I would certainly not object to their hearing what I could tell a gentleman, he yielded, fortunately for my peace of mind, and told all.

I can't repeat it. I was too horrified to hear all, when they told me. What struck me as being most shocking was my distorted explanation about the letters. It now set forth that I was not allowed to write myself, but would be happy to have him write to me; then there was an earnest assurance that my *feelings* toward him had not changed in the least —

Here I sprang from my chair and rushed to the window for a breath of air, wringing my hands in speechless distress. How a word more or less, an idea omitted or added, a syllable misplaced, can transform a whole sentence, and make what was before harmless, really shocking!

And if it had not been for Ada and Marie —! Blessed angels! they entreated him not to deliver any of his messages, insisting that there must be a mistake, that if he knew me he would understand that it was impossible for me to have sent such a message by a stranger. And although at first he declared he felt obliged to discharge the task imposed on him, they finally succeeded in persuading him to relinquish the errand, promising to be responsible for the consequences.

"Ah me!" I gasped last night, making frantic grimaces in the dark, and pinching myself in disgust, "why can't they let me alone? . . . O women — women! I wish he could marry all of you, so you would let me alone! Take him, please; but *en grâce* don't disgrace me in the excitement of the race!"

Friday, 25th.

Write me down a witch, a prophetess, or what you will. I am certainly something! All has come to pass on that very disagreeable subject very much as I feared. Perhaps no one in my position would speak freely on the subject; for that very reason I shall not hesitate to discuss it.

Know, then, that this morning, He went North along with many other Confederate prisoners, to be exchanged. And he left — he who has written so incessantly and so imploringly for me to visit his prison — he left without seeing me. *Bon!* Wonder what happened?

. . . .

Evening.

I have learned more. He has not yet left; part of the mystery is unraveled, only I have neither patience nor desire to seek for more. These women —! Hush! to slander is too much like them; be yourself.

My sweet little lisper informed a select circle of friends the other night, when questioned, that the individual had not called on me, and, what was more, would not do so. "Pray, how do you happen to be so intimately acquainted with the affairs of two who are strangers to you?" asked a lady present. She declined saying how she had obtained her information, only asserting that it was so. "In fact, you cannot expect *any* Confederate *gentleman* to call at the house of Judge Morgan, a professed Unionist," she continued. So that is the story she told to keep him from seeing me. She has told him that we had turned Yankees! All her arts would not grieve me as much as one word against Brother. My wrongs I can forget; but one word of contempt for Brother I *never* forgive! White with passion I said to my informant, "Will you inform the young lady that her visit will never be returned, that she is requested not to repeat hers, and that I decline knowing any one who dares cast the slightest reflection on the name of one who has been both father and brother to me!" This evening I was at a house where she was announced. Miriam and I bade our hostess good-evening and left without speaking to her. Anybody but Brother! No one shall utter his name before me save with respect and regard.

This young woman's father is a Captain in the Yankee navy, and her brother is a Captain in the Yankee army, while three other brothers are in the Confederate. Like herself, I have three brothers fighting for the South; unlike her, the only brother who avows himself a Unionist has too much regard for his family to take up arms against his own flesh and blood.

Tuesday, October 6th.

I hope this will be the last occasion on which I shall refer to the topic to which this unfortunate book seems to have been devoted. But it gives me a grim pleasure to add a link to the broken chain of the curious story, now and then. Maybe some day the missing links will be supplied me, and then I can read the little humdrum romance of What might have been, or What I'm glad never was, as easily as Marie tells her rosary.

Well! the prisoners have gone at last, to my

unspeakable satisfaction. Day before yesterday they left. Now I can go out as I please, without fear of meeting him face to face. How odd that I should feel like a culprit! But that is in accordance with my usual judgment and consistency. Friday, I had a severe fright. Coming up Camp Street with Ada, after a ramble on Canal, we met two Confederates. Everywhere that morning we had met gray coats, but none that I recognized. Still, without looking, I saw through my eyelids, as it were, two hands timidly touch two gray caps, as though the question "May I?" had not yet been answered. In vain I endeavored to meet their eyes, or give the faintest token of greeting. I was too frightened and embarrassed to speak, and only by a desperate effort succeeded in bending my head in a doubtful bow, that would have disgraced a dairy maid, after we had passed. Then, disgusted with myself, I endeavored to be comforted with the idea that they had perhaps mistaken me for some one else; that having known me at a time when I was unable to walk, they could have no idea of my height and figure, or walk. So I reasoned, turning down a side street. Lo! at a respectable distance they were following! We had occasion to go into a daguerreau salon. While standing in the light, two gray uniforms, watching us from the dark recess at the door, attracted my attention. Pointing them out to Ada, I hurried her past them downstairs to the street. Faster and faster we walked, until at the corner I turned to look.

There they were again, sauntering leisurely along. We turned into another street, mingled in the crowd, and finally lost sight of them. That fright lasted me an hour or two. Whose purse have I stolen, that I am afraid to look these men in the face?

But what has this to do with what I meant to tell? How loosely and disconnectedly my ideas run out with the ink from my pen! I meant to say how sorry I am for my dear little lisper that she failed in her efforts to conquer the "Hero"; and here I have drifted off in a page of trash that does not concern her in the least. Well! she did not succeed, and whatever she told him was told in vain, as far as *she* was concerned. He was not to be caught! What an extraordinary man! Dozens fighting for the preference, and he in real, or pretended ignorance.

I must do him the justice to say he is the most guileless, as well as the most honest of mortals. He told the mother of a rich and pretty daughter what he thought of me; that my superior did not exist on earth, and my equal he had never met. Ha! ha! this pathetic story makes me laugh in spite of myself. Is it excess of innocence, or just a rôle he adopted? Stop! His idle word is as good as an oath. He could not pretend to what he did not believe. He told her of his earnest and sincere admiration — words! words! hurry on! She asked how it was then —? Here he confessed, with a mixture of pride and penitence, that he had written me letters which absolutely required answers, and to which I had never deigned to reply by even a word. That, mortified beyond measure at my silent contempt, he had tried every means of ascertaining the cause of my coldness, but I had never vouchsafed an answer, but had left him to feel the full force of my harsh treatment without one word of explanation. That when he was paroled, he had hoped that I would see him to tell him wherein he had forfeited my esteem; but I had not invited him to call, and mortified and repulsed as he had been, it was impossible for him to call without my permission. . . . Did my little lisper change the message when the little midshipman told her it had been intercepted because too friendly? I know she met this martyred Lion frequently after that and had many opportunities of telling him the simple truth, but she evidently *did not.*

He has gone away with sorely wounded feelings, to say nothing more; for that I am sincerely sorry; but I trust to his newly acquired freedom, and his life of danger and excitement, to make him forget the wrongs he believes himself to have suffered at my hands. If it was all to be gone through again (which thank Heaven, I will never be called upon to endure again), I would follow Brother's advice as implicitly then as I did before. He is right, and without seeing, I believe. They tell me of his altered looks, and of his forced, reckless gaiety which, so strangely out of keeping with his natural character, but makes his assumed part more conspicuous. No matter! He will recover! Nothing like a sea voyage for disorders of all kinds. And we will never meet again; that is another consolation.

"Notice: The public are hereby informed through Mrs. ——, Chief Manager of the Theatre of High Tragedy, that Miss Sarah M., having been proved unworthy and incompetent to play the rôle of Ariadne, said part will hereafter be filled by Miss Blank, of Blank Street, who plays it with a fidelity so true to nature that she could hardly be surpassed by the original."

Monday, November 9th.

Another odd link of the old, stale story has come to me, all the way from New York. A friend of mine, who went on the same boat with the prisoners, wrote to her mother to tell her that she had formed the acquaintance of the most charming, fascinating gentleman among them, no other than my *once* friend. Of course, she would have been less than a woman if she had not gossiped when she discovered who he was. So she sends me word that he told her he had been made to believe, as long as he was on parole in New Orleans, that we were all Unionists now, and that Brother would not allow a Confederate to enter the house. (O my little lisper, was I unjust to you?) He told her that I had been very kind to him when he was in prison, and he would have forgotten the rest and gladly have called to thank me in person for the kindness he so gratefully remembered, if I alone had been concerned; but he felt he could not force himself unasked into my brother's house. . . .

She told him how false it was.

Sunday, November 22d.

A report has just reached us that my poor dear Gibbes has been taken prisoner along with the rest of Hayes's brigade.

November 26th.

Yes! It is so, if his own handwriting is any proof. Mr. Appleton has just sent Brother a letter he had received from Gibbes, asking him to let Brother know he was a prisoner, and we have heard, through some one else, that he had been sent to Sandusky. Brother has applied to have him paroled and sent here, or even imprisoned here, if he cannot be paroled.

Monday, November 30th.

Our distress about Gibbes has been somewhat relieved by good news from Jimmy. The jolliest sailor letter from him came this morning, dated only the 4th instant from Cherbourg, detailing his cruise on the Georgia from leaving England, to Bahia, Trinidad, Cape of Good Hope, to France again. Such a bright, dashing letter! We laughed extravagantly over it when he told how they readily evaded the Vanderbilt, knowing she would knock them into "pie"; how he and the French Captain quarreled when he ordered him to show his papers, and how he did not know French abuse enough to enter into competition with him, so went back a first and second time to Maury when the man would not let him come aboard, whereupon Maury brought the ship to with two or three shots and Jimmy made a third attempt, and forced the Frenchman to show his papers. He tells it in such a matter-of-fact way! No extravagance, no idea of having been in a dangerous situation, he a boy of eighteen, on a French ship in spite of the Captain's rage. What a jolly life it must be! Now dashing in storms and danger, now floating in sunshine and fun! Wish I was a midshipman! Then how he changes, in describing the prize with an assorted cargo that they took, which contained all things from a needle to pianos, from the reckless spurt in which he speaks of the plundering, to where he tells of how the Captain, having died several days before, was brought on the Georgia while Maury read the service over the body and consigned it to the deep by the flames of the dead man's own vessel. What noble, tender, manly hearts it shows, those rough seamen stopping in their work of destruction to perform the last rites over their dead enemy. One can fancy their bare heads and sunburned faces standing in solemn silence around the poor dead man when he dropped into his immense grave. God bless the "pirates"!

Thursday night, December 31st, 1863.

The last of eighteen sixty-three is passing away as I write. . . . Every New Year since I was in my teens, I have sought a quiet spot where I could whisper to myself Tennyson's "Death of the Old Year," and even this bitter cold night I steal into my freezing, fireless little room, *en robe de nuit*, to keep up my old habit while the others sleep. . . .

> "Old year, you shall not die;
> We did so laugh and cry with you,
> I 've half a mind to die with you,
> Old year, if you must die."

No! Go and welcome! Bring Peace and brighter days, O dawning New Year. Die, faster and faster, Old One; I count your remaining moments with almost savage glee.

Wednesday, February 3d.

Last night we were thrown into the most violent state of commotion by the unexpected entrance of Captain Bradford. He has been brought here a prisoner, from Asphodel, where he has been ever since the surrender of Port Hudson, and taking advantage of his tri-weekly parole, his first visit was naturally here, as he has no other friends.

Poor creature, how he must have suffered! The first glance at his altered face where suffering and passion have both left their traces unmistakably since we last met, and the mere sight of his poor lame leg, filled my heart with compassion.

. . . .

How he hates Mr. Halsey! I could not forego the pleasure of provoking him into a discussion about him, knowing how they hated each other. He would not say anything against him; understand, that as a gentleman and a companion, Mr. Halsey was his warmest and best friend; there was no one he admired more; but he must say that as a soldier, he was the worst he had ever seen — not that he was not as brave and gallant a man as ever lived, but he neglected his duties most shamefully while visiting Linwood so constantly, eluding the sentinels daily as he asked for neither pass nor permission, and consulting only his inclinations instead of his superior officers or his business. And that last night at Linwood, when he absented himself without leave, why could he not have signified to him, his Captain, that he wished to say good-bye, instead of quietly doing as he pleased? When the Colonel sent for a report of the number of men, quantity of forage and ammunition, etc., and it was discovered that John Halsey was absent without leave, with the books locked up and the keys in his pocket — even after this lapse of time, the fire flashed through the ice as the Captain spoke. Sergeant Halsey, I am sorry for you when you reported yourself next day! All the fun that could have been crowded into an evening at Linwood could not have repaid you for the morning's scene. And after all, what was it beyond very empty pleasure, with a great deal of laughter? He could have dispensed with it just as well. Looking back, I congratulate myself on being the only one who did not ask him to stay.

5th.

Not dead! not dead! O my God! Gibbes is *not* dead! Where — O dear God! Another?

Only a few days ago came a letter so cheerful and hopeful —we have waited and prayed so patiently — at my feet lies one from Colonel Steadman saying he is dead. Dead! Suddenly and without a moment's warning summoned to God! No! it cannot be! I am mad! O God, have mercy on us! My poor mother! And Lydia! Lydia! God comfort you! My brain seems afire. Am I mad? Not yet! God would not take him yet! He will come again! Hush, God is good! Not dead! not dead!

O Gibbes, come back to us!

11th.

O God, O God, have mercy on us! George is dead! Both in a week. George, our sole hope — our sole dependence.

March.

Dead! Dead! Both dead! O my brothers! What have we lived for except you? We, who would have so gladly laid down our lives for yours, are left desolate to mourn over all we loved and hoped for, weak and helpless; while you, so strong, noble, and brave, have gone before us without a murmur.

God knows best. But it is hard — O so hard! to give them up. . . .

If we had had any warning or preparation, this would not have been so unspeakably awful. But to shut one's eyes to all dangers and risks, and drown every rising fear with "God will send them back; I will not doubt His mercy," and then suddenly to learn that your faith has been presumption — and God wills that you shall undergo bitter affliction — it is a fearful awakening! What glory have we ever rendered to God that we should expect him to be so merciful to us? Are not all things His, and is not He infinitely more tender and compassionate than we deserve?

We have deceived ourselves wilfully about both. After the first dismay on hearing of Gibbes's capture, we readily listened to the assertions of our friends that Johnson's Island was the healthiest place in the world; that he would be better off, comfortably clothed and under shelter, than exposed to shot and shell, half fed, and lying on the bare ground during Ewell's winter campaign. We were thankful for his safety, knowing Brother would leave nothing undone that could add to his comfort. And besides that, there was the sure hope of his having him paroled. On that hope we lived all winter — now confident that in a little while he would be with us, then again doubting for a while, only to have the hope grow surer afterwards. And so we waited and prayed, never doubting he would come at last. He himself believed it, though striving not to be too hopeful lest he should disappoint us, as well as himself. Yet he wrote cheerfully and bravely to the last. Towards the middle of January, Brother was sure of succeeding, as all the prisoners had been placed under Butler's control. Ah me! How could we be so blind? We were sure he would be with us in a few weeks! I wrote to him that I had prepared his room.

On the 30th of January came his last letter, addressed to me, though meant for Lavinia. It was dated the 12th — the day George died. All his letters pleaded that I would write more frequently — he loved to hear from me; so I had been writing to him every ten days. On the 3d of February I sent my last. Friday the 5th, as I was running through Miriam's room, I saw Brother pass the door, and heard him ask Miriam for mother. The voice, the bowed head, the look of utter despair on his face, struck through me like a knife. "Gibbes! Gibbes!" was my sole thought; but Miriam and I stood motionless looking at each other without a word. "Gibbes is dead," said mother as he stood before her. He did not speak; and then we went in.

We did not ask how, or when. That he was dead was enough for us. But after a while he told us Uncle James had written that he had died at two o'clock on Thursday the 21st. Still we did not know how he had died. Several letters that had been brought remained unopened on the floor. One, Brother opened, hoping to learn something more. It was from Colonel Steadman to Miriam and me, written a few hours after his death, and contained the sad story of our dear brother's last hours.

He had been in Colonel Steadman's ward of the hospital for more than a week, with headache and sore throat, but it was thought nothing; he seemed to improve, and expected to be discharged in a few days. On the 21st he complained that his throat pained him again. After prescribing for him, and talking cheerfully with him for some time, Colonel Steadman left him surrounded by his friends, to attend to his other patients. He had hardly reached his room when some one ran to him saying Captain Morgan was dying. He hurried to his bedside, and found him dead. Captain Steadman, sick in the next bed, and those around him, said he had been talking pleasantly with them, when he sat up to reach his cup of water on the table. As soon as he drank it he seemed to suffocate; and after tossing his arms wildly in the air, and making several fearful efforts to breathe, he died.

. . . .

"Hush, mother, hush," I said when I heard her cries. "We have Brother and George and Jimmy left, and Lydia has lost all!" Heaven pity us! George had gone before — only He in mercy kept the knowledge of it from us for a while longer.

On Thursday the 11th, as we sat talking to mother, striving to make her forget the weary days we had cried through with that fearful sound of "Dead! Dead!" ringing ever in our ears, some one asked for Miriam. She went down, and presently I heard her thanking somebody for a letter. "You could not have brought me anything more acceptable! It is from my sister, though she can hardly have heard from us yet!" I ran back, and sitting at mother's feet, told her Miriam was coming with a letter from Lydia. Mother cried at the mention of her name. O my little sister! You know how dear you are to us! "Mother! Mother!" a horrible voice cried, and before I could think who it was, Miriam rushed in, holding an open letter in her hand, and perfectly wild. "George is dead!" she shrieked, and fell heavily to the ground.

O my God! I could have prayed Thee to take mother, too, when I looked at her. I thought — I almost hoped she was dead, and that pang spared! But I was wild myself. I could have screamed! — laughed! "It is false! Do you hear me, mother? God would not take both! George is not dead!" I cried, trying in vain to arouse her from her horrible state or bring one ray of reason to her eye. I spoke to a body alive only to pain; not a sound of my voice seemed to reach her; only fearful moans showed she was yet alive.

Miriam lay raving on the ground. Poor Miriam! her heart's idol torn away. God help my darling! I did not understand that George *could* die until I looked at her. In vain I strove to raise her from the ground, or check her wild shrieks for death. "George! only George!" she would cry; until at last, with the horror of seeing both die before me, I mastered strength enough to go for the servant and bid her run quickly for Brother.

How long I stood there alone, I never knew. I remember Ada coming in hurriedly and asking what it was. I told her George was dead. It was a relief to see her cry. I could not; but I felt the pain afresh, as though it were her brother she was crying over, not mine. And the sight of her tears brought mine, too. We could only cry over mother and Miriam; we could not rouse them; we did not know what to do.

Some one called me in the entry. I went, not understanding what I was doing. A lady came to me, told me her name, and said something about George; but I could not follow what she said. It was as though she was talking in a dream. I believe she repeated the words several times, for at last she shook me and said, "Listen! Rouse yourself! the letter is about George!" Yes, I said; he is dead. She said I must read the letter; but I could not see, so she read it aloud. It was from Dr. Mitchell, his friend who was with him when he died, telling of his sickness and death. He died on Tuesday the 12th of January, after an illness of six days, conscious to the last and awaiting the end as only a Christian, and one who has led so beautiful a life, could, with the Grace of God, look for it. He sent messages to his brothers and sisters, and bade them tell his mother his last thoughts were of her, and that he died trusting in the mercy of the Saviour. George! our pride! our beautiful, angel brother! *Could* he die? Surely God has sent all these afflictions within these three years to teach us that our hopes must be placed Above, and that it is blasphemy to have earthly idols!

The letter said that the physicians had mistaken his malady, which was inflammation of the bowels, and he had died from being treated for something else. It seemed horrible cruelty to read me that part; I knew that if mother or Miriam ever heard of it, it would kill them. So I begged Mrs. Mitchell never to let them hear of it. She seemed to think nothing of the pain it would inflict; how could she help telling if they asked? she said. I told her I must insist on her not mentioning it; it would only add suffering to what was already insupportable; if they asked for the letter, offer to read it aloud, but say positively that she would not allow any one to touch it except herself, and then she might pass it over in silence. I roused Miriam then and sent her to hear it read. She insisted on reading it herself, and half dead with grief held out her hands, begging piteously to be suffered to read it alone. I watched then until I was sure Mrs. Mitchell would keep her promise. Horrible as I knew it to be from strange lips, I knew by what I experienced that I had saved her from a shock that might cost her her life; and then I went back to mother.

No need to conceal what I felt there! She neither spoke nor saw. If I had shrieked that he died of ill treatment, she would not have understood. But I sat there silently with that horrible secret, wondering if God would help me bear it, or if despair would deprive me of self-control and force me presently to cry it aloud, though it should kill them both.

At last Brother came. I had to meet him downstairs and tell him. God spare me the sight of a strong man's grief! Then Sister came in, knowing as little as he. Poor Sister! I could have blessed her for every tear she shed. It was a comfort to see some one who had life or feeling left. I felt as though the whole world was dead. Nothing was real, nothing existed except horrible speechless pain. Life was a fearful dream through which but one thought ran — "Dead — Dead!"

Miriam had been taken to her room more dead than alive — Mother lay speechless in hers. The shock of this second blow had obliterated, with them, all recollection of the first. It was a mercy I envied them; for I remembered both, until loss of consciousness would have seemed a blessing. I shall never forget mother's shriek of horror when towards evening she recalled it. O those dreadful days of misery and wretchedness! It seems almost sacrilege to refer to them now. They are buried in our hearts with our boys — thought of with prayers and tears.

How will the world seem to us now? What will life be without the boys? When this terrible strife is over, and so many thousands return to their homes, what will peace bring us of all we hoped? Jimmy! Dear Lord, spare us that one!

November 2d, 1864.

This morning we heard Jimmy is engaged to Helen Trenholm, daughter of the Secretary of the Confederate States. He wrote asking Brother's consent, saying they had been engaged since August, though he had had no opportunity of writing until that day — the middle of September. I cried myself blind. It seems that our last one is gone. But this is the first selfish burst of feeling. Later I shall come to my senses and love my sister that is to be. But my darling! my darling! O Jimmy! How can I give you up? You have been so close to me since Harry died!

Alone now; best so.

NO. 19 DAUPHINE ST.,
Saturday night, December 31st, 1864.

One year ago, in my little room in the Camp Street house, I sat shivering over Tennyson and my desk, selfishly rejoicing over the departure of a year that had brought pain and discomfort only to me, and eagerly welcoming the dawning of the New One whose first days were to bring death to George and Gibbes, and whose latter part was to separate me from Miriam, and brings me news of Jimmy's approaching marriage. O sad, dreary, fearful Old Year! I see you go with pain! Bitter as you have been, how do we know what the coming one has in store for us? What new changes will it bring? Which of us will it take? I am afraid of eighteen sixty-five, and have felt a vague dread of it for several years past.

Nothing remains as it was a few months ago. Miriam went to Lilly, in the Confederacy, on the 19th of October (ah! Miriam!), and mother and I have been boarding with Mrs. Postlethwaite ever since. I miss her sadly. Not as much, though, as I would were I less engaged. For since the first week in August, I have been teaching the children for Sister; and since we have been here, I go to them every morning instead of their coming to me. Starting out at half-past eight daily, and returning a little before three, does not leave me much time for melancholy reflections. And there is no necessity for indulging in them at present; they only give pain.

NO. 211 CAMP ST.,
April 19th, 1865.

"All things are taken from us, and become portions and parcels of the dreadful pasts." . . .

Thursday the 13th came the dreadful tidings of the surrender of Lee and his army on the 9th. Everybody cried, but I would not, satisfied that God will still save us, even though all should apparently be lost. Followed at intervals of two or three hours by the announcement of the capture of Richmond, Selma, Mobile, and Johnston's army, even the stanchest Southerners were hopeless. Every one proclaimed

Peace, and the only matter under consideration was whether Jeff Davis, all politicians, every man above the rank of Captain in the army and above that of Lieutenant in the navy, should be hanged immediately, or *some* graciously pardoned. Henry Ward Beecher humanely pleaded mercy for us, supported by a small minority. Davis and all leading men *must* be executed; the blood of the others would serve to irrigate the country. Under this lively prospect, Peace, blessed Peace! was the cry. I whispered, "Never! Let a great earthquake swallow us up first! Let us leave our land and emigrate to any desert spot of the earth, rather than return to the Union, even as it Was!"

Six days this has lasted. Blessed with the silently obstinate disposition, I would not dispute, but felt my heart swell, repeating, "God is our refuge and our strength, a very present help in time of trouble," and could not for an instant believe this could end in an overthrow.

This morning, when I went down to breakfast at seven, Brother read the announcement of the assassination of Lincoln and Secretary Seward.

"Vengeance is mine; I will repay, saith the Lord." This is murder! God have mercy on those who did it!

. . . .

Charlotte Corday killed Marat in his bath, and is held up in history as one of Liberty's martyrs, and one of the heroines of her country. To me, it is all murder. Let historians extol blood-shedding; it is woman's place to abhor it. And because I know that they would have apotheosized any man who had crucified Jeff Davis, I abhor this, and call it foul murder, unworthy of our cause and God grant it was only the temporary insanity of a desperate man that committed this crime! Let not his blood be visited on our nation, Lord!

Across the way, a large building, undoubtedly inhabited by officers, is being draped in black. Immense streamers of black and white hang from the balcony. Downtown, I understand, all shops are closed, and all wrapped in mourning. And I hardly dare pray God to bless us, with the crape hanging over the way. It would have been banners, if our President had been killed, though!

Saturday, 22d April.

To see a whole city draped in mourning is certainly an imposing spectacle, and becomes almost grand when it is considered as an expression of universal affliction. So it is, in one sense. For the more violently "Secesh" the inmates, the more thankful they are for Lincoln's death, the more profusely the houses are decked with the emblems of woe. They all look to me like "not sorry for him, but dreadfully grieved to be forced to this demonstration." So all things have indeed assumed a funereal aspect. Men who have hated Lincoln with all their souls, under terror of confiscation and imprisonment which they *under-*

stand is the alternative, tie black crape from every practicable knob and point to save their homes. Last evening the B——s were all in tears, preparing their mourning. What sensibility! What patriotism! a stranger would have exclaimed. But Bella's first remark was: "Is it not horrible? This vile, *vile* old crape! Think of hanging it out when —" Tears of rage finished the sentence. One would have thought pity for the murdered man had very little to do with it.

Coming back in the cars, I had a *rencontre* that makes me gnash my teeth yet. It was after dark, and I was the only lady in a car crowded with gentlemen. I placed little Miriam on my lap to make room for some of them, when a great, dark man, all in black, entered, and took the seat and my left hand at the same instant, saying, "Good-evening, Miss Sarah." Frightened beyond measure to recognize Captain Todd[1] of the Yankee army in my interlocutor, I, however, preserved a quiet exterior, and without the slightest demonstration answered, as though replying to an internal question. "Mr. Todd." "It is a long while since we met," he ventured. "Four years," I returned mechanically. "You have been well?" "My health has been bad." "I have been ill myself"; and determined to break the ice he diverged with "Baton Rouge has changed sadly." "I hope I shall never see it again. We have suffered too much to recall home with any pleasure." "I

[1] A cousin of Mrs. Lincoln.

understand you have suffered severely," he said, glancing at my black dress. "We have yet one left in the army, though," I could not help saying. He, too, had a brother there, he said.

He pulled the check-string as we reached the house, adding, "This is it," and absurdly correcting himself with "Where do you live?" — "211. I thank you. Good-evening"; the last with emphasis as he prepared to follow. He returned the salutation, and I hurriedly regained the house. Monsieur stood over the way. A look through the blinds showed him returning to his domicile, several doors below.

I returned to my own painful reflections. The Mr. Todd who was my "sweetheart" when I was twelve and he twenty-four, who was my brother's friend, and daily at our home, was put away from among our acquaintance at the beginning of the war. This one, I should not know. Cords of candy and mountains of bouquets bestowed in childish days will not make my country's enemy my friend now that I am a woman.

Tuesday, May 2d, 1865.

While praying for the return of those who have fought so nobly for us, how I have dreaded their first days at home! Since the boys died, I have constantly thought of what pain it would bring to see their comrades return without them — to see families reunited, and know that ours never could be again, save in heaven. Last Saturday, the 29th of April, seven hundred and fifty paroled Louisianians from Lee's army were brought here — the sole survivors of ten regiments who left four years ago so full of hope and determination. On the 29th of April, 1861, George left New Orleans with his regiment. On the fourth anniversary of that day, they came back; but George and Gibbes have long been lying in their graves. . . .

June 15th.

Our Confederacy has gone with one crash — the report of the pistol fired at Lincoln.

THE END

Reading this for the first time, in all these many years, I wish to bear record that God never failed me, through stranger vicissitudes than I ever dared record. Whatever the anguish, whatever the extremity, in His own good time He ever delivered me. So that I bless Him to-day for all ot life's joys and sorrows — for all He gave — for all He has taken — and I bear witness that it was all Very Good.

SARAH MORGAN DAWSON.

July 23d, 1896.
CHARLESTON,
SOUTH CAROLINA.

EDITOR'S NOTES

Page 1. The first twenty-five pages of the diary are omitted. They treat of her father's death from a severe attack of asthma, and the events connected with her brother's death "on the field of honor." Henry W. F. "Harry" Morgan had just set up a medical practice in New Orleans when he became involved in a minor dispute with the father of James Sparks, with whom he had attended the University of Louisiana (now Tulane University). The former classmate issued the challenge; the duel was fought at the Louisiana Race Course, north of Baton Rouge, May 1, 1861. Both men must have had an utter contempt for death, since the contest was fought with double-barreled shotguns. Sparks emerged uninjured; Morgan, mortally wounded, was borne home and died a few hours afterward. The best accounts of the affair are given in the Baton Rouge *Daily Advocate*, May 2, 1861, and in James A. Renshaw, "Recollections of Yesterday," *Louisiana Historical Quarterly*, VIII (1925), 431-432.

Pike's Clock, a landmark in the city, hung atop the bank of William S. Pike on Third Street. Pike himself was probably the wealthiest man in the city at this time.

Sophie Brunot was the widow of James M. Brunot, a prominent local attorney. Their home was located on North Boulevard, three blocks from the Morgan residence. Still standing, it is presently occupied by Mrs. Brunot's granddaughter, Miss Laura Duchein.

Page 5. The U. S. Arsenal at Baton Rouge surrendered to Louisiana militia January 12, 1861. Twelve days later Louisiana seceded from the Union. For an account of the siege and surrender of the Arsenal, see William Watson, *Life in the Confederate Army* (London, 1887), 76-80.

The "Mr. McG——" to whom Sarah referred was William C. McGimsey, son of Dr. J. W. P. McGimsey, a local physician. At this time Sarah had little affection for him. In a passage omitted from that day's entry she wrote: "If one fold of my dress had touched him, I *know* I should have hated him." (See also page 241.)

Page 6. "The graveyard" is Magnolia Cemetery, located nineteen blocks from the river and in the midst of the grounds over which the Battle of Baton Rouge was waged. Most of the Morgan family is buried here.

Sarah's youngest brother, James Morris Morgan, at this time was a midshipman in the Confederate States Navy. His war memoirs, *Recollections of a Rebel Reefer* (Boston, 1917), are among the best personal narratives of the war. For an excellent sketch of his life, see M. L. Bonham, "The Rebel Reefer Furls His Last Sail," *Louisiana Historical Quarterly*, XI (1928), 582-606.

Commodore George N. Hollins, a former officer in the U. S. Navy, was commander of the Confederate flotilla (16 ships) in the Mississippi.

Page 7. Second Lieutenant James H. Trezevant of the 1st Louisiana Infantry suffered a slight head wound at Shiloh (April 6-7), came home on furlough and, on April 27, married Fanny Davidson, the daughter of Colonel Thomas G. Davidson, mentioned on page 12. In most instances the military achievements of Louisiana soldiers have been taken from Andrew B. Booth, ed., *Records of Louisiana Confederate Soldiers and Louisiana Confederate Commands* (4 vols., New Orleans, 1920).

At the time of his death Captain J. T. Wheat commanded Company G, 1st Louisiana. (Henceforth, all infantry regiments will be listed only by number and state. Others, such as cavalry and artillery units, will be so designated.)

Pages 8-9. Buck Bradford was the brother of J. L. Bradford, the captain who paid Sarah so many unwanted attentions beginning late that year (see pages 270 *et seq.*). Sarah's "little golden calf" was Captain Thomas Butler of the 1st Louisiana, and "that rattle-brain" was Mr. Trezevant.

Page 10. Dr. A. V. Woods at that time was a twenty-nine-year-old bachelor who, according to several unpublished entries in the diary, was infatuated with Miriam Morgan. He later served as Surgeon of the 1st Louisiana Cavalry. His closeness to the Morgan family originated with his medical care of Sarah's father in his last days.

Page 12. Although Thomas Green Davidson lived and practiced law in Baton Rouge, he had extensive land holdings in Livingston Parish, which adjoined East Baton Rouge Parish. He also served one term as a U. S. Congressman.

Editor's Notes

Page 13. Greenwell Springs, a few miles northeast of Baton Rouge, was once a popular resort area. An old road and a small cluster of houses are all that now bear its name.

Page 14. Everyone thought the disagreement between Morgan and Sparks had been settled, since the district attorney had placed both men under peace bonds. Baton Rouge *Daily Advocate*, May 2, 1861.

Page 16. Forts Jackson and St. Philip, on opposite banks at a bend in the Mississippi, were all that stood between Rear-Admiral David Farragut's Union fleet and New Orleans. In operations lasting April 18-24, Farragut's flotilla broke through the makeshift Confederate defenses, which consisted of the forts' guns, a few maneuverable boats, and several ships sunk in an attempt to block the channel. Once past the obstacles, the Federals had clear sailing to New Orleans, which surrendered April 24. Four days later the forts themselves capitulated. See *War of the Rebellion: Official Records of the Union and Confederate Navies* (31 vols., Washington, 1894-1927), XVIII, 253-446. Cited hereafter as *Navy OR*. A detailed discussion of the role played by the forts may be found in Ernest A. Landry, "The History of Forts Jackson and St. Philip, With Special Emphasis on the Civil War Period" (unpublished master's thesis, Louisiana State University, 1938).

Page 18. As the 1860 census returns for the Baton Rouge area list neither a Mr. Hutchinson nor a Dr. Moffat, both gentlemen evidently were passing through town and merely stopped at the Morgan home to give the family news of Jimmy.

The *McRae* was Commodore Hollins's flagship. It was crippled on April 24 by telling fire from the *Iroquois*. Many sailors considered the ship jinxed, for on its maiden voyage up the Mississippi late in 1861, it became lost in the fog and rammed into the pier of Jefferson Davis's plantation. Morgan, *Rebel Reefer*, 61-62.

Page 19. Lieutenant Thomas B. Huger, a widower, was mortally wounded when Farragut broke through the river defenses. His wife was a sister of General George G. Meade, the Federal victor at Gettysburg.

Page 21. William E. Pinkney (so erroneously spelled in all official records) served originally with the 1st Louisiana Heavy Artillery, later became a lieutenant-colonel in the 8th Louisiana Battalion. Captured in 1864, he escaped and served under

General Richard Taylor until the latter's surrender May 6, 1865. Will and Miriam once discussed marriage, but Sarah was instrumental in dissolving the proposed union on the grounds of Miriam's youth. Unpublished entry for January 19, 1863.

Major-General Mansfield Lovell commanded New Orleans until its fall. He was a Confederate leader who always had difficulty in securing a post small enough to fit his talents. See Jefferson D. Bragg, *Louisiana in the Confederacy* (Baton Rouge, 1941), 251-253.

Page 22. Sarah's allusions are to the slow-motion struggle (April 27-May 30) for Corinth between Confederate General P. G. T. Beauregard and Federal General Henry Halleck. A good concise account of this campaign is in Shelby Foote, *The Civil War: A Narrative* (New York, 1958), 374-376, 381-386.

The commander of the *Iroquois* was Captain James S. Palmer, who sent a demand for surrender to the newly installed mayor, B. F. Bryan, on the morning of May 9. Although Mayor Bryan refused to surrender the city voluntarily, Federal forces nevertheless moved in and occupied it. Sarah's account of the affair, while basically true, is a trifle overdramatic. See Charles E. East, "Baton Rouge Mayors Are Forgotten Men," Baton Rouge *State-Times*, November 14, 1956.

Page 26. Lieutenant Alexander F. Warley was as daring as Sarah described him. This South Carolinian performed wonders while commander of the *Manassas*, the first ironclad ram propelled by steam. On April 24 it rammed the *Brooklyn*, a U. S. steamer sporting twenty-four guns, but the impact was not enough to sink the Federal ship. The following day the unpredictable *Manassas* ran ashore, and was scuttled. *Navy OR*, XVIII, 182-199, 335-345, 758-764.

Page 28. The State House was Louisiana's capitol. A turreted castle-like structure, it burned in December, 1862, while being used as a Federal prison. Rebuilt in the 1880's, it is today one of the principal landmarks of Baton Rouge.

Page 29. Colonel William Wilson's 6th New York Zouaves were recruited mostly from the rougher elements of New York City's East Side, and were as prone to fight among themselves as they were to take on Confederates. Their notoriety came from service in Florida, described in William W. Davis, *The Civil War and Reconstruction in Florida* (New York, 1913), 121, 129-133.

Editor's Notes

Page 31. Major (later Colonel) Richard C. Drum was Adjutant-General of the Department of the Pacific. He met and wed Lavinia Morgan while stationed at the Baton Rouge Arsenal in the 1850's. For his wartime activities in the Far West, see *War of the Rebellion: Official Records of the Union and Confederate Armies* (128 vols., Washington, 1880-1901), L, pt. 1, 1110-1116. Cited hereafter as *OR*. In 1880 Drum was appointed Adjutant-General of the United States by President Hayes; he retained the post until his retirement eight years later.

Page 33. The Federal move toward Vicksburg was little more than a reconnaissance.

Page 35. Major-General Benjamin F. Butler was the Federal commandant of New Orleans. When the ladies of the city refused to display the courtesy to Federal troops Butler felt his men deserved, he issued on May 15 the infamous General Orders No. 28, which decreed that any lady exhibiting any degree of contempt toward his troops would be treated as "a woman of the town plying her avocation." President Jefferson Davis retaliated by branding Butler "an outlaw and common enemy of mankind," subject to death if ever captured. Butler's order, and Davis's rejoinder, are in *OR*, XV, 426, 906-908.

Page 36. Norfolk was evacuated by the Confederates on May 9 and occupied by Federal troops the following day.

Page 40. Henry A. Castle, Jr., a youth of eighteen, was finally captured on July 7 and imprisoned in New Orleans. Butler planned to execute him as a spy, despite the fact that he was a private in Company H, 1st Louisiana Partisan Rangers. When General Daniel Ruggles, the Confederate commander in that area, threatened severe retaliation if any harm came to Castle, Butler changed his mind. *OR*, XV, 519-521. Young Castle evidently escaped from prison, for Sarah recorded the arrest of Dr. John Nolan as a hostage pending Castle's recapture (see page 146). Henry's younger brother, sixteen-year-old Nathan Castle, also got into trouble with Federal authorities, as Sarah explained on page 72.

Page 41. Dr. Castleton was either Thomas Castleton, the Presbyterian minister in Baton Rouge, or his son Henry, a local physician.

Page 47. Felix R. Brunot was a second lieutenant in Company K, 3rd Louisiana. He was killed in the closing operations around Corinth.

Howell Polk Carter, son of the sire of Linwood, later became a prominent New Orleans attorney. He recounted his experiences in the 1st Louisiana Cavalry in *A Cavalryman's Reminiscences of the Civil War* (New Orleans, n.d.).

Francis Edmond Badger was the son of Wallace and Mary Carter Badger, and a first cousin of Howell Carter. "Ned," as Sarah called him, served in Company F, 1st Special Battalion (Rightor's), Louisiana Infantry.

Page 48. Seth David owned a large farm just outside Baton Rouge.

Page 51. The bombardment occurred when Confederate guerillas fired on a dingy as it was putting to shore with a message from Farragut to the mayor. In his official report Farragut said he tried to shoot only where he thought the guerillas might be, and added: "I spared the town as much as possible." *Navy OR*, XVIII, 520.

Caroline E. was the wife of William D. Phillips, a local merchant.

Page 53. The Wisconsin colonel to whom Sarah alluded was Lieutenant-Colonel Sidney A. Bean, commander of the 4th Wisconsin, the only Badger unit in the occupying force. Bean was killed the following year at the siege of Port Hudson.

Page 55. Brigadier-General Thomas Williams commanded the Second Brigade in Butler's Department of the Gulf. This unit, composed for the most part of five infantry regiments (14th Maine, 7th Vermont, 21st Indiana, 4th Wisconsin, 6th Michigan), was entrusted with the occupation of the Baton Rouge area. Williams himself was a controversial officer. One Confederate said he was "a brave, upright, and strict officer, and did not allow any insult or outrage to be committed on the inhabitants." Watson, *Confederate Army*, 394. On the other hand, the officers of the 6th Michigan were almost unanimous in their dislike of him. See Edward Bacon, *Among the Cotton Thieves* (Detroit, 1867), 6-29. Sarah liked him very much, and went so far on one occasion as to assert: "If all the Yankees are like him, hurrah for Lincoln, then!" Unpublished entry for July 24, 1862.

Camp Moore, Louisiana's largest camp of instruction, was sixty miles northeast of Baton Rouge near Tangipahoa. A member of the 13th Louisiana described the base as "the hottest, most uncomfortable camp I have ever known." Frank L. Richardson, "War As I Saw It," *Louisiana Historical Quarterly*, VI (1923), 91.

Page 60. In April, 1862, the widow Mary C. Daigre purchased the home and property adjoining the Morgan residence on the northern side from T. G. Morgan, Jr., who had obtained it from William S. Pike. The Lucy Daigre referred to on page 135 was the daughter of Mary and Gilbert Daigre.

William G. Waller, a civil engineer, later became administrator for the estate of Sarah's mother.

Dr. J. Bertrand Duchein, a Baton Rouge physician, married Eugenia Brunot, the "Dena" mentioned in the diary and the daughter of Sophie and James Brunot.

Page 61. Lice were as prevalent in the army as the tales of their voracity. A Confederate once swore he saw his discarded shirt moving back and forth as the lice scampered around "hunting for a soldier." Quoted in Bell I. Wiley, *The Life of Johnny Reb* (Indianapolis, 1943), 250-251.

Page 63. General Beauregard retired to Tupelo and went no further southward.

Page 64. The "Mr. Tunnard" mentioned was one of the three sons of William F. Tunnard, a respected carriage-maker and also a major in the Pelican Rifles. All three sons served in Confederate armies. One of them, William H., recounted much of the action around Baton Rouge in his war memoirs, *A Southern Record: The History of the Third Regiment, Louisiana Infantry* (Baton Rouge, 1866).

Page 65. Lieutenant James C. Biddle was an aide to General Williams. On page 118 Sarah records hearing of his death at Vicksburg. This report was untrue. When the war ended Biddle was a brevet colonel and aide to General George G. Meade. See *OR*, XLVI, pt. 3, 1241.

Page 66. Colonel James W. McMillan was later promoted to brigadier-general and placed in command of a brigade. He evidently was a crusty warrior. Once ordered to confiscate several barges loaded with cotton and to use them as troop transports, McMillan told his men to "fling overboard every damned pound of cotton — and fling the damned proprietors over after it."

Homer B. Sprague, *History of the 13th Infantry Regiment of Connecticut Volunteers* (Hartford, 1867), 206-207.

Page 67. Sarah erred slightly in her reports of action in the East. With the Confederate victory at Winchester, Virginia (May 25), General T. J. "Stonewall" Jackson drove General Nathaniel Banks from the Shenandoah Valley. Seven miles from Richmond, on May 31-June 1, General Joseph E. Johnston stopped General George B. McClellan's advance up the Peninsula at Seven Pines and Fair Oaks.

Page 71. Leon Bonnecaze emigrated to Baton Rouge from France and became one of the city's leading merchants.

Colonel McMillan led a detachment into the interior to capture Lieutenant Josiah Roberts of Bynum's Battalion of guerillas. McMillan was shot by the youth's father, Major Steven Roberts, as he crossed the threshold of the Roberts home. The son was killed; the father, imprisoned for three years at Fort Jackson, was released shortly before his death at the age of seventy-four. Baton Rouge *Tri-Weekly Advocate*, October 27, 1865.

Page 72. No record could be found of the depositions of William Garig or Nathan Castle. Apparently little came of the arrests, for after the war Garig acquired large holdings and became president of a Baton Rouge bank.

The Michigander with whom Sarah talked was either a noncommissioned officer or else was leading Sarah on. No commissioned officer by the name of "Bee" is listed in the comprehensive roster found in John Robertson, *Michigan in the War* (3 vols. in 1, Lansing, 1880), pt. 3, 1-255. "Our General" was Hamilton P. Bee, commanding the District of Texas and a brother of General Bernard E. Bee, killed at First Manassas.

Page 73. Major Joseph A. Haskins, 1st U. S. Artillery, was in command of the Arsenal at the time of its surrender. During prewar days he was always a welcome guest in the Morgan home. The fact that he had lost an arm caused Sarah to feel maternal pity for him. Unpublished entry for October 16, 1862.

Page 74. A Prussian emigrant, George Heroman, owned a brick mercantile store at the corner of Church and Florida Streets, not far from the Morgan home. The building, or part of it, had apparently been converted into a hospital.

Page 75 Sarah closed her entry for June 10 by saying: "If I can do anything on earth for that man [Col. McMillan], I'll do it if I die for it! . . . Mobs shall never govern my opinions, or tell me how much I may be allowed to do."

Page 78. The quotation at the top of the page is the last line of a Negro spiritual. It was written in the journal prior to the time Sarah began using it for her diary.

Page 81. William Pinckney has already been mentioned in the note for page 21. Although he was married, Sarah had a deep affection for him and devoted the last four pages of her June 17 entry to praise of his virtues.

Page 82. Sarah is expressing the unfounded but consistent rumors of English and French intervention in the war. Neither country ever officially pledged itself to the Southern cause.

Page 86. Jeanne Manon Phlipon became famous in the French Revolution as the wife of the Jacobin statesman, Jean Marie Roland. Guillotined during the Reign of Terror (1793-1794), Madame Roland is reputed to have gone to her death apostrophizing: "O Liberté, que de crimes on comment en ton nom! (O Liberty, how many crimes are committed in thy name!)"

Page 90. Major-General Earl Van Dorn succeeded General Lovell as commander of the Vicksburg defenses on June 22. His General Order No. 1, the proclamation to which Sarah referred, was issued on the 24th. Because his strict martial rule of the area incurred the wrath even of his fellow-Mississippians, Van Dorn was subsequently replaced by Lieutenant-General John B. Pemberton.

Page 92. Butler came to Baton Rouge on an inspection tour. He returned to New Orleans with five citizens who, he stated, "had threatened citizens of Baton Rouge who profess favoritism for the Union." Jessie A. Marshall, ed., *Private and Official Correspondence of Gen. Benjamin F. Butler during the Period of the Civil War* (5 vols., Norwood, Mass., 1917), II, 13.

Page 93. In an omitted passage for that entry Sarah wrote: "If this is American Liberty, Despotism in a foreign land, I accept you in preference! Dearly as I love Louisiana, it can never be my home, under such a sway. . . . God have mercy on us and deliver us from the hands of our enemies!"

Pages 95-96. A cotton-planter and slaveholder, Thomas Overton Moore carried Louisiana into secession and the Confederacy.

He resigned from office when Federal troops overran his state in the spring of 1862. Edwin Warren Moise was a former state attorney-general appointed to the state supreme court just after the outbreak of war. He seems to have been the most dedicated Confederate on that tribunal.

The Reverend N. A. Cravens was pastor of the Methodist church. The largest house of worship in the city, it stood on the corner of Church and Laurel Streets and was, in the words of one Federal soldier, "a handsome and commodious edifice." Henry T. Johns, *Life with the 49th Massachusetts Infantry* (Pittsfield, Mass., 1864), 137. On March 2, 1863, the same writer stated that "the pastor . . . is somewhere within the rebel lines." *Ibid.*, 145.

Page 97. Solomon Benjamin was a middle-aged merchant and brother of the Confederacy's famous Secretary of State, Judah P. Benjamin. Butler classified Solomon as one of "the most violent of the rebels" in that area, though he proved to be one of the first to take the loyalty oath. *OR*, XV, 502.

Pages 102-103. Jackson did not surround McClellan's forces; in fact, with the Confederate defeat at Malvern Hill (July 1), which ended the Seven Days' Campaign, General Robert E. Lee acknowledged his failure to annihilate the Federal army, as he had planned. No authority could be found to substantiate the assertion that the 7th Louisiana was given a battery of artillery for its valor. This unit was attached to Jackson's division, and he made no mention of it in his official report. *OR*, XI, pt. 2, 552-559.

Great Britain's prime minister, Henry John Temple, Viscount Palmerston, came within a hair of proposing active aid to the Confederacy. Only the skillful diplomacy of the American ambassador, Charles Francis Adams, saved the day for his government. Of Butler's General Orders No. 28 Palmerston said: "It authorizes proceedings revolting to every manly feeling and without example in the history of nations," and added that "it is an outrage upon the feelings and practices of Christian nations." Quoted in Herbert C. F. Bell, *Lord Palmerston* (2 vols., London, 1936), II, 316.

Page 104. Mrs. Philip Phillips, once imprisoned in Washington for "traitorous proclivities," again reprimanded for teaching her children to spit at Federal officers, was finally sent to Ship Island for the crime of standing on her New Orleans balcony and shouting insults at a funeral procession bearing the body of Lieutenant George DeKay, mortally wounded while chasing guerillas along the Mississippi. *OR*, XV, 24, 510-511. Ship Island was an army station and prison camp just off the coast of Mississippi. For a description of its barrenness, see John W. De Forest, *A Volunteer's Adventures*, edited by J. H. Croushore (New Haven, 1946), 3-12.

Page 105. The action to which Sarah referred was an expedition from Ponchatoula by a company of Confederate sharpshooters under Lieutenant Alfred Bradley. His report of the affair is in *OR*, XV, 120-122.

Page 107. Sarah was very depressed during this period. In omitted entries for July 5-6, she spoke of death being preferable to the existence she then had, but concluded that the coming of peace would assuredly bring her contentment.

The Reverend John Gierlow was rector of St. James Episcopal Church, where the Morgans had worshipped since their removal to Baton Rouge.

McClellan's army, though wounded by the pounding of Lee's efforts to destroy it, did not surrender, nor was its commander wounded.

Page 108. Dr. Richard H. and Lavinia E. Day lived on Church Street just to the south of the Morgans. Dr. Day moved to the city from Baltimore; Mrs. Day, his second of three wives, was a member of the prominent Elam family of Baton Rouge.

Page 112. Major E. Augustus Scott commanded Company I, 3rd Louisiana Cavalry. Captured in November, 1864, he was exchanged too late to see further service.

Page 113. The 1st Louisiana was in A. R. Wright's Third Brigade of Benjamin F. Huger's division. For praise of its conduct in the Seven Days, see *OR*, XI, pt. 2, 807. If Jackson lauded its actions, he did so privately. There is no reference to the unit in his official report, cited earlier. Port Republic, fought on June 9, was one of Stonewall's typical Sunday victories: waged with the fury of Old Testament prophets and afterwards conceded by Jackson to have been the handiwork of God.

Page 117. The Penitentiary stood a few blocks east of the Morgan home on the site where now is the main post office. After the Battle of Baton Rouge, in which it was a strategic point, its cotton looms were removed to Clinton for safekeeping (see page 184).

Page 119. In General Van Dorn's Department of Southern Mississippi and East Louisiana, Brigadier-General Daniel Ruggles commanded the First District, which encompassed all of Louisiana and the coastal counties of Mississippi.

Page 120. John L. Wolff was a cabinet maker. Louis Sheppers listed himself in the 1860 census returns as a "gentleman," which means he probably had retired from business.

Page 123. Sarah's reference to "our Ram's recent exploits" pertains to the famous *Arkansas* and her dash through Farragut's fleet in one of the more colorful episodes of the war. See H. Allen Gosnell, *Guns on the Western Waters* (Baton Rouge, 1949), 101-135.

Page 124. The omitted passage in the July 21 entry recounted a most embarrassing experience to Sarah. While she was crossing a street under the fixed stares of Union officers standing on nearby balconies, a breeze suddenly lifted her skirts and exposed her feet "to the admiration of all."

Page 126. The Asylum was a four-storied, state-maintained school for the deaf and dumb on St. Ferdinand Street, a few blocks south of the business district. At that time it was regarded by at least one soldier as "a dangerous fire trap." B. F. Stevenson, *Letters from the Army* (Cincinnati, 1886), 294.

Page 128. Mary W. was the wife of Richard H. Loucks, who had served as both state attorney and superintendent of schools for East Baton Rouge Parish. For reasons still unknown, Loucks left Baton Rouge sometime before the war and went to New York, leaving behind his wife and four children all under sixteen years of age. Mrs. Loucks opened a boarding house and gained both profit and respectability. One newspaper article referred to her as an "estimable lady, so well and favorably known to the people of this place." Baton Rouge *Daily Advoeate*, October 18, 1857.

Page 134. Philadelphia Nolan was the daughter of Dr. John T. Nolan of West Baton Rouge Parish.

Page 135. Mrs. E. E. Flynn was a permanent resident at the inn of William and Mary Elder (see page 173). The hotel apparently was on the Baton Rouge-Port Hudson road.

Editor's Notes

Page 136. Ambrose Baumstark, originally from Baden, was the city's principal cabinet-maker and undertaker. His place of business stood at the corner of Church and Laurel Streets.

Page 137. Sarah was not alone in her contempt for the Home Guard. See also Morgan, *Rebel Reefer*, 77, and Frank L. Owsley, "Local Defense and the Overthrow of the Confederacy," *Mississippi Valley Historical Review*, XI (1924-1925), 490-525.

Page 144. Early in August, as a first step toward the recapture of New Orleans, Major-General John C. Breckinridge moved on Baton Rouge from Port Hudson with his division of 5,000 men. The summer heat was intense; every spring of water along the way was stagnant. At least one-third of the men were without shoes, and a majority of them were almost naked. Each mile of the march was strewn with men who had dropped from heat, thirst, and fatigue. Breckinridge pulled up before Baton Rouge with barely 2,600 men. Yet early on the morning of August 5, he launched a two-pronged assault from the north and east on the city's defenses (many of which Williams had constructed closer to the city than his camps). The main Confederate assault struck McMillan's 21st Indiana, the only unit on the Mississippi armed with breechloaders. Fighting on both sides quickly became desperate and costly. Slowly the Federals were driven through the town to the river's edge. There they took shelter in the Arsenal and barracks and under cover of the gunboats anchored at the wharves. Breckinridge kept them pinned there while he waited for the *Arkansas* to steam downriver and clear the gunboats, thus enabling the ground forces to clinch the victory. But the Confederate ram, constructed and held together by a conglomeration of materials, floundered to within four miles of the city, broke down and crazily ran ashore. She was now helpless, and her crew was forced to destroy her. Breckinridge then retired to Port Hudson, but less than two weeks later, owing to Butler's concern for the safety of New Orleans, the Federals abandoned the Louisiana capital and moved southward closer to the Gulf. The best concise account of the battle for Baton Rouge is in *Southern Historical Society Papers*, VIII (1880), 324-332. Cited hereafter as *SHSP*.

Page 145. "Miss Walters" was probably Margaret Walter, the daughter of the lady mentioned on page 161. Margaret, aged twenty-one, had a sister Fanny, four years her senior, but it is reasonable to assume Sarah was referring to the girl nearer her own age.

Page 147. Mrs. Adelaide La Noue was the widow of Hypolite La Noue. She had two children: a daughter, Noemie, and a son, Charles, who married Eliza Morgan.

Page 148. The report that two Federal regiments surrendered on the field was false. Near the end of the fighting, however, General Williams personally led the 6th Michigan in a frenzied counterattack to save the day. The assault failed, and Williams was killed.

Page 149. The *Essex* was a Union ironclad which, with two small gunboats, had protected the Federal troops at Baton Rouge. The morning after the battle, when it was obvious that the *Arkansas* was disabled, the *Essex* moved upstream to take advantage of her foe's ensnarement. It was then that the Confederates destroyed the ship that had done so much during a total naval service of twenty-three days. For a narrative of her saga by one of her crew, see *SHSP*, XXXIII (1905), 1-15.

Page 151. Lieutenant Henry Stevens was in command of the *Arkansas* because of the illness of her regular skipper, Captain Isaac N. Brown. Charles W. "Savez" Read, a lieutenant at this time, later commanded the ram *W. H. Webb* as a lieutenant-commander. His own war memoirs, "Reminiscences of the Confederate States Navy," are in *SHSP*, I (1876), 331-362.

Page 152. Midshipman Daniel B. Talbott was later promoted to lieutenant and, in 1864, was transferred to the James River Squadron.

Page 156. "Mr. Stephenson" was probably the Henry Stevens who commanded the *Arkansas.* Midshipman Dabney M. Scales subsequently served on the famous *Shenandoah,* which did not strike its colors until December, 1865. After the war he became a notable Memphis attorney. "Mr. Barlaud" apparently was Lieutenant Alphonse Barbot, a native of Louisiana. A complete roster of the *Arkansas*'s officers is in *Navy OR*, XIX, 132.

Pages 159-160. Albert Gallatin Carter had been commissioned a general of the Louisiana militia soon after the conclusion of the Mexican War. A prominent planter in East Feliciana Parish and owner of Linwood plantation, he served a prewar term in the state legislature. His second wife, Frances Priscilla Howell, was a cousin to Varina Howell Davis, wife of the Confederate President.

Federal casualties at Baton Rouge totaled 383 men; Confederate losses numbered 456. R. U. Johnson and C. C. Buel, eds., *Battles and Leaders of the Civil War* (4 vols., New York, 1884-1887), III, 584. Cited hereafter as *B & L*.

The casualties of the 14th Maine were 119 men, second only to the 126 losses sustained by the 21st Indiana. *OR*, XV, 51.

Thompson J. Bird was a lieutenant in the 11th Louisiana. By the end of the war he had risen to the rank of major and commanded the 1st Battalion, Trans-Mississippi Cavalry. *OR*, XLI, pt. 3, 971.

"Piper's" was the mercantile shop of Jacob Piper.

Nathan A. M. Dudley was colonel of the 30th Massachusetts but intensely disliked by his own men (who dubbed him "Gold Lace"). Soon placed in charge of a brigade, he was removed from command for incompetence in Banks's 1864 Red River Campaign. Sarah closed her August 9 entry by writing: "What a brute of a man he is! Among all those who have done their best to disgrace their cause and country, Col. Dudley's name has the honor of standing first on the list of infamy."

Page 161. Mrs. Joseph B. (Victorine) Durald was the wife of the sheriff of West Baton Rouge Parish.

Page 162. George Washington Watson owned a small piece of property near the Lobdell plantation. He sold out in 1866 and left the area.

Page 163. In describing what she called "rockets," Sarah evidently was referring to mortar shells, whose arching flight toward their targets gave them a meteoric appearance. See Robert V. Bruce, *Lincoln and the Tools of War* (Indianapolis, 1956), 164-167.

Page 164. Leocadie Walter was the widow of Joseph Walter. Like the Morgans she fled into West Baton Rouge Parish when fighting began in the city. Her son William married Virginia K. Nolan, the "Ginnie" Sarah mentioned often in her diary.

Page 167. The *Lewis Whiteman*, a Federal troop transport, was carrying General Williams's body to New Orleans when it collided with the gunboat *Oneida* at 1 a.m. on August 7. There were few survivors. According to one source, all hope of recovering Williams's corpse was given up until, late the following afternoon, a piece of wreckage supporting a box was sighted floating downriver. Examination showed the box to be the General's coffin, its contents intact. Wickham Hoffman, *Camp, Court and*

Siege (New York, 1877), 52-53. See also *Navy OR*, XIX, 138-139, 780.

Abraham and Caroline Broussard Lobdell lived on a large plantation in West Baton Rouge Parish. Their daughter-in-law, Angelina Bird Lobdell, was the one who had the misfortunes described on page 169. She was married to James L. Lobdell.

Page 172. Dempsey P. and Mary Ann Hereford Cain owned a large tract of land on the west bank of the Mississippi near the Lobdell estate. As Sarah stated, their home was six miles from Linwood. Their only child was Dempsey J. Cain, who, until November, 1863, served as First Sergeant, Company B, 1st Louisiana Cavalry. After that date he is listed as absent without official leave. Booth, *Louisiana Confederate Soldiers*, II, 217.

Sarah here erroneously attached the rank of general to Colonel Henry Watkins Allen of the 4th Louisiana. Shot in the face at Shiloh, Allen then had both legs shattered by canister at Baton Rouge. He was promoted to general in 1863, and elected governor of Louisiana the following year. After the war he went to Mexico City, where he lived out his last days as editor of *The Mexican Times*. See Sarah A. Dorsey, *Recollections of Henry Watkins Allen* (New York, 1866).

Page 173. Luther R. Ronaldson owned considerable property along the east bank of the Mississippi not far from Port Hudson. He operated a ferry which crossed the river where East Feliciana and East Baton Rouge Parishes adjoin. This was the "Randallson's Landing" Sarah mentioned on page 165.

Page 174. Dr. Peter Mortimer Enders was a highly respected physician in the area. He was probably the father of Frank Enders, mentioned often in the diary. Records show that the doctor had a large number of children.

Page 177. Colonel Andrew Matta was one of Baton Rouge's wealthiest citizens. The "Minna" to whom Sarah referred two lines later was his daughter. On page 259 Sarah characterized her as "stout, good-natured Minna." Descendants of the family say Minna objected heatedly to Sarah's allusions to her size when the diary appeared in 1913. Letter to the editor from Charles E. East, March 11, 1959.

The Baton Rouge *Daily Advocate* suspended publication from 1862 to August, 1865, when it was reissued under the title *Tri-Weekly Advocate.*

EDITOR'S NOTES

Sarah's account of the burning of Baton Rouge is verified in an article, originally published in a September, 1865, issue of the *Tri-Weekly Advocate*, and republished in the Baton Rouge *State-Times*, January 14, 1959.

Page 179. Lieutenant-Colonel Thomas H. Shields of the 30th Louisiana was subsequently killed at Ezra Church, Georgia, July 28, 1864. Colonel Gus A. Breaux, who took over Henry Allen's 4th Louisiana when the latter fell wounded at Baton Rouge, proved one of Louisiana's most capable officers. Sarah liked him immensely, and once wrote in her diary: "O Col. Breaux! If all the unmarried men were as charming, what a pleasure society would be!" Unpublished entry for October 7, 1862.

Page 181. Anna Badger was the sister of "Ned" Badger, who is mentioned conspicuously in the diary.

Page 183. Lieutenant (later Captain) Charles H. Luzenberg was officially a member of the 13th Louisiana, but he served through most of the war on various detached duties. See Booth, *Louisiana Confederate Soldiers*, III, pt. 1, 815.

Page 184. Although Dr. Jehu Perkins owned much property in Baton Rouge, he was listed in the 1860 census returns as a farmer.

Page 185. By this time Louisiana's capital was a shambles. One Federal soldier wrote after visiting it: "Baton Rouge, once fresh and pretty, is now curled up and withered by the heats of war." James K. Hosmer, *The Color Guard* (Boston, 1864), 118. Another prophesied: "It will require fifty years of peace, with all its arts, and labors, and expenditures, to restore the city to its primal beauty." Stevenson, *Letters from the Army*, 302.

Colonel W. T. Withers then commanded the 1st Mississippi Light Artillery. A few months later he was appointed chief of artillery for the Vicksburg defenses.

Page 189. The man labeled "A—— de J——" by the original editor was William St. Martin, son of Alexander St. Martin, a local brewer and captain of the "Home Guard" in 1861. Records show that on August 5, 1861, the twenty-three-year-old St. Martin deserted in New Orleans from Company D, 21st Louisiana. Booth, *Louisiana Confederate Soldiers*, III, pt. 1, 900. Sarah concluded her August 24 entry by writing: "He talked brave enough to be General of the —— home brewed."

Page 193. Mrs. S. E. Jones operated the Central House, at the corner of Laurel and Church Streets near the Morgan home, and she had done so for at least a year. Mrs. Jones apparently knew Sarah's mother. The fact that Sarah herself seemed unacquainted with one who lived so close was probably due to a disassociation with a proprietor of a boarding house.

Page 194. The Union officer was probably Captain Charles E. Clarke of the 6th Michigan, since he appears to have been the only Captain Clark(e) in the several regiments stationed at Baton Rouge.

Page 198. Oscar Barbee owned property just to the east of the Penitentiary.

Page 201. Mrs. Ripley lived on a plantation a few miles south of Baton Rouge. After visiting the city late in August she wrote: "Judge Morgan's was the only vacated house I entered. It was enough: I was too heart-sick and indignant to seek another evidence of the lengths to which a conquering army can go in pitiless, unmeaning destruction, when nothing can result from such vandalism but hatred and revenge." *From Flag to Flag: A Woman's Adventures and Experiences in the South during the War, in Mexico, and in Cuba* (New York, 1889), 49-50.

Page 206. Henry Marston was the sire of a large and prominent family in the Clinton area. The antebellum homeplace still stands.

Page 210. Sarah somewhat distorted the military events in the East. The battle of "Stonebridge" refers to the famous Stone Bridge that figured strategically in the Battle of First Bull Run (or First Manassas), the opening, large-scale land engagement of the war. Cedar Run, or Slaughter Mountain (August 9), as it is often called, was a preliminary but bloody engagement prior to the Second Manassas Campaign (August 28-30), fought between Lee and Major-General John Pope. Neither General McClellan nor General Ambrose P. Burnside took part in the battles.

Page 213. William P. Carter was the son of William D. Carter and the nephew of General Carter of Linwood. He served in Company A, 4th Louisiana. His torrid love affair with Miriam Morgan begins on page 290.

Theodore Pinckney was a private in Company G, 4th Louisiana.

Page 214. Mrs. Eliza McCay was a fifty-nine-year-old widow living in East Feliciana Parish. Her daughter Delia married

Bythell Haynes, a Clinton attorney. Eliza Haynes was their daughter. Included in Mrs. McCay's family, as shown in the 1860 census returns for that parish, was Jane Forester, the orphan girl Sarah mentioned on page 215.

Pages 221-222. Donaldsonville, midway on the Mississippi between Baton Rouge and New Orleans, was set ablaze by gunfire from three Federal ships on August 9. It was eventually occupied by Union forces on October 25, 1862. Bayou Sara was situated on the river near the present town of St. Francisville. Once an important landing for traffic to and from East and West Feliciana Parishes, it no longer exists, though a bayou and highway in the vicinity still bear its name. The *Essex* bombarded it on August 10 but did no appreciable damage.

The Confederates might have had titular control of Arlington Heights, overlooking Washington, but their main army at the time was in Maryland on Lee's first northern invasion.

In the middle of August Major-General E. Kirby Smith and four divisions went slashing into Kentucky as part of a two-pronged assault to bring the Bluegrass country into the Confederate fold. After taking Lexington, Smith made threatening moves against both Louisville and Cincinnati, but then was forced to fall back when the other wing, under General Braxton Bragg, fell prey to the over-cautiousness of its commander and suddenly retreated.

The "nice little affair" was probably the September 8-9 encounter between Colonel James McMillan's two regiments and a Confederate cavalry detachment near St. Charles Court House. The Rebels were routed. *OR*, XV, 135-138.

No positive identification for Lieutenant Bourge could be made.

Page 226. Mrs. Cornelia Barr was a first cousin to Joseph Bernard's several daughters, one of whom was the person Sarah mentioned.

Again Sarah was victim of attaching importance to rumors of the action in the East. Baltimore was never occupied by Confederate troops, and Maryland proved surprisingly cool to its Southern invaders. Lee and his lieutenant, Major-General James Longstreet, were at that moment gathering their forces at the sleepy hamlet of Sharpsburg to fight one of the climactic engagements of the war—and Lee would hardly have relinquished his valiant Louisiana regiments on the eve of his Maryland campaign.

Ponchatoula, fifty miles east of Baton Rouge, was raided and burned by Federals during an expedition, September 13-15. *OR*, XV, 138-141. An interesting description of the village is given in Bacon, *Among the Cotton Thieves*, 63-65.

Page 230. Dr. A. Porter Brown was a twenty-eight-year-old physician in the Port Hudson area.

Page 231. Private Eugene Fowler of the Louisiana Grand Artillery was killed at Weelford's Ford, Virginia, during Lee's retreat from Maryland. In the omitted passage in her September 20 entry Sarah wrote of her great love for him: "He was always so good and affectionate to Miriam and me, and was much at home, that we shall miss him sadly."

Page 234. The 4th Louisiana lost 42 men at the Battle of Baton Rouge. While its appearance may have left much to be desired, its complement in October was listed at 397 men, which was about average Confederate strength for a normal 1,000-man regiment. *OR*, XV, 93, 841. Sketches of the 4th may be found in *Confederate Veteran* (40 vols., Nashville, 1893-1932), IX (1901), 210-212; XVI (1908), 261, 299.

Pages 236-237. The "Sarah Morgan. X." at the top of the page is the mark to which she alluded on pages 213-214.

"Wool's defeat" evidently referred to the surrender of Harpers Ferry, Virginia, to Stonewall Jackson's forces on September 14. The Ferry was a part of the Department of the Eastern Theater, commanded by Major-General John E. Wool, a bluff old regular who had served with Anthony Wayne in the War of 1812.

Three battles comprised Lee's Maryland invasion. On September 14, while Jackson's men gobbled up the arsenal and 11,000 Federals at Harpers Ferry, Major-General D. Harvey Hill's division prevented five Union divisions from gaining the mountain passes at South Mountain, Maryland. Then, on Wednesday the 17th, occurred the bloodiest one-day struggle of the war at Sharpsburg. General McClellan with a numerically superior Federal army assailed General Lee's forces, dug in with the Potomac River dangerously close behind them. Had McClellan launched a full-scale attack on the whole, thin Confederate line, sheer weight of numbers might have brought him success. Instead, he delivered three uncoordinated assaults, one at a time, at various sectors of the defenders' works. Lee parried each by the skillful use of his reserves and the unbreakable courage of his men. By day's end the Confederate position was battered and breathless, but unbroken. It had lost 8,000 men. McClellan's "strategy" had cost 12,000 Federals. With one-fourth of his army gone Lee retired to Virginia. President Abraham Lincoln saw enough victory in the battle to justify the issuance of the Emancipation Proclamation, which transformed the war into a struggle for humanitarian principles.

On September 7 the *Essex* steamed past the blazing guns of Port Hudson and joined the Federal fleet just below Vicksburg. Commodore W. D. Porter, commander of the *Essex*, stated in his official report that his ship was struck fourteen times by the 35-40 guns of the fort, which lay between Vicksburg and Baton Rouge. *Navy OR*, XIX, 181-182.

Page 240. Two Baton Rouge sisters, Mattie and Mollie Castleton, were of the same age as the Morgan girls and apparently very envious of them. From several omitted passages in the diary, the Castleton girls ostensibly spread malicious gossip about the over-friendliness of the Morgan sisters with Federal soldiers.

Page 241. "Mrs. S——" was Mattie Castleton, who married James Stith in Baton Rouge in 1860. "Mr. McG——" was the William McGimsey identified in the note for page 5.

Page 242. Dr. Addison's companion was Samuel Milliken, formerly Acting Master on the *Arkansas*.

Page 244. Captain Charles E. Morrison, Company D, 30th Louisiana, also served on Colonel Breaux's staff.

Page 245. Esther Worley, General Carter's niece and wife of Caleb Worley, lived near Linwood. Her husband was a merchant in the Port Hudson area.

Page 251. First Lieutenant Thomas Gibbes Morgan, Jr., joined the army at the age of twenty-four in June, 1861. Elected lieutenant and then captain of Company C, 7th Louisiana, he was wounded at Sharpsburg and sent home on a recuperative furlough. His death is recorded on page 426, with further explanation in the accompanying notes.

Page 253. Lieutenant McGimsey was serving in the 8th Louisiana at the time of his wounding. Captain Andrew S. Herron, a native of Tennessee and Baton Rouge attorney, commanded the "Baton Rouge Fencibles" in the 7th Louisiana. After the war he served as state attorney general, then was elected to one term in Congress.

Page 254. Artemus Ward was the pen-name of one of America's outstanding humorists, Charles Farrar Browne. Sarah was probably referring to his work *Artemus Ward: His Book* (New York, 1862), which sold 40,000 copies.

Pages 256-257. Mordecai Powell was a middle-aged planter in the Port Hudson area. His son, L. M. Powell, was a private in Company G, 4th Louisiana, and was so wounded at Baton Rouge that he was officially discharged from service in November, 1862.

Page 270. Sarah's additional remarks, omitted in the text, about Colonel H. W. Allen were: "Monsieur struck me as being the last person one could be fascinated by. A dough face stood in the place of a handsome one; and as I looked at it, I could not help thinking, 'My friend, I know nothing of your history or tastes, but if you are not vicious, then I shall no longer believe in intuitive aversion.'"

At this time Captain J. L. Bradford commanded Battery F, 1st Mississippi Light Artillery. Captured at Port Hudson, he was exchanged and closed out the war as a battery commander in the Department of Mississippi and East Louisiana. Sarah seemed to have a difficult time making up her mind whether or not she really liked the captain. In omitted passages for November 3-4, she thought him "amiable . . . charming . . . intelligent" and "much more agreeable than his brother" (cited on pages 8-9). Four months later she wrote: "He bores me, and I take no pains to conceal it." Unpublished entry for March 27, 1863.

Page 271. Second Lieutenant Henry W. Fowler, 1st Louisiana Heavy Artillery, was captured at both Fort St. Philip and Vicksburg, but ended up the war as a captain in the Trans-Mississippi Department. See Booth, *Louisiana Confederate Soldiers*, II, 910.

Private Frank H. O. Enders of Captain Fenner's Battery, was subsequently captured near Vicksburg October 6, 1863. He was one of Sarah's most ardent callers during her stay at Linwood.

Lieutenant (later Captain) B. Morgan Harold was an artillery liaison officer attached to Brigadier-General Martin L. Smith's staff. He was taken prisoner at the fall of Port Hudson.

Editor's Notes

Page 275. Brigadier-General William N. R. Beall of Arkansas was Confederate commander of the Third District, which comprised most of Louisiana and western Mississippi. His headquarters was at Port Hudson. His exact jurisdiction is given in *OR*, XV, 768, 840.

Page 280. Commander of a battery in the Louisiana Light Artillery, Captain Charles E. Fenner later served in General Samuel Maxey's brigade in the Third District. After the war he became a noted New Orleans jurist. It was in his home that ex-President Jefferson Davis died.

Lieutenant Thomas B. Harris, Company K, 4th Louisiana, was among those captured when Port Hudson fell.

Page 281. Colonel I. G. W. Steedman commanded the 1st Alabama, which was reorganized at least four times during the war and served as both infantry and artillery. Its war service is recounted in one of the better regimental histories: Edward Y. McMorries, *History of the First Regiment, Alabama Volunteer Infantry, C. S. A.* (Montgomery, 1904).

Page 285. Captain Thomas M. Lenoir was commander of a group from two Alabama counties known as the "Mathews Guards" (later Company I, 3rd Alabama Cavalry). This unit often worked in close association with the 1st Alabama. Information supplied by Peter A. Brannon, Director, Alabama Department of History and Archives.

Page 286. Dr. John C. Miller was president of Centenary College, now in Shreveport but located during the Civil War at Jackson. An energetic administrator, Dr. Miller also acquired a reputation for lengthy orations. One historian characterized a six-hour baccalaureate he delivered in 1854 by saying that "people were too hungry to give the professor's address such a hearing as its merits deserved." William H. Nelson, *A Burning Torch and a Flaming Fire* (Nashville, 1931), 152. See also *ibid.*, 167-168.

Page 288. Dr. Madding (initials unknown) was Assistant Surgeon of the 1st Alabama.

Page 289. The omitted passages in the November 16 entry contain Sarah's conviction that Port Hudson would soon fall. She based her belief on the apparent apathy of the defenders, for one Johnny Reb had told her if the fort fell, the men all knew the paths by which they could escape to safety. "That is no way for soldiers to talk," Sarah wrote. "I expected the answer that always makes my heart swell with enthusiasm, 'We'll conquer or we'll die!' Fancy my disappointment!"

Page 290. Dr. Caleb W. Dortch was a thirty-two-year-old physician living near Linwood who paid both social and professional calls on the Morgan girls while they were in the vicinity. He was the half-brother of Will Carter.

In the footnote Mr. Dawson explained the card game of love staged between Miriam Morgan and the General's nephew, Will Carter (who was residing with his half-sister, Mrs. Esther Worley). Sarah wrote that Will was crazy enough in love with Miriam "to blow his brains out." Unpublished entry for November 24, 1862.

Page 292. The "Mr. G——" was the Reverend John M. Geary, pastor of The Plains Presbyterian Church in East Baton Rouge Parish near the East Feliciana line.

Page 306. First Lieutenant Thomas J. Duggan was an officer in Captain Fenner's battery; he later commanded the unit in the 1863 Chattanooga campaign.

Thirty-year-old John H. Halsey was a second lieutenant in Company I, 1st Louisiana Cavalry. He was another of Sarah's more persistent callers.

Page 311. Lieutenant-Colonel M. B. "Mike" Loucke was Steedman's second-in-command of the 1st Alabama. Major D. P. Buckner was a member of General Beall's staff.

Page 313. The two unnamed gentlemen Sarah identified only as a Captain McClure and a Mr. Gwynn.

Lieutenant Alcée Lewis Dupré was an aide-de-camp to General Franklin Gardner. He and Miriam Morgan were married in the summer of 1866, after which Dupré became a brilliant but inebriate Memphis newspaper editor. Because of his over-fondness for drink, Miriam left him through legal separation and rejoined her family in Charleston, South Carolina. Letter to the editor from Warrington Dawson, February 9, 1959.

Page 316. "Brother" was Judge Philip Hickey Morgan, Sarah's half-brother and a New Orleans jurist.

As for Butler's October decree, Sarah was probably referring to General Orders No. 82, issued October 17, 1862. This was but one of several orders issued by the Federal commander and designed to confiscate the assets of all Confederate sympathizers. See *OR*, XV, 571-576, 581.

Page 321. Major Sprately (initials unknown) was General Gardner's Chief Quartermaster during the Port Hudson operations. *SHSP*, XIV (1886), 345.

Page 323. Much earlier in her diary Sarah had speculated on the type of man she would marry, and had concluded: "I have the greatest penchant for widowers and lawyers." She got the former when she married Francis Dawson. Unpublished entry for May 6, 1862.

Page 335. On March 14 Federal land and naval forces made their first coordinated move against Port Hudson, which stood between them and Vicksburg. Federal strategy called for the army to create a diversion while Farragut ran his fleet past the river batteries. Only four of the Federal ships successfully ran the gauntlet, and two of these—*Monongahela* and *Richmond*—were crippled, the former seriously. For an interesting account of this expedition, see Johns, *49th Massachusetts*, 165-175.

Page 339. In her frantic dash to get past the Port Hudson batteries the cruiser *Mississippi* plowed into a sand bank, where she came under the withering fire of three Confederate batteries. Literally blasted loose from her ensnarement, the helpless ship began drifting downriver perilously close to the remainder of the Federal fleet. The *Mississippi* was then abandoned and blown up to prevent her from supplementing the damage being done by the Confederate batteries.

Page 345. Major-General Franklin Gardner, a native of New York and veteran of the Mexican War, was in command of Port Hudson. Just prior to the Federal assaults on his position, Gardner is reputed to have told his men: "The enemy are coming, but mark you, many a one will get to hell before he does to Port Hudson." McMorries, *1st Alabama*, 58. After surrendering the fort Gardner was exchanged and served out the remainder of the war in General Richard Taylor's Department of Alabama and Mississippi.

Major T. Friend Wilson was a member of Gardner's staff. In an omitted passage for that entry Sarah wrote of the difficulty she experienced in attempting to converse with the Major, who gazed at her so fixedly she kept undergoing "suffocation and despair."

Editor's Notes

Page 346. It was almost customary for persons on both sides of the Mason-Dixon Line to refer to Lieutenant-General Thomas J. Jackson as "Old Stonewall." In reality, this Cromwellian Confederate who won his nickname at First Manassas was only thirty-nine years old. Two months later he died of complications from wounds received at the Battle of Chancellorsville (May 1-4).

Page 350. George A. Neafus, formerly of New York, was a Clinton merchant.

Page 351. Samuel H. Gilman was the first captain of Company E, 7th Louisiana. He resigned from service in January, 1862.

Pages 354-355. Major George T. Howard was a member of the 1st Mississippi, commanded by Colonel John M. Simonton.

Page 356. Mrs. Charles E. "Mertie" Cate was the wife of a prominent Hammond landowner who also ran a shoe factory and sawmill.

Page 359. The "straggling, half-deserted town" Sarah mentioned was Madisonville. As the 1860 census returns for that district show no Mrs. Greyson living in the area, it could be assumed she was a refugee who had fled from New Orleans when the Federals occupied the city.

Page 362. "Mr. J——" is given in the diary as a Mr. Carter.

Page 364. There were several Christmas families in Ponchatoula at the time, which makes positive identification of this particular one difficult. In all probability, it was Richard Christmas, a youth of nineteen.

Like Mrs. John B. Grayson, Mr. Worthington was evidently a refugee from another part of the state.

Dr. Auguste Capdevielle left his New Orleans practice to seek safety in the Louisiana interior. After the war he returned to his native city and became one of its most prominent physicians. Apparently he was a skilled linguist, for the doctor and Sarah conducted many of their conversations in French. The unpublished entry for April 4, 1863, is an example.

Page 366. On October 1, 1862, Lieutenant-General John B. Pemberton replaced General Van Dorn as commander of the Department of Mississippi and East Louisiana, with headquarters at Jackson, Mississippi. Pemberton, regarded by many as being another of "Davis's pets," was strongly criticized for his surrender of Vicksburg early in July, 1863. For example, see

John K. Bettersworth, *Confederate Mississippi* (Baton Rouge, 1943), 194-195, 205.

Colonel Ignatius Szymauski, formerly with the Charmette Regiment, Louisiana Militia, was at this time a member of Pemberton's staff. He later was in charge of prisoner exchange for the Department of the Trans-Mississippi.

Page 375. According to Sarah's entry for April 19, a Mrs. Ryan's husband had conspired with a Mr. Breedlove to pilfer some funds belonging to Judge Morgan. The same Mrs. Ryan was the lady to whom Sarah alluded on pages 378-379.

Page 384. Brigadier-General James Bowen was Provost-Marshal of the Federal Department of the Gulf.

Page 387. Dr. Warren Stone of New Orleans is also the "Dr. S——" referred to on page 397.

Page 388. The Edict of Nantes, issued in 1598 by Henry IV, granted religious toleration to all French Protestants. In 1685 the Edict was revoked by the absolutist Louis XIV, who wished all Frenchmen to conform to his own Catholic faith. The net result of the Revocation was the driving from France of thousands of Huguenots, many of whom, like the father of Paul Revere, came to America.

Page 391. The Federal raid that isolated Lydia Carter Morgan was a slashing expedition through central Louisiana by Colonel Benjamin Grierson in early June. The Federal cavalry turned back short of their destination (Baton Rouge) after a fight at Clinton with two Arkansas regiments. *Confederate Veteran*, XIII (1905), 122-123.

Page 393. In the middle of June General Lee embarked upon his second invasion of the North, and by the 26th he was approaching Chambersburg, Pennsylvania. His plan was not to move directly on Washington, as Sarah implied, but to strike further to the north. The Confederate army is variously estimated at between 50,000 and 75,000 men, while the Federal Army of the Potomac, under Major-General George G. Meade, was moving in pursuit of Lee with 97,000 soldiers.

Major-General John B. Magruder, dubbed "Prince John" because of his bearing and theatrical antics on the battlefield, was commander of the District of Texas. In January, 1863, he captured Galveston and moved up the coast, stamping out the small Federal strongholds along the Gulf. Sarah was expressing the hopeful speculation that he might move into Louisiana via Fort Jackson, but Magruder remained in the Lone Star State.

At this time Rear-Admiral Farragut was with the Federal fleet bombarding the crumbling Vicksburg defenses. No "English ironclads" were threatening the mouth of the Mississippi.

Page 394. Brashear City was a Federal outpost one blueclad described as "a city which consists of a wharf and a railroad-depot, and but little besides." Hosmer, *The Color Guard*, 118. On June 23 a Confederate raiding force under Major Sherod Hunter sacked the town, capturing 11 cannon, 2,500 small arms, and 1,300 prisoners. *OR*, XXVI, pt. 1, 227-232. The village, located to the west of New Orleans, was renamed Morgan City in 1876.

Page 395. On July 4 General Pemberton surrendered Vicksburg and its 29,396 defenders to Federal forces under the command of Major-General Ulysses S. Grant. The best account of the Vicksburg operations is in Kenneth P. Williams, *Lincoln Finds a General* (5 vols., New York, 1949-1959), IV, 346-425.

The New Orleans *Era* was the pro-Union newspaper that replaced the popular *Daily Delta* after the city fell. A devout Confederate of the fairer sex classified the *Era* as "a shameful thing, not even genteel," and said it was "filled with insolent braggadocio." *The Journal of Julia LeGrand*, edited by Kate M. Rowland and Mrs. M. L. Croxall (Richmond, 1911), 128, 231.

Page 396. Realizing the futility of trying to hold out after the fall of Vicksburg, General Gardner surrendered Port Hudson to the Federals on July 8. This opened the entire Mississippi to Federal shipping. The defenders at Port Hudson and Vicksburg ate both mules and rats to keep from starving. For varied opinions over the tastefulness of mule meat, see McMorries, *1st Alabama*, 67-68; *SHSP*, XIV (1886), 339; *Confederate Veteran*, XVII (1909), 512.

Page 397. The flamboyant Unionist to whom Sarah referred was a Dr. Schuppert.

Page 399. In what many historians consider to have been the climactic battle of the war, General Meade hurled back Lee's attacks for three days (July 1-3) at Gettysburg, Pennsylvania. The combined casualties of the two armies exceeded 43,000 men.

After the fall of the last two river fortresses Sarah's diary reflected the dreariness and monotony of life that she experienced in New Orleans. Thenceforth, the journal was devoted more and more to personal and family feelings that possess little value to the general narrative. (This explains in part why the original editor omitted large portions of almost every entry.) For example, in her December 20, 1863, record Sarah wrote: "O my dear diary, what a dull monotonous life this is where one cannot find a day to mark with a white stone, and say 'this day is worth remembering.'"

Page 403. Dry Tortugas was a notorious Federal prison camp off the Gulf coast of Florida. Treatment of Confederate prisoners there often reached barbaric depths. See *Florida Historical Quarterly*, XXII (1934-1944), 98, 102.

"Captain C——" is the same Captain McClure Sarah first mentioned on page 313.

Page 422. On recounting the capture of Hays's brigade in her November 22 entry, Sarah added: "I can hardly believe it. If it is so, they have taken the bravest set of men any army ever held." Most of the Louisianians under Major-General Harry T. Hays were captured at the Battle of Rappahannock Station, Virginia, November 7, 1863.

For a more detailed discussion of the cruises of the *Georgia*, see Morgan, *Rebel Reefer*, 114-183.

Page 424. Asphodel was a plantation home on Carr's Creek near the village of Jackson in East Feliciana Parish. Restored in recent years and presently occupied by Robert Couhig, the home was a location setting for the 1957 filming of the movie, "The Long, Hot Summer."

Page 426. Captain Gibbes Morgan rejoined his 7th Louisiana still unwell from the wounds received at Sharpsburg. After his capture at Rappahannock Station he was taken to Old Capitol Prison in Washington, then transferred to Johnson's Island, Ohio, where he died. He was twenty-eight years old.

Page 430. Captain George Mather Morgan was three years younger than his brother Gibbes. Enlisting in New Orleans in April, 1861, he had risen in the ranks to commander of Company D and regimental assistant quartermaster of the 1st Louisiana. He died at Orange Court House, Virginia, from what Sarah described as "inflammation of the stomach, induced by the necessity of eating Pork." Unpublished passage in that same entry.

Page 435. Both Richmond, Virginia, and Selma, Alabama, fell into Federal hands on April 2. Mobile surrendered on April 12, and General Joseph E. Johnston's Army of Tennessee (what was left of it) laid down its arms near Durham Station, North Carolina, April 26.

Page 436. Henry Ward Beecher was a clergyman and outspoken abolitionist who initially gained the hatred of the South by promoting the transportation of New Englanders to the newly opened Kansas territory to prevent that area from being dominated by proslavery elements. The new rifles the abolitionists carried with them into Kansas were nicknamed "Beecher's Bibles."

President Lincoln was assassinated while attending a stage comedy at Ford's Theater on the evening of April 14. At the same time, Secretary of State William H. Seward was so seriously wounded by fellow assassins under John Wilkes Booth that his life hung in the balance for several days.

The Corday-Marat episode is one of the famous murders of the French Revolution.

Page 438. The Bells were the family in tearful mourning.

Captain John W. Todd was Chief of Ordnance for the Department of the Gulf. In June, 1865, he was placed in command of the Baton Rouge Arsenal. *OR*, XLVII, pt. 2, 746.

Pages 339-340. The ten regiments, all infantry, serving with Lee's army were the 1st, 2nd, 5th, 6th, 7th, 8th, 9th, 10th, 14th and 15th. The parole lists compiled at Appomattox account for only 374 men present in these units at the time of their surrender. *SHSP*, XV (1887), 4, 6, 230-237, 456, 472.

Sarah continued her June 15 entry by writing: "It is incomprehensible, this change. Seeing familiar faces on the street is an oddity to which I cannot reconcile myself.

"Miriam came in from the Confederacy with Charlie, Lilly, and all the children on the nineteenth of May. And since then, every one seems to follow. There is Dr. Woods who seemed silently attracted to the spot, for he walked in a few days after as though we had parted hours, instead of years ago. Then in came Captain McGimsey, O *so* naturally, that I was insensibly carried back to the days when he rather liked me; and I came near being ever so civil to him. Miriam's adorer, Colonel Dupré, came next. Our cousins Gibbes Morgan, Walker, and Phil, and dozens that we did not know so well, followed in rapid succession, until the unusual sensation of receiving visitors makes me dizzy. And then, who should step in a week ago, but John Halsey!! Dear John! Twice a day he comes. Why, I would grow alarmed if twenty-four hours passed without bringing his good, honest face."

The diary continues through the latter months of 1866, and ends with a postscript Sarah added years afterward about her marriage to Francis Dawson. The entry, dated January 27, 1906, reads: "Saturday. Thirty-two years ago today — only it was a Tuesday — 1874, Jan. 27th — we were married. Nearly seventeen years I have been alone. My beloved is Mine, and I am His, and Love is stronger than Death."